BEYOND THE CALL OF DUTY

MEMOIRS OF AN EXCISEMAN

H.A.B. Sheppard M.B.E.

To Jim
from
Horace   16th June 1999
with Best wishes
    from
Mother and Father
    3rd October 1999

Published by
THE OLD MUSEUM PRESS

BEYOND THE CALL OF DUTY
MEMOIRS OF AN EXCISEMAN

First published by The Old Museum Press Limited
The Old Museum, Bramber, West Sussex BN44 3WE
England
1998

A catalogue record of this book
is available from The British Library

ISBN 1 84042 012 X

Cover design and format by StewART

Printed and bound by Antony Rowe Ltd
Bumpers Farm, Chippenham, Wiltshire.

CONTENTS

DEDICATION
To the memory of Dorothy.

This book is not an autobiography. It has been written almost entirely from memory, hence its sub-title, "Memoirs", although I have had access to some old family records. In addition, I have had recourse to personal notes made at the time of my various periods serving in H.M. Customs & Excise, simply to record 'where', 'period', 'for or with whom and in what capacity'. Also I have the records of examinations taken in pursuit of a career. For this reason my "Memoirs" do not contain material requiring approval to be published, in the nature of official secrets. The remainder of the "Memoirs" is simply a record of my progress, if this is the right word, as a child, a school boy, an apprentice and my involvement in various organisations before and after retirement. All taken in an effort, in my view, to improve or foster pleasure and enjoyment for my fellow beings as well as for myself, by associating together.

This book is dedicated to the memory of my dear wife, Dorothy, who despite that she declined to wait for five minutes for me to make my first journey from Birmingham to Chatham to meet her, a distance of around 150 miles on my motor cycle, in 1928, agreed later, in 1930 to accompany me through the next 61 years of happy married life. Also to my two sons, who have fully repaid in love and affection, all I expended with the help of Dorothy, on their education, from which they have fulfilled every hope I ever expected.

My thanks go to all my friends I have made throughout my life, many of whom I have failed to mention in my "Memoirs". My apologies to them. Particularly I thank those who helped me stage the little shows we put on for the Civil Service Motoring Association members in Gillingham; to the members of the Probus Club of Bournemouth who assisted me in its formation in 1979; to the members of the West Hampshire Masonic Bowling Association for so much enjoyment on the bowling green. Sincere thanks go to Margaret Green of P.b.S Chislehurst, who has typed and retyped my script, so many times that she probably knows it by heart! Correcting my endless mistakes in spelling and syntax besides offering advice on what to put in and what to leave out. Without her my "Memoirs" would never have been completed. Also my thanks to Graham Buckingham of Buckingham Photographic for so carefully reproducing the many photographs, to enable them to be included where appropriate in the "Memoirs". To the staff of the Royal Masonic Benevolent Institution Home in Chislehurst for seeing to my needs at all times, go my appreciation for keeping me fit to enable the "Memoirs" to be completed. But to the Police Force at Maidstone and to the Police prosecuting service that dealt with the case of dangerous driving against a police constable when I was severely injured in 1967 and which resulted in his acquittal so preserving his career, I still feel that justice failed, so I offer no thanks!! As Dorothy said at the time "you are still alive" and I have lived to tell the tale!

FOREWORD

Horace Sheppard was twenty-one years of age in 1927 and one of the first to join Her Majesty's Customs & Excise - probably the oldest government department as an 'Unattached Officer of Customs and Excise'. His subsequent career in Customs, spanning forty-two years, involved a wide variety of jobs and postings to different parts of Britain. In this engaging account of his working life, Horace has set out, with great humour, the changes that came to pass in that time - what he calls "the variety in an Exciseman's life".

I am proud to have been asked to write this foreword. I too joined Customs as an Officer of Customs & Excise and, like Horace, found the lure of investigation work impossible to resist. I and my colleagues in the present day National Investigation Service - the 1800- strong criminal investigation arm of the modern Department - do regard our investigation duties, like Horace, as "easily the most interesting period" of our careers. What a contrast between the cases that Horace investigated and the tax frauds and drug trafficking cases that we deal with in the late 1990's. I am fascinated by his accounts of the Golden Plovers smuggled into London in a consignment of pigeons, the chance 'raid on two genteel ladies selling smuggled foreign watches and the duplicitous 'nark' who made off with a suit-case full of nylon stockings. But professionalism and integrity have always been the hallmarks of Customs investigators and those quali-ties prevail today. The frauds we investigate and the drug trafficking rings we dismantle result in many of the most serious cases brought before the British courts.

For those of us that have followed Horace there is a sense of envy at reading these pages. The computer age is partly to blame for the loss of many of the characters that Horace had to deal with on a daily

10

basis - the redoubtable Bob Luck and his cider farm must have been charming as well as one to keep a close eye on !

Outside of his busy 'official' life, Horace led an immensely satisfying family life. Sixty years of marriage to Dorothy and the raising of two fine sons, Colin and Brian, still gave Horace time to play an active role in all manner of social, fraternal and charitable circles.
The very essence of the saying, "if you want a job doing, ask a busy man"

In the year that this book is published, Horace will be 92. Many of the characters he mentions will no longer be with us. Those that remain will read this account with great interest. Others, like me and many others in Customs & Excise, will be engrossed and seduced by this insight into another era.

DICK KELLAWAY
Chief Investigation Officer
HM Customs & Excise

Custom House
London
February 1998

CHAPTER ONE
History and Family background.

16th June 1906	To Horace William Barnabas Sheppard and Florence Beatrice Sheppard, nee Cox, at 57 Grove Road, Chatham, Kent - a son.

The above announcement did not appear in the issue of The Times for that date. What did appear under 'births' was the arrival of 24 babies (12 boys and 12 girls) to various couples able to afford the charge of six shillings for six lines or less, plus one shilling and sixpence for each additional line. Of the girls, two were twins. Of the rest, one unfortunately was still born. One baby girl was the new daughter for Fleet Paymaster J.H.F. Campion, R.N. H.M.S. Mercury. I wonder whether he eventually became an Admiral or whether his daughter survived to the age of 90?

Another interesting item in The Times of the 16th June 1906 was an advertisement for a house in Beckenham, Kent which area had the lowest death rate in the Kingdom. The house had 10 bedrooms, 3 reception rooms, a conservatory, electric light, a linen room, 2 bathrooms, 4 W.C's, a tennis lawn, 2 summer houses and a lease of 70 years to run, at a price of £3,000 or near offer!

Also reported was that Kent had beaten Surrey at the Oval by one wicket and for Kent's success the team was indebted to its young professional, Woolley, whose game was a triumph "not likely to be overlooked even when Blythe is able to come back into the side". 1906 was the year when Kent won its first county championship. Since then Woolley went on to become second only to Jack Hobbs, in scoring 58,969 runs to Hobbs' 61,237 in County First Class Records, besides exceeding 2,000 runs each season for many successive years. He also took over 100 wickets in the years 1914, 1912, 1922 and 1923 plus over 2,000 runs in each of those years. Even W. G. Grace cannot equal Woolley's records.

As for 16th June, in other years, it saw the birth of Edward 1st who later as a Prince, defeated Simon de Montfort at the Battle of Evesham. Later still when he ascended the throne in 1272 he became a great legislator codifying many laws and statutes with the effect that the House of Commons attained a great place in the constitution. Edward 1st is also remembered for his expulsion of the Jews who had become the national money lenders. June 16th was the birthday of Adam Smith the economist and author of "The Wealth of Nations". He was a Commissioner of Customs in Edinburgh. His father had been a Comptroller of Customs and his uncle a Customs Collector. Hence my date, 16th June had been important in the eighteenth century. Much later it saw the birth of Stan Laurel the comedian and also of Tom Graveney the England Cricketer.

Politically the year 1906 was one of tremendous change. The Liberal party won a landslide victory over the Conservatives. Mr Arthur Balfour, the outgoing Prime Minister lost his seat. Sir Henry Campbell-Bannerman succeeded him with Mr. Asquith as Chancellor of the Exchequer. Mr David Lloyd George became President of the Board of Trade. Mr. Phillip Snowden who had been an Excise Assistant before he had to retire due to a cycle accident, was elected as one of the earliest Labour MPs. His election was to have a profound effect on the work of the Excise when legislation was passed to provide universal Old Age Pensions. It was because of Phillip Snowden's knowledge of the fact that the Excise Department had a complete coverage of every parish and town throughout the country with its system of "rides" by Excise Officers, that the task of investigating all claims to the pension was placed upon Excise Officers who then reported to Old Age Pension Committees set up to award a pension at the appropriate rate according to the income of the claimant. A "means test" that lasted until the proposals for a universal retirement pension came into force under the Beveridge scheme in 1945 when the Social Security Department took over control.

In 1906 the first moves were afoot to reform the House of Lords which is still being discussed!! More vociferous was the call for votes for women. Mr Asquith speaking at Nottingham on the subject of the Education Bill before Parliament was interrupted by women in the balcony shouting for "Votes for Women". This was amid laughter from the audience and cries of "Chuck 'em out". Mrs Pankhurst the suffragette leader was this year released from prison in Holloway gaol.

Such was 1906 as reported in The Times Newspaper and elsewhere.

57 Grove Road, Chatham where I was born, was a small terrace house. It has since been demolished. The area is now the site of modern post war 1939/45 Council houses.

My father was the only child of William and Annie Sheppard (nee Astle). My mother was the second daughter of Albert Edward John Cox. So far as I have been able to ascertain her mother's maiden name was Little or Liddle, one of, I believe, 7 sisters living in the Luton, Chatham area of Kent. My mother was born on the 25th February 1886, probably in Maida Road, Luton, Chatham. She had three sisters, Lilian the eldest married George Ayears and became the mother of 5 sons, George, Horace (who lost his life in the evacuation from Dunkirk in the 1939/45 war), Albert, Cyril and Ronald. Later 'Aunt' Lil, adopted a baby girl named Joan. My mother's younger sister, Edith, married George Morgan, a Royal Marine. They had 3 children, Edith, George and Edward. Edward died in childhood. The youngest sister was Ethel who married another Royal Marine, Charles Gedge. They had one child, a daughter Ethel, known always simply as 'Babs'. My mother also had a brother, younger still, named Albert John William Cox who married Eliza Eva Ralph. They had three children, Albert Horace George Cox, Dorothy Maud Cox and Joan Doreen Mary Cox.

My grandfather, William Sheppard was born at Stratton St. Margarets, near Swindon, Wilts, of farming stock, in about 1862. About 1865 or so the Great Western Railway was developing its engineering works in Swindon. Later the parents of my grandfather, of whom I have no information, decided to apprentice him to work in the railway workshops. But grandfather William Sheppard had no desire to be an apprentice so he ran away and tried to join the Royal Marines at Chatham. Being under age for service in the Royal Marines he was refused enlistment and was returned to the railway workshops. Being still unhappy he ran away a second time to Chatham. This time his parents decided to let him stay, so he was duly accepted into the Marine Regiment. In Chatham he met my grandmother Annie Eliza Astle, the eldest child, daughter of Barnabas Astle, whom he married. Their only son, my father, was born 25th June 1886, and christened Horace William Barnabas Sheppard. My mother was christened Florence Beatrice Cox.

My great grandfather, Barnabas Astle was born January 30th 1845 at Hilton, Derbyshire. My great grandmother Emma Astle, was born at Tuxford Nottinghamshire on January 24th 1847. The date of Barnabas and Emma's marriage is not known to me. My grandmother, Annie Eliza Astle was born at Tuxford, Nottinghamshire on 28th September 1867. Soon after this my great grandparents, the Astles, must have moved to Chatham, Kent for Barnabas to join the Royal Marines. During the next 17 years they proceeded to produce and raise most of a large family of 11 children. The first son, Frederick William Astle was born at Chatham on March 18th, but died one month later. Next came Alfred, born 6th July 1871 in Cage Lane, Chatham. Minnie Elizabeth, born October 28th 1872 at Forton, Gosport, then Herbert Barnabas born 8th May 1874 also at Forton. Next Edith Emma born May 14th 1876 at Forton. Then Ernest James born April 16th 1879 and Edward Henry born 20th February 1881; Lewis, born April 5th 1882; Daisy Adelaide, born October 1883 and finally May Eugene born 8th May 1885. The last five children were all born in the Marine Barracks at Chatham.

It has to be appreciated that all these children were born at regular intervals, obviously not unconnected with Barnabas Astle's periodic returns from his numerous 'commissions' at sea with the Royal Navy serving as a Royal Marine (the naval police force) on board navy vessels. These 'commissions' took him to various parts of the emerging British Empire.

The Astle Family (c.1880) showing Great grandfather, Barnabas Astle, his wife, Emma, on left, with 7 children, including Annie Sheppard, (nee Astle) eldest daughter, with son Horace father of auther on her lap, on right.

15

An interesting 'side-light' to this is that during the second half of the nineteenth century European countries were commencing to trade with the various Pacific Islands in the wake of the missionaries who had been attracted to them. Captain Cook in his search for the mythical "Terra Australis Nondum Cognita" or great southern continent had discovered many Pacific Islands besides surveying the coasts of both Australia and New Zealand. He had also surveyed Hawaii and Tahiti where he spent a considerable time, plus the Fiji Islands. Hawaii eventually became a U.S.A. possession. France was particularly keen on establishing possessions in the Pacific. The British Government was unwilling to accept responsibility. France acquired Tahiti which Cook had surveyed. The British Government had taken over Australia to which convicts from the UK were transported and New Zealand from the Maories. Tahiti and the Fijis has been discovered by the Dutchman, Tasman, but it was Captain Cook who surveyed their coasts. In 1858 the chiefs of the Fijis asked for annexation by the British, which was declined. However, after protracted efforts to avoid responsibility, in 1874 the British Government finally proclaimed annexation. Naval squadrons were sent out. One of these was commanded by Admiral Sir Charles Beresford. My great grandfather, Barnabas Astle went with Sir Charles Beresford as his 'batman'. I have no record of Barnabas going on other 'commissions' or to Australia with the convicts as a 'policeman' but his visit to the Fiji Islands with Admiral Sir Charles Beresford was well known in the Astle family. As an interesting facet of Barnabas Astle's stay in the Fiji's, I am reminded that few years ago the Fiji Islands sent a rugby football team to play in England. The Captain of the Fiji team was a Mr Barney.

When Barnabas Astle eventually retired from the Royal Marines, he became the licensee of the Dockyard Arms in Wood Street, Old Brompton, later part of the Municipal Borough of Gillingham. He became a Mason as a member of the Brownrigg Lodge, meeting in Old Brompton. In 1891 a new Lodge was formed in Chatham. Barnabas Astle was one of the Founders and became the first Hon. Treasurer. The name chosen for this new Lodge was 'Lord Charles Beresford'. Sir Charles had by 1891 been raised to the Peerage. He had by then been raised to Grand Rank in the United Grand Lodge of England, a very signal honour in Masonry. I have little doubt that the name of the new Lodge stemmed to some extent from Barnabas Astle's association with Sir Charles, later to become Lord Beresford.

My grandmother, Annie Sheppard, nee Astle, Barnabas's eldest daughter, passed to me two Masonic aprons worn by her father at meetings. The cases bear the two names, Brownrigg and Lord Charles Beresford. The aprons so far as I am aware have no intrinsic value. My grandmother also gave to my father a few years back, two spittoons, taken from the bar of the Dockyard Arms. The name aptly describes for what they were used. My father passed them to me and I in turn to my elder son. They are now more than 100 years old and in good condition. As antiques they possibly are of some value. One is made of brass and the other copper and are now 'installed' in my son's "listed cottage" in Chislehurst as a family heirloom.

Barnabas Astle died on the 1st November 1901 at the Dockyard Arms. He had got up to open the premises for the early customers on their way to work in the dockyard. He complained of feeling unwell. His wife Emma, my great grandmother asked a customer to look at him. A doctor was called who pronounced Barnabas was dead. The subsequent inquest recorded a verdict of death from natural causes. He was 56 years old and was buried in the cemetery near St. Mary Magdalene Church. My great grandmother Emma Astle went to live in Leonard Road, Luton, Chatham. I once saw her there when I was a small boy about 5 or 6 years old. She was then living I believe with her youngest daughter May Bell, nee Astle. To me she appeared then a very frail old lady but was actually only about 66 years old.

Emma Astle, (C 1890), author's great grandmother.

Of the entire Astle family, I never met Herbert and Edith. Possibly they died in childhood. My father never mentioned them to me. Ernest I once visited at this house near East Street, Chatham. I met one of his sons who was a librarian at the Public Library in New Road, Chatham, near to the Technical School where I was attending at the time.

It has to be remembered that my father who was born 25th June 1886, was only 13 months younger than his Aunt May, his mother's youngest sister. He was also only 2 years and 8 months younger than the next sister, Daisy. His 'uncle' Lewis was 4 years and 2 months older than my father and even Edward only 5 years and 4 months older. Because the eldest daughter, my grandmother Annie had a baby, (my father) soon after her mother Emma had her last few babies and that they were all living together in the Royal Marine Barracks, it is little wonder that my father looked on his young aunts and uncles as his sisters and brothers. I, for my part regarded my 'great' aunts and 'great ' uncles as my ordinary aunts and uncles.

Aunt 'Min' Astle married 'Bob' Philbrick who was a book binder for the Royal Engineers and the Admiralty. The Philbricks lived at 12 Granville Road, Gillingham near to Gillingham Railway Station. My father may have been living with them at the time of his marriage to my mother on Christmas Day 1905. My mother gave as her address 20 Granville Road, probably an 'accommodation' address to ensure the wedding took place in the St. Mary Magdalene Church, nearby. The officiating clergyman was the

"Florence and Horace Sheppard (C.1905) Author's parents."

Vicar, Canon Robins who was totally blind. My mother used regularly to say that a blind man married her! A little play on words!

St Mary Magdalene Church, Gillingham is close to where the 'Great Chain' was thrown across the River Medway to Upnor to act as a barrier against the Dutch fleet. Unfortunately the precaution failed; the Dutch broke the chain and sailed on to destroy the English fleet anchored at Chatham. Close by also is the hamlet of Grange, a limb of the Cinque Port of Hastings in distant Sussex. Grange contained one small licensed public house. This raised problems for me years later when, as the officiating Excise Officer for Gillingham, I had to ensure that the licence duty paid for this single public house was credited to Hastings in Sussex instead of to Gillingham in Kent. History existed in this tiny area!

Many times I went with my parents to Granville Road to see Aunt 'Min' and family. It was a very long walk, the normal system of travel at the time. From Luton, up steep Stoney Alley to cross Chatham Hill into Windmill Road and then down the long Gillingham Road to the railway level crossing. To me then, it was an adventure. Aunt 'Min' suffered terribly from asthma. It was very distressing to see her gasping for breath. But a charming lady, pleased to see us when we called. 'Min' and Bob Philbrick had two children. The elder, Dorothy, a little older than me, and George about the age of my sister Doris. Dorothy married a Mr Howie. They lived in Grange Road afterwards and she used to keep in touch with 'Aunt' Daisy who had emigrated to Australia, marrying a Professor Jordan. George, I believe became a doctor in the Birmingham area. The Howies had children but I have not heard from Dorothy Howie since December 1972 when she last wrote to tell me she had lost touch with Aunt 'Daisy' in Australia and her two daughters Grace and Ruth Jordan. Dorothy Philbrick attended Chatham Commercial School which had a loose connection with Chatham Technical School as well as premises at Fort Pitt in Rochester. I saw her quite frequently when the girls had classes at the 'Tech'

I knew Edward 'Uncle' Ed. Astle very well. He was the manager of the butcher's shop in Chatham High Street and so, was able to supply my father and mother with a suitable joint for Sunday dinner! Edward was married to Sarah, a very pretty lady. They had two children, "Young" Edward and Hilda. "Young" Edward was a few years older than me and Hilda younger. It was a great tragedy when Sarah committed suicide from post natal depression following the birth of Hilda. 'Aunt' Min brought up Hilda almost as a sister to her own Dorothy. This tragedy brought great depression and sorrow to all the family. 'Young' Edward was determined to join the Royal Marines following in his grandfather's footsteps.

Unfortunately 'Young' Edward was very small and too short to be accepted into the Royal Marines. The story goes that he tied his legs to the foot of his bed and attempted to increase his height by stretching himself! But was unsuccessful in getting any taller! So in due course he joined the Royal Marine Band as a drummer boy. From such he progressed, still quite short, to become the Bugle Major and finally the Drum Major of the Royal Marine Band stationed at the Chatham Barracks. My father took me on occasions to watch the band playing on the Marine Barracks parade ground where I saw cousin Edward proudly marching at the side as Bugle Major and in front as Drum Major. Eventually I believe, during the second world war he was granted a commission in the Royal Marines as an Officer. His grandfather, no doubt would have been proud of him. 'Young' Edward married but I have no further information on his career.

'Aunt' Daisy who after becoming a nurse at Charing Cross Hospital, eventually attained the rank of Assistant Matron. She later emigrated to Australia to marry Professor Jordan. The Australian Government authority declined to let her continue her nursing career unless she took a fresh set of examinations in nursing in Australia. This she declined to do. She had two daughters, Grace and Ruth but I have no information about them. 'Aunt' May married a man named Tom Bell. I think he was a soldier. They had two children, Thomas and Cyril. I have no knowledge of their life, although I met them at 'Aunt' Mins!

My grandparents, William and Annie Sheppard, when he retired secured a position as caretakers and in charge of security at the premises of Ellis and Ellis who were Parliamentary Solicitors at 10 Little College Street, Westminster, London, close to the Houses of Parliament. My grandfather was recalled to the services for 1914/18 war, but my grandmother continued in the service of Ellis and Ellis. She was a collector of postage stamps and gave them to me for my collection. No doubt she collected them from the 'commissions' to

20

foreign parts of both by her father, Barnabas, and her husband. Among those I received were two envelopes addressed to Ellis and Ellis at 10 Little College Street. They bore stamps from the inception of the postage system in 1840, 'Penny Reds' with the date 1840 showing. Hence they could not have come from letters sent by either my great grandfather or grandfather. I attempted via the Law Society to contact the successors to Ellis and Ellis, but without success. The envelopes are still in my possession and may possibly be of some value. They should have been of interest to Ellis and Ellis or their successors., had I succeeded in tracing them.

Occasionally I went to stay with my grandmother Annie Sheppard, at Westminster, London. My grandfather was then serving in the Marine Barracks at Deal, where he was acting as the Provost Marshall. With my grandmother, sometimes I went to the gardens adjoining the Parliament buildings and it was there I saw the River Thames for the first time, a

William and Annie Sheppard (nee Astle).
Parents of Author's father
(Author's grand parents) (c 1913).
outside their residence, at
10 Little College Street, Westminster,
near to Houses of Parliament.

river I was to be connected with much in the years after I became a official in H.M. Customs and Excise Department. While I was in Westminster on one occasion 'Aunt' Daisy took me (when she was wearing her nurses uniform) to see the paintings in the National Gallery near to Trafalgar Square. Being in her uniform, onlookers appeared to think that I was a young "gentleman" being shown round the paintings by his guardian nurse! Partly true! Another time when I returned from Westminster to Chatham during the first world war, I found that crowds of people were looking at the damage caused by a Zeppelin that had dropped a bomb on some dwellings near to Christ Church, Luton, where I served as a choir boy. The damage was not far from where I lived with my parents in Alexandra Road and even much nearer to Luton Council School where I was a pupil. This bomb was possibly one of the first ever dropped by the Germans in England, probably meant for Chatham Dockyard which it had missed by several miles. A foretaste of what was to occur much later in my life during 1939/45! On another occasion I saw a Zeppelin in the glare of searchlights. It was later 'brought down' in flames, I believe over Essex.

My grandfather died on the 20th April. 1919 while still serving in the Marines, in the Royal Naval Hospital in Gillingham. He was then probably in his late 50's. He was rather a formidable looking man. On the occasions he came to visit my parents in Alexandra Road, great preparation had to be made for his meals etc., with special cheeses and wine. Similarly when my grandmother arrived for a visit, Madeira wine had to be available. She always seemed to me to be dressed in outlandish clothes. She had a puppy dog pet which went astray on one

Annie Sheppard, (nee Astle),
Author's grandmother

visit causing great distress to everyone. It was never found despite advertisements in the local press offering a reward. She never got over her loss of the dog. In Deal on one occasion I went to stay on holiday with my mother's younger sister, Edith, who had married George Morgan and was living in the married quarters for service men. As children we played on the parade ground when not being used. I was playing there with others when a shout went up "Its old Sheppard", and all the other children ran away! I did not have to - it was my grandfather, pleased to see me! He was held in awe by the residents in the married quarters being the Provost Marshall! It was said that should he find washing by the wives still hanging after the lowering of the flag at dusk, on the clothes lines near, he would cut the ropes for the washing to fall to the ground. True or false? I do not know, but the story illustrates how he was feared as Provost Marshall! My grandfather had two sisters, the elder, Emma, was a housekeeper for the Jardine family at Goring-on-Thames in a large house. This was the family of Douglas Jardine who captained the English cricket team for the famous, (or infamous) 'body line' bowling Tests in Australia. I visited this great aunt Emma at Goring soon after I was married in 1930. She was a charming, to me old lady who made Dorothy and I very welcome. Quite different when he was alive from her martinet brother!. The other sister was was my great aunt Kate who lived in Swindon. She had married an ex-miner, invalided from working in the pits in South Wales. They had no children. I also visited my grandfather's younger brother, George. He had several grown up children, and I believe owned a haulage business. I was shown some antique Staffordshire pottery acquired I was told from journeys to the potteries by canal barges. I have no further information about the Wiltshire side of the Sheppard family. However a man did write to me on one occasion about 'Sheppards' in the West country. I gave what information I could but heard no more from him. I have always understood that the name 'Sheppard' has nothing to do with sheep. My information is that 'Sheppard' stems from ships and shipbuilding. The "Shepway" district of Romney March, Kent, certainly is connected with ships and seafaring.

My grandmother eventually retired from the service of Ellis and Ellis. At first she came to live with my mother and father at Century Road, Rainham but she later bought a house at 44 King Edward Road, Gillingham, near to St. Mary Magdalene Church and lived there with her younger brother Lewis, who was unmarried. The name 'Lewis' undoubtedly stems from 'Lewis' the nomenclature for a son born to a Mason after joining the organisation. Great grandfather Barnabas Astle, no doubt had this in mind when Lewis his last son was born. I took my new girl friend, Dorothy Brown to see my grandmother at King Edward Road. She was very interested in my progress through Chatham Technical School, then at the Royal Naval Dockyard School, and finally in the Customs and Excise Department. She was thrilled when eventually Dorothy and I were married in 1930 and even more so when our first son Colin was born in 1936. When too, in 1933, I joined the Masons my grandmother was overjoyed. No doubt she was thinking of her father's Masonic career. It was then that she passed to me the two old Masonic aprons in their original cases I have referred to earlier. I have a very interesting photograph taken in the garden at Century Road, Rainham, of the "Four Sheppards" together - grandmother, father, myself and Colin, the baby. My mother is shown 'watching'.

When I joined the Masonic organisation in 1933 I had, as one of the reasons, the opportunity to attend Masonic Ladies' Nights. My father-in-law, William Brown was a member. He organised and 'ran' these functions for several Lodges to which the ladies could attend. I wanted to attend with my wife.

The youngest son, Lewis continued to live with my grandmother in King Edward Road until her death. He stayed on there and later married late in life but had no children. He was employed in the Naval Store Department in Chatham Dockyard and from there, in fact, supplied me with a "fear-nought" jacket to keep out the cold when I first became an apprentice.

My grandmother died on 28th October 1938. She had developed a rupture from turning her old fashion mangle, used for wringing out her clothes after washing. There were no 'spin dryers' in those days although she could easily have afforded a more up-to-date 'wringer'. She received a pension from Ellis and Ellis, the Westminster solicitors, plus her service pension. Also possibly the Widows Pension which came into force under legislation in 1930. I had been actively engaged on investigating claims for this new pension, in Southampton and Romsey, Hampshire, where I was then stationed. But not in Gillingham, Kent! My grandmother passed away in St. Bartholomew's Hospital in Rochester and was buried in the family grave she had purchased in Chatham Cemetery, alongside her husband.

This concludes the 'history' of the Barnabas Astle family, except for that of my father, who was, however, a Sheppard!

My grandfather, Albert Cox was a hammerman employed in the smithery in Chatham Dockyard. This was quite a skilled job in the nineteenth century for making parts and equipment for vessels of the Royal Navy. I have no knowledge of his parents or earlier ancestors. Albert Cox had at least two brothers. One lived in Leonard Road, Luton, Chatham. The other lived in Sheerness on the Isle of Sheppey. My mother's elder sister, Lilian resided with her uncle in Sheerness for a while. Grandfather Albert Cox died at a relatively early age, I believe from tuberculosis, a prevalent disease at the time. The young son Albert, known as Bertie, was placed in an orphanage in Ashford, Kent. Subsequently Grandfather Cox's widow, my grandmother Mary, became involved with a man named Wellard whom she eventually married. I have little knowledge of this Mr Wellard except that he was not accepted by the daughters. I called to see my grandmother a few times when I was a small boy living in Alexandra Road, Luton. She was living in very poor circumstances on Chatham Hill and relying on agricultural work such as apple and cherry picking in the seasons. If cherries were around I always received a large basket full to take home. She also worked in the Kentish hop gardens and was an expert picker. With Mr Wellard, my grandmother went to live in very poor surroundings in Selling near Canterbury where my parents and I went to see her. I was very sorry to see her in such poor surroundings. Later with Mr Wellard they returned to live in Old Brompton near to where her son Bertie, then married, was living with his wife and children. My grandmother Mary was buried in Chatham cemetery quite close to where my grand-mother Annie Sheppard lies also buried, in the Sheppard family grave. For some time I tended Mary's grave when visiting also, the Sheppard family grave. It has now been grassed over by the cemetery authority.

All the Cox daughters were exceptionally clever seamstresses. My mother and her sisters Edith and Ethel, all worked in the clothing factory, known as the "X Brand", close to where I later went to school at the "Tech". Their employment was mainly on men's clothing, the major portion of which was uniforms for the Royal Marines. Work had to be perfect for the eagle eye of the Master Tailor's critical examination at the Royal Marine Barracks. Putting the red stripe down the side of trouser legs, part of the uniform had to be done exactly. I visited the factory to see my Aunt Ethel before she was married. The woman employees all seemed to be singing as they worked their machines. My mother continued working at the factory after I was born. My Aunt Lilian cared for me and fed me during the day until my mother came home, although I have no recollection of this. Aunt 'Lil' had herself had a third son, Albert, three months after I was born. Within two years of my birth, my mother again became pregnant. We moved from Grove Road to the house next door to that where Aunt 'Lil' and Uncle George lived in Constitution Road, Luton, Chatham. My sister Doris Florence Lilian was born there on 13th August 1908.

My father had attended the Royal Marine School near to Chatham Town Hall as a boy. Entitlement to attend was allowed to sons of Royal Marines. Recruits were also instructed there in the "3-Rs" if necessary. My father as a senior boy was eventually chosen to help in teaching recruits requiring tuition to bring them up to the standard required for admission to the Regiment of the Royal Marines. On leaving school my father was first employed as a shop assistant at the Maypole Dairy Company in Chatham High Street close to where Uncle Edward Astle had his butchers shop. Later my father commenced working with George Ayears, the husband of his elder sister Lilian. George Ayears was a very capable bricklayer. He was then employed building terrace houses in Coronation Street, Luton, Chatham.

Pupils at Royal Marine School, Chatham (c1893)
Author's father Horace is probably the small boy in a sailor suit,
5th from left in front row.

After a while this contract was completed. George Ayears obtained employment at the Curtis and Harvey explosive factory then being constructed on the marshes at Cliffe-at-Hoo near Rochester. He built the very tall chimney stacks necessary for safety reasons. He was employed there for the rest of his life. Aunt "Lil" had two more sons, making five in all - George, Horace, Albert, Cyril and Ronald. She finally adopted a baby girl named Joan and they were all a very happy family.

Meanwhile after two years in the house in Constitution Road, my mother and father moved to a terrace house at 34 Alexandra Road, Luton, Chatham. My father, once the building work in Luton was completed, obtained employment in the Works Department in Chatham Dockyard. Soon he was transferred to the Electrical

26

Department and became a 'wireman', quite an advancement in his status. My mother for her part had ceased employment in the "X-Brand" factory but carried on as an 'out-worker' still making uniforms for the Royal Marines. Her sister Edith had gone to live at Deal in the married quarters for Marines and their families. She had married George Morgan, a Marine. They had three children, Edith, George and Edward. Unfortunately the last named died in infancy. Later on the family returned to Chatham where I saw them all very frequently. My mother's youngest sister Ethel also married a Marine, Charles Gedge. Prior to her marriage my aunt Ethel continued working at the "X' Brand" factory. She came to live with us at Alexandra Road. After her marriage she lived in Connaught Road, Luton adjoining Alexandra Road. They had one child a girl christened 'Ethel' but known throughout her life as 'Babs'. Charles Gedge was groom to a Royal Marine officer. The officer's horse was exercised on the nearby Coney Banks at the end of Alexandra Road. Occasionally Uncle Charlie would give me a ride on his big black horse sitting in front of him on his saddle. Later on my mother's young brother Bertie left the orphanage at Ashford and came to live with us at Alexander Road. He obtained employment first as a tram conductor and later at the Oil and Cake Meal factory at Strood, Rochester. He too married and went to live in Old Brompton.

My mother's employment as an outworker on uniforms for the Royal Marines was more remu-nerative than working in the "X-Brand" factory. The uniforms were made using a treadle machine operated by her feet. No electric machines in those days. In fact electricity had not been installed in small terrace houses. I can see her now working away, all day and every day, singing all the time much as the women workers in the "X-Brand" factory did.

The Sheppard family, (c.1910) Horace, father; Florence, mother; Doris, sister, and Author.

27

Material for the uniforms was supplied from the Royal Marine Barracks. The finished uniforms were taken back for examination and passing by the Master Tailor at the barracks, and to receive payment for the work.

My father who had been advanced to grade of "wireman" in the Electrical Department received a further advancement by being selected to fill a vacancy for a shift engineer whose task it was to connect an electricity supply to ships of the navy when they came into the dockyard for a refit or other reasons. As such he worked periods from 6.00am to 2.00 pm; 2.00pm to 10.00pm and 10.00pm to 6.00am on a rotation of three weeks. Extra shifts were worked at weekends to allow for "change-overs". This meant having only one weekend in three at home. But the arrangement for extra working at two weekends out of three regularly, meant that he earned extra pay for overtime and brought more money into the family total.

At one period during the war, before my father became a shift engineer, he was required to go to Salcombe in Devon where a German submarine off shore was being salvaged after being sunk. He was one of the electricians operating the pumps for supplying air to the divers. He was a poor 'sailor' but managed to complete the task in hand. I understand that the various explosives on the sunken submarine made it a hazardous operation. It was after his return from Salcombe that he commenced as a shift engineer.

Also at this time my mother and later her younger sister Ethel had acted for a 'credit' firm by name of 'Bows' as agents collecting payments in arrears for goods the factory girls in the "X-Brand" works had obtained from local retail shops. I presume that my mother or Aunt Ethel received some payment from 'Bows' for their assistance in collecting the weekly payments. My mother decided that she would be better off running such a system for herself especially as she had ready access to potential customers at hand in the clothing factory. With my father she secured the approval and co-operation in a 'credit' scheme from two shops in the Luton Road. One was a clothing and general outfitter by the name of Seager and the other, a boot and shoe shop next door to Seagers, by the name of Baldock.

The system was to issue a 'ticket' to a customer for a fixed amount in round pounds which when presented at the retail shop enabled the holder to obtain goods to the total on the 'ticket'. The customer paid my mother a sum of one shilling for 21 weeks for each pound sterling on the 'ticket'. In effect it was 5 months before my mother was repaid but she made a profit of one shilling in the pound. Additionally of course, she received a discount of approximately 10% on the total of customer's accounts each month from the retail shops. So my mother received some three shillings in the pound profit for money lent to customers. Of course they took the risk of a customer failing to pay on time or not paying at all. They also had to pay the shopkeepers at the end of each month for goods purchased and for which full payment had not been received from customers. It became known as the 'tallyman' or credit purchasing. The customers obtained goods in advance and paid for them afterwards by instalments. At the start of the business my parents had to meet bills from the shops well in advance of having collected the weekly sums from customers. But the business prospered and eventually other shops were obtained willing to enter the system. Customers recommended other likely purchasers but my parents were very careful whom they accepted as customers. They went round together sometimes, 'collecting' the weekly payments. Messrs Bow who had themselves a retail grocery shop were not pleased but were unable to take any action. Eventually my parents had accumulated enough capital from their business plus work from the Marine Barracks during the war for Marine uniforms, plus my father's enhanced position in the dockyard to enable them to consider moving to a better house. This they did in 1919 when they purchased at an auction a bungalow in Century Road, Rainham. The paid £820 for the bungalow, a huge sum in those days but they secured a loan from the owner of the bungalow who lived in the house next-door in 16 Century Road. I lived at 14 Century Road, Rainham until I entered H.M. Customs and Excise Department in 1927, and I was married from there in 1930. My sister Doris was also married from there to Robert Craske who lived in Maidstone and was an electrician for Maidstone Borough Council.

Front door of 14 Century Road, Rainham,
Gillingham, Kent, showing clematis in bloom. Home
of Author, 1919 to 1927 and 1930, for marriage.

My parents continued to live at 14 Century Road until their deaths, my father at nearly 82 years of age and my mother at 88.

CHAPTER TWO
Childhood.

When we first moved to Alexandra Road the lighting in the house was from oil lamps carried from room to room as necessary. It was some years before gas mains were connected to small rented terrace houses. The rent then was five shillings a week. The landlord was a Mr Auger, farmer 'cum' carrier. Eventually the gas main was connected and lighting supplied by a burner with gas mantles. My father usually performed the job of lighting a new gas mantle, quite a delicate operation. The gas would be ignited and the mantle glowed giving much better illumination of a room than the old oil lamps we had previously. But there seemed always to be flies buzzing round the room particularly near the gas although this had a shade protecting the mantle. So a fly paper with a sticky surface was hung from the gas bracket. Once the flies settled on the fly paper they were doomed and could not escape. In 1912 when six years of age I was taken ill with the 'flu' epidemic prevailing at that time. Fortunately I recovered but strangely enough many years later when undergoing a routine check for the Civil Service, a 'scar' was detected on my lungs and I was told it was the effect of my early bout of 'flu' after a second X-ray examination had been called for, and carried out at King's College Hospital, London.

As school children we played in the street at various games. For the boys it was sometimes 'tip-cat''. A small piece of wood was prepared by sharpening the two ends to form points. This was placed in a small ring drawn on the road. The game was to strike the end of the small piece of wood with a long stick so that it flew in the air towards another ring drawn on the road some distance away. The winner was the boy whose piece of wood arrived nearest the second ring. Or a variation was to hit the piece of wood as hard as possible and strike it in the air with the long stick. The winner was the one that travelled

31

the greatest distance. It was sometimes a dangerous game should the piece of wood travel towards a window in a nearby dwelling. Another game was playing with spinning 'tops'. 'Tops' were conical round pieces of wood about three inches long which could be spun with the fingers on to the road and then were struck with a piece of cord or string fastened to a long stick. By whipping the 'top' with the string it could be made to spin faster and travel along the road. One had to be careful not to whip it into the air and possibly into a window frame! We also played 'hopscotch', chalking the squares on the road. This game is still played by children, but not in the road today!

We also skipped a lot turning the rope faster and faster. Sometimes even so fast as to be able to pass it under one's feet twice while they were in the air. The girls were usually better at this that the boys. We sang "salt, mustard, vinegar, pepper" as we skipped. In the evenings sometimes we played under and around the gas lamp at the corner of the road. The 'gas man' would come round at dusk and turn on the gas, lighting it with his special taper. There were other games. Nothing of this nature is now played in the street. In any case traffic is far too prevalent and with cars lining every road on both sides no room remains. Open spaces and playing fields are now the order of the day.

On Sundays a street trader, (her name was Whittaker) came round the houses selling shell fish from a basket she carried on her arm. The contents were mainly shrimps and winkles. She called out her 'wares' as she walked along the road. Shrimps and certainly winkles were a favourite item for 'Sunday tea' among the working population of Chatham. (My youngest girl cousin married one of the Whittaker family. She was my uncle Berties' youngest daughter!!).

While in Luton School I recall seeing boys from the gypsy encampment situated at the top of Beacon Hill, who came to school wearing heavy clogs or in a few cases with no boots on at all, just bare feet. The gypsy encampment consisted of numerous caravans of the horse drawn type but which had not moved for years. The gypsies had long standing rights of tenure there. Most of the caravans housing the gypsies were kept clean and tidy and they caused little trouble to other residents in the area. Eventually, many years after I lived in Luton, the Council obtained authority to clear the site and the gypsies had to move away.

There was a working windmill nearby, I presume grinding corn. The beacon site was the highest in the area at some 600 feet above sea level. It was where a beacon could be ignited as a warning or message to pass on across the country. It stands where a spur of the North Downs is broken by the valley of the River Medway. Ahead is the area known as the "Great Lines" where in the past troops have been reviewed. Below the Great Lines lies the Medway and a view of the dockyard with various naval and military establishments. Around are the many forts designed to protect the Medway and the dockyard in the past. Fort Amherst is directly beneath the Great Lines. In the distance, Forts, Luton, Pitt, Darland, Borstal etc. with Upnor Castle standing guard. Charles Dickens in the Pickwick Papers writes of Mr Pickwick seeing a review on the Great Lines.

From Alexandra Road we had one or two trips down the River Medway in the paddle steamer starting from Sun Pier Chatham and travelled down to Southend-on-Sea. Then the long walk on the pier into Southend before returning to Chatham again. My father took me below deck to see the ship's engines at work turning the paddles to propel the ship forward. Sometimes the paddle boat went on to Margate but we never took the longer journey, preferring to stay in Southend until the ship came back for returning to Chatham after picking up passengers still in Southend.

Sometimes two of my cousins from Cliffe-at-Hoo, sons of Aunt "Lil", came to stay with us at Alexandra Road, Chatham. We had to sleep three in a bed, but it was fun. I recall that in the bedroom at the back of the house was kept a 'penny farthing bicycle', possibly what my grandfather Cox had used to go to work in Chatham dockyard. What became of it I have no knowledge, possibly thrown out when we moved to Rainham.

Living in Luton my parents became members of the Chatham Co-operative Society which once a year paid a dividend, as did all co-ops, to their customers on the basis of the purchases made during the past year. But more important to the children of customers, the Co-op had an annual fete for the children. Tickets for admission had to be collected at the head-quarters office. Part of each admission ticket was a portion entitling the holder to cakes and a mug of tea at the venue of the fete. This venue was normally at Luton Recreation Ground near to the Wagon-at-Hale public house on the Capston

Road. Once, however, it was held on Chatham Football Club ground. All the children attending had to assemble at the Co-op H.Q's and march in a long procession to the venue for the fete. The procession was several hundred yards long and attracted crowds of on-lookers. At the venue, swings and roundabouts had been erected prior the fete. Also attached to the admission ticket was a portion to be presented to the man in charge of the swings or roundabouts for a ride on the 'apparatus'. The man in charge had to push the swings to ensure it sailed higher and higher, but not too high! It was a very popular section of the fete. My father was generally one of the men responsible for operating the swings so my sister and I generally got more rides that we were entitled to. There were also races for the older boys and girls with prizes for the winners. All the children had to sit on the grass in lines to receive their cakes and mugs of tea. "A good time was had by all" unless it was a wet day which I cannot recall. The fete was always held in the summer time!

Many years later I found out that the parents of my future wife were members of Gillingham Co-operative Society and from their membership she had attended the Gillingham Co-op fetes for children. She was a champion runner and high jumper. She had won the Kent 100 yards junior Championship at a Gillingham Co-op Fete, as well as the high jump. She proved her running ability also when we were married and attended a Civil Service Holiday Camp at Corton near Lowestoft. In the race put on for parents, she ran away from the field to win easily. I fell over in the race for fathers!!

While a pupil at Luton School I became a choir boy at Christ Church Luton and also joined the Boy Scout troop started by two young men at the church by the name of Biss. As a choir boy my mother clothed me in a nice jacket and with a Windsor collar. I also had a mortar board hat to wear but I was the only choir boy with this head gear! As choir boys we received the magnificent sum of two shillings per quarter for attending. Should we miss a choir practice, held twice a week in the evening we lost one penny from our 'salary'. One could be out of pocket if one failed to attend many choir practices for a whole quarter, even if one sang in the choir on Sunday morning and evening. The choir master was a Mr Newport who was also a teacher at Luton boys school and the organist at the church. The organ was activated by wind from bellows worked by a pumping mechanism behind the organ. Mr Newport selected two choir boys to pump the organ for music for each church service. It was a privilege to be selected to pump instead of singing in the choir, but sometimes 'pumpers' became forgetful and failed to keep up the pressure from the bellows. Mr Newport was not pleased when this occurred and the music faded!

I had a happy time in the Scouts and rose to be a Patrol Leader. The rest of my patrol were all taller than I was. We held little meetings and also had a camp at Lidsing sleeping under canvas. Lidsing was a former parish outside Luton on the road to Boxley and Maidstone. The parish was later incorporated into the Municipal Borough of Gillingham. The parish church had been pulled down but there were tombstones still standing in the former churchyard. It was among the gravestones that we camped and lit our campfires for cooking our meals! I passed for my 'cook's badge' at the camp. I also qualified for a 'path-finder badge'. Later I obtained a laundry-man's badge. All these to sew on my uniform to show my skills!

My mother decided that I should be taught to play the piano. A piano has been purchased and stood in the 'front room'. I was sent to learn to play with a teacher, Mrs Much, who lived on Luton Road near to the church. I had to practice the little pieces of music set by Mrs Much ready for the next weekly lesson. My mother also commenced learning to play with Mrs Much. Being very small I was unable to reach the pedals of the piano and also I had small hands so could not stretch an octave. Not the best type of pupil and I did not enjoy 'practising'. Fortunately for me I ceased taking lessons when we eventually moved to Rainham in 1920. We took the piano with us but not for me to play unless I was pressed. I did learn to play a few pieces but gradually forgot all of them. Piano playing was not my forte!!

All the roads around Alexandra Road were named after Queen Victoria's family. There was even a Victoria Road as well as Albany, Clarence, Connaught, and Edinburgh and a Coronation Street. We had moved from Constitution Road. It was like living among the Royals! Whoever chose the names must have been a true royalist. But one street name is as good as any other so long as it can be pronounced and located.

We moved to Century Road, Rainham, early in 1920. I was then 13 years old and my sister Doris, 11. We cycled to and from school and my father cycled to his work in the Dockyard at Chatham. The tramway system was then in operation but we all cycled except for occasional pleasure trips. The trams ran from the top of Frindsbury Hill, part of Strood, and Rochester, to the terminus outside the Cricketers public house at Rainham. The track from Rainham to the top of Barnsole Road, Gillingham, was via a runway behind the hedge apart from a small portion at Rainham Mark where built up houses were in the way. For this the trams went out onto the main road. The main road, now the A2 had high hedges on the left hand side going towards Chatham, which gave protection from bad weather. Should a lorry come along my sister and I attempted to catch hold of the back so getting a 'tow' to school. This was not very dangerous because lorries in those days went fairly slowly and were not very numerous. Conditions today are far different. The road has been widened taking in most of the old tramway track, the rest is now a boulevard with pretty flower beds.

The depot for the trams was at the end of the Luton Road, almost opposite Christchurch church. The track ran along Luton Road until it met the longest track running from Rainham to Frindsbury, at the Luton Arches. This is where the main railway line crossed the road by a series of arches before entering the tunnel under 'The Great Lines' to reappear again at Gillingham Railway Station. This was the old South Eastern and Chatham Railway before it merged and eventually became part of national railway systems. The tramway system had a series of 'points' which had to be altered by a 'point boy' who stood there but if absent the tram conductor had to get off his tram and alter the points before the tram could proceed on its journey along Chatham High Street or up Chatham Hill. There were branch tramways at the Jezreels at the top of Canterbury Street allowing the trams to go down Canterbury Street, Gillingham instead of on to Rainham. The Canterbury Street tram went down to Gillingham High Street and on to Richmond Road and the Strand by the river. At the bottom of Canterbury Street it met another branch line that had come via Old Brompton en route for Gillingham Railway Station and to Gillingham Green near to St. Mary Magdalene church. Another branch line went from Chatham Town Hall along Railway Street up the Maidstone Road past Chatham cemetery towards Bridgewood. Another branch line went on from Rochester through Delce up to Borstal village the site of the 'Borstal' establishment. It is the prison from which all 'Borstal' establishments take their name. From the terminus at the top of Frindsbury Hill, one could walk down the lane to Upnor and the beach opposite to Gillingham on the other side of the River Medway. Here there is a good view of Chatham Dockyard across the river. Here also one can see the training ship 'Arethusa', an old wooden vessel which receives visitors to see how seamen in past years existed in such primitive conditions. Upnor Castle is close by and is the location where the "Great Chain" was stretched across the river from Gillingham.

Also from the tramway terminus at Frindsbury Hill, one commences the walk to Cliffe-at-Hoo if willing to undertake a long journey. Our whole family did it sometimes to visit Aunt Lilian and Uncle George Ayears and their five sons at Reed Street, Cliffe-at-Hoo. The 'Jezreels' mentioned in the preceding account of the tramway system was a tower erected by a religious sect known as the Jezreelites as a temple in 1885 in which they intended to assemble when the end of the world was nigh. It was supposed to be fireproof to protect the adherants from the fire and brimstone forecast to be due in the not too distant future. Unfortunately it was never completed and stood as a sad memorial to man's folly! The sect ran out of money! It was a very large solid building inside of which were later two hard tennis courts. I played on these a number of times but being still open to the elements were not an 'all-weather' facility. The Jezreelites were still in existance even up to the start of the 1939 war, conspicuous by their flowing locks which they declined to cut. But they had lost their temple intended to save them from Armageddon! It finally fell into the ownership of the firm of Robinson which manufactured the Jubilee clip invented by Mr Robinson who was an Artificer in the Royal Navy. Patented, he made a fortune. Mrs Robinson during the early years of the 1939 war contributed the required sum of £5,000 for a Spitfire aeroplane to take part in the 'Battle of Britain' contests. The Jezreels tower was finally demolished in 1960 and the site is now occupied by the offices and factory for 'Jubilee' clips!

George and Lilian Ayears lived in a small terrace house overlooking Cliffe Marshes and the River Thames. "Great Expectations" country! Cooling not far away. In the distance, the Curtis and Harvey explosive works where Uncle George worked building the tall chimney stacks etc, necessarily on the marshes away from the village. To get there one had to walk past a number of chalk pits filled with water, relics of former workings for chalk for the cement works in the area. My cousins went swimming in these old pits but I was unable to swim. I spent a number of holidays in Cliffe-at-Hoo with my cousins. It was very crowded, I had to share a bed with at least two cousins. The house had an outside lavatory and no main drainage. It smelled to 'high heaven', there apparently being no cesspool either. Digging a cesspool was, I imagine, impossible due to proximity of the marshes'. There was a large walnut tree with plenty of walnuts in the season at the end of the garden. Uncle George was a keen bird fancier and kept many singing birds in very small cages on the wall outside the back door. They were mostly linnets or finches of various kinds which he showed in singing competitions. It seemed to me a very cruel method of keeping little birds in such small cages. He caught the birds in nets on Cliffe marshes. The practice of keeping such birds has since been outlawed in the United Kingdom but such singing birds may be seen nowadays in the small lanes in Palma, Majorca where the birds seem to enjoy singing in the cramped conditions. The Cliffe marshes had many ditches draining the ground. With my cousins we went catching eels, using a long pole with a specially spiked metal end with flanges that prevented the eels from escaping when the pole was thrust into the ditch and struck an eel lurking there. There were plenty of eels. Those we caught we took home to Aunt 'Lil' to cook for a meal. We also went bird nesting on the marshes looking for eggs in the grass nests from birds such a plovers and lapwings. These I took home for my own collection of birds eggs. Another activity now prohibited. My holidays in Cliffe-at-Hoo were most enjoyable with my five cousins particularly cousin Horace, older, Albert, three months younger and Cyril younger still. I had no brothers and their company was most enjoyable to me. The road to Cliffe passed over the level crossing on the railway that ran from Gravesend to Port Victoria on the Rivers Thames and Medway. Port Victoria was named after the Queen at the time and intended as a port for ships at the mouth of the River Thames. It was never a financial success, it has now been closed and the railway discontinued. 'By Dr. Beeching'.

At the end of Alexandra Road stretched the Coney Banks for some miles to Snowledge Bottom and Walderslade, not then built up. So named after the many rabbits or 'coneys' that existed there. The horses from the Royal Engineers' stables located at the other side of the Coney Banks were exercised there as well as horses owned by Officers in the Royal Marines. As a result of the presence of the horses, mushrooms could be collected there by the basketful. Also the hedgerows were full of blackberry brambles. We children collected many jarfuls as well as playing games there. At the outbreak of the 1914 war the banks were used for digging trenches as practice for war. Live grenades were thrown so the area became dangerous. One boy from Chatham Technical School named Hawkins picked up one that had failed to explode on impact. It 'went off' and he lost his hand. Later he opened a garage selling petrol and for repairs to the emerging flood of motor cars, using the compensation he received. Eventually he was a prosperous business man. Such was his fortunes of war but no doubt he would have preferred to have the use of two hands.

During the war soldiers began to be billeted on householders. A troop arrived one day and billeting began in Alexandra Road. The Sergeant in charge allocated men according to accommodation available in each house. The first ones we received in No. 34 were raw recruits with little knowledge of how to put on their equipment. Fortunately my father was well acquainted with "putties" and packs etc. from his association with the Marines. So was able to give advice enabling them to parade properly dressed. In due course the Sergeants and Corporals knew a good billet when they saw one and we seemed always to get one or other of such as our 'guests'.

CHAPTER THREE
Early Schooldays

From Alexandra Road at age 5 I started to attend the Luton Road Council School. There were three sections. The Infants and the Big Girls, both entered from Luton Road and the Big Boys entered from Alexandra Road. I was a very small boy. My sister Doris, two years younger was taller than I was. I attended the Infants for my first year, then I was considered bright enough to go up to the Big Boys. However, being so young and so small it was felt not advisable for me, so as an alternative, I was sent to the "Big Girls" school. I think I must have been the only boy to have been in the 'Infants', the 'Big Girls' and then the 'Big Boys', where I was sent at the age of seven straight into Form 2. There were 10 Forms and I progressed steadily through 2, 4, 6, 8 and 10 which I reached at just about 11 years of age. In Form 10 were boys of nearly 14 about to leave school. I only had one setback to my progress. When in Form 6, in the play-ground I was set upon by a big bully boy. A master appeared so I and the bully were sent to the Headmaster, a strict disciplinarian named Francis White who was known for his propensity for caning boys. I refused to submit to punishment for something I had not done, so I struggled with the Headmaster and I understand damaged his pocket watch. He was furious and decided to lock me in the stationery cupboard. I began to climb out of the window but was stopped and sent to Form 5 for punishment. Next day my father went to see the Headmaster and the outcome was that I was returned to Form 6 and no other action was taken.

While in Form 8 the whole school received a visit from a lecturer from the Education Department of Kent County Council who addressed each Form on the subjects of drinking and smoking. Afterwards we all had to write an essay on the lecture. A prize was awarded, one for the whole school and I was the winner. It was a book entitled "Done and Dared in old France" which I found most uninteresting. In Form 10, I was usually top of the class and at 11 years of age was entered for a scholarship to the Chatham Technical School. I was the only successful entrant from the school There were 20 scholarships awarded among all the schools in the Borough of Chatham.

Class four at Luton Road Council School, Luton Chatham Kent (c.1913)
Author is small boy standing next to teacher

When we received the letter from Kent County Council to tell my parents that I had been awarded the scholarship, my mother immediately bought me a new dark blue school cap with the distinctive light blue cross on the crown. Also an enamel school badge from the Technical School with the Invicta insignia. I soon found that it was the practice for older boys to take off a new boy's cap with badge on it just to strike it against the wall and to break the enamel of the badge, spoiling it. A funny sort of joke, but then boys will be boys especially if their actions can cause distress. I tried to keep my enamel badge intact as long as possible but it was finally damaged. I was so proud of my new cap that I walked up and down Alexandra Road for every one to see it!"

CHAPTER FOUR
Technical School.

And so on 1st May 1919 when I was 12 years of age, I commenced a new era and real education at Chatham Technical School.

The intake was divided into two streams, the older boys in Division 'A' and the younger ones in Division 'B'. I was in Division 'B'. We all took the same exam at the end of each term. The results were published with order of merit on the reverse of each scholar's report. Division 'B' had most of the scholarship boys in it so competition was keen. I attained second position in my first year and the first in the second year. Finally I gained first place in the third year. All tuition was towards securing a good result in the examinations held by the Admiralty for apprenticeships in the Dockyard at Chatham or for entry into the Royal Navy as "boy artificers". This examination was very competitive. Boys from all the schools in the Medway towns plus others from away, sat the exam. Similar examinations were held in the other naval areas, Portsmouth, Plymouth, Rosythe etc. The higher a boy came in the dockyard exam, the better the trade he could chose to follow. Almost invariably the top passes took trades such as electrical fitter, engine fitter, sometimes shipwright. Lower down the scale were, plumber, joiner, pattern maker, etc., all recognised trades. The apprenticeship scheme had been set up by the Board of Admiralty in the early 19th century so to ensure that there were skilled craftsmen in training for constructing the ships and vessels for the Royal Navy. The "Navy Artificer" scheme came later. The training was entirely separate, although only one comprehensive entrance examination was held. A boy could opt to enter either or both and then choose. I opted when my turn came to take the exam, to be a dockyard apprentice, but in any case I was too small in height for entry as a naval artificer apprentice. At the 'Tech' tuition was concentrated on the subjects for the dockyard exam.

The important subject was of course mathematics with the related disciplines of arithmetic, geometry, algebra and trigonometry. We also had to study machine drawing plus the more ordinary subjects of physics, chemistry, history, geography, free hand drawing, English and literature. No foreign languages were taught during my period at school at the 'Tech', although these were started after I had left when a teacher of German was appointed We also had sessions of physical training (PT) at which I was more or less useless being so small. The PT instructor was an ex Major from the army and to my mind too fierce a person to be in charge of small boys. His name was Selby and I disliked him.

Major Selby was keen for our class to give a display of gymnastics. One display was of a pyramid with the big boys at the base, then a second tier of less tall boys. On the top were three boy exceptionally short, of which I was one! At practice I usually fell off the pyramid! Much to Major Selby's annoyance. We also had to do high jumping which again I disliked. I was no favourite of Major Selby!

We also had sessions for instruction in woodwork and metalwork. I enjoyed these immensely. The woodwork master was a Mr Thurston who had previously taught at Luton Council Boys School so he knew me. He gave me some awkward jobs sawing up planks for the other boys to use. The metalwork master was a Mr Haigh, a much more pleasant man than either Major Selby or Mr Thurston. In my last year at the Technical School I made a useful metal salver of beaten copper about 13 inches in diameter. This I kept and it is now in the possession of my younger son, Brian. Well polished it stood in the hall of my flat in Bournemouth for many years. Now as it is 75 years old it will soon rank as an antique.

The metalwork and woodwork rooms were situated in the basement of the Technical School and from both, the boys could see the traffic passing along Chatham High Street. It was most unfortunate that when these classes were held in the morning after the school opened, the vehicles conveying the contents of cesspools in Chatham could be seen and smelt as they passed along the High Street on their way to a dump known as Snowledge Bottom on the outskirts of Chatham in the Walderslade area. This is now a heavily built up residential area. Main drainage has now taken over from cesspools. There was no main drainage in those days of 1918.

For sport, the classes had to climb the very steep hill, Institute Hill, immediately opposite the school, carrying the cricketing gear, stumps etc., on to the "Great Lines". We had no sports ground until much later after I had left, when the School was moved to Holcombe, a large residence off the Chatham-Maidstone Road.

I was really not much good at sports or cricket, being far too small in my case. The master who taught drawing and literature was quite popular with the boys. But he was a betting man! On occasions he lowered me out of the window on the ground floor class room on to the High Street to get him a newspaper with the racing results! I was small enough for this task. One year at Christmas time the school put on a play. It was Dicken's "Christmas Carol". Being small I was quickly chosen as one of the school boys to cheer 'Tiny Tim', son of Bob Crachett if my memory is correct.

Although I was no cricketer, I was very interested in the fortunes of Kent County Cricket Club. On one occasion with others, I walked, pushing my bicycle from the school on a half day holiday, to see Kent playing at the Bat and Ball ground at Gravesend. I was able to ride my bicycle home for the return journey. The same happened when some in the class walked to the Mote ground at Maidstone to see Kent play. We went via Boxley Hill passing across the Pilgrims Way. Each of these walks was about 8 miles to the grounds.

However, despite my failures at PT and sports in general I was always near the top in what mattered, the position in scholastic subjects.

We moved from Luton to Century Road, Rainham early in 1920. I was then 13 years old and my sister Doris 11. From Alexandra Road, Luton it had been very easy for me to walk to school at the 'Tech'. Similarly Doris who had been awarded a scholarship to the new County School just inside the Chatham boundary had been able to get there fairly easily, but from Rainham it was not so easy. So we all had bicycles. Father rode his to and fro to the dockyard. Doris and I rode to school along the London Road which had high hedges on one side and the tramway track on the other. Doris went to the top of Chatham Hill and I to the bottom. My distance was about 4 miles and Doris's 3 miles. Father had about 7 or 8 miles each way. Sometimes Doris and I 'hitched' a lift from a slow lorry going our way by clinging on the back. Not too dangerous in those days with little motor traffic and the lorries travelling at slow speeds.

44

After a while at Rainham, our parents decided that we should all have a holiday. We all went to Ramsgate on our bicycles!! 40 miles there and 40 miles back, journeys made without an accident going via Sittingbourne, Faversham, and Canterbury, towns I had never seen before. Neither had I seen the sea as such before. These holidays, and we made two of them in successive years, were a great success. Doris and I built sand castles. We had never seen so much sand as exists at Ramsgate. I won a prize given by the Daily Mail in a sand castle building competition. My effort was of a map of the world using small pebbles to show the continents. Quite different from most of the other entries. I have always been interested in geography even in my early days in Luton School and I regularly took first place in the subject at the Technical School examinations.

We bathed in the sea in our bathing costumes. These all had skirts, even mine and my father's. Skirts down to our knees for men and women! Nothing like the bikinis for the girls and the trunks for the men and boys worn today. To bathe we had to enter a wooden bathing hut on wheels which was pulled in and out of the water by horses far enough to go up and down the steps from the hut on wheels into the see. All undressing and dressing by both sexes had to be performed inside each hut individually away from prying eyes. It was all a very serious matter. A strange corollary of this performance on Ramsgate sands so long ago, occurred at the Cumberland Hotel in Eastbourne, where and when Dorothy and I were celebrating our Diamond Wedding of 60 years duration. A friend of ours, a hotel proprietor from Goudhurst in Kent came to see us at our hotel. I was showing him round the hotel when on the wall of a small reception room were pictures, photographs, of horses in the sea. He was astounded. The horses, he said, were those his father used during the winter to pull the carts delivering coal to his customers. His father had been a coal merchant in Lewisham. During the summer his father regularly sent his horses down to the sea at Ramsgate for a "holiday" and to pull the bathing huts into and out of the sea. Horses, my friend said, loved to go in the sea so they too had a bath. My friend was Frank Owen who later retired to Headcorn in Kent where his bungalow was destroyed in a disastrous fire caused by his cat knocking over a portable stove.

At Ramsgate, there was open air entertainment performed by a concert party on a stage erected on the sand. Payment had to be made to sit in a deck chair in rows in front of the stage. However, onlookers could view and hear the show by standing at the back for which there was no payment required. One of the performers did, however, come round with a hat for voluntary contributions. We often stopped and watched from the back. The performers were generally dressed as pierrots and sang popular songs of the times. Also comedians cracking jokes. To us a nice free show.

The first time at Ramsgate we stayed on the East Cliff and next time the West, in small boarding houses of which there were plenty in the town. From the West Cliff we could see Pegwell Bay where the Vikings had landed centuries before. Beyond Pegwell was Sandwich where though I did not know it at the time I was to be stationed in the Excise for quite a long period while in charge of the port and of a brewery at Ash nearby. The Excise Station had become vacant due on retirement so I was sent there until the new appointee arrived. Our little family eventually returned from these two holidays on our bicycles.

14 Century Road, Rainham was a great improvement on the terrace house in Luton. It was lit by gas, and had more modern cooking and heating facilities. There was a large garden with cherry, apple and plum trees, also a row of damson trees which bore loads of fruit. My mother made gallons of damson wine although the family were not drinkers of alcoholic beverages. Most of the wine was given away to friends and relatives. Much later my future brother-in-law, Robert Craske became very fond of mother's wines. My father cultivated the garden producing vegetables for the house. We kept chickens and at one time I had also a flock of homing pigeons as a hobby. There was a nice lawn behind the bungalow on the edge of which father planted a vine which produced some edible grapes. There was a wooden garage at the end of the garden approached from a passageway between the houses in Century Road and the next road Salisbury Avenue. We were now living "in style"! The garage became very useful when my father purchased an 'Omega' motor cycle and even more so when some years afterwards, his first motor car. When I was given a motorcycle, an A.J.S. make, I too was able to use the garage although this was some time later.

The house had two large bedrooms leading off the entrance hall and with a large 'front' room, also the sitting/dining room both leading off the entrance hall. Behind the dining room was a large kitchen having an opening from a rear door to the lawn. There was also a small room, we called it the vestibule, from which there was a stairway leading to a third bedroom and an enormous loft over the downstairs rooms. From the kitchen there was a toilet and bathroom. The kitchen contained a large stone 'copper' heated by coal for mother to do her washing. Eventually this was dismantled and a more modern boiler installed. So too was the toilet and the bathroom to be replaced by altering the vestibule by a different approach stairway to the third bedroom and loft. A new up-to-date toilet and bathroom was then installed replacing the old vestibule.

My parents occupied the front bedroom; my sister the back bedroom and I had the small bedroom at the top of the stairs. It was all very comfortable. My father had purchased the bungalow from a Mr Thompson by auction. It had previously been occupied by the local schoolmaster. Mr Thompson who lived next door in a very large house known as White Cottage, 16 Century Road. He allowed my father a loan to complete the purchase, which was paid off by instalments over several years. This was convenient to all concerned. Mr Thompson had a large timber business in Chatham as well as having two of the new fangled motor char-a-bancs. These he hired out. This was a new feature of travel in the early 1920's. There were two Thompsons sons both about my age and we became friends. I recall hearing a piano being played soon after we moved into Century Road. Whoever was playing was extremely expert. I later discovered that what was being played was a pianola which produced music mechanically, hence the expert playing. Sometime later when I got to know the Thompson family I was permitted to play the pianola, which was easy, producing perfect music. The two Thompson boys started to attend the Mathematical School in Rochester on a fee paying basis, so we did not mix so much once I had began to get involved with more advance studies at the 'Tech'.

At the Headmaster's suggestion, I took the open examination for apprentice in the Royal Air force. This was a fairly new examination with the opportunity to go to Cranwell College. I secured 3rd place in all England, quite an achievement but I had no desire to go into the Royal Air Force. I did not attend for interview but being under 5 feet in height it is doubtful if I would have passed the medical examination. In 1922 I sat the long awaited Dockyard Examination for apprenticeship. I secured the highest pass from the Technical

School with 10th place among all the contestants from all the schools in the area and beyond. I particularly wanted to be an electrical fitter apprentice but there were only 8 vacancies for such. However, some boys in the nine ahead of me opted for engine fitter apprenticeships so in the end I obtained my first choice, that of electrical fitter.

CHAPTER FIVE
Apprenticeship years

So another era closed, that at the Technical School and a fresh one opened. I started in the Chatham Dockyard in September 1922.

From having to cycle just 4 miles to school at the 'Tech', I now had a 7 mile ride to Chatham Dockyard and the necessity to arrive by 7.00 am. This meant arising at about 6.00 am. Arriving on time was essential because employees had to 'clock on' at the muster point just inside the dockyard gate, pick up a metal identity disc and deposit this at one's particular work place inside the dockyard. This also needed to be done by 7.00 am A bell tolled inside the dockyard as 7.00 am approached and stopped precisely at that time. The apprentices too had evening sessions at the Dockyard School so it was a very long day away from home. I was unable to get home between the time of leaving the workplace and starting the evening school sessions. I usually went as far as Chatham High Street and had a snack 'tea-break'. Most of the other apprentices and all of the 'electricals' could easily get home between the time of leaving the work place and getting to school. But for me, my periods away from home lasted from just after 6.00am to near 10.00 pm 3 days a week.

Being small I had been in short trousers, so my mother with her expertise made me a long trousered suit to start work. The whole point of wanting to be a dockyard apprentice was to be able to attend the Dockyard School which was considered equal to a degree course, especially if one completed the full four year course. When I arrived for my first day in the electrical fitting building it was found that I was too short to reach the bench, so I was given a wooden box to stand on. I was then only 4ft 11inches tall. There were 7 other apprentices starting the same day, but one, named George Lawrence was absent for some time. (He later became my 'best man' at my wedding in August 1930). The others were Harold Attwood, Horace (Dusty) Doust, from Richmond Road School, Gillingham. William Holloway from the Mathematical School, Rochester, Frank Smallwood from Rochester Technical School, Chris James from Byron Road School, Gillingham, Leslie Ansell from Napier Road School, Gillingham. George Lawrence was from Ordnance Place School, Chatham. No other boy from Chatham Technical School secured a place high enough to choose to be an electrical fitter apprentice. Of the seven other apprentices only one, Chris James was as small as I but whereas I started to grow quickly, he remained short. I seemed quickly to catch up with Attwood, Holloway and Ansell, nearly so with Lawrence. Doust and Smallwood were both very tall boys. We all became good friends apart from Smallwood who was something of a 'loner'. My first year 'at the bench' was mainly occupied repairing parts of gun firing equipment from a warship. For the second year all the apprentices 'went afloat', in other words on to vessels under construction or refitting, installing electrical equipment. I was attached to a fitter who was qualified particularly on gyroscopes then coming into use especially on submarines. He was an excellent technician but a very poor instructor so I never really learned what the gyro system was all about. The arrangements for teaching apprentices their trade was to be attached to a technician known as one's 'skipper'. He received the princely sum of two shillings per week extra on his wages for instructing his protégé. A qualified craftsman in those days received wages of three pounds two shillings per week, so the extra two shillings was very welcome. For work considered dangerous an extra two shillings was paid and also for work considered to be 'dirty'. These extras were paid on recommendation from the Inspector in charge of the Department. We apprentices received fourteen shillings in our first year which went up to sixteen shillings in the second year. It should have been more but the Admiralty imposed a cut in wages in our second year. For the third year, it was eighteen shillings and fourth year twenty-five. On coming out of 'one's time' we became craftsmen on the three pounds two shillings level. There was little hope of any increase unless one passed the examination for 'draughtsman' in the Department's Drawing Office with a much better salary. Or a craftsman could be selected by the management to be a 'chargeman' superintending the work on the shop floor or on the ships etc. There were higher ranks of Inspector and Engineer. I never discovered how such advancement was obtained. The main desire of all apprentices was to take advantage of the exceeding high standard of education in the Dockyard School which could lead to obtaining a better position in society away from the dockyard. For those apprentices not so ambitious, serving an apprenticeship at any trade ensured a 'job for life' as a tradesman within the dockyard. It has to be remembered, that in those days, the dockyard was the major employer in the Medway Towns with over 10,000 artisans at work, the envy of many in less secure occupations.

All apprentices of whatever trade, attended the Dockyard School for two afternoons each week plus three evening sessions. Instruction in all engineering subjects was given although history was taught in the first two years. After that it was purely engineering, mathematics to a very advanced stage, chemistry, physics, metallurgy and electricity. Exams were held half yearly. At the end of the first year, approximately half the apprentices were released from attending school. These were those below the required pass mark. Again at the end of the second year another half, approximately, left, a similar procedure at the end of the third year. By this means the Admiralty weeded out all but the top twenty or so apprentices and retained only those likely to be of value for future use within Admiralty service as draughtsmen, engineers, constructors, electrical engineers etc., controlling the workforce employed in building and maintaining the Royal Navy vessels. It was a very competitive and indeed almost a vicious system but it ensured the Admiralty having the highest trained men available to carry on the tasks of building and maintaining vessels for the Royal Navy. Originally the trade of shipwright was considered to be the most superior. This in the days of sailing vessels when minor trades of carpenter, caulker, sailmaker etc., were of less importance although quite necessary for building a complete sailing ship. Similarly blacksmiths, coppersmiths, ropemakers, sailmakers etc. all had to be trained. However, the most important trade was that of shipwright responsible for the task of designing and building a vessel. For this reason the apprentice obtaining first place in all the naval dockyards throughout the country, Chatham, Portsmouth, Devonport etc., of whatever trade, be it engine fitter or electrical fitter was persuaded to change trades at the end of his fourth year to that of shipwright and to attend full time at the Royal Naval College at Greenwich and to become a Naval Constructor. A top placed shipwright apprentice would naturally not need to change his trade. Only one apprentice throughout the whole country was selected each year for such a prize appointment. One such, originally an engine fitter apprentice from my old school, the Chatham Technical, who was a year senior to me, took first place throughout his period in the Dockyard School over all apprentices in all the Royal Dockyards. He changed his trade to Shipwright and was awarded a place at the Royal Naval College at Greenwich to become a Naval Constructor. He also gained a scholarship to a University. His name was Morley and I subsequently made a brief acquaintance with him at the Royal Military College located at Shrivenham, Wiltshire when visiting my wife's uncle who was a draughtsman there. Morley was a professor at the college. The college had been moved from Woolwich to Shrivenham during the war.

Another boy, one year junior to me in the Dockyard School who was selected to go to the Greenwich Naval College to be a Naval Constructor, lived in Upchurch, a village a few miles from Rainham where I lived. We used to cycle home together from our studies in the Dockyard School. This late in the evening. We had many discussions of mutual interest. His name was Baker. After qualifying as a Naval Constructor at Greenwich Naval College he was seconded to the Canadian Government for service in the Canadian Navy then under construction. He became the authority on nuclear powered submarines. Eventually I learned that he had been given a knighthood by the British Government and became Sir I Baker. I quote these examples to demonstrate what could be achieved by apprentices of outstanding ability from passing through the Dockyard School. Other opportunities occurred from Whitworth Scholarships given by the firm of that name to engine fitter apprentices to attend a university. At one time these scholarships were also available to electrical fitter apprentices but were discontinued and awarded only to engine fitter. Competition was very keen among all the apprentices throughout their various periods in all the Royal Naval Dockyard schools throughout the country be they Chatham, Devonport, Portsmouth, Rosythe etc.

What also happened of course, was that other apprentices of high calibre, scholastically obtained from their training in the Dockyard Schools very frequently left at the conclusion of their apprenticeships to posts in industry, commerce, civil service etc. The Admiralty, however, still retained artisans qualified to fill higher posts such as draughtsman, overseer, inspector, constructor, engineer etc. for Admiralty service within each dockyard.

My second year apprenticeship 'afloat' with my artisan instructor was mainly spent on submarines undergoing a 'refit', in other words, refurbishment, overhauling the electrical apparatus throughout the vessel including the installation of a gyroscope used for steering purposes. The experimental submarine, the 'X.I'. was such having an installation. As it turned out much later, the 'X.I.' was not a success proving too slow and unwieldy and no further submarines of this type were constructed. I also spent a considerable time on the submarines M.1, M.2, and M.3 and also on the very small submarines of the H. Class. For the M. Class submarines reconstruction was taking place to mount a gun in front of the conning tower of one and apparatus for allowing a plane to 'take-off' on another. How the plane would return I do not know. Maybe it was for a small seaplane. I believe both projects failed to materialise. I also worked on some smaller submarines of the 'H' class, but mainly on the 'X.1.' I never really got to know much about gyros for steering the submarines. My 'skipper' was not too keen to explain. He had had a course of instruction at Sperry Gyroscopes Ltd. on behalf of the Admiralty. We had had other work to do in any case. For a time we were on the 'mother' supply ship for submarines, H.M.S. Hermes. Because our tasks were not completed when the Hermes was due to leave Chatham dockyard to go to sea 'my skipper' and I had to sail with the ship down the Medway to Sheerness to allow enough time to complete our work. Eventually we had to descend down a rope ladder into the Liberty boat for return to Chatham. This was a scary experience for me that I would not like to repeat, the Hermes being a vessel with decks a considerable height above sea level.

After my second year I returned to the Electrical Engineering 'shop' for instruction in 'fitting and turning'. This was on a lathe and did not require much brain power except to take great care not to spoil the article being turned, or to have an accident with the machine or of the materials. My next transfer was to the electrical power station which provided all the electrical power for the whole dockyard and for the ships undergoing refit or construction throughout the 'yard'. This was an interesting year where I obtained an insight into the 'boards' controlling the distribution of electrical power and of the reciprocal type steam powered engines driving the dynamos to produce it. Also the large coal fired burners producing the steam to drive the reciprocal engines. During my stay in the power station the start was made in replacing the steam powered engines with more modern diesel powered machines, I was the only one of my year sent to the power station. The other apprentices went to a different aspect of electrical work such as telephones, cable distribution, instrument testing etc. My final year was in the drawing office as a draughtsman for some designing of parts required; drawing the complete layout of the electrical apparatus throughout a vessel under construction, or refitting, plus designing or modifying apparatus. My 'Instructor' was very knowledgeable on literature but it seemed to me, not very good at passing on knowledge of electricity. We apprentices spent most of our time when in the drawing office in studying. Throughout my third, fourth and fifth year I attended the Gillingham Technical School in the evening further to study electrical engineering and related subjects. From this I was awarded National Certificates by the Institution of Electrical Engineers. I would have found these of value had I continued in this career.

During our years as electrical fitter apprentices we engaged in a number of joint activities. I believe the first suggestion for forming a cricket club came from Horace (Dusty) Doust (he was known to everybody as 'Dusty' because of his dark skin although there was no suggestion of African or Asian ancestry). 'Dusty' was a very good bowler. We had a little meeting and I was appointed Treasurer which I was willing to accept since I was no good as a cricketer! We brought the 12 'electricals' from the 1921 entry into our scheme plus a few others from the 1923 and later entries. After our first year as a team we were very fortunate to receive strength from an apprentice who had transferred from Gibraltar when his father who had been employed in the Naval Dockyard there, returned to employment in Chatham yard. The son's name was Bert Tippen and he was an exceptionally good cricketer. He attended the Dockyard School with those from the 1921 entry but so far as I know he was not very successful as a scholar. At first we played on the 'Great Lines' on a portion of grass which we cut with a lawn mower I carried up from Rainham and then stored at the residence of Chris James who lived near the 'Great Lines'.

I had a very old cricket bat but a good set of stumps. Several of the other apprentices had their own cricket bats. We paid in about tuppence a week. We played amongst ourselves at first when time away from school permitted, generally at weekends. We approached

54

the Superintending Electrical Engineer and through him received permission to play cricket on a proper cricket pitch on St. Mary's Island within the dockyard. Soon we felt strong enough to enter the Medway Cricket League for youths in the area. We were moderately successful although we never succeeded in winning the championship. It was very nice to have a real cricket pitch to play on for 'home' games. When the 1921 entry retired during their fifth year we were able to recruit apprentices from later entries. Bert Tippen, our 'transferee' from Gibraltar was the star player in our team. He won the trophies awarded by the League for best batsman, best bowler and as such for best 'all-rounder' in the second year we played in the League. On one occasion we played a match against the Engineers and other officials of the Electrical Department. Our entry of 1922 was certainly a 'go-ahead' crew. The only one who did not join in our 'extra mural' activities was Frank Smallwood. He was a motor cycle enthusiast.

My father purchased a motorcycle and sidecar and allowed me to remove the sidecar to ride the motorbike solo. For my mother it was very comfortable in the sidecar. However, when I took it off to ride solo I invariably omitted to put it back on! In the end my father bought me my own motor cycle, an A.J.S., very powerful. Father's machine was an 'Omega', a make now almost unknown. It was a big two-stroke motorcycle that made lots of noise, but easy to manage. With my A.J.S. I was able to get about very easily but I never took it into the dockyard. On one occasion Smallwood with Les Ansell as pillion passenger and with me on my A.J.S. with 'Dusty' Doust on my pillion, went for a weekend to Margate into 'Bed and Breakfast' accommodation. We felt awfully 'grown-up'. This was the only time that Frank Smallwood entered into any activities with the other 7 apprentices of our year. Having found accommodation to take four youths in one room, we went for a walk around the town but did not find anything of great interest. We then went back to our 'accommodation'. The other three had had a glass of beer in a public house and I had had a lemonade. The room had four single beds. When we decided to retire we had no idea where the toilet was situated, and we all wanted to pee, but we did find two chamber pots!! So we used them. I strongly objected to the chamber pots remaining in the room! We thought about putting them outside the bedroom door. In the end we decided to put them outside on the window sill. The bedroom was on the first floor and not very high above the pavement outside. When we arose next morning we found that the pots were in full view of passers-by. We hastily rescued the pots and left them in the bedroom for the landlady to deal with!

As apprentices we were allowed one week away from work and school during each summer, with pay. Other leave could be taken without pay. I suggested that we have a camping holiday. I had heard of a suitable site near Maidstone at Allington on the River Medway. This was owned by Mr. Tyrrit Drake, Mayor of Maidstone who let us camp in his orchard close to the river. We knew of a scout troop who would lend us a bell tent. My mother provided all the cooking utensils. Her brother, my Uncle Bert, had a friend with a covered van who kindly conveyed us to the site. We hired a rowing boat from the hire firm at Maidstone for the week we were under canvas. About one dozen went on the camping holiday, some from my year, one or two from the engine fitter apprentices and also from the 1921 entry. It was a very successful venture. 'Skippers' from the electrical department came out the first year to see how we were faring. The next year we repeated the camp at Allington. Mr Tyrrit Drake by this time had received a knighthood. The following two years we went on the camping holiday to Haysden near Tonbridge on the Medway. We did not need a boat at this site. Shopping was done in Tonbridge. Our final camp was held at Reculver on the North Kent coast near Herne Bay. All our camping holidays were highly successful but they ceased when we finished our apprenticeships in 1927.

Another activity I engaged in with other apprentices was attending the Unitarian Church on Sundays with Harold Attwood and Bill Holloway. This church stood at the top of Hammond Hill in the New Road, Chatham. The parson was The Rev. Will Hayes. He was very knowledgeable on other religions and beliefs throughout the world. This I found very interesting on a subject I had not thought about since I was a choir boy in Christ Church, Luton. As a child, one generally believed without questioning the teaching at Sunday School and also the religious service one was attending. I enjoyed listening to The Rev. Will Hayes' discourses.

In the early 1920's "wireless" was in its infancy. The crystal set with a 'cats whisker' to pick up signals was in use. Then the sets using valves came into use. The valves were almost as big as electric light bulbs. Sets were built using valves, condensers and transformers, etc. I became quite adept at building a wireless set using valves, as also did George Lawrence. None of the other apprentices were interested. I built a very large set using five valves which stood out on top of the cabinet holding the other parts of the set. The five valves when switched on were almost bright enough to light up the room. I erected a long outdoor aerial stretching from the bungalow roof down the garden to my mother's clothes pole. The signals such as music received from the set were very loud and could easily be heard by the neighbours if the window was opened. My 'skipper' in the dockyard knew nothing about radio and was completely at a loss when I drew out a radio circuit showing the valves, condensers, etc. George Lawrence was equally knowledgeable. We purchased the parts to build a radio set from radio shops that were springing up in the district. George and I decided to advertise ourselves as the 'Radio Doctors' in the local press. We obtained a few customers but the cost of advertising nullified any real profit. In any case people owning a purchased set usually took it back to the supplier should it develop a fault. So the Radio Doctor venture was discontinued. Our school studies were paramount.

Soon after my father had given me the A.J.S. motorcycle, 'Dusty' Doust and I conceived the idea of going on a motorbike trip to Oxford and Cambridge just to see what these university towns looked like should we ever succeed in getting to either as students. 'Dusty' came as my pillion passenger. We went via Surrey passing through a little village called Mickleham. Here I was stopped by a policeman for exceeding the 10 miles per hour speed limit! Eventually I was fined the sum of two pounds by a local court. I did not appear to dispute the case. There was little traffic on the roads in those days but two pounds was quite a sum for an impecunious apprentice. I paid up. We duly reached Oxford and were impressed by the exteriors of the many ancient colleges. We then went on to Birmingham where we spent the night. Next day we set out for Cambridge. 'Dusty' got off the pillion at a small town called St. Neots to check from the signpost, the direction for Cambridge. He hesitated about something and I thought he had got back on the pillion so set off at speed for Cambridge. I chatted to him for a while but getting no response, turned round to find he was missing. This was after I had travelled a considerable distance. I retraced my 'steps', eventually finding 'Dusty' continuing his journey towards Cambridge on foot!

The road being a country lane, 'Dusty' was dusty in fact as well as in name. We reached Cambridge in time to look round as we had at Oxford, at the exteriors, before returning to Gillingham and Rainham.

We sometimes attended the musical concerts in the Central Hall in Chatham. These were generally vocal and were a great attraction to older people as well as to the younger generation. My companion at this time was a boy I had known named Cyril Cox at the Council School in Luton where he was in my class for Forms 6, 8 and 10. He did not take the scholarship exam in the year I was successful. But my father persuaded him to compete the following year so he started at the Chatham Technical School a year later than me. However, he took the examination for Dockyard Apprentice in 1922 and succeeded in obtaining an apprenticeship as a joiner and carpenter. We often attended the Central Hall concerts together and made friends with two sisters named Violet and May Wren. This was our first experience of feminine company but it did not last very long. The Wren girl's father was very suspicious of boys so the girls were required to return home early whenever they went out. But in any case Cyril Cox and I were far too busy with our Dockyard School studies and we also had other interests. Cyril Cox also had a friend at the Technical School named Arthur Holbrook whose parents kept a sea-food restaurant in Chatham. Arthur Holbrook took the examination for Dockyard Apprentice in 1923. He too became a joiner and carpenter apprentice. After finishing their apprentice-ships both Cyril Cox and Arthur Holbrook took examinations set for The City and Guilds Certificate which they both secured. They then both became handicraft teachers at schools in Chatham. They were both first-class footballers and cricketers so were able to instruct the school children in their respective schools in these skills as well as in handicrafts, particularly woodworking. I kept in touch with them both until their deaths especially with Arthur Holbrook in his membership of a masonic lodge.

Although my mother's maiden name was Cox, Cyril Cox was not related to my mother's family in any way. He came from the little village of Burham nestling under the North Downs where the Pilgrims Way crosses the River Medway en route from Winchester to Canterbury.

During my 4th and 5th years as an apprentice I became, through George Lawrence and Bill Holloway, a member of the crew of a motor vessel owned by two senior ex-apprentices employed as electrical fitters.   They had purchased from the Admiralty at a sale of surplus boats after the 1914/19 war, a 30 foot pinnace.   This they fitted with a petrol engine and propeller.   They also built on to the boat, cabins for eating and sleeping.   It was called the 'Venetia' and was an exceedingly comfortable seagoing vessel.   The two owners were Alf Fuller and Percy (Tich) Higgins.   Bill Holloway later married 'Tich' Higgins's sister, Olive.   I will mention them later in these memoirs.   Alf Fuller was George Lawrence's "skipper" for a year and later became Power Station Engineer.   'Tich' Higgins who was very short, later became an Admiralty draughtsman.   The boat "Venetia" was moored at Rochester on the River Medway.   Fuller and Higgins were members of the Medway Cruising Club.   Alf Fuller some years later married a girl named May Kirk that I had been friendly with as my dancing partner.   George Lawrence and I were fairly regular members of the 'crew' when we 'sailed' up the River Medway to Maidstone.   Alternately we 'sailed' down the Medway to Queenborough on the Isle of Sheppey.   Four could sleep comfortably in the two cabins.   If 'Tich' Higgins came he was able to curl up easily in the prow of the "Venetia" when four taller young men were occupying the berths for sleeping at night on board. 'Tich' Higgins was so very short.   He later married a publican's daughter from Luton Road and they had a son who was quite tall.   This son entered the army in due course and attained the rank of a Brigadier.   When he finally retired from the army many years later he secured an appointment as Manager of the Royal Naval Hospital in Gillingham where my grandfather and later my father died.   The Hospital had come under the alterations in management scheme brought about by political action when the National Health Service was changed.

'Dusty' Doust was also a crew member at times and we shared out the trips we made, up and down the river.   Once or twice we ventured across the mouths of the Rivers Medway and Thames to Leigh-on-Sea from where we could go into Southend.   Our most ambitious trip was when we went as far as the River Blackwater on the East coast.   From Queenborough we had intended to cross to Essex early in the morning to reach Havengore Creek farther up the Essex coast in order to get into the River Roach separating Foulness Island from mainland Essex.   Alf Fuller was in charge of the trip.

The crew was George Lawrence, 'Dusty' Doust and myself. It was necessary to cross the Maplin Sands on high tide, unfortunately we started out too late and the tide was dropping. This meant we had to go farther and farther out to sea until we came to where the River Crouch of which the River Roach is a tributary, flows into the North Sea at the north end of the extensive Maplins. It was a very hazardous journey for our small boat especially when a storm blew up and darkness descended. We had no lights but eventually in the darkness we saw a faint light somewhere on the shore side of the Maplins. This we made for and found that it was a barge sheltering from the storm, off Foulness Point at the mouth of the River Crouch. We had sailed right round the Maplins towards the River Blackwater. We sailed back into the River Crouch between the Dengie Flats and Ray Sands and finally reached the River Roach to anchor off Foulness Island. This is a naval gunnery practice area. Fortunately no guns were firing at the time. We went ashore to obtain fresh water from a solitary farmhouse, passing several pieces of shrapnel and other evidence of gunnery practice. Next day we set out for the Blackwater but on high tide! We spotted a small object floating about and found it was a small dinghy which apparently had come adrift from a boat in the previous day's storm. So we took it in tow and sailed up the Blackwater to West Mersea with our own dinghy in tow and behind it the smaller dinghy we had found at sea. We dropped anchor but were soon approached by a man who was obviously a sailor. He was irate since we had anchored over his oyster bed so we had to a anchor again farther up the river. We approached an obviously sea-going man to enquire whether he was interested in purchasing a dinghy we had picked up at sea. He went away but soon afterwards we were interviewed by an official in Customs uniform wanting to know about the dinghy we had found. He explained that he was the Receiver of Wreck for Customs and he took the dinghy away. The upshot of this episode was that some months later we each received the princely sum of three shillings and sixpence from the Customs as our share of the prize for rescuing the dinghy, the owners having been found and required to reward the finders. We stayed a couple of days at West Mersea before returning to Queenborough on the Medway, this time crossing the Maplins on high tide! Altogether this was a most venturesome journey which we were perhaps lucky to have survived without coming to harm.

The interesting facet of this encounter with the Receiver of Wreck for West Mersea, for me personally, was that 10 years or so later I was appointed among other duties, the Receiver of Wreck for the Port of Rochester in Kent. The official we saw at West Mersea was an Assistant Preventive Officer of the "uniform wearing" branch of the Customs Preventive Service. He was probably the only Customs official in that part of the Essex coast. The Customs service that I subsequently joined covered all types of revenue matters, both Customs and Excise. Rochester being an important port had four Customs and Excise Officers with a Surveyor in charge. This staff covered every aspect of Customs and Excise work, raising revenue in both branches besides controlling the area. Such officers did not wear uniforms. The responsibility for receiving wreck, in any, was a very minor section of the work of the port and surrounding area of Kent. There were some uniform wearing Customs Preventive Officers and Assistant Preventive Officers at Rochester but they were of a lower grade, controlled from Gravesend in the Port of London. I mention the encounter with the Customs official at West Mersea since it was a strange quirk of fate that occurred to bring me into contact with the Customs Service at a time when I had no thought of changing my career. Incidentally while at Rochester and elsewhere in the Customs Service I had no occasion to deal with a dinghy found at sea!

George Lawrence, 'Dusty' Doust and I commenced to take up dancing. We attended wherever a public dance was being held, even in Frindsbury (part of Strood, Rochester) and in Tonbridge. We had no permanent partners but relied on finding a girl to dance with when we followed the usual practice of watching to see how the girls danced and then crossing the floor at the commencement of a dance to request a girl as a partner. 'Dusty' was quite a good dancer being tall; George improved slowly. I had danced before in the village hall in Rainham with my sister and her friends, so found no difficulty in dancing with any girl that I requested to partner me. None of the other apprentices in our year were interested in dancing.

One year, however, Chris James's father who owned and ran dances in the Paget Hall in Gillingham offered the apprentices' cricket team the use of his hall for a 'New Year's Eve' dance. It was very generous of him since New Year dances always attracted crowds of dancers. 'Dusty' was a very good violinist. There was another apprentice, a year senior, Charles King, who was excellent as a drummer. He brought with him another friend who could play a saxaphone. Another apprentice, Tommy Hewson who was a ship fitter was a first-class pianist. He too joined our 'orchestra'! A senior ex-apprentice, Joe Hills, also helped with the arrangements for the dance. I took over the admissions at the door. Also we made sandwiches, which with lemonade, we sold at a profit from the kitchen window to the hall. The 'New Year Dance' was a great success so we made quite a sum for the cricket club's funds. We were very grateful to Mr. James who was an ex-marine! Once more I was appointed Treasurer.

Around this time I became friendly with a young lady named Elsie Edmonds who lived in Chaucer Road, Gillingham. Sometimes I found time to go to the cinema with her but it was a difficulty to fit in with my studies in the Dockyard School plus the extra sessions at Gillingham Technical School on some evenings. On some Sundays Elsie came to Century Road, Rainham to have tea with my family. She was very well liked by my parents. Elsie once came with my sister Doris for a trip with me on the boat "Venetia" and with George Lawrence and Alfred Fuller. Also she came to see 'we apprentices' camping near Tonbridge. I was sorry when our friendship finished. It was mainly due to the fact that she was not interested in going to dances whereas George Lawrence, 'Dusty' Doust and I were keen. An interesting facet of my association with Elsie was that I used to call to see her sometimes on my way home to Rainham from school in the dockyard or from the 'Tech'. We would be at the backdoor at Chaucer Road. I learned subsequently that Elsie's brother was talking to a young lady at the front door in Chaucer Road. The brother later joined the Royal Air Force as an apprentice, but the girl he was with was a Dorothy Brown. Elsie Edmonds was studying commercial subjects at Gillingham College of Commerce. She became employed first in the office at Gillingham Laundry in Richmond Road, Gillingham, and later in charge of the branch of the laundry in Delce, Rochester. Dorothy Brown also studied commercial subjects at the Gillingham College of Commerce. After a short period working in Chatham for a 'rogue' debt collector against whom she had to give evidence when the police were investigating his activities, Dorothy Brown was also employed in the office at the Rochester branch at Delce of the Gillingham Laundry. Dorothy Brown became my dancing partner.

At the end of my third year when I was due to sit the examination for selection to be admitted to attend the Dockyard School for the fourth year, there appeared the first signs of a nation-wide recession. For the Admiralty, particularly in the naval dockyards, it created doubts on the necessity to employ so many men. All trades were under threat of contraction. Discharges were possible of excess staff in all Departments. The threatened recession had repercussions on the number of apprentices required in the future. An outcome was that whereas 12 electrical fitter apprentices were taken on from the 1921 entry, the number for 1922 (my entry) was 8. For 1923 the number was reduced to 3. Of the 12 electrical apprentices from 1921, an exceptionally high number of 10 were admitted to complete a fourth year in the Dockyard School. There was therefore what might be considered a 'glut' of the more highly skilled young men ready and able to fill vacancies in the hierarchy of senior posts in the Electrical Department.

During my first three years in the School I had secured a place varying from 4th to 10th each term among all the different trades competing. I had therefore reasonably high hopes of being selected for the 4th year course. A total of 20, which included the 10 'electricals' had succeeded in the previous year. But for my year only 8 apprentices were selected from all trades. Of these 8, Doust was the sole 'electrical' success. I was placed 10th and had therefore failed. Or put it another way, the recession had failed me. The position was further illustrated by the 1923 entry for all trades when only three were required for electrical fitter apprenticeships. Of these three, eventually, when their time came, only one again was accepted for the fourth year course.

I have little doubt that in the case of Doust, without decrying his success, since he was an exceptionally clever boy, his whole life had been steeped in dockyard lore. His father was a Constructor in the Shipbuilding Department. His two elder brothers had both been apprentices passing through the Dockyard School. The eldest had obtained a university degree and became subsequently a Naval Commander in the Educational Department of the Royal Navy.

At this time, also, the General Strike called by the Trade Union Congress in support of the miners, caused some ferment among dockyard employees who belonged to a trade union, but were anxious about their position as Government employees. Visits were made to London by Electrical Trade Union representatives to seek advice. Soon, however, the General Strike was called off to the relief of the employees who were then more concerned with the threatened recession and its effect on the work force.

The threatened recession also had an effect on artisans in other trades, particularly for shipwrights. Some of these from my year of entry (1922) were discharged in 1927 when they had completed their apprenticeships. The position regarding former dockyard trained apprentices who entered during the years prior to 1921 for all trades and now serving as artisans at their various trades was very critical. Considerable reductions in overall employment of apprentices was likely. A movement was started to ensure that ex-apprentices who had been trained at Admiralty expense should be retained. This would be to the detriment of other employees including artisans from elsewhere who had secured employment within the dockyard. The matter was hotly debated. Leaders of the movement for retention of dockyard trained ex-apprentices called a meeting in the Assembly Rooms in Gillingham to which all dockyard trained ex-apprentices were invited to attend.

Apprentices still undergoing instruction were also invited. The upshot was that an ex-apprentices "association" was proposed and agreed. A committee was appointed to press for the protection of continued employment of all dockyard trained ex-apprentices by the Admiralty. I recall that I made a speech, the only one by an apprentice still under training, supporting the proposal. The meeting was well attended. Several of my fellow apprentices were present. As a result of my speech I was appointed to the committee. I made some attendances. The only activity I recall carrying out for the Dockyard Ex-Apprentices Association was organising a motor coach tour of the River Medway valley where I had a meal 'laid on' at Igtham on the road to Tonbridge. It was successful but not repeated because I left dockyard employment, but in any case school work came first. The Secretary of the Committee was a Mr Bert Cheshire, a well known employee who was also Secretary of the National Deposit Friendly Society which made provision for sick pay when a person was away from his employment when ill. The Dockyard Ex-Apprentices Association did not achieve any successes in preserving employment for members. It was obvious that discharges were in the hands of officials within the dockyard who were able to decide which employee was to be made redundant, whether an ex-apprentice or recruited from employment elsewhere.

The other side of this problem arose when some years later at the beginning of the 1939/45 war, efforts were made by the Government to trace the whereabouts of former dockyard employees. If and when found, these men were directed as far as was possible, back into Admiralty or other services employment. Chris James one of my colleagues who had become a draughtsman at the Admiralty but subsequently became an official of the Inland Revenue, was so directed back into Admiralty employment at Bath where the Admiralty had been transferred at the outbreak of the war. A similar fate occurred to some ex-dockyard apprentices who had entered the Customs and Excise Department some years after I had done so. Fortunately my service in the C & E was retained. Of my fellow apprentices from the 1922 examination, Doust went to Vickers in Barrow-in-Furness, from there to Whites in the Isle of Wight. He then emigrated to Australia to be employed on Navy work, then back to England to be employed at the Air Ministry. Attwood went first to Malta and then to Bermuda in charge of Admiralty telephone systems. Ansell became an Admiralty Overseer visiting firms engaged on Admiralty work. Lawrence, Smallwood, Holloway and James all became draughtsmen at the Admiralty. Later they were transferred to Bath at the outbreak of the 1939/45 war. James only after he was recalled from the Inland Revenue Department again to serve as a draughtsman. He had become an amateur grower and exhibitor of sweet peas. On one occasion, the show for this flower was at Bournemouth. He came to stay with my wife and myself during the period of the show. I visited him at his home in Bath was well as George Lawrence (my best man) and Bill Holloway with whom we stayed several times, in Bath after the war. James eventually returned to his employment with the Inland Revenue.

An entrepreneur named Forsythe came to Rochester and re-opened the former Rochester Casino as a dance hall employing the top dance bands, to supply the music. The Casino became a veritable 'Mecca' for dancers. At this time 'Dusty' Doust and I had become quite proficient dancers, George Lawrence was not quite so. I can remember him trying to practice the 'Charleston' on the roof of the cabins of the boat "Venetia" when we had beached it at Upnor near

Rochester to scrub and clean the boat's bottom. We three apprentices attended the Casino dance hall regularly on Saturday evenings in our last year as apprentices. Sometimes I took a partner, May Kirk, but we youths preferred to dance with any girl who appeared to be a good dancer. It was at the Casino that I first met Dorothy Brown, later my wife, who was a marvellous dancer. May Kirk, incidentally, married Alfred Fuller, the "Captain" of the pinnace "Venetia" in which we had made our trip to West Mersea, skirting the Maplin Sands!!

After I had obtained my National Certificates in Electrical Engineering, I was selected by the Principal of Gillingham Technical School evening classes, to accept a position with the seaplane manufacturers, Shorts, at Rochester. I declined the invitation since I had no desire to enter the aircraft manufacturing industry. The vacancy was then offered to another apprentice in my year, an engine fitter named Hambrook who had obtained selection for a fourth year in the Dockyard School. He accepted and left Admiralty employment. Later the firm of Shorts moved to Belfast taking Hambrook with them. I heard subsequently that he had attained the position of Manager of Shorts in Belfast. I have no regrets on this score.

Since I had not obtained selection for a fourth year in the Dockyard School, following from Admiralty policy in the light of the probably recession, I decided to attempt to obtain an external degree from Oxford University. I understood, however, that one needed then to have a pass in a foreign language. I therefore started on a correspondence course with Wolsey Hall in Oxford, in French language. I also commenced evening classes at Chatham Technical School in oral French and Latin.

CHAPTER SIX
Examination for Appointment as Officer of H.M.Customs and Excise.

My plans though, were suddenly changed when I observed an advertisement in the Daily Mail newspaper to the effect that 2,000 vacancies were to be available in the Customs Department. I wrote off to the advertiser and learned that it was from Loreburn College in Manchester. The college told me that the examination for the vacancies was imminent and I should apply to sit the examination immediately. This I did but I found that the estimate of 2,000 vacancies was woefully inaccurate. Actually only 50 vacancies existed but my application to sit the exam due in 10 weeks time was accepted. Loreburn College had offered me a 12 week correspondence course covering eight different subjects in the examination; weeks eleven and twelve to be squeezed into weeks nine and ten. The subjects for the examination were English, Elementary Mathematics, General Intelligence, Science, Further Mathematics, French, German or Latin, History and Geography, Economics and Elementary Politics plus a Viva Voce test. Loreburn College's offer to me was that for a fee of three pounds I would receive the tuition in eight subjects but would only have to send in answers to any four. From the tuition I had received in the Dockyard School I decided that I did not need to send in answers to either of the Mathematics subjects. Also I had been quite proficient in History and Geography and in Science during my days at the Chatham Technical School from 1918 to 1922. I would be able to "brush up" my knowledge in these subjects from the correspondence course without sending in answers, so I would then be able to concentrate on the English and General Intelligence correspondence tuition. The examination was to be in six of the eight subjects, with 200 marks for each, except General Intelligence which was for 100 marks. I brought the matter of the correspondence course and the examination, to the notice of the other apprentices who were in the drawing office at the time. Of these Dusty Doust, and Chris James of my year (1922 entry) were interested. Also a boy named Carey from the 1923 entry who had obtained a fourth year in the Dockyard School. Between us we decided to take the Loreburn College correspondence course contributing fifteen shillings each to meet the three pounds total fee. I sent off for the course and duly received the first week's tuition papers in eight subjects. These I circulated so that all four participants saw all the instruction documents and we chose which of the four answers we would submit. The other three apprentices submitted their applications to the Civil Service Commission to sit the examination. The problem then arose in submitting our answers to the tuition papers from Loreburn College. They necessarily had to be in the same handwriting so it was agreed that I should copy out all the answers from the other three and submit them in my handwriting to Loreburn. The plan was for all to see the instruction papers, choose one to answer from any of the eight available; let me have it for copying and submission to Loreburn, regularly each week. None of the four needed to pay much attention to the mathematics instruction sheets, but I had to submit answers to Loreburn in four different subjects. These were generally, English, Science, History and Geography and General Intelligence. I recall that when the results of the examination were published and I had passed at position 44th, having dropped 14 places in the 'viva voce' from 30th, Loreburn College made great play in their subsequent publicity that I had scored 87% in Elementary Mathematics and 82% in Further Mathematics. So the teaching I had received in the Dockyard School had also proved useful. I also scored the 13th highest place in Science and 8th highest place in History and Geography (my favourite subjects) among the successful candidates. So Loreburn's "brush up" instructions had proved useful. Of the other three candidates Doust, James and Carey, Doust dropped out at the last minute and did not sit the examination saying he had no desire to become a Customs Officer. (Actually the exam was for Officer of Customs and Excise, a higher grade than the ordinary uniform Customs Officer). James failed the examination because of a very low mark in the Viva Voce test. Carey on the other hand, although scoring 17 more marks than I did in the written exam, scored a very low mark of only 67 out of 200 for Viva Voce and was not in the first 50 places. He attained the 62nd position. However, the Board of Customs and Excise subsequently extended the number of vacancies available to 100 and he was accepted. One feature of this examination that gave me some satisfaction was that two apprentices from my year in the Dockyard School who had secured the four years when I had not, failed the Customs and Excise Examination. One was Hambrook who had taken the post offered for Shorts the seaplane manufactures in Rochester which I had declined.

I received the result of the examination for appointment as an Officer of Customs and Excise showing I had been successful. I was then working on H.M.S. Kent, a cruiser I had seen launched at Chatham Dockyard some months earlier. The Kent was undergoing 'fitting out' prior to service at sea. I was engaged in installing electrical equipment at a salary of £3 and 2 shillings per week. Ahead of me was the prospect of sitting the examination for appointment as a draughtsman for a higher salary or possibly finding employment elsewhere.

H.M.S. Kent, which Author witnessed being launched at Chatham Dockyard in 1926, and afterwards worked on it installing electrical apparatus when his father came to tell him that he had passed the examination for appointment as an Officer of H.M. Customs and Excise in 1927

My father brought the Customs and Excise examination result in to me because he was starting his 2.00 pm to 10.00 pm shift. I was over-joyed. Subject to a medical examination I was appointed an Unattached Officer at a salary of about three pounds ten shillings per week rising by annual increases to over eight pounds per week. A higher salary than that of a draughtsman and possibly of an Inspector in the Electrical Department. I lost no time in going to the main office of the Electrical Department to tell them I would be leaving. In due course I passed the medical examination and ceased working for the Admiralty in Chatham Dockyard on 10th December 1927. I was to report to the Excise Office in Maidstone on the 12th December 1927 for instruction in my future duties.

So commenced my next career. I had taken a step which I never regretted. An important factor was that my salary was to rise annually. I was to receive 6 weeks leave annually plus a pension when I finally retired. Paid sick leave if necessary was also one of the conditions of employment. For me everything in the garden had come up 'Roses', as the saying goes!!

My father bought me a brand new Ariel motor bike. It was a very powerful machine of high horse power. It had two exhaust pipes, made plenty of noise and I was very proud of it. I rode it to the dances at the Casino. My father continued to use the Omega motorbike and sidecar so we were able to go on visits to the seaside together. My sister Doris, sometimes came as my passenger on my pillion seat. Dymchurch sands were a favourite venue at weekends when my father was off work for the weekend.

CHAPTER SEVEN
Relief work in Excise and instruction in procedure.

On the 12th December 1927 I duly travelled to Maidstone to commence employment in H.M. Customs and Excise Department. The office was in Earl Street, Maidstone practically next door to Fremlins Brewery. There I received a gigantic array of instruction books on every subject the Customs and Excise was responsible for. These together with piles of 'amendments' to these "instruction books". It was all rather daunting especially as I was told that I had to paste in the amendments so to be 'au fait' with the 'up-to-date' procedures. Also there was a large pile of what were termed 'General Orders' which also had to be studied since they covered aspects of Customs & Excise work not shown in the instruction books. I was told that I was to be instructed in the Excise by Mr Wallace Wood in charge of the Maidstone 2nd Station which covered the control of Fremlins Brewery and a portion of the town of Maidstone but did not extend into the surrounding countryside. Mr Wood introduced himself to me and told me "not to worry", and that I should soon "pick it all up". There were three other Excise Officers in the office plus a Surveyor who was in overall charge, named Releen. I was introduced to him and he seemed rather elderly, understandingly so, because he retired soon afterwards. A new Surveyor named Battison was appointed. This was after I had left 'on my travels' as an Unattached Officer. Mr Wood was a very gentlemanly man. He took me round Fremlins Brewery to explain how the Excise controlled the duty to be paid on the beer produced there. My periods of instructions was from December 12th to January 14th 1928. With Mr Wood I went round his 'Station' visiting public houses. Mr Wood explained to me that all licensees of a public house were required to enter in the 'Spirit book' kept on the premises, the receipt of all spirits which had to be accompanied by a 'spirit certificate' from the sender. Also the premises had to be surveyed for a number of other reasons, one of which was to check that no smuggled goods were on the premises, visiting if thought necessary the cellar. Any casks were to be examined to confirm that no 'grogging' was taking place, i.e. putting water into an empty cask to extract any spirits remaining in the wood of the cask. To see also if any dilution of beer was taking place in the cellar. All these checks were relics of past times and completely out of date in 1927. We visited the premises of bookmakers (for the betting tax then in force), plus a cinema for entertainments duty. All very confusing to an erstwhile electrical engineer. I began to get the gist of the structure of the Customs and Excise Department with its 'Stations' 'Districts', 'Collections' plus the Head Office situated then in the Custom House in London. There were also the many ports throughout the country but knowledge of these was to come much later. After a while Mr Wood allowed me to go out into the town alone to visit a few public houses for Excise supervision. Eventually towards the end of my instruction period I visited one licensed public house and found that the licensee had failed to enter the spirit certificates in his book. Also I noticed two small casks on a shelf behind the bar and asked the licences to get them down so I might check the contents. All this was being rather officious but I was a 'new boy'. Mr Wood was rather amused when I told him, but promised to look into the matter. I realised now that the whole system of 'surveying' public houses once in each year ending 31st March was out of date, relics of the nineteenth century and before, but in 1927 still being carried out. It has now been discontinued. There are far more important revenue matters than surveying public houses and shops selling methylated spirit etc. I was told to survey Fremlins Brewery alone as a test of my knowledge obtained as Mr Wood's pupil. I took so long that the Surveyor came to find me, but I was being careful not to make any errors! He duly passed me satisfactory. I then had to assist Mr Wood for about a fortnight. It struck me that if my assistance was compensation for the time taken to instruct me, it was a rather back-handed way of repaying him.

Actually as a new Unattached Officer I was something of a novelty. There had been no examination by the Civil Service Commission since 1914, before the outbreak of the first world war. All appointments to the Department from 1919 onwards for a few years had been of ex-service men from the armed forces considered academically qualified. The exam, I sat in 1927 was the first after the war and I was one of the first to be appointed from it.

Mr Wood took me to his home in Maidstone to show me his collection of bird's eggs. He was a keen collector and when I told him I had a collection gathered in some cases on Cliffe-at-Hoo marshes when I was a boy, he was most interested. He explained that it was likely that I would be sent to Scotland later in my service for instruction in distillery control. If so he said, perhaps I would be able to collect some eggs from birds there for him! This did not appeal to me but I was careful not to disabuse him!

Although Alfred the Great is generally considered to the be first to have imposed a Customs Duty, near the conclusion of the ninth century, there is a 'Charter' of 742 which shows the grant of "dues" from two ships, by Aethelbald, King of Mercia to "Collectors in the Hithe of London Town".   Excise, on the other hand, was first charged by the Parliamentarians and by Charles I in 1643, for each side to help pay for the Civil War, 1642 to 1646.   The Parliamentarians first limited their Excise to beer and a number of foreign articles, but later in 1643 extended the duties to many other items. The King's Excise was levied on hay and straw, hops, 'larkes' eggs and fish, to be collected by the King's Excisemen in the markets. In 1648 a petition was presented by the "Knights, Gentry, Clergy, and Commonality, of Kent" urging the immediate abolition of the Excise as being contrary to the Petition of Right". No notice was taken of the petition. The Excise duties were finally placed on a permanent footing at the Restoration of Charles II.   At the Restoration the rules for collecting Customs duties were also revised. Records show that at this time, on the orders of the King, payment of £500 per month was made to "Mistress Eleanor Gwynne", today worth several hundreds of thousands of pounds per annum. "Mistress Nellie" was doing very well out of the Excise!

Doctor Johnson some 100 years or so later, in his Dictionary, described Excisemen collecting the tax as "wretches hired by those to whom the Excise is paid". So I became in Doctor Johnson's eyes a wretch!!

I duly received from C & E H.Q's, my Commission appointing me as an Officer of Customs and Excise plus another authorising me to deal with obtaining Probate for small estates on application by legatees or others involved. Also another Commission appointing me an Inspector of Corn Returns. All these documents made me feel important but I was strongly enjoined to take great care of them since they gave the holder authority to do all manner of things, in excess even of the powers held by the police. It has to be remembered that the Customs is the oldest authority in the land originating from Alfred the Great with power to operate the 'custom' of securing a portion of any goods coming into the country, for the King. The Excise on the other hand is much younger, having been imposed by Charles the First and gave authority using the Dutch word for excising a portion for the Crown. There were no police forces when either Customs or Excise were originally imposed.

Both Departments were separate prior to 1909, the Excise being part of the Inland Revenue. It was decided to amalgamate the Excise with the Customs to form the all embracing C & E Department. The Inland Revenue department continued to be responsible for income tax and related matters. 1909 saw also the start of the universal Old Age Pensions paid on a means tested basis, already mentioned in these memoirs and which was placed under the control of the Excise which covered every parish throughout the country.

It is appropriate that I attempt to describe the peculiar system of time notation used in the Excise, to record arriving at the office to commence work and for notifying attendances at particular 'traders' such as a brewery. Also to record departures away from the office to parishes outside of the town of appointment. Leaving the office for surveying or other business did not have to be recorded provided the visit was within the town. The system was "e.p and m.p". meaning " evening past" if after noon and "morning past" if before noon. No precise time was used such as 4.15 pm. if the time intended to be recorded was quarter past 4 in the afternoon. Just e.p.4 was sufficient. Similarly if one arrived at the office, say at 10 minutes past 10 o'clock in the morning or left to go on survey to an outlying parish at this time it was recorded in the office 'Journal' simply as m.p.10. Minutes of the hour were never shown. Simply record whether after a precise hour as m.p. or as e.p. Again when apparently visiting an important trader such as a brewery the Officer drew a line in the brewing book showing it was made at either e.p. or m.p. possibly from the last time the *parish clock struck the hour!* How this most peculiar system came about I do not know, but it allowed Excise staff extreme flexibility in recording times. The office 'Journal' was kept for recording the times as indicated. In an office where several Officers were housed, they all used one office 'Journal' for signing 'in' or 'out' - 'm.p.' or 'e.p.'!

Did this most peculiar system of time notation arise from when pocket watches or wrist watches were non-existent, before Harrison invented the chronometer which allowed Captain Cook to determine exact Longitude in his voyages to and in the South Seas? Throughout my time in the Customs and Excise Department the e.p. and m.p. system of time notation was sacrosanct. Any attempt to change it was vigorously opposed. Whether it now is used with the imposition of Value Added Tax and a complete change in Excise procedures I do not know. For the Customs side of the Service it does not apply. Customs Officers work to exact hours on which any overtime due is based!

I started my first leave on February 1st and immediately received an advice from the Collector responsible for Maidstone district, whose office was in South London, that I was to be transferred at the end of my leave to Birmingham Collection. So my travels commenced!

Meanwhile I had continued to attend with George and 'Dusty', the dances held in the Casino. Early in February I saw a nice girl dancer on the floor so at the first opportunity I went over and requested a dance. She agreed immediately and her first question was whether I had come to the dance on my motorbike! I had, but had brought there May Kirk! The upshot of this question was that I agreed to take the nice dancing girl to her home in Gillingham on my motor-bike! Her name was Dorothy Brown and this is how I first met my future wife! How Dorothy Brown knew of my motorbike, the new Ariel I never discovered. Probably from Elsie Edmonds who was in charge of the office in Delce, Rochester. After taking Dorothy home to Wellington Road, Gillingham, I had to explain to her that I was about to be transferred to Birmingham in the C. & E. She was well aware that I had been an apprentice in the dockyard. Her father was employed there also but in the Engineering Department. He did not know of me. However, I promised to return from Birmingham the following Saturday so that we might go to the Casino dance together. I said that I would meet her "under the clock" at Chatham Town Hall at 5 o'clock. I had to travel down from Birmingham and did not know at that time what my duties would be there. I managed to get away in time and arrived "under the clock" at five minutes past five! There was no Dorothy Brown in sight. I went to Wellington Road, Gillingham and her father opened the door. He announced to those inside that a strange man dressed in a 'Sidcot' suit (worn by motorcyclists) was outside who was asking for Dorothy. She came to see me and explained that she had waited until the Chatham Town Hall clock had struck five precisely and then went home! I had been five minutes late in getting there from Birmingham about 150 miles away! We often discussed this episode during our married life which lasted 61 years after we were wed in August 1930. "She couldn't wait for five minutes". We went to the dance after all, when we had both dressed for it! And on my motorbike. Dorothy was a glutton for pillion riding, until years later when I brought a side car for her to be more comfortable, later still to change over to a car.

In Birmingham, when I arrived there on February 11th 1928, I stayed at the same hotel that 'Dusty' and I had used years before when we went on our trip to Oxford and Cambridge via a stop in Birmingham. I called at the Excise Head Office to report to a Mr Jackson who was the Collector. I had not been in contact with a Collector before but found him quite reasonable. He seemed pleased to see one of the first 'new boys' from the recent exam. I must admit that in those days I looked very youthful. The Collector enquired about how much I knew of the Excise. Particularly he wanted to know whether I knew anything about Betting Duty. I told him that I had visited a bookmaker's office with my instructor in Maidstone. This seemed to satisfy him and I was put in charge of a vacant Excise Station dealing solely with betting duty. Fortunately there were 6 other Unattached Officers in the building all engaged on control of the betting duty, paid by bookmakers in the whole of the Birmingham area. All these U.O.s as the Unattached Officers were known, were ex-service men from the 1914/18 war and considerably older than me. They were all very helpful in showing me the 'ropes' particularly in writing reports to the Board of Customs and Excise. These had to go via the Surveyor in charge of the Betting Duty District, set up especially to deal with the new Betting Duty brought in by Mr Winston Churchill in 1926. Writing reports had to commence - "Honourable Sirs ...." since they were going to the Honourable Board of Customs and Excise. This was an art in itself. Legal jargon entered into every phrase in making a report to the Board especially if it involved a possible fraud having to go ultimately to the C. & E. Solicitor's Office for preparing the evidence then to go to the law courts.

I had one special problem. My area of control included the Birmingham Law Courts so that when a prosecution of a bookmaker for fraud was agreed by the Board on the advice from the Solicitors Office, the 'file' came to me to "exhibit" the documents for the case to be heard. This was also for all the other areas of control besides being from my own area. It kept me busy. I had to line up in the court room with all other applicants for all types of reasons which had nothing to do with betting. I remained in control of my particular betting duty area until May 1928 when a Fixed Officer arrived who had been appointed to take over permanently. By this time I was well acquainted with betting duty control and even had reported some frauds I had uncovered. But so far as general Excise control was concerned I was still very much a 'tiro'. It was all a far cry from being a prospective Electrical Engineer!

I continued to go home to Rainham every weekend to see my parents who were very interested in my new career which obviously, I was enjoying in that it had given me a completely new outlook on life in the outside world and of commerce in general. My friendship with Dorothy Brown ripened. We went dancing every Saturday at the Casino or the newly opened Pavilion dance hall in Gillingham. She was well liked by my parents. My sister Doris had developed a friendship with a young man from Maidstone whom she had met at the Casino. With my parents we often went on Sunday to the seaside, as a party of six. This after dancing on Saturday night. I then returned late on Sunday evening to Birmingham ready for the next day back in the Excise Office. Quite a strenuous weekend but I thought little of travelling down from Birmingham and back again. I was still seeing my old colleagues, the electrical fitter apprentices from time to time. They were all then out of 'their time' and working as artisans in the dockyard but all still studying, this time for a coming examination by the Admiralty for appointment as draughtsmen. I did not envy them. I was more than satisfied with my new career. I did, however, return into the Electrical Department main office to collect some pay due to me from work I had started on H.M.S. Kent after I had completed my apprenticeship and ultimately completed by another electrical fitter when I had left dockyard employment. The work involved had been on a 'contract' under which an additional payment was made when completed 'on time'! A proportion was due to me for my part of the 'contract' hence I saw no reason why

I should not be paid my proportion. It presented no problem at the office. I duly received my share. My salary in the C. & E. was already in excess of that being received by my fellow ex-apprentices!

Dorothy Brown was an excellent dancer. With my sister she entered a competition for two girls dancing together. They easily won and received two free hairdressing 'perms' from a local hairdresser. Dorothy's mother was a teacher of dancing. She held classes in the Masonic Hall in Gillingham. Dorothy's father was also competent. He regularly acted as MC for the Masonic Ladies Nights for several Lodges meeting in the same building. Many apprentices and ex-apprentices attended what was commonly know as "Brownies Hop" on Saturday afternoons, learning to dance. Dorothy's cousin Ivy, who was a graduate pianist supplied the music. Dorothy assisted in the teaching. Quite a family affair, but very popular. Strangely though, I had never attended these classes, otherwise I would have met my future wife much earlier.

Dorothy had a sister, Marjory, two years younger. She was pretty and a vivid 'red-head'. Red hair seemed to 'run' in the Brown and Goddard family. (Goddard was her mother's maiden name). Dorothy, though and her mother Amelia, known to all as 'Min', were natural blondes, as was her younger brother Frederick, two years younger than Marjory. But John the baby was another vivid red-head. Interestingly, my only grandson, Adrian, is also a vivid red-head, although there are no red haired 'Sheppards' prior to Adrian. The "Browns" were a very happy family, I enjoyed going to their home. 'Min' was what is known as a 'scream' otherwise always happy and cheerful, full of quaint sayings. Nothing worried her. William Brown, known to all as 'Bill', Dorothy's father, was a very quiet man. Apart from his work in the Engineering Department of the dockyard, he was only interested in sport. He had been a good cricketer and was still playing tennis very competently up to the time of his death at 60 years from a heart attack sustained on a tramcar when he was returning home from his employment. This happened many years later, after Dorothy and I were married.

I continued to travel home from Birmingham to Rainham every weekend. It was no problem getting away from the Betting Duty Station I was filling, on Saturdays. Work in the Excise is based on a particular system of what are termed 'units', calculated on the time taken to carry out any particular item of work. The total arrived at from adding up the various units for all the tasks to be completed in a year determines the area of country to be allocated to an Officer as his 'Station'. It sounds very complicated to any person not engaged in Excise work. It takes some time for a newly appointed Officer to understand what 'Units' mean, suffice to say that it works!! It ensures that all Officers are working to a figure for the amount of work in a whole year which can be completed within a single year without requiring attendance at any particular time. Except of course, that some surveys or items of control might be required to be carried out weekly, monthly or quarterly etc. The units allocated for such work would go into the total for the year. I became, at the later part of my career in the Excise, the staff association representative for negotiating the figures for units, with the Board of Customs and Excise through its supervising officials. I was then the Association's "Units Secretary" among many other positions I held. It is difficult for me to explain the 'Units System' in more detail. Negotiations with the Board were conducted through Whitley Councils and Committees set up by the Treasury in the various Government Departments throughout the Civil Service as a whole. The Units system in the Excise was but a small outcome of the Whitley Council operating in the C. & E. Department covering negotiations with the staff on all matters affecting such staff. Complicated?? The answer is "Yes", but it worked in the main, to the satisfaction of both the Board and the staff. All this was up to the time I finally retired from service in the C. & E. What occurs now is certainly different but that is not now my responsibility!

For me at any time I was free to perform my work when I chose to do it on any appropriate day. Provided that I ensured any urgent matter that arose was performed on a particular day, I was free to come and go at any time. The whole system was a matter of trust in an Officer to carry out his work throughout the geographical area to which he had been allocated within a complete year. All areas of the country termed 'Stations' had as far as could be calculated an equal number of 'Units' for a year's work.

Under this system I could go home on Saturday and return on Monday. Occasionally, of course there could be items of work to be performed on a Sunday. Such would have been included in the overall total of 'Units' for the Station. All Excise 'General' Stations were calculated using the units assessed for a legal parish. Every 'Parish' was used to calculate the units within it, and the total for the 'Station' was duly arrived at by adding up all the parish totals. Under this arrangement parishes with the units within such, could be transferred from one Station to another to bring them as far as was practical into equilibrium. This was termed 'rescheming' and was carried out on the Collector of C. & E. instructions for the appropriate area of the country whenever necessary. This was infrequent because Rescheming was time consuming. This system I had to become acquainted with, particularly when in due course I was appointed an Excise Fixed Officer with my own area of control. But as an Unattached Officer I was not involved in Rescheming unless I was "filling" (i.e. responsible for) a vacant Station awaiting the appointment of the next Fixed Officer to be permanently in charge. I was often sent to assist Officers anywhere in the Collection who by some chance had too much work to do. This happened frequently within any Collection, (the area of a large section of the country under the control of the Collector.) The Collector would select Unattached Officers who were available for 'assisting' and send them off to 'assist'. Should, however, a Collection be understaffed and in need of Unattached Officers, such were selected from another Collection solely on a seniority basis. The juniors "had to go" from one Collection to another in strict order of 'juniority' and then only on the direction of the Board of C. & E. from the advice from the Establishment Division of Head Office. When the first appointments of new recruits from the open examination of 1927 arrived they were welcomed with open arms by the much older men, many with family commitments, who had been appointed after the end of the 1914/18 war. These men, still Unattached Officers had been bearing the brunt of inter-Collection moves at great inconvenience for many years. On the other hand when the new young men commenced to take up their appointments and became in their turn subject to inter-Collection moves these were often welcomed as a means of gaining experience and at the same time reaping some financial reward in the shape of transfer allowances for moving. Also they were seeing the country at the Board's expense!!

When I first commenced in Birmingham and was allocated to a vacant Betting Duty area, I was taken under the wing of an older U.O. (term for an Unattached Officer) by the name of Bonnar Williams, a Welshman from North Wales. He quickly contacted the landlady where he was in 'digs' and secured me similar 'digs' in the same premises. So I left my hotel immediately and moved in to great comfort with Mrs Aaron in the Small Heath area of Birmingham. She was a marvellous cook and produced such marvellous meals as I ever enjoyed!! She had a charming daughter, a schoolteacher, with whom I think Bonnar Williams was in love but showed no signs of such affection. I learned, years later that he married her! Bonnar and I were the only two boarders. I was able to store my motorbike in the back garden, highly convenient for me. Bonnar soon bought himself a Matchless motorcycle. He used it to go off regularly to play golf, a game I had not at that time any knowledge of. He often quipped that whereas I had an Ariel manufactured in Birmingham he had a Matchless made in Kent. Both makes have now become almost unknown. Asking my name, Bonnor was not inclined to accept 'Horace' and chose instead my third name 'Barnabas'. Whether my grandmother was pleased is not difficult to say! She was overjoyed. so 'Barney' I became and this remained with me for many years among my contemporaries. One young new U.O. invariably called me 'Barney' throughout my whole time in the C. & E. He was a devout Catholic named Lewes. I nicknamed him "Angel" although he never quoted the scriptures to me. The name "Angel" caught on and he was 'Angel Lewes' throughout his entire service of over 40 years in the C. & E. He had been a librarian in Southampton prior to the 1927 exam, where he was placed 39th, 7 marks ahead of my total. 'Angel' attended my wedding in 1930 in Gillingham and actually travelled on the same train as did Dorothy and I going on our honeymoon to Bournemouth. 'Angel' travelled only as far as Southampton but not in the same compartment of the train!

Assessing the amount of work to be performed by an Officer in a betting duty Station was based on the number of betting slips the bookmaker received from 'punters' plus the time agreed via the Whitley Committee negotiations for the clerical work involved. The bookmaker made a periodic return of the total sum staked on all his betting slips and from this paid the amount due to the Collector. The bookmaker's 'return' was then passed to the verifying Officer. He had to check the total on the 'return' by adding up all the amounts of individual betting ships. A laborious task! For a 'course' book-maker, he produced his book compiled on the race course. This too had to be checked by adding up the amounts staked. Bookmakers employed their own individual methods of recording amounts staked on the race course. Some might show 5 with a dot along side which the bookmaker knew meant 5 pounds and ten shillings. They all had their own secret codes on which a course bookmaker paid out on winning bets. The C. & E. employed a staff of inspectors, mainly ex-policemen, who visited race courses and placed a distinctive stamp on a bookmaker's course book record. These 'inspectors' passed back the information about the bookmaker's books they had stamped to the appropriate Officer. On one occasion the wife of a bookmaker away on a race course produced to me a 'phoney' set of books. This bookmaker was duly prosecuted and fined for his offence. The weakness of the whole system of the 1926 betting duty was that office bookmakers produced the betting slips from their 'runners', i.e. men who stood in the road and took bets from 'punters' made out on odd pieces of paper, even on cigarette packets! 'Street' betting was illegal in the days before betting shops were legalised, so in effect we in the Excise Department were legally accepting betting tax based on an illegal action. i.e. betting slips brought in to the bookmaker by his street 'runners'. Eventually the 1926 betting duty was abolished due to the difficulties of collecting it and verifying it from an illegal action. The more recent betting duty is based on betting shops legally operating, but even these produce many problems for verifying Officers.

Before the 1926 betting duty was discontinued, Fixed Officers had been appointed to the Birmingham Betting Duty Stations. They eventually lost their 'Station' and became 'displaced' (allowing them to take a pick of any vacant Station in the country). Meanwhile a Fixed Officer arrived to take over the area I had been 'covering'. So I became a real U.O. available to fill or assist in any Excise Station in the Birmingham Collection. My first 'stop' was at a Bonded warehouse and employed on stocktaking, i.e. checking visually the contents of the warehouse and comparing this with the warehouse book record. Shortages had to be accounted for. The Officer in charge of the bonded warehouse was something of a "character". Each lunch time he made a specially brewed soup for himself and other acquaintances who knew where to come! The 'soup' was laced with remnants of wines and/or spirits he knew how to "acquire" in the warehouse. No questions were asked. All bonded warehouses were fastened with two locks when closed. One the official Excise lock and the other the lock belonging to the warehouse owner. One partner in this system could not gain access without the other's knowledge.

After my period in the bonded warehouse I was sent by the Collector around a series of General Excise Stations in Birmingham and in Erdington, Handsworth and West Bromwich. For all these except West Bromwich I retained my 'digs' in Small Heath with Mrs Aaron. Bonnar Williams was a great help in advising me on problems. He was 'filling' a vacant Station at Ansells Brewery. All the Officers I met were most helpful, particularly a Mr Cross at West Bromwich. He strangely enough had formerly been a dockyard apprentice in Plymouth long before the 1914/18 war. Not only did he instruct me over problems when assisting him, he also provided me with accommodation in his lovely house in West Bromwich. Because I had moved more than 3 miles from my last place of assisting I was entitled to receive 'disturbance allowance' of thirty shillings plus six shillings for the first 5 nights away from my normal residence (Small Heath). A most welcome payment of £6!! Eventually the Collector sent me to take over the Station at Redditch in Worcestershire when the Fixed Officer was going on annual leave for three weeks. I received my £6 Disturbance Allowance, but the task of 'officiating' in a vacant station for 3 weeks was quite a challenge. I was learning the job the hard way in having to officiate for a Fixed Officer. In addition to the normal Excise work I had also in Redditch to deal with Old Age Pension investigation of claims plus issuing pension books by hand throughout the area at the same time confirming that each pensioner was still entitled to the pension under the means test regulations. On the Fixed Officer's return from his holiday I was directed back to Birmingham again with the receipt of the £6 Disturbance Allowance there to officiate in other Stations in Birmingham Collection. I was enjoying life in the Excise!!

With 'Angel' Lewes and another U.O. named Barry I attended a few public dances. But no-one could dance like my Dorothy back in Gillingham. I saw her every week-end when possible and we went to the Casino in Rochester. Once when I was in Redditch I was directed to 'make a detection' on a Saturday at the local cinema to check the Entertainment's Duty was safeguarded. This prevented my early departure on my Ariel motorbike for the 150 miles or so journey to Gillingham and Rainham. But I duly make the 'detection' when the cinema opened and I enjoyed the experience.

My prowess at dancing had become common knowledge in the Collection. The Assistant Collector also named Williams had a presentable daughter and they went to dances! Mr Williams invited me to attend with him the dances held at the West End Tennis Club on some week-ends. These were rather exclusive functions and I could hardly refuse. So I went several times, I am sure just to dance with Mr William's daughter!! Maybe he saw in me a likely suitor for his daughter who was about my age. 'Bonnar' back in Small Heath digs was all for my attendances. No other U.O.s received such invitations. I also met two charming girls at dances. They were both employed at Birmingham's Assay office for certifying the figure for gold and silver. Both were nice dancers especially the one 'Bonnar' always referred to as "The Naylor". She was exceedingly pleasant to me. I visited her at her home in Edgbaston. Both these girls came out with me at different times on my Ariel motorbike. But my thoughts were always with Dorothy in Gillingham.

Once a year the Birmingham Collection held a Dinner/Dance at a smart hotel in the town. The Assistant Collector, Mr Williams, invited me to attend and to sit at his table. I had sent home for my evening dress suit, so was fully prepared for the dinner/dance. Champagne was served and a good time had by all! Once more I was dancing with his daughter! But in September 1928 I was informed by the Collector, Mr Jackson, that I was to be transferred to Liverpool Collection.

In 'digs' at Small Heath with Mrs Aaron, I had been paying three pounds and fifty shillings per week which was quite a large sum for me. At West Bromwich where I had collected my 'disturbance allowance' of six pounds I paid a nominal sum of thirty shillings for my stay with Mr Cross. I then had to go to Redditch, again changing my residence. I secured 'digs' for two pounds per week. I decided that when I returned to Birmingham I would look for accommodation at a lower figure than the three pounds thirty shillings I paid at Small Heath even if the food was not up to the standard I received from Mrs Aaron. I had in mind a need to save money with a view eventually of getting married (to Dorothy!). The U.O. named Barry had found some digs in Edgbaston where he was paying just twenty five shillings a week. On return from Redditch I too went to these digs and found it was a veritable rabbit warren of boarders, but it was cheap! Every room had more than one bed. I shared a room with an oldish man who had been in the Klondyke gold rush at the end of the nineteenth century. He told me lurid tales of fights for fortune which he had not secured! But the most interesting thing that occurred was when the landlady's husband who was a Commercial Traveller invited Barry and I to see the items he 'travelled' in. Up to then we had seen brooms and brushes of all shapes and sizes as samples of his 'wares'. The landlady and husband slept in a glass conservatory! The only space remaining from all the boarders! Barry and I were shown into a spot off the kitchen where stood a coffin!! The landlady's husband travelled as his main product, in 'coffin furniture'!!! These comprised silk etc, linings, brass knobs and handles, head rests, in fact anything except an actual coffin. His brooms and brushes were just a sideline. Fortunately there were no bodies!! I remained in these digs at a cheap rate until I went off to Liverpool and betting duty work again in October 1928.

I saw the Higher Collector who asked if I knew anything about Betting Duty!! From my reply I was immediately sent to take over a vacant Betting Duty Station which included Littlewoods Pools and Vernons Pools in the centre of Liverpool. I made two separate journeys back to Birmingham to give evidence in two prosecutions against bookmakers where I had discovered fraud in my verification of their accounts. Also I received another invitation from Mr Williams, the Assistant Collector in Birmingham again to attend the Annual Collection Dinner/Dance. So another trip back to Birmingham on my Ariel again to dance with Miss Williams!! Back in Liverpool I was sent to Excise Stations to assist or officiate, in St Helens and Newton-le-Willows. Each time I moved my digs, I received the welcome payment of £6 Disturbance Allowance! Often I had to go back to Liverpool for betting duty work or stocktaking in a warehouse, again Disturbance Allowance!

On one period of stocktaking at a warehouse, I found an enormous deficiency on the stock of casks actually in the warehouse compared with the book record. Eventually I solved the problem by finding that at one stage, the Officer recording totals when turning over a page, had added in the date, which then showed over 1900 casks short! It was easily corrected.

Mr Williams was promoted to be Collector of Swansea Collection. He was a Welshman so probably welcomed his move up the promotion ladder. He duly went and I heard no more from him or his daughter or received any more invitations to the Birmingham Annual

Dinner/Dances! Neither did I hear any more of the two Assay Office young ladies. But I had enjoyed my time in Birmingham sharing 'digs' with Bonnar Williams and enjoying Mrs Aaron's cooking. I heard much later that Bonnar married Miss Gladys Aaron!

In Liverpool I had spells of officiating or assisting in a variety of Stations. One was the B.A.T. tobacco factory ensuring that the duty paid on tobacco that had been imported with a moisture content of 10% and re-exported with a moisture content of 14% was not over-paid -the import duty or as the C. & E. term it, the drawback. I was also employed for a period at Bryant and Mays match factory veri-fying the Excise duty paid on boxes of matches. The work was very varied and I was rapidly becoming Excise minded. Electrical engi-neering was forgotten. I was well able to get away from most of my periods of employment in Stations for me to make the 250 mile journey on the Ariel to Rainham and Gillingham via Chester, Whitchurch, Newport etc, round the back of Birmingham on the A.5, (the old Roman Road to North Wales) through London to Kent. There to attend a dance or go to the cinema (or both) with Dorothy. Sometimes also on Sunday down to the coast at Dymchurch for a dip in the sea. Then the return late on Sunday night on the Ariel to arrive in Liverpool around 8.00 am via the Mersey tunnel. It seems difficult to imagine such a journey and return now-a-days, but then traffic was much lighter and especially during the night almost non-existent.

On one occasion in early December 1928 on a visit to the Casino dance hall in Rochester, we entered a dancing competition. The judge was Santos Casani the most prestigious dancer in the country. There is a film strip, or was, showing him dancing the 'Charleston' on top of a taxi proceeding up the Strand in London!! Dorothy and I were chosen to dance in the local final of the Columbia Championship to be held at the Pavilion Dance Hall in Gillingham later in December. To be so chosen for the final was something exceptional. Five other couples were picked out by the judge although Dorothy and I were the first couple chosen. I returned to Liverpool to be told I was to officiate for a Mr Orme, who strangely enough was the Officer for Ormskirk a small town a little farther up the coast from Liverpool. The period for officiating for Mr Orme was December 15th to 29th which meant over the Christmas holiday period. Mr Orme was not a man one could 'take to'. In the first place he had no official office. In those days many Excise Stations were controlled from the Officer's private residence for which they received a monetary payment of about 7 shillings per week. At his residence he held all the Excise books and records including all the old age pension books for issue to pensioners as they fell due. Often an Officer with such a Station with 'office at his residence' would allow a U.O. sent to officiate for his leave, to use his office in the house. So he did no lose his office allowance. But not Mr Orme!! He insisted that I transfer all the records, books and everything else connected with Ormskirk Station to my digs. For this I had to organise the local brewers to loan me a brewer's dray to carry all the Excise records to my digs in the town. These digs had no gas or electric lighting so work in the evening which was necessary for a U.O. to keep up to date, had to be carried out by the illumination of an oil lamp on the table!! Primitive conditions indeed! I found too that Mr Orme had left me quite a number of tasks to be carried out that quarter due to end on 31 December which could easily have been carried out by him at any time from 1st October onwards. Included for example was the "taking of the quarterly samples" from the local cake factory for submission to the Department of the Government Chemist for determination of sugar content for 'drawback' of duty when exported. Simple enough to carry out but why leave it until the last two weeks of the quarter? Another task he left was taking the samples from the brewery for testing original gravity of a brew. I found too that an old age pensioner who had lost her pension book had not been dealt with as required by the Old Age Pension Officer (Mr Orme). Instead it was the local postman, a friend of the pensioner who actually had lost the book while drawing the pension for the old lady instead, had been paying the pension to her out of his own pocket! The whole business had been reported to Mr Orme but he had done nothing about it except to draw my attention to the problem and leave me to deal with it. The loss had been reported by the postman some weeks before. Enquiries and information by me had to be carried out with the Post Office and report made before the problem created by the passage of time could be solved. Just examples of Mr Orme passing the buck!! On the day I 'took over' the Station from Mr Orme and had transferred all the records to my digs he asked me to have a drink with him in the local British Legion Club where he was a member. I did not consume alcoholic drinks so consented to have a lemonade. He had a glass of beer. He chose a double whisky at my expense! Such a man was Mr Orme of Ormskirk!!

Then I received news from Dorothy that the final for the Columbia dance championship was to be held just before Christmas and I was in Ormskirk over 250 miles away. I duly set out on the Ariel but the weather was against me, fog all the way! I reached Gillingham and the Pavilion Dance Hall just in time to see the other 5 finalists on the floor with their competing numbers pinned to their backs. I was too late through no fault of my own! Dorothy and I duly received our medals as finalists but lost the opportunity to compete and to go to London for the "All England" Final. Such is bad luck. We may not have won but would like to have tried.

In Newton-le-Willows Station, I was delivering pension books to pensioners and at the same time re-checking entitlement to a full pension under the means test operating in those days. I called at a house with a book for a Mrs Mary Smith. The old lady who answered said she was Mrs Mary Smith but did not require a new book - "She already had one". I insisted that a new book was due to Mrs Mary Smith. Then the 'penny dropped'. The Mrs Smith I was talking to was over 70 but upstairs in bed was her mother-in-law, also named Mrs Mary Smith, who was over 90 years old! Such incidents make for variety in an Exciseman's life.

In St Helens I shared digs with a Mr Hutchins a much older man, unmarried, who liked his liquor!! He seldom went home to lunch at the digs, preferring to spend his time in the local hostelry, "The Fleece". He had charge of the local brewery. One evening he invited me to go round the brewery with him on his 'survey'. When he reached the desk where the brewer made his 'declarations' of the amount of 'wort' (i.e. unfermented beer) in the fermenting tanks, an employee produced a quart tankard of beer which Hutchins immediately consumed. The employee then produced a second tankard filled to the top. Hutchins drank almost all of it. I drew his attention to the fact that he 'had left some'. His reply was "Manners my son, Manners". Unfortunately for Hutchins his drinking habits became known to the Board of Customs and Excise. He was removed under censure to a tobacco factory in London. Maybe he took up chain smoking!! I never met him again, but he had a sense of humour as exemplified by his "Manners my son, Manners" reply about the beer he left in the second tankard.

At a second spell of officiating in St Helens, another U.O., older than I, was in Hutchins old Station. I was also the Probate Officer, dealing with obtaining Probate for applicants to control small estates. It is necessary at the finalisation of the paperwork for the applicant to swear an oath of correctness, using the bible kept in the office for this purpose. We could not find the bible! In the end, the other U.O. and I carefully wrapped up a 'Hams Year Book' which shows the composition of every Excise Station throughout the country. "Swear on this" said the other Officer. The applicant did so, none the wiser, and all was well! Such is life in the Excise. I had periodically to return to betting duty work. Under the units system the amount of work placed upon any Officer in a betting duty Station was based mainly on the number of betting slips received by the bookmaker. So many seconds allocated to each betting slip to be checked and added up to arrive at the time for each bookmaker. By this units system the total for all the bookmakers made up the year's work in a Station. An Officer was required to check a fixed percentage of the total 'slips' received. When I first went to Littlewoods Pools to verify the tax paid I said I would like to check all the slips under the letter 'S'. This was just a random choice. I was told that all the slips starting with letter 'S' took up all the room and were filed on the second floor! I then said I would restrict my check to those starting with the letters 'SH'. This also proved impractical because the whole of one room on the second floor was used for the letters 'SH'. In the end I was reduced to trying to check the totals for 'Sheppard' to apply verification under the approved 'Unit' system. But even this would have taken me roughly 6 weeks in any *month!!* Eventually I received official permission to reduce my control check to whatever I considered practical! Now of course checks are made using computer records. There were no computers in 1928! The 'Unit' system could not in 1928 be applied to Littlewoods Pools. *And* I had Vernons Pools also in the Station I was filling temporarily.

In May 1929 I was told to report to Albert Dock, Liverpool for instruction in the Customs side of the Department. Birmingham was a completely Excise Collection. Liverpool on the other hand was both Customs and Excise. In the main the Excise work in a Station was based on a total for a year's work under the 'Units' system. Customs however was organised on fixed hours such as 8.0 am to 4.0 pm ; 9.0 am to 5.0 pm, 10.0 am to 6.0 pm to meet the requirements of shipping. Or other hours equally necessary. Overtime was paid at an agreed rate in excess of the normal. 'Overtime' working was much sort after by some Officers to boost their salaries!

I never liked the 'overtime' system and avoided it as far as was possible even when at one stage in my career I was employed solely on Customs work. Officers of Customs and Excise on Customs duties did not wear uniforms. Uniforms were worn by members of the Waterguard Service of the C. & E. Their work was to deal with passenger's baggage, rummaging, i.e. searching on board ships for contraband etc and generally in control of very small ports where large vessels with cargo did not berth, such as at West Mersea already described in these memoirs. Officers of Customs and Excise at ports dealt with cargoes or in control of bonded warehouses, in or near the docks where vessels discharged cargo. This is a very broad description. All Officers of Customs and Excise had to be conversant with both Customs and Excise work and to meet any problem that arose. Those men who liked overtime or working to fixed hours chose a Customs Station when time came for appointment. Those who preferred the freedom to work at one's own choice and with no fixed hours opted for the Excise. Since appointment to Stations that were vacant was entirely in order of seniority and compulsory only when a U.O. reached the top of the list. It often happened that a U.O. had to take a vacant Station as a Fixed Officer in the side of the service he did not prefer. However, all vacant Stations were advertised to the whole C. & E. Service each week so any Officer could apply for a transfer provided he had served a year in his present Station. By this system 'desirable' Stations were quickly filled by the senior applicant by transfer. The transferee's Station then became vacant and was advertised for filling either by a further transfer or by the senior U.O. should there be no applicant for transfer. Stations filled by transfer were at the applicant's expense, but Stations filled by compulsory appointment by a U.O. were at the Crown's expense. I had a great deal to do with changing the system of compulsory appointments years later when I became a voluntary official in my staff association. This I will deal with later in these memoirs.

In Liverpool I had secured digs in the Anfield district fairly near to the football ground of Liverpool. But I was no football enthusiast although I did go to watch the team play once or twice. My landlady's name was Mrs Ward and was the next door neighbour of a friend of my mother we had known in Gillingham. She was easy enough to get on with but did not cook as well as did Mrs Aaron away in Birmingham! I was contented enough there but wished that I was employed nearer to Gillingham, in Dover Collection. Mrs Ward's daughter was being courted by a young man employed in shipping. Eventually another U.O. named Taylor who had been dockyard apprentice in Portsmouth obtained digs nearby, so I had a companion. We went to a dance or two but nothing of moment resulted.

I duly reported to Albert Dock in Liverpool at the beginning of May 1929. It was a dock where casks of wines and spirits were discharged from vessels, or were received 'under bond' i.e. in locked containers or guaranteed liability, for any duty due. All the casks had to be 'gauged' to assess content on which duty due could be calculated. For spirits the duty was arrived at from the alcoholic strength using 'proof spirit' as the base from which duty could be calculated, what 'proof' spirit is I will describe later in these memoirs.

At the time of my introduction to the Customs at Albert Dock I only knew that 'proof' spirit was approximately 50% pure alcohol and 50% water. Officers at the dock could assess the strength of the spirits in the casks by use of an hydrometer. Samples had to be drawn from the casks by means of a valinch, a narrow tube that would go into the orifice (the bung hole) of the cask when, by holding on to the small opening at the top end of the valinch, a quantity of spirit could be held to transfer it to a sample jar for transmission, when sealed to the local chemical Station in the docks. The amount remaining in the valinch after the sample had been drawn to test for strength, had then to be put back into the cask. There is a story told that a member of the trader's staff who had drawn the sample under supervision of the Officer who had to be present, when told to put it back promptly put it into a glass which he then drank. 'Putting it back' has more than one meaning!! For wines, the duty on these was assessed on scales for 'less than 25% proof, over 25% but under 42% and over 42%. If over 42% the wine was considered to be a spirit. All this was completely new to me but more so was the gauging of the casks to determine content. This was an art in itself. There were gauging tools, such as large callipers to ascertain length and diameter. Other tools to determine the thickness of the wood of the cask, both of the staves and the ends. From all the measurements, content was estimated from tables. But most important, allowances had to be made for irregularities and the appearances of each cask, whether slim, or fat. All this knowledge was only obtained from experience. It was possible also to weigh casks both full and empty. This was generally necessary only exceptionally for casks of spirits. I was truly mystified and vowed never to become an Officer on such a Station. At Albert Dock in Liverpool, large drums of raw tobacco were imported. These had to be weighed and samples drawn to ascertain percentage of moisture. Albert Dock has completely disappeared as such, and is now a 'Leisure Centre' for the inhabitants of Liverpool.

I was next transferred to Alexandra Dock at the other end of the town. Here general cargoes of all descriptions were discharged from vessels from all parts of the globe. Such cargoes were examined by Officers comparing the description given on the ship's 'Captain's Report' describing the cargo carried, with the individual 'Entries' made by merchants for their goods which they wished to take possession of. Such descriptions by merchants were physically checked by Officers. 'Entries' were submitted to the Collector's staff at the Custom House, duty paid and the 'Entries' sent to the Officer at the dock for comparison with the actual goods. Discharges of goods from the ship went into 'Transit Sheds' deemed for legal purposes to be part of the ship, so that physical examination of cargoes could be undertaken by Officers. Meanwhile the ship was checked physically, known as 'rummaging' by the Waterguard staff who could arrive at any time to conduct the 'rummage' searching the vessel for contraband. Waterguard staff were also under the control of the Collector (in Liverpool by a Higher Collector, being a large port), assisted by Waterguard higher staff such as Inspectors. I found the work at Alexandra Dock most interesting but I had no desire to be appointed to a Customs Station.

One thing that saddened me in Liverpool at the docks was the sight of rows of men, would be dock workers lining up at the dock side waiting to be taken on for work by a 'ganger' who walked up and down the rows picking out the men he preferred to work in his 'gang'. The look on the faces of men not selected was very sad. They had no alternative but to return home or to do whatever they could find to occupy their time, still unemployed. Unemployment in 1929 onwards was a feature of the country as a whole and especially so in Liverpool.

Also in the USA prohibition was in force. But one would not have thought so from the activities in Liverpool dockland. Ships were being piled high with wines and spirits and even beer, destined for the American market to contravene the prohibition laws in the USA. "Bootlegging" was at its height and the gangsters reigned supreme.

In June 1929 I was examined in Customs work by the Collector, passed as competent and immediately transferred to Chester Collection. I had sent a petition to the Board of C. & E. asking for removal to another Collection in the South! Such petitions were in order, but removal just a few miles south to Chester did not exactly meet my wishes. Fortunately, however, my first assignment in Chester Collection was to the Parcel Post Depot in Stafford, a little nearer south. Stafford town had a large parcel post depot which had been taken over by the Customs for examination of goods sent from abroad to recipients in England. Similar depots existed in Scotland and Ireland, probably also in Wales. The largest depot for such work was in London at Mount Pleasant. There was one in Southampton. At Stafford parcels for the north and midlands came under scrutiny. All parcels from abroad needed to have a Customs declaration attached describing the contents. There were six fixed Officers at the Stafford depot plus a host of U.O.s assisting in the work. A Post Office employee produced the parcels to the Officer and opened it for the Officer to check whether the 'declaration' was correct. If so duty, if any was assessed from the published 'Tariff'; the parcel resealed with a label announcing that it had been opened by Customs. The assessed duty, if any, was collected by the postman delivering the parcel, and transferred to the 'coffers' of the C. & E. 'Angel' Lewes my U.O. friend from Birmingham was also employed at the P.P. Depot. Most of the U.O.s were in digs together, with a Mrs Cumming who charged us thirty shillings if there all the week but only twenty five shillings if away for the weekend. This suited me because I went back to Rainham and Gillingham every Saturday returning on Monday am. The Ariel was in constant use. One U.O. in the digs, by the name of Brooks was a good pianist, but insisted on singing the song "They'll never believe me ... etc" all the time to his music on Mrs Cumming's piano. He was in love somewhere else in England! I was entitled to summer leave for three weeks in July and August and went home to Rainham.

On return I was directed to the town of Newport, Shropshire for a Mr Hodgson. This was a great experience and I was glad to get away from the Parcel Post Depot in Stafford. When at Stafford I had had a chance to visit the Potteries and to row on Trenthem Park Lake with another U.O. named Egan. He was an ex-apprentice from Plymouth and eventually obtained a Fixed Station at Paignton in Devon where he remained wisely, for the rest of his service in the C. & E.

The Office in Newport, Shropshire was in the Officer's house, as had been the case in Ormskirk, Lancs. But Mr Hodgson was a far different man than had been Orme of Ormskirk!! He could not have been nicer to me. I found digs across the road from Mr Hodgson's house. He let me use his home for the three weeks I was there to deal with Excise work. He had two breweries, small ones, in the Station. One was on the road towards Stone in Staffordshire, the other on the road towards Wellington in Shropshire. "Angel" Lewes and another U.O. named Ewens whose father was a brewer in Bristol were both officiating in Wellington.

Soon after I started officiating in Newport, Salop, I was returning from a visit to the brewery on the Wellington Road when a van came round a corner on the wrong side of the road and struck me on my right leg. It was very painful. Mr Hodgson had not yet left for his holiday due to start in a day or so, so he took me in his car to Stafford Hospital and conveyed me round the casualty ward to have my leg x-rayed. I was in a wheelchair and it was a strange experience to be pushed around by the Officer I was supposed to be 'relieving'. The x-ray showed that I had slightly splintered a bone in my leg. It was bound up at the hospital and we returned to Newport, Salop. I felt well enough to carry on and Mr Hodgson left for his holiday. In his house he had a magnificent library of books on many subjects. He had given me permission to read any of them. Callers on Excise or Old Age Pension business came to the house to see me as necessary. There was a small cinema in the main street which I visited on a 'survey'. All was in order.

In the Station, scattered all over the area around Oakengates, now the built up town of Telford, there were around 400 'private brewers'! These were ordinary households that brewed their own beer most of them free of licence duty. Larger houses depending on their rateable value had to have a licence to brew but did not pay beer duty. Under the rules a private brewer brewing beer for his family's consumption had to be surveyed once in each twelve months. With this number under 'survey' it meant the Officer had to visit at least one every day of the week excluding Sundays. I did my share without ever finding a householder actually brewing! Some were doing their weekly wash in the copper they could use for brewing beer! This also happened at the brewery on the road to Stone. I found the brewer's wife soaking her washing in the tank where any beer brewed was fermented.

Lilleshall which was then a small athletic ground was in the Station. It has now expanded to a National sporting centre. My life officiating in Newport, Salop was very pleasant. I decided that this would be the life for me whenever I became fixed in a Station. I sometimes met up with 'Angel' and Ewens. We went to Wenlock Edge and the Wrekin. Also on one occasion into Wales to Montgomery and Newtown to walk on the hills. Ewens had a Rover car and I had my Ariel. We visited Buildwas Abbey (a ruin but well worth seeing). Also Ironbridge built 1777/9, the first to be built using cast iron. I was really seeing England at the Board's expense! For using my motorcycle I received a mileage allowance based on the miles covered on official business. "All grist to the mill!"

My digs across the road from Mr Hodgson's home was kept by the wife of the local ironmonger whose shop was at the front of the building in the High Street. Her name was Mrs Holloway. There were several other boarders, two male schoolteachers, an engineer from a factory in the town and a man employed at Lilleshall. Meals were very formal, to be taken to fit in with shop hours. Mr & Mrs Holloway's daughter was paying a visit during my stay, with her husband a South American from Brazil. We all sat round a large long table for our meals. With all meals we had to have home grown tomatoes from the garden, no matter what else was on the menu! Additionally there was a formal procedure. Mr Holloway went down to his cellar and duly appeared with a large jug of Hereford Cider. We all had to have this cider with every meal. It was insisted upon. The other boarders enjoyed it, but for me it was a penance I could easily have done without.

Pension work consisted of investigating any new claims received. Then for submission to the Old Age Pension Committee for the area. If agreed a new book had to be made out and issued to the claimant. Existing pensioners were issued with a new book when necessary. Once every two years books, had to be delivered personally and the pensioner's means checked to see if he or she was still entitled to whatever rate he or she was receiving. Over 90% of all pensioners received the full rate of ten shillings per week. On alternate years a new book was sent by post with the requirement that the recipient signed for no change in means. In a Collection such as Birmingham or Liverpool the pension work for the town was carried out by a specially recruited staff of Women Pension Officers under the control of the C. & E. Surveyor for the District. Hence I did not have to do pension work in the Centre of Birmingham or Liverpool when officiating in a 'town' Station. But in West Bromwich, Redditch, St Helens, Newton-le-Willows and Ormskirk the pension work fell to be performed by the Station Officer. I had quite a few pensioners under my control in Newport, Salop. I invariably maintained a private record of every pensioner I visited to deliver a book should the occasion arise for me to confirm that I had carefully re-investigated each one in order to confirm continued entitlement to the pension. On one occasion I was able to produce my private record so to confirm that I made the required re-investigation. This was when a pensioner had been found later to have means above the figure on which his pension had been based.

At the end of my spell in Newport, Salop, possibly one of the best I ever had, when Mr Hodgson returned from his holiday, I was immediately transferred to London West Collection for instruction in distillery control, a very important section of Excise work. This was to be at Hammersmith Distillery. For me it was a great disappointment because the large majority of U.O.s were sent to Scotland for distillery instruction at a Highland still. This was a great experience for U.O.s and brought them into contact with the most enjoyable aspect of life in the Excise.

Distillery Officers in Scotland, in the main lived in 'provided houses' i.e. houses that had to be provided by the distiller under the law, if the distillery was more than the allowed distance from a market town. Practically all distilleries in Scotland are situated near to suitable streams to provide the right water for any whisky produced. U.O.s sent to Scotland for distillery instruction had a very enjoyable time in the Highlands. Suitable digs were well known. It was often said that a Scottish landlady wanted nothing better than to get her daughter or daughters married to a 'Gauger'. 'Gauger' being the well known description of an Exciseman employed at a distillery. But for me it was Hammersmith, like it or lump it!! I disliked it intensely.

Industrial alcohol was produced at the Hammersmith distillery for use in industry.   Nothing like the whisky, mostly 'single malt' produced in the Highlands of Scotland.   Barges came up the River Thames loaded with molasses, generally from the West Indies.   The molasses were transferred to the distillery tanks, there to be mixed with water and allowed to ferment to produce alcohol.   A small proportion of the alcohol could then be transferred as required to a refinery adjoining the distillery to be re-distilled to make gin using the required flavouring substances.   This process too, was under Excise control but not by the Hammersmith Distillery Officers who worked on a shift system to maintain continuous control.   I never understood the procedure for manufacturing industrial alcohol from the pure alcohol produced at the distillery rendering it non-potable for use in industry, neither did I want to!   The place was one big mass of pipes and tanks.   I quickly made up my mind never to get appointed to such a soul destroying place.

I found some digs with other U.O.s in Ealing but was able to go home very frequently to Rainham and Gillingham only about 30 miles away. After a desultory examination by the Surveyor for Hammersmith District I escaped and went to assist an Officer in the Strand Station, London for a few days.   I recalled the visit I had made many years earlier to the National Gallery with my 'Great Aunt' Daisy.   The Strand Excise Office was immediately behind the National Gallery.

On the distillery course with me were two other U.O.s named Bagot and Mills. Bagot looked normal when sitting down.   But he had extremely short legs so that when he arose he was dwarf like.   Still he was affable.   Mills on the other hand was devoid of conversation. He later was appointed to Tonbridge Station in Kent but I did not need to contact him.   Bagot I believe finished as an Officer in Liverpool Customs but I saw him no more.   I petitioned the Board of C. & E. knowing that it was unlikely that I would remain in London West Collection, for transfer to a number of Collections in order of preference.   Dover was first on my list, then Brighton, but eventually I secured Southampton.   I travelled there early in October 1929.   I took over digs from Bill Hook who was a dockyard apprentice for the year senior to me (1921 entry).   He was an electrical fitter apprentice who had obtained a fourth year in the Dockyard School, (one of the 10 mentioned earlier).   He had secured 78th place whereas I had obtained 44th.   Such are the fortunes of examinations. Bill

Hook was well known to me being one of the apprentices cricket team and a member of the campers 'brigade'. The landlady was Mrs Brookbanks whose husband was a Departmental Clerical Officer in the Collector's office in Southampton. Bill Hook left the 'digs', due to having to go on an instruction course elsewhere in England. Whereabouts not known to me. I know that he eventually became a Fixed Officer in Southampton and finally retired to live in the Isle of Wight. He once appeared on a television programme where the contestants in a quiz game were required to identify the name of the person having a name similar to something else. It was called 'The names the same'. Bill Hook was the name and a bill hook was the article. I do not recall whether his name was guessed correctly. I knew him very well. I am sure that Mrs Brookbanks found him a suitable boarder.

In Southampton after first reporting to the Higher Collector, I was directed to assist in the King's Warehouse Station. This is where goods seized from passengers or other importers are taken into customs possession until such time as any duty due or fine imposed is paid. Unless of course the goods are forfeited because of a major irregularity to become the property of the Crown. Goods on which a passenger or importer is unable to meet the duty due may be left until such is paid, with a charge for storage. Goods which are not 'cleared' or have been seized are eventually sold by auction. These are held publicly although nowadays sales of goods from the Queen's warehouse are conducted mainly on a tender basis after prospective buyers have been allowed to inspect or have been adequately described in the press or other announcements.

In Southampton an Officer by the name of Bolitho (a Cornishman) was 'lotting' goods to be sold at a public auction due to be held later. Bottles containing spirits had to be over three years in the warehouse before being sold. All spirits in Great Britain, such as whisky from a distillery have to be over three years old before being released from Customs control. The same applied even to bottles of whisky or gin etc., stored in the King's warehouse. My job was to assist in the 'lotting' and in due course to act as the auctioneer's clerk when the actual sale was held. Mr Bolitho was in addition redesigning the shelves on which goods were stored in the warehouse. I was a welcome help in this since I was able to measure and draw up an entirely new storage system. Eventually my plans were put into an official file and submitted to the Higher Collector. He submitted the proposals to the Board of C. & E. Eventually the proposals were approved and the file came back. However, the proposals appeared as coming from the Higher Collector and nothing revealed that they had come from me. My name did not appear!! The Higher Collector eventually became the Chief Inspector of the Department, the highest position to which an official can attain. He was a very clever man in all respects. My dockyard training in machine etc. drawing had been helpful in designing the layout of Southampton's King's warehouse.

I spent over two months assisting in the King's warehouse Station and then had a short spell on the docks where liners were discharging such cargo as they carried. At that time the new Southampton docks were under construction, draining much of the marshlands to the west of the old docks. My next spell was at the parcel post depot where I was quite acquainted with procedure. After this I was granted leave over the Christmas period and went home to Rainham and Gillingham.

Dorothy took me to see her grandfather who was the Superintending Engineer at the Crossness works on the Thames marshes beyond Erith and Abbey Wood. He lived on the works and was a very clever man with a large garden able to be 'fertilised' from the Crossness works which dealt with sewage etc. from the whole of London. Some barges also came down the River Thames carrying rubbish etc. Dorothy's Aunt and Uncle also lived on the site. He was also an engineer at Crossness.

This was my first acquaintance with Dorothy's father's family. She also had another Aunt living in Abbey Wood whose husband was a draughtsman in Woolwich Arsenal. On the way back I proposed to Dorothy that we should become engaged to marry. She accepted me and so did her mother and father. We proposed to marry in the coming August (1930) and made plans accordingly. I returned to Southampton again to the King's warehouse for a week and then to my joy was sent to assist in the Excise Station at Romsey for two weeks. I did not change my residence, travelling there on the Ariel. Romsey was the only Excise Station in the Collection outside of Southampton. The Officer was a Mr Skelt easily the most gentle man I ever encountered in the Department. His normal relief for leave was a senior U.O. named Gibbons who also officiated in the few Excise Stations in the town of Southampton. This was under a scheme set up by the Board where officiating could be carried out by a U.O. not requiring changes of residence. But I was sent to assist so travelled daily the 8 miles from Southampton to Romsey. Romsey Station contained Strong's brewery and this was expanding rapidly. Mr Skelt was in need of considerable assistance. I also assisted in the Excise Stations within Southampton. These covered the country as far east as Eastleigh. Beyond was Portsmouth Collection. To the West was Weymouth Collection and to the North, Salisbury. Southampton therefore was a very small Collection in area but important because of being a major port. In early 1930 came the new Widows Pension legislation giving all widows over 50 years of age a 'widow's pension'. The whole of the work involved in bringing in the scheme was placed upon the Excise to investigate claims and administer the first payments. All Excise Stations were affected. None more so than Mr Skelt at Romsey whose area covered practically all of the New Forest. He was already burdened with the expansion of Strong's brewery. Eventually I was sent to assist him for two weeks in every four. Between these two weeks I assisted in Southampton Excise and in the special Widows Pension Station that had been set up in Southampton and was staffed by a U.O. named Wilkinson. In fact I became also a Widows Pension expert. My officiating notices from the Collector simply said I was to assist in Romsey, then return to Southampton and so on. I considered that since Southampton to Romsey was 8 miles and changes of residence were allowed for 3 miles or more, I should be allowed changes of residence when I went to Romsey and when I returned to Southampton. The officiating notices I received were very old prints from about 1911 since no-one up to the time I received mine had required one which specified 'change of residence allowed'. I approached the Chief Clerk in the Custom House who consulted the Higher Collector. My changes of residence were approved! I went to and fro to Romsey a number of times collecting the approved Disturbance Allowance each time, there and back.

Meanwhile when assisting in the Excise in Southampton I adopted my practice of doing whatever I felt necessary without regard to time and going home to my digs with Mrs Brookbanks for lunch at a precise predetermined time as did her husband employed in the Collector's Office. I stayed out working as I thought necessary. Mrs Brookbanks was a very nice lady and I was quite happy in her home as a boarder. But her attitude on returning each day at a precise time annoyed me and I told her so. The upshot was that I gave her my notice to leave as a boarder. I looked round in Southampton for fresh digs and found some with a Mrs Thorne not far off the Romsey Road. Mrs Brookbanks had charged me thirty two shillings and sixpence per week. Mrs Thorne's were twenty two and sixpence, but I agreed to pay twenty five shillings to include the daily use of the bath! Mr Thorne was employed with the gas authority and was a very good cricketer playing for his team each Saturday in 'The Parks' in Southampton. They had no children and obviously to me, Mrs Thorne wanted to 'mother' me! I was very happy with her and did not have to pay for digs when I was away in Romsey.

But the Accountant and Comptroller General in Head Office in London queried my continual changes of residence which attracted Disturbance Allowance for such a short journey as 8 miles. The A. & C.G. took it up with the Higher Collector who agreed that he had sanctioned the changes of residence on the officiating notices. I argued that if I had to travel daily the Station Officer in Romsey would lose because of the time taken to travel backwards and forwards. In the end it was agreed that the Station Officer should receive extra assistance for the travelling time involved. So I lost my Disturbance Allowance but in return spent more days in Romsey. We win some, we lose some!

Much more important was the fact that Mr Skelt allowed me to take over all work in the countryside leaving him with just the work in Romsey town plus the brewery. So I was roaming the New Forest on my motorbike dealing with old age pensions and all Excise work plus the new Widows Pension investigations. Mr Skelt undoubtedly appreciated my work in the station and I frequently stayed late in the evening completing all the paper work involved. The office was in one of a row of shops in the town. One shop was a fish and chip business. Over the shop was a hall and this was occupied most evenings by a religious sect known then as 'Hot Gospellers', probably the Elim religious people. They ranted and raved all the evening stamping their feet and calling out to "Praise the Lord!". I could hear it all in my office down below. I do not think that Mr Skelt knew about the matter. Unfortunately when the religious meeting was concluded the 'worshippers' rushed straight down the stairs into the fish and chip shop! Then they stood in the doorways of the various shops in the row consuming their fish and chips. They seemed to take pleasure in stuffing their used fish and chip wrapping paper, mainly newspaper, through the letter boxes of the shops in the row including that of the Excise Office! I stayed at a hotel in the town. Romsey stands on a small stream that runs in gullies through the town. There was no main drainage so each night a suitable vehicle came round to collect the 'night soil'. In the hotel this 'collecting' caused a smell far worse than that I had experienced as a schoolboy at Chatham 'Tech' when engaged in woodwork or metalwork in the workshops below ground level when the 'carts' went by and we had hurriedly to close all windows facing Chatham High Street!!

Work on the new Widows Pension finally came to an end. For all Officers who had had to perform this extra work additional to their normal duties, a 'one off' lump sum was paid based on the number of claims dealt with. For U.O.s, however, filling Stations that had been set up especially to deal with the work, no payment of a lump sum was allowed. This on the basis that the work had been carried out solely as a daily duty not as work on top of the ordinary Excise duties. Mr Skelt considered that I had carried out all his Widows Pension work additionally dealing with all the Excise work in the New Forest including ordinary Old Age Pensions, so he claimed the allowance per claim for a Widows Pension made in the whole of Romsey Station as if he had carried out the investigations etc. So he received the lump sum. He immediately gave the whole amount to me as a wedding present plus a pair of brass book ends stands which I still possess. He was a gentleman of the highest order. The lump sum which was considerable, I now cannot recall the exact figure, but it was between £40 and £50. This to me at that time was most helpful since I was getting married in August. Mr Gibbons the usual offici-ator was eventually appointed to Stowmarket Station in Suffolk. Dorothy and I later went to stay with him and Mrs Gibbons and their baby daughter. Unfortunately he later contracted multiple scle-rosis from which he eventually died.

I was very happy living with Mr and Mrs Thorne. They treated me like a son. I helped them re-paper their dining room. I also assisted in the garden, actually grafting some briar rose stems with buds from my father's standard rose trees. While with the Thornes in Percy Road Shirley, Southampton, another boarder came to stay. He worked in the local brick making factory. After the first week he had failed to pay his board and lodging money. He had a suitcase in his room which Mrs Thorne said indicated he would be back after failing to turn up for the second week. Eventually Mrs Thorne opened the suit case. It contained several bricks!! We never saw him again. Mr Thorne knew of a flat that would be available belonging to a colleague in his gas office. It was owned by Mr and Mrs Swash who lived downstairs.   The flat was on the first floor. I agreed to bring Dorothy down to Southampton to view it. Eventually we decided to take it when we were married in August. My last visit to assist in Romsey was in June. Thereafter I was assisting in various Stations both Customs and Excise in Southampton, including further spells in the Parcel Post Depot, the King's Warehouse, Landing and shipping Stations in the port, Excise Stations in the town and one period at the British American Tobacco factory in Shirley near to the flat I had agreed to take. In July I took my annual leave to last until August 9th. Dorothy and I were to be married on August 2nd. I was then 24 and 6 weeks over my 24th birthday. Dorothy was then 19 but would be 20 on August 5th. She often said jokingly that she was 5 years younger than me when we were married but in fact it was only 4 years apart from the odd 3 days between August 2nd and 5th.

CHAPTER EIGHT
Employment in Southampton and marriage.

We were married in St Barnabas Church in Gillingham. Maybe my great grandfather Barnabas Astle would have approved of our choice of church. My grandmother Annie certainly did. St Barnabas Church was actually Dorothy's parish church. The Rev. H Treacher officiated. He was a friend of my father-in-law and had been employed in Chatham dockyard before taking holy orders and becoming vicar of St Barnabas Church. Since then he had been appointed Head of the Church Army and was based in Gravesend. He came back to his old church to perform the wedding ceremony for Dorothy and me. Dorothy had six brides-maids. Her sister Marjory; a friend Sheila Sugarue whose father was a colleague of Dorothy's father; my sister Doris and my cousin Edith Morgan, daughter of my mother's younger sister. Also two small bridesmaids, my little cousin Joan Cox daughter of my mother's brother Bertie Cox. (Joan Cox was the girl who married into the Whittaker family!), and Joan Ayears the adopted daughter of my mother's elder sister Lilian. Altogether quite a retinue!. My mother made all the frocks for the wedding, including Dorothy's wedding dress and her going away outfit. My best man was my former apprentice colleague, George Lawrence, (he of the 'wireless doctor' venture!). Our honeymoon was to be at the Wrenwood Hotel in Bournemouth, but we planned to spend the first night at our flat in Southampton. The wedding reception was in the Masonic Hall in Acasia Avenue in Gillingham. Caterers were arranged for the wedding breakfast and a dance band for the dance that was to follow. Several of my old dock-yard apprentices came to the reception and also 'Angel' Lewes from officiating somewhere in the Midlands.

The main speech at the Wedding Breakfast was given by Mr Jack Phillips a friend of my father-in-law. He was the owner of the largest mineral water manufacturers in the Medway Towns, Messrs Dove, Phillips and Pett. (Dove and Pett had departed.) I had been to school at Chatham Tech, with Reg Phillips, son of Jack Phillips. Another son, Ivor became Mayor of Rochester after attending the Rochester Mathematical School, founded centuries earlier by Sir Joseph Williamson. Dorothy's sister, Marjory Brown, who was Dorothy's chief bridesmaid later became secretary to the mineral water firm. Mineral

Wedding photograph of Author and Dorothy on 2nd August 1930 at St Barnabas Church Gillingham, Kent

waters were subject to Excise survey due to the Excise duty levied on them. Some years later when employed in the Excise in Gillingham I had to 'survey' the Dove, Phillips and Pett branch factory in Gillingham. Dorothy's sister Marjory married later Jack Littlejohns who was the nephew of Robin (known everywhere as 'Tiny' due to his large stature). 'Tiny' was an Officer of Customs and Excise appointed from the post - 1914/9 war ex-service men. He was at the time of my wedding serving at Tilbury Docks in the Port of London. Later he transferred to the Customs station in Rochester to take charge of a bonded warehouse. Marjory's husband from being employed in Chatham dockyard in civil engineering later obtained a civil engineering post with a large Danish Civil Engineering firm. Marjory and Jack Littlejohns had one son, Michael who attended Gillingham County School where David, (later Sir David) Frost, (the television personality), was also a pupil. David Frost was the son of a Methodist church minister in Gillingham. Michael Littlejohns became a graduate at Nottingham University, then joining the large engineering firm of Lucas, serving in the U.S.A. later to become eventually a Director. He now resides in Birmingham.

Following the wedding breakfast a dance was held in the Masonic Hall, (the venue of many 'Brownies Hops' in the past, attended by numerous dockyard apprentices). When the time approached for Dorothy and I to set out on our journey to Southampton and then to Bournemouth, she did not want to go because she preferred to stay to continue dancing! Eventually we went off by train, with 'Angel' Lewes in the next compartment! After a night in Southampton in our flat above that of Mr & Mrs Swash we went off to Bournemouth on my Ariel motorbike. We were booked to stay at the Wrenwood Hotel. When we came down to our first breakfast, an immediate query from the next table was "Are you on your honeymoon?" We both looked so youthful! We explored Bournemouth; one day to be our home when I retired! Dorothy said to me that she liked "this place". Adding "shall we retire here one day?" My response was that I had to do some work first and for many years! We paid a visit to Swanage, but the weather was so unpleasant that we both had to wear overcoats to keep out the wind and cold. Eventually the honeymoon was over and we went back to Southampton, but not before we had danced in the Pavilion Ballroom in Bournemouth to Victor Sylvester's dance band. A fore-taste of future events if I did but know it.

Later in the summer of 1930 after our honeymoon, with my parents we decided to take a short holiday together to visit the West country. Dorothy and I went on my motorbike. We met my parents travelling down by motorcycle and sidecar from Rainham, to near Salisbury and went on to view Stonehenge. Then on towards Lynton and Lynmouth, the scene in later years of serious flooding. We stayed two nights and then crossed to Torquay skirting Exmoor and Dartmoor to stay another two nights before returning to our homes. It was a very enjoyable trip despite the steep hills in Somerset to reach Lynmouth. Countesbury and Porlock were particularly awesome to my father who had never before ventured so far or met such hills to negotiate. I was so glad to have given him the opportunity to see another part of the country and to go farther than he had ever been before on his 'Omega' motorcycle with my mother in the sidecar!!

For me, back to spells of officiating or assisting in either Customs or Excise Stations: in the Kings Warehouse, Parcel Post Depot, Landing and Shipping Stations at the docks and some Excise work which

I preferred. At the Parcel Post Depot was an Officer who had been a dockyard apprentice in Portsmouth before the 1914/18 war. His name was Pridham and he still lived at Portsmouth from where he travelled back and forth every day. It was the town where he had been an apprentice. I had a spell assisting at the B.A.T. tobacco factory very close to our flat. Dorothy found favour with Mrs Thorne my former landlady who wanted to 'mother' us both! Mrs Thorne had been a nurse at a Southampton hospital. She spoke with a very pronounced Somerset accent, coming as she did from Frome. On the other hand the Swashes living below our flat were not the ideal landlords. They complained about the slightest noise we made including the headphones of our 'wireless' set which I hid in saucepans to reduce the sound from our pillows when we went to bed. They also complained of the noise made when we moved a chair across the room just to sit down. Nothing would please them except total silence in the flat upstairs. I found that Dorothy was not the best of cooks!! She had never been required to cook meals at home. Her mother did it all. I suggested that Dorothy take some lessons in cooking at the nearby evening classes arranged by the Borough Council Education Authority. She was quite willing. It was just a case of learning what to do. At home I had watched my mother cook, sew and do all the work of a housewife and could do them all quite well. I suggested to Dorothy that she cook some rice for an 'after pudding' at lunchtime. When I arrived home from the docks the rice she had cooked 'rattled' on the plates. It became quite a joke with us. But she improved tremendously as the result of her evening classes so all became well. Dorothy was something of an exception being so young among the wives of the other much older men at the Parcel Post Depot. She was invited out to afternoon 'get-togethers' in various homes. But the wives all wanted to play Bridge; not Dorothy's choice of a party. However, we both played badminton with other C. & E. staff at the local badminton club. I also played cricket on one occasion to fill a vacancy in the Customs team against another Government Department. We played on the Hampshire County Cricket Ground, quite an experience. I did not distinguish myself but then I did not have to bat because the other side was dismissed cheaply! I held a catch at square leg position when fielding, much to my amazement as well as to the rest of the team! I was still not much good as a cricketer, but I was appointed Treasurer of the Badminton Club! I did a short spell in the Collector's office employed on calculating the drawback of duty due by longhand from first principals of arithmetic. I found that I was as quick in my calculations as some of the clerical staff were with their machines!

When employed at the docks I rode an ancient pedal bicycle given to me by an Officer. I fitted it with two 'steps' on the back wheel so that Dorothy could stand on them while I worked the pedals! I 'laid up' the Ariel for the winter to save the licence duty until the Spring! We had friends from Gillingham living at Totton near Southampton and I rode there with Dorothy on the 'steps' of the bicycle, a distance of about 4 miles. Fortunately no hills! But when we went to Bitterne in the other direction to visit Mr and Mrs Gibbons (ex Romsey) it was mostly uphill, quite a 'push' with Dorothy on the 'steps'! We managed!!

Eventually the blow fell. I was informed by the Higher Collector that I was to be transferred to Manchester Collection. Dorothy and I had furnished our flat following a visit to the Daily Mail Ideal Home Exhibition in London. We were very comfortable living in Southampton and had no wish to go north to Manchester. I had learnt that some U.O.s could be seconded and appointed to the Government Chemist Department to work in London. Such a secondment would be for three years when the appointee would be sent to fill a 'Chemical' Station. These specialised Stations were located in the larger ports. London, Glasgow, Bristol, Southampton and Liverpool had such, staffed by two Officers. Their work was to test any article either imported or exported where duty or 'drawback' was involved. Spirits and wines were especially subject to test at the Chemical Station on goods sent by Landing and Shipping Officers. What attracted me was that I would be free of being transferred to any Collection in the country for three years and thereafter appointed to fill a Chemical Station for several more years. I would thus gain seniority until such time as I became due for appointment elsewhere to an ordinary Station. I had obtained a good mark in Science, which included chemistry, in the entrance exam, so my application was granted. Dorothy and I then had the decision to make; where to live for the purpose of working in London.

Dorothy's grandparents had by this time retired from Crossness outfall works. Her aunt and uncle had left Crossness to live at Bexleyheath although still employed at Crossness. We decided to settle for Bexleyheath area. We found a flat just off the main road near enough to the railway to London Bridge or Cannon Street. It turned out to be unsatisfactory so we quickly moved to a nice house to rent at Barnehurst, very near another railway station connecting to London, and backing on to the local golf course. Strangely enough our next door neighbour was a banking official who hailed from Gillingham so we were very happy with our choice. We were close enough to visit her aunt in Bexleyheath and her grandparents in Abbey Wood. Also only about 20 miles from Gillingham. We went there frequently to visit our parents.

CHAPTER NINE
Government Laboratory.

I made a firm friendship with another U.O. named Eddie Standingford who had previously been employed in a city bank. He lived in Leytonstone, his father being a post office official at Post Office Headquarters in the City. Eddie had been at the Government Chemist's Department for a few months and was most helpful in showing me the testing procedures. This was more involved than was the work carried out at London Port Chemical Station situated at St Katherine's Dock close to the Tower of London. The Government Laboratory had a section situated on the fifth floor of the Custom House which was the Headquarters of London Port and some of Customs & Excise Headquarters Divisions. Others were in Eastcheap with a connecting walkway to the Custom House in Lower Thames Street. Next door to the Custom House was Billingsgate Market, the centre for the fish distributing industry. The 'Fish Porters' with their quaint headgear designed to allow them to carry large heavy boxes of fish on their heads, were very much in evidence especially early in the morning. Billingsgate fish market attracted more interest to visitors to the Capital than did the ancient Custom House next door. By the afternoon all was quiet, the fish having been sold by auction or tender to be taken away, until the next day's early start for disposing of the various catches brought in by boat, but more so by road and rail from ports throughout the country.

From the laboratory there was a grand view of the River Thames, the Tower of London, the Monument marking the end of the Great Fire of London so aptly described by Pepys. Across the Thames some of the ancient wharves such as Butler's. In the river the 'Harpy' landing stage, Headquarters of the London Waterguard service of the Customs. Also the two Dutch vessels allowed to anchor there under an ancient charter. Not to be vacant, so when one vessel went away another came to replace it. History was written here.

I was assigned to the laboratory bench, testing for strengths of wines. This by use of a spectrometer and by light to determine strength. Samples sent up from the local Chemical Station for confirmation were received for a second check if found of border line strength, but most tests were on wines on import from farther afield in London Port. Hundreds were received every day so I was kept busy. Next I was transferred to the bench testing spirits for strength. In the case of Liqueurs, the strength could only get determined by distillation of part of the sample using intricate sets of tables to consult. All remnants left after strength had been established had to be destroyed "by pouring down the common sewer". This under the eye of the Senior Chemist!! It was said that the fish regularly gathered below, in the Thames for a destruction 'session'. The laboratory 'common sewer' emptied into the Thames!! Quite untrue but a nice comment!

The Department of the Government was formed after many years being just a part of the Excise to give figures for strengths of spirits etc. The staff came from Excise Officers. Testing for other purposes followed until eventually the Excise and other testing had become large enough to be made into a separate Government Department. But Excise staff remained. The secondment arrangement was adopted to ensure that the Excise continued to safeguard the Revenue. Other staff was recruited to carry on testing for precise details of composition etc. for any Government Department. An Excise official remained for a time as head of the new Government Department but eventually the appointment of the Chief Government Chemist was filled by a scientist chosen by the Government and not by the Board of Customs and Excise.

In the laboratory at the Custom House, spirits, wines and beers were tested for alcoholic content. The room adjoining this section was devoted solely to examining tea imported from abroad. This, for the presence of adulteration constituent would amount to a fraud. This testing was carried out by an expert senior chemist. Seconded U.O.s never took part in such work. Other specialised testing took place for saccharine or other substances in an article e.g. toothpaste where health problems could exist. U.O.s on secondment were employed solely on testing where revenue of customs or excise was involved. These were intoxicating liquors, sugar and tobacco. After a spell in the spirits etc. section, I went over to sugar content testing. This, mainly for establishing percentages of sugar in goods such as cakes and biscuits exported on drawback of the duty, whether Excise duty paid on sugar manufactured in British beet sugar factories or on Customs duty paid on molasses for example, imported from abroad. Cakes had to be immersed in water and left to soak overnight to allow the solution to be tested the next day for percentage of sugar to be compared with the declaration of sugar content by the exporter to be confirmed or otherwise. I found that the work involved in the Custom House laboratory interesting but not exactly brain stretching. Next I was transferred to the Government Laboratory Headquarters at Clements Inn in the Strand, London, near to the Law Courts. Here I was employed testing tobacco, mainly cigarettes for export on drawback. Samples of cigarettes sent from the docks in small sample jars were weighed and then placed in an oven overnight to establish by re-weighing, the percentage of water contained when thoroughly dried. The dried cigarettes were then roasted to destruction. The residue was weighed to establish if sand had been included in the weight so to enhance that on which drawback was claimed. Shops were also visited around the capital for purchase of cigarettes, to be minutely examined under a microscope for impurities. Cabbage leaves have been known to be shredded to resemble tobacco! This microscopic examination of samples was carried out, again by a scientist in the Department who had expert experience of what might be found, to defraud the public. There is a valuable trade in exporting tobacco products to India of cheap cigarettes manufactured partly from the stalks and stems of tobacco leaves. Such are not used in cigarettes for home consumption. Similar tests were applied to 'pipe' tobacco. Occasionally snuff made from finely ground tobacco including the stalk, came under checking, but this again was carried out by experienced staff.

The jars of cigarettes sent from the docks invariably contained sufficient numbers of individual cigarettes to enable a second test to be carried out should the first prove unsatisfactory. Also for a third test to be made by a senior chemist if both were unsatisfactory. Such ensured that evidence was available in the event of a dispute with an exporter. However, this meant that should the first test be satisfactory, a quantity of cigarettes remained for disposal. As a non-smoker I was entrusted with the task of taking such into the basement to be destroyed by burning in the fires of the boilers heating the laboratory. I had many 'friends' among smokers in the Department wanting remnants from jars for them to do the destroying by smoking! I did not become a popular member of the laboratory staff!

112

After I had been seconded to and serving in the Department of the Government Chemist for about two years, the Board of Customs and Excise, in response to pressure from the staff association, agreed to discontinue the secondment scheme and return all the U.O.s in the laboratory to the 'Outdoor Service'. This was to be carried out at the rate of two U.O.s per month. The Government Chemist was also in favour of the discontinuance of the secondment scheme. It had become an anomaly in an important section of Government policy for the protection of public health and other matters. It was often said that the employment of Officers of Customs and Excise in the Department of the Government Chemist, once that body had been set up, was simply because the Board of Customs and Excise did not trust the Government Chemist to safeguard the revenue in the way the Board had so done over the years before the new Department was set up! It was certainly a small waste of man power for Officers to be employed on work that could easily be carried out by laboratory assistants at a much lower salary but who could from the experience gained, attain promotion to the higher ranks in the Laboratory. The Government Chemist was also keen to gain control over the small number of Stations throughout the country where Officers formerly in the Laboratory on secondment, were employed on testing. These were gradually to be phased out, by staffing with Laboratory assistants. In June 1933 I was 'released'. The U.O.s involved were all allowed, when their turn came for return to the Outdoor Service, to choose whichever Collection they preferred. I chose Dover and reported to the Collector there on 1st June 1933. I had been on secondment since February 1931. I did not regret my period in the Government Laboratory. It had given me additional seniority, taught me much about revenue testing but I had lost nearly two and a half years of experience. This, however, was soon regained. I was now in the Collection of my choice and had not had to move to a Chemical Station after the normal three years. My friend Eddie Standiford, chose Cardiff Collection and was soon enjoying life in the Welsh mountains and valleys! I proposed a scheme for the former "seconded U.O.s." to write a letter once a month to be circulated in a folder to pass round, describing our experiences in the wide world of H.M. Customs and Excise. This suggestion was accepted by the majority of the U.O.s in the Government Chemist Department and was continued for several years. I finally found the file among Eddie Standingford's documents after he passed away a few years later.

While in the Government Laboratory, cuts in salary were imposed on Government employees, the armed services, teachers, police etc. due to the recession. I was affected in-as-much as the yearly increment to my salary was withheld as my contribution to meet the financial crises affecting the country. Dorothy did not think much of what was happening! I contacted the landlord of the house we had just started to occupy and he agreed to reduce the rent! As an employee of the local authority, he too, probably had to accept the 'cuts' imposed, but he was very fair to me.

At Barnehurst, Dorothy and I now had a very nice residence where I could store my motorcycle. I had a garden I could cultivate to grow produce for the house. I once planted a new row of small cabbage plants for them to grown on to maturity. Nearby were some old cabbage "stumps" left behind by the previous tenant. These had newly grown 'sproutings' which were available for cutting and using. I told Dorothy to cut them off for use at our evening meal. When I arrived home we had very nice spring greens to eat but they were from the tops of the newly planted small cabbage plants instead of from the 'sproutings' from the old stumps nearby! Our meal was nice and green and tender! Dorothy had no experience of gardening. Her father hated gardening. His sole thoughts were on sport. Her grandfather on the other hand was the best gardener I ever met. His garden at Crossness was a picture and a riot of colour. He grew everything in the vegetable line that they consumed.

We continued to attend dances in the Medway Towns. On one occasion we went together to judge a dancing competition in a hall near to Chatham Town Hall. This completed, we set out on my motorbike to return to Barnehurst. Unfortunately on the main road I ran out of petrol. When I stopped I was looking into the petrol tank, with my right leg steadying the machine when another motorcyclist went by at speed striking my right leg with his footrest. He did not stop. I rolled over to the ground. A passing motorist stopped and assisted me to get to my feet, but the pain was intense. The motorist went away and came back with a supply of petrol. This he poured into my empty tank; the motorist assisted me to sit on the motorbike. He started the engine and I rode away after thanking him. All that night after we returned home to bed I was in pain, so as early as possible I arose and on my motorbike set out for hospital at Woolwich. There I was examined and a broken leg above the ankle was diagnosed. My leg was bandaged and I again drove my motorbike home and went on sick leave for about two weeks. Eventually my leg healed and I went back for duty. An outcome was that I claimed on a free insurance, sponsored by the Daily Mail newspaper and received the sum of ten pounds for my broken leg which had been certified by Woolwich Hospital! I also received sick pay benefit from the Tunbridge Wells Equitable Friendly Society of which I was a member, from a recommendation I had received from the Officer in West Bromwich, Mr. Cross, who had also advised me to take out a term insurance policy with the Scottish Widows Fund. This policy proved of use later when I was paying the fees for my two son's education at the King's School in Rochester; the second oldest public school in the country after the King's School at Canterbury. Both were founded following the conversion of England to Christianity by bishops from Rome, centuries before.

While at Barnehurst, with Bill Holloway, one of my former apprentice colleagues, we decided to install electric light in my parent's bungalow in Rainham. Previously the lighting was by gas. I purchased all the electrical cables and switches, lamp fittings etc. I had retained most of my knowledge of how to wire premises although Bill Holloway's expertise was invaluable. The installation was a great success. Double pole switching to allow for entering and leaving the dining room by different doors was arranged. Similarly too for going up and down the stairs to my former bedroom. Bill had by then married Olive Higgins, sister of 'Tich'. We went occasionally camping to the seaside together. I had purchased a small four seater motor car, a "Clyno" model with fabric body, unknown now-a-days. It would not fit into the small wooden garage attached to the house, so instead I dug out the earth floor so that it would drop in and fit! Once on our way with Bill and Olive Holloway to Dymchurch to camp, we stopped on the London Road between Gillingham and Rainham because of a large crowd gathered there for the opening of a new Civil Service Sports Council sports ground for use by dockyard employees and other Government Departments employing Civil Servants in the Medway Towns area. Little did I know then that later, both I and my mother, were to have close associations with this project. With the 'Holloways', Dorothy and I went as far a Lulworth in Dorset to camp overlooking the Cove. But for the rain that descended in the night, it would have been a great success. We purchased 'Lilos' for use as mattresses. Dorothy and Olive regularly consulted together to plan the menus for our camping trips! (Memories of the Boy Scouts and of apprentice camps on the bank of the Medway).

At Barnehurst also, colleagues in the C & E on secondment, particularly Eddie Standingford and another U.O. named Tom Mollett came to visit us. Dorothy and I went sometimes to Leytonstone to stay there with Eddie's parents. His mother was a 'charmer' but his father a cantankerous man. Eddie told us that sometimes, when a member of the family put more coal on the dining room fire for heat, his father would straight away take the new coal off because the coal which was still there wasn't fully consumed! Eddie took his 'winter' leave when possible, so to act as a temporary postman for the Christmas mail. His father was at Post Office H.Q's. Eddie had two sisters both younger and unmarried. The elder eventually married a scientist and they emigrated to Australia. The other daughter Elizabeth, remained unmarried as also did Eddie. Both would have made excellent parents. Eventually the Standingford family transferred their residence to the Hayes area of Kent and Eddie cultivated there a nice garden. Dorothy and I, also sometimes, Marjory, Dorothy's sister, attended local dances, staying overnight with Eddie's parents. Eddie after release from the laboratory and following his period again as a U.O., was eventually appointed to an Excise Station in South London. I finally visited him in the Charing Cross Hospital when it was removed to the Fulham area of London. He passed away before he was due to retire, from thrombosis affecting his legs. A sad end to such a grand chap and good friend over the years. While at Barnehurst I erected a badminton net on the lawn for visitors to play with us at badminton. I also received 'presents' of golf balls lofted over into my garden from the adjoining course. If asked for their return I would comply, but if left as 'lost', I gained a present. At that time I had not taken up the game although I had what was the 'kit' in the shape of 'plus fours' I had had made in Southampton before my wedding. ("Hardly worn", as second hand clothing advertisements are framed!!).

116

CHAPTER TEN
Contact with Customs and Excise Federation.

While in the laboratory I joined the Customs and Excise Federation, a staff organisation, formed many years earlier for the protection of the interests of Officers and Surveyors. Officers constituted over 90% of the membership. In general all Officers joined the Federation, also some Surveyors, but they also had a separate Surveyors' Association. Collectors had a Higher Grades Association. All met the representatives of the Board of C & E regularly to discuss matters, via the Whitley Council system for negotiation between Government representatives, which, in the case of the C & E was the Board. Sometimes all three staff associations met under what was termed the Outdoor Service Sectional Whitley Committee. Each of the three Associations sent delegates according to their strength of membership. The Federation was always well represented in discussions. More often the Federation met the Board separately via the Officer Grade Whitley Committee when all the delegates on what was known as the "Staff Side", were Officers.

The Federation had branches throughout the country mainly on a territorial basis equal to the individual Collections, but not necessarily so. Branch areas could overlap Collection boundaries or include more than one Collection. Local Whitley Committees were representative of all grades in the Collection, Surveyors, Waterguard, Clerical Staff, Watchers and cleaners, met for negotiations with the local Collector. The Federation held a conference annually, known as the "Council" which on meeting, duly elected an Executive Committee, a General Secretary, and two Assistant Secretaries plus the Treasurer and a President. Councils were held in different towns throughout the country each year at the invitation of a branch, for the privilege of staging the Council. This generally lasted three days, but the Executive Committee met for an additional day either side of the Council Meeting. London was the largest branch of the Federation including as it did the Collections of London Port plus the Four Excise Collections of London Central, West, North and South. Delegates to Councils were based on membership within each individual Branch. London, obviously sent the largest delegation of up to 10. Smaller Branches might send one, two or three. U.O.s had a separate representation. The elected Executive from the previous year attended the next year's Council in their capacity as members of the Executive as did the elected Secretaries, and Treasurer. Discussions at Councils were fast and furious. Decisions arrived at had to be accepted and if necessary negotiations on such were passed to the Whitley representative to negotiate with the Board, or locally with Collectors.

I attended my first Federation meeting in the Essex Hall off the Strand and saw there the Federation officials who represented me. Of necessity the officials were all members of London Branch, serving as Officers in one or other of the London Collections. U.O.s seconded to the Government Laboratory were regarded as members of London Port staff. At the first meeting I attended, doubts were raised from the floor on the non-representation of U.O.s generally at Councils. I did not enter the discussions, but at the subsequent election of delegates to attend the forthcoming Council to be held in Harrogate, Yorks, I was elected as a U.O. delegate. At the council meeting in Harrogate I met the delegates from all over the country, English, Scottish, Irish and Welsh. It was a veritable "talk shop" but to me most interesting. I duly made my speech for the 1927 entrants and said on this subject that these young men were now quite capable of performing all the duties of the Officer Grade, seeking no special favours. I was in fact the first post 1927 delegate to be elected as a delegate. Special leave was granted by the Board for delegates to attend the Council. Expenses were paid by the Federation.

At Councils there were a number of outside activities plus 'fun and games' in the local hotel where all were staying. The Harrogate Council was at the invitation of Leeds Branch. Most of the Council delegates were well known "characters", attending Councils year after year and generally able to make competent speeches to put their points of view. Leeds Branch staged a Council dinner one of the evenings. Leeds branch also took the delegates by coach to see the ruins of Fountains Abbey. Also out on to Ilkley Moor (Baht-tat), also

118

to see Mother Shiptons caves where dripping water solidified nearby objects. I was really seeing more and more of England's 'pleasant land'. A move was afoot in London to ensure that U.O. problems were being dealt with by the Federation. I was not aware of what these were but at a meeting was called to discuss, I was invited to act as Secretary and take the minutes. Shortly afterwards my tenure of employment in the Government Laboratory ended. I duly reported to the Collector in Dover, for instructions for my future employment.

Dorothy and I went to Dover to look for accommodation. Every landlady or house agent who showed us what was on offer made a categorical assurance that there was "a good view of the castle" from the premises we were inspecting! At one in fact, the castle could only be seen from the W.C. if one stood on the seat to look through the small window! Eventually we found a flat in the Folkestone Road. It had gas lighting so I approached the local electricity office to have electricity installed. Without this, how were we to operate the electrical equipment we had accumulated in our Barnehurst house? This accomplished, I went to see the Collector and was directed to go forthwith to Hythe, a Cinque Port, to assist the Officer there. So no early occupation of the flat we had secured. I was in Hythe for 14 days, apart from one day on special leave to attend an Officer Grade Whitley Committee meeting in London to which I had been elected at the Harrogate Council. Dorothy had secured some accommodation in a small terrace house. It was her first experience of being 'on the road' in the Excise. But I received the expenses for our transfer at the Board's expense from Barnehurst to Dover. Our furniture duly arrived but we still had not occupied the flat secured in the Folkestone Road. I then received an "officiating note" from the Collector to assist in Herne Bay Station, followed by another to go to Maidstone to officiate in the 4th Station there. I was now seeing Kent at the Board's expense! Every move attracted the payment of Disturbance Allowance, including that to Maidstone when the Collector gave me authority to live at Rainham, travelling to Maidstone daily. I managed to perform the officiating in Maidstone 4th Station without mishap. Fortunately there was no brewery in the 4th but 'country' to 'survey' plus Old Age Pension work. This accomplished, I was directed to go to Dover Customs, but on arrival I was re-directed to proceed to Canterbury to officiate. Dorothy had taken my proposed stay in Dover on customs work to do her 'laundry'. I arrived back at our flat to say "off to Canterbury". In

came the laundry off the drying line. It was back as far as Canterbury.
There the Cricket Week for Kent County Cricket had commenced so
accommodation was difficult to find. Dorothy found some near the
centre of the town. She was becoming an accomplished finder of
accommodation and enjoying it. After a fortnight in Canterbury,
directions were received to proceed to Ash near Sandwich.

We went back to Dover 'to confirm' that our flat in the Folkestone
Road still existed!! The landlady wanted to know when we were
coming to live in it. We never did. The electricity supply had been
installed but to my dismay, I found that at that time Dover electricity was based on 100 volts Direct Current (D.C). One of the few
places using out-of-date voltages. All our electrical equipment was at
220 volts Alternating Current (A.C.). With my background I should
have known better! But I did not enquire when I arranged for the
electric supply to be installed. The landlady took us down into her
cellar to show us the fish her husband had caught off the Western
Dock in Dover. It was an enormous cod. She promised to ask him
to catch us some fish. He did, but it was so large we would not eat
it at our Ash accommodation, so we took it to Gillingham for
Dorothy's father to consume. He liked fish. We departed on the
road to Ash near Sandwich.

Ash was the most interesting Station in which I ever officiated. It
contained a small brewery, (Gardiners), the Cinque Port of Sandwich,
with a small amount of customs work, mainly timber from the Baltic,
a cinema and much country with many Old Age Pensioners, a Corn
Market that never operated!   Plus varied ordinary Excise work,
licensed premises etc. The main concern was the brewery. In the
distance was Sandwich Bay with opportunity to bathe provided one
had a pass to enter the private area constituting the Bay. We were
given a pass! The Officer, Mr Vining, had been in the Station for
thirty four years. It was originally a 'Ride' i.e. the area that could
be surveyed with a horse as the means of getting around the countryside. For this, a 'Ride' Officer received an allowance of some £40.
Additionally Ash Station records were maintained in the Officer's
residence, for which he received the magnificent sum of seven
shillings per week. The term 'Ride' had been discontinued. Mr
Vining also had a Clyno car, this, my father ultimately purchased
from him. What happened to the 'Omega' motorbike and sidecar
I cannot remember! Mr Vining was retiring, so once again I had the

task of removing all the Excise records plus all the Old Age Pension books to such accommodation as I could secure. This had fortunately been arranged with the local grave digger! Dorothy and I had two rooms in his house, one to be the Excise Office as well as our living quarters. Besides being the Excise Officer, Mr Vining was a market gardener sending his produce regularly to market. He was also a member of the Church Council and Chairman of the parish council. I really think that the Excise was a secondary occupation for him! Ash Station was originally a "Second Class Ride", i.e. it contained less work than one in a large town and so received a lower salary for the Officer in charge. First and Second Class Rides, (later Stations) disappeared as descriptions at the amalgamation of the Customs and Excise to form one Department. All became Stations on 1st class salary basis. No wonder Mr Vining remained there! I was approached one evening by the Vicar to ask if I would like to serve on the parish and church councils! He was under the impression that I too would stay for many years! Such was the Excise "in the old days" when an Officer was on a "par" with Solicitors, doctors and others who controlled their businesses from their residences. Now no more! Having moved all the records, Dorothy and I daily awaited the post to see what our journeys were to be for that day. Sometimes this decision was made in bed when the post arrived early! The Officer for Deal Station, named Usher, lived in nearby Sandwich. Dorothy and I soon made friends with him and Mrs Usher. Unfortunately I was only officiating in Ash Station for about eight weeks, because I was due to take my entitlement of leave. So had to hand over to another U.O. named Button, also an ex-dockyard apprentice who knew Dorothy well. He was sent to take over from me and to occupy the premises we had found so suitable. He was unmarried, but I believe, though, he fell in love with Ash landlady's young daughter! Nothing came of it. He subsequently married much later, a female employee in the C & E headquarters' staff but had no children. One interesting occurrence in Ash station. The Station included a corn market which never operated, or had not for many years. However, a record was maintained which showed "Nil" sales every week. The return of sales of corn had to be sent to the Ministry of Agriculture weekly. One week I omitted to send in the 'Nil' return. Within a day I received a telegram requesting me to send in a 'Nil' return. Bureaucracy demanded a 'Nil' return to be filed with all the other previous 'Nil's' made over many years for a non-operating Corn Market! One night in accordance with the instructions relating to brewery surveys, I made the required annual visit after midnight to the small Ash brewery. The staff was on duty preparing for the next day's brew. They told me that they had never known such a visit by Mr Vining the whole time that they had been employed there! It was just as well that no illegal brews had taken place, unrecorded in the official brewing books during Mr Vining's tenure of Ash Station.

I received notification from the Board of Customs and Excise that I was entitled to claim the seven shillings per week allowance for the use of my accommodation in Ash as the official office. This was the amount that Mr Vining had received for many years before retiring. I had not claimed such an allowance for the period I had had to use my accommodation in Ormskirk Station when I transferred all the Excise and Old Age Pension records from Mr Orme's residence when he went on leave. From my acquaintance with Mr Orme I am sure that he would not have willingly surrendered his seven shillings a week allowance because of going on leave although he had insisted that all the records had to be transferred to my 'digs'. He was not a pleasant man for whom to officiate. The difference was of course that Mr Vining had retired so he was obviously no longer entitled to receive the official office allowance. The problem did not arise when I officiated in Newport, Salop, Station. Mr Hodgson allowed me to use his office in his home. Quite a different man to Mr Orme.

From my attendance at the Harrogate Council I had been appointed to the Officer Grade Committee of the Departmental Whitley Council. At the 'Staff Side' meeting I proposed that the 'Fixed Officiator' scheme be re-introduced and revised. My proposal was that a 'Fixed Officiator' be appointed in the Excise where six Officers were conveniently near to each other. The Fixed Officiator would relieve for leave for the six Officers in turn with his own leave this would occupy most of his time. Days for 'taking over' and 'handing over' had also to be allowed for. In the Customs where six Officers were very adjacent, in fact often working in the same office or building, the officiating scheme would be extended by the appointment of a 'Fixed Relief Officer'. This would be a fixed appointment and the F.R.O. would not have to accept appointment compulsorily elsewhere at any time.

The Board approved the proposed scheme for relief both for the Excise where a U.O. appointed would be a 'Fixed Officiator' (F.O.)

and for the Customs where the appointed U.O. would be a Fixed Relief Officer' (F.R.O.). Certainly in the Customs the scheme gave more fixity of service. For the Excise an Officiator would have continuous knowledge of his future commitments until he was appointed to a Fixed Station.

In the Department, a special scheme of absences on leave was applied. Leave was granted for three weeks in the 'summer' and three weeks in the 'winter' on a precise 'rota'. The rotation was in the order, 1,4,7,2,5, (8) (if necessary), then 3, followed by 6, and back to 1. In other words add the figure 3 each time. This 'rotation' was applied to the summer leave periods, then applied in reverse for the winter. Summer and winter were naturally 6 months each. By this rotation each Officer obtained a first choice of summer leave once in 7 (or 8) years, but if at the 'tail end' (7th or 8th) for summer, he received 1st choice for winter. The scheme had been put into operation at Staff Side request, when it was found that senior Officers were regularly using their 'seniority' to claim first choice every year, both for summer and winter. Staffing problems, particularly in the Customs necessitated that there was always sufficient staff on duty. With a 'F.R.O.' available in the Customs and a 'F.O.' in the Excise, there would always be sufficient staff with no posts vacant. The '8' rotation figure generally only applied for Unattached Officers who might be entitled to less than the normal annual leave of 6 weeks. U.O.s too, were placed on a similar list to ensure that not too many were on leave at any one time. U.O's on first appointment had a slightly reduced scale of annual leave.

At the inception of the F.O. scheme a U.O. named McKirdy, was regularly officiating in the Rochester area. He was then appointed F.O. upon application. He was an ex. 1914-19 war entrant. In due course he became due to take a Fixed Station. When the Rochester Group was re-advertised as vacant, I applied and was appointed. The seniority I had obtained by service in the Government Laboratory had stood me in good stead and in time secured me a modest amount of fixity at Rochester until I had to accept appointment to a Fixed Station. It could be to Tilbury dock as a 'F.R.O.' whereby I could avoid appointment to a Station which might be to any part of the country. Service in the C & E was always at the Board's discretion where it was to be, but it was possible to apply some thought to the problem so to avoid fixity in an unwanted area.

Since the recruitment of staff to the Department was nation-wide there was always some possibility of a member of the staff being willing to accept fixity in an area others wished to avoid. Fixity in a South coast area was always attractive, but these Stations invariably were filled by senior applicants on transfer. I had my eyes firmly fixed on a particular area in Kent as an Excise Officer! It was many years before I achieved my objective!

CHAPTER ELEVEN
Employment at Rochester
Customs and Excise.

Having handed over the control of Ash Station to U.O. Button I took delayed leave in October 1933 followed by a short spell of assisting in Sheerness Station for an Officer named Cook who was a friend of mine. He later became a Surveyor and then an Inspector at Head Office. I was required to take further leave in November, but finally I commenced my duties in the Rochester Fixed Officiator Group on December 1st 1933. It was to last until March 31st 1935. During that time I officiated in all the six Stations within the Group, but I was awaiting the time when I knew that I would be required to take a Fixed Station, possibly anywhere in the country. I had a preference within the Group, for officiating in the Excise; Gillingham 1st and 2nd. Rochester 2nd and Strood. The other two Stations were in Rochester 1st and were Customs. The Officer for Gillingham 1st was a Mr Armstrong who had been there many years, knowing all the 'short cuts'. He always arranged that during my periods in his Station, I did not have to visit the N.A.A.F.I. warehouse, a very suspicious arrangement, but I could not alter it. I was at that time too innocent to query his instructions. On the other hand the Officer for Gillingham 2nd was a Mr Shaw, who literally 'hit the bottle' frequently. On one occasion I had to go to his private residence to obtain the office keys. These from his wife, Mr Shaw being too incapacitated to see me. For all that, he was a very friendly man, quite different from Mr Armstrong. Gillingham 2nd Station took in the area to the south of the town including Rainham and Wigmore as well as the country area around Hartlip and Stockbury which I knew so well. Mr Nash who was the Officer for Strood Station was a very secretive person. On arrival in the morning he would lock his office door and paper over the key-hole preventing others from attempting to discover whether or not he was in his room! Often the Surveyor, Mr Jewett, wanting to discuss something with him, would hammer on the door calling out, "Mr Nash, are you in there". It was a regular performance! All drawers in his office were locked. I never discovered their contents. The compensating factor for me was that Strood Station covered the area of Kent eastwards to the Isle of Grain including the villages of Cliffe-at-Hoo and Cooling; the riverside at Upnor and other areas I knew so well from my boyhood with my cousins, plus the spots visited years before in the boat 'Venetia'. Rochester 2nd Station was under the control of Mr Wakeling, a very jovial person, easy to get on with. He was the Inspector of Corn Returns for the area, so I regularly visited the Corn Market in the City, to receive Corn Returns on Saturday. He was also the Probate Officer for the area so in his Station I had to deal with applications for Probate on small estates. His country area extended along the Medway Valley almost to the old camping ground of the dockyard apprentices but on the other side of the river. Mr Ottaway, the Customs Officer for the Long Room was responsible for all Customs work on the river. As well, he controlled the Long Room work including maintaining the Registry of Shipping. He seems always to have sent out enquiries regarding hulks and derelict vessels lying in the river or on its banks just before proceeding on leave, requesting that recorded owners should have the registration cancelled! Those replies that were returned, I had to deal with while officiating. Work was then required by me on the Register ready for the signature of the Surveyor who was the 'official' Registrar of Shipping but did no actual work other than to sign and ensure that no mistakes had been made in recording the changes of ownership of 'shares', or cancellations in the Register.

Registry of Shipping was a very involved subject, being the legal record of the ownership of a boat or ship. Some Registers contained details of numerous ships, as for example in London. Others very few, if for a small port maintaining a Register. Rochester was not a very large port but it contained a fair number of vessels on its Register. The Registry of Shipping was akin to the registry maintained for establishing the ownership of a property by its Deeds. In the case of a vessel, however the ownership was divided into 64 parts, any of which could be bought or sold individually, but all such transactions had to be recorded in the Register, otherwise they were not legal. A ship or boat had to have a legal "Master" known as the "Ship's Husband". This person, too, was recorded in the Register.

Equally involved, too, was the 'signing off' of crews after a voyage when the Captain or his representative attended at the Custom House with members of the crew. Their employment record had to be endorsed to signify the conduct of each member. The Register of members of the Royal Navy Volunteer Reserve was also maintained for the Port. Mr Ottaway was entitled to the rank of Commander of the R.N.V.R. Whether he had the uniform for his rank I did not discover. He was, of course, the Receiver of Wreck for Rochester Port!! He also paid pensions to retired Dockyard employees. There were so many different tasks to be performed when necessary that I was always glad when each period of officiating in Mr Ottaway's Station came to and end. He had as well, the Landing and Shipping on the Medway from Sheerness in the Isle of Sheppy as far up river to Maidstone, all within the official Port of Rochester and with the oil refinery of Berry Wiggins on the Grain peninsular. Here thick heavy oil was received from Trinidad in South America. The large tanks had to be dipped on each visit to establish amounts received and used in the manufacture of asphalt substances for roads etc. I detested having to climb to the top of the tanks for the dipping to be performed personally by the Officer to check receipt and usings. Mr Ottaway was, of course, well versed in his tasks over the many years he had been in the Station. I have to record that Mr Jewett, the Surveyor kept well in the background, and was more interested in the Excise side of his District. The Long Room had a staff of two Clerical Officers, carrying out the clerical work of the 'Long Room'. (The Custom House Office is always referred to generally throughout the entire Customs and Excise Department, as 'The Long Room'. It is so called from the actual 'Long Room' in the Custom House for the Port of London in Lower Thames Street, which is in fact a long room). The two Clerical Officers at Rochester were both very efficient and gave me all the assistance I needed when officiating for Mr Ottaway. He was very much an old fashioned Customs and Excise Officer from pre-1914 war days. An old boy of the Mathematical School at Rochester, of which he was very proud; a member of the Masonic organisation in Gillingham, but not of my Lodge, of which he was unaware of my membership. He was contemptuous of the Waterguard staff when they appeared on the River Medway referring to them as 'boatmen', an old term for that staff before it was upgraded. Mr Ottaway's knowledge of the Excise side of the Department was nil, but he was an excellent Customs Officer.

The remaining Station in the Rochester Group was Mr Allison who was soon to retire. He was in charge of the two bonded warehouses. One was owned by Owen J Carter and relatively small. It supplied dutiable wines and spirits to ships for the Royal Navy as well as to merchants in the area, on payment of duty. The other warehouse was much more important, in that it supplied taxable wines and spirits and other goods to most of the Embassies in the U.K. The head office was in Gibraltar. The owners were Saccone and Speed, having connections world-wide. Goods for Embassies could only be released on the express orders of the Board. Files arrived authorising each individual consignment. This had to be carried out very meticulously. Taxable liquors were also supplied to ships of the Royal Navy, as well as were tobacco products. Very little duty was collected since deliveries were to Embassies or to naval vessels. Mr Allison's work was relatively simple compared to the other Customs Station at Rochester occupied by Mr Ottaway. It was an easy Station in which to officiate.

The Rochester Group of Stations was the most varied one could imagine, with General Excise, including a 'dry Goods' warehouse (which I never visited!), much Old Age Pension work, Probate, and a Corn Market requiring returns to be sent. The Customs side carried responsibility for a 'Long Room', Registry of Shipping, Registrar of the Royal Naval Volunteer Reserve, signing off of crews after a voyage. Receiver of Wreck, and payment of Admiralty Pensions to former Dockyard employees preferring to take their entitlement in cash rather than by cheque, post, or attend in person at the Dockyard. Plus all the Landing and Shipping work on the River Medway between the Isle of Sheppy and Maidstone, including an Oil Refinery at Berry Wiggins. There were two Bonded Warehouses both dealing with the Navy, one also a specialist for Embassy deliveries. The Navy was always in the background for 'facilities'. Seizures of 'periques' detected at the Post Office were common of tobacco supplied duty free to naval personal on board ship, but posted to relatives in the U.K. These had to be sent to the King's warehouse in London after seizure.

Once I had officiated in all six Stations, I considered that I knew generally as much about the Customs and Excise as did the whole as all the six Officers in the Group put together! This is not boasting. I had to do both Customs and Excise work whereas they were all specialists in their own fields. In any case they were all fairly elderly but from being in their individual Stations for many years, in effect had no experience of anything other than their own day to day Customs or Excise controls. But being an Unattached Officer required one to work anywhere at any time on any task, that was what U.O.s were for! Unattached Officers were in effect permanently under training. The only item of work missing in Rochester was of 'gauging' such as I had performed at Albert Dock, Liverpool. It is possible that either Mr Ottaway or Mr Allison, could 'gauge' a cask but such expertise was not required at Rochester.

I was instructed by the Surveyor to carry out a number of 'detections' in the Medway towns area on Refreshment Houses that had failed to renew their annual licence of ten shillings and sixpence despite 'reminders' and warnings from the Collector's Office. I therefore set out after 10.30 pm, the time at which a licence became necessary allowing premises to stay open to supply refreshments to the public. At each place visited the owner could not produce to me his licence. I had ordered a light meal at each, but did not necessarily have to consume it! Eventually all were prosecuted at Chatham Police Court and all pleaded 'guilty', so I had no need to give evidence. All subsequently took out the required licence after a nominal fine. The local press displayed a 'banner' headline on the "Customs man who had six suppers in one evening" topic. I had not eaten six suppers but it made good reading for the readers of the paper! I had also when in Ash Station, made a detection of failure to charge entertainment duty by a very small travelling circus that had stopped in a village field nearby. I was very loath to do this but I could not take the risk of the circus proprietor claiming he had not been involved in an offence at his previous site when he moved on the next venue for his show, quoting Ash. He was let off with a caution. From the size of the audience at Ash, the circus would not survive very long!

As soon as I was appointed to Rochester F.O. Group, Dorothy and I commenced looking for a residence in the Medway Towns. We gave up the flat in Folkestone Road, Dover, which we had never occupied but for which I had had electricity on a voltage of 100 D.C. installed! We found a flat on the ground floor in Osprey Avenue, Chatham immediately across the boundary with Gillingham. In fact everybody imagined that it was in Gillingham. Fort Darland was opposite so we were not over-looked. It was another of the Forts surrounding the Medway Towns from Napoleonic days. Dorothy's mother was for a time unwell so Dorothy and I opted to stay with her family in a new residence they now occupied in Canterbury Street, Gillingham. When Dorothy's mother recovered, we took up our residence in Osprey Avenue. The owners of the house were named Donovan whom Dorothy knew. They occupied the upstairs flat. They had no children so we were quite happy and quiet there. I had become a Mason in November 1933 so we were now able to attend Masonic Ladies Nights together with Dorothy's parents.

My sister Doris who had taken up training as a nurse in the Homeopathic Hospital in London, had married Robert Craske and was now living in Maidstone. My father still a Shift Engineer in the dockyard Electrical Department suffered an accident one morning on his return home from work. He was struck by a lorry, which fortunately stopped and conveyed him to the Royal Naval Hospital. He had sustained a broken pelvis and he remained in hospital for some time. I was now able to assist my parents in the promotion of their business as 'Credit' suppliers to customers in the Medway Towns. Their business had prospered and they now had many more 'customers' from whom to collect credit payments plus many more retail shops prepared to use the system. I visited my parents at least once a week to keep their business accounts which my sister Doris had been doing for a while before her marriage. During my father's stay in hospital I was able to cultivate his garden, growing the usual vegetables for the house.

My former colleagues as apprentices in the Electrical Department in Chatham Dockyard were now studying for the Draughtsman' Examination. 'Dusty Doust' was now at Vickers in Barrow-in-Furness as a draughtsman but planning to emigrate to Australia for service with the Australian Government. Chris James was now employed in the Inland Revenue Department. The other ex-apprentices I saw from time to time. George Lawrence, my 'best man' had married. So had Harold Attwood. Alfred Fuller, the 'captain' of the boat, "Venetia" had married my former dancing partner, May Kirk, and was now a Station Engineer in the Electrical power Station in the Dockyard. Quite an important position.

The Federation Council was again held, this time on the invitation of Liverpool Branch at Southport. I was appointed the U.O. delegate from Dover Branch. On this occasion Dorothy came with me and we stayed in sumptuous accommodation in Southport that had been occupied the previous week by Gracie Fields The usual Council Dinner was held at the invitation of Liverpool Branch. Visits were to be made to 'Beauty Spots' in the area as a relief from the Council proceedings. There were two other post - 1927 U.O. delegates so this time I had support in putting forward ideas from the younger delegates. I was quite near to my 'bete noire,' Mr Orme, the Officer for Ormskirk Station but I did not care to visit him. I was again appointed to the Office Grade Whitley Committee. After the Council Dorothy and I decided to visit Blackpool which Dorothy had never seen. I once paid a brief visit there with 'Angel' Lewes on the pillion of my Ariel motorbike. I did not like the town and 'Angel' did not like the pillion! Dorothy did not like Blackpool either, so we went East to Corton near Lowestoft where there was a Civil Service Holiday camp. We broke our journey overnight in Peterborough but also took the opportunity to visit Chatsworth, home of the Duke of Devonshire, with its beautiful garden and house full of treasures. We made a brief visit to Corton and vowed to come again since it was a well run holiday camp fully under the control of the committee of Civil Servants elected from the 'campers' each week. We returned then to our flat.

I then heard that due to some reason there was now a vacancy on the Federation Executive Committee. The Secretary of Dover Branch nominated me and I was elected. The first post 1927 entrant to be so appointed. I then began to attend Executive Committee meetings and regularly attended all the future Council meetings until I was appointed to a Fixed Station. Due to the scarcity of Excise Station vacancies in the South I had no option but to accept appointment to Tilbury Dock in the Port of London Collection. This was the nearest I could get to Gillingham so to avoid a compulsory appointment elsewhere and possibly having to move our home. As a Fixed Relief Officer under the scheme I had put to the Board via the Federation I could not be moved except voluntarily to another Fixed Station. I was in the Rochester Fixed Officiator Group for less than three years but it was a very enjoyable period of my service.

Dorothy and I started to look for a house instead of living in a flat. We found one in Cecil Avenue, Gillingham, very near to the Civil

Service Sports Council sports ground we had earlier seen opened. It was a semi-detached villa newly built, facing a large open square expanse of park land given to the town by a former Mayor. It was known a Vinall Park after the Mayor. We could not be overlooked. The builder lived in a similar 'semi' just three doors away. It had a nice garage for keeping my car. We were very happy there. We considered that it was time to start a family! But this came later. After a year, the builder came to see me and to offer to sell me his house because he was leaving to build elsewhere. The price was £750. The builder's house had better fittings such as the picture rails, the flooring of Bruce Oak strips etc. and with a similar garage. I approached the Civil Service Housing Association for a loan on mortgage and they offered to let me have £700. This meant I had to find £50 myself. However, I then saw the builder and offered him £700 since that was all the Housing Association would let me have. The builder accepted so we went ahead and bought our first property and we had not to move very far! Just three doors away!

Dorothy and I look a motor tour to Scotland to visit a U.O. there who had been in the Government Laboratory, going via Birmingham and Liverpool also to visit former acquaintances. We visited Loch Lomond and other beauty spots and Stratford-on-Avon to see a Shakespeare play. It was our first real holiday away from home.

Dorothy and I had once before been on a holiday together. With George Lawrence and my sister Doris, before we were married, we went abroad as far as Ostende. The two girls shared a room on the first floor but George and I were stuck in a small room near the attic! We did not think much of Ostende, but the trip up the coast to see the 'Mole' at Zeebrugge with the guns still there after being 'spiked' by our forces in the Zeebrugge raid during the 1914/18 war was more interesting. Dorothy proved to be a very poor sailor. She was even sick in Dover Harbour before the ferry cast off! And violently sick on board all the way over, having to stay below in a cabin. The same performance on the return journey. But strangely enough she was perfectly well once she had her feet on dry land. It was always the same every time we went abroad by a sea journey, later in our married life. The worst one was when we once toured Scandinavia and had to take a voyage from Gothenborg in Norway to Aalborg in Denmark. I suppose it was psychological; she thought she would be sick even on a short voyage, and was!!

132

I had one piece of disturbing bad news while I was at Rochester Fixed Officiator Group. A young U.O. formerly a dockyard apprentice, but several years junior to me, had been sent to Northern Ireland to help man the boundary with the Irish Free State. This was about the time of the 'partition'. At the land boundary post he had to take duty on goods being brought into Northern Ireland from Eire. Foolishly he had put the money involved into his own pocket and attempted to hide the evidence. He had not reckoned with the expertise of the C & E accounting system where checks are carried out by the Accountant General's Office. As a result, his duplicity was discovered and he was prosecuted and dismissed from the Service. He returned to Gillingham and took up accounting with a firm of Chartered Accountants in London where he made good! It was a disgrace though, for an ex-dockyard apprentice to behave in such a foolish manner.

About this time, Dorothy's younger brother John was attending my old school, Chatham Technical which was now at Holcombe on the Chatham-Maidstone Road. The teacher for German by the name of McWillie arranged for a party from the school to go to Germany. John Brown was one of the party of schoolboys making the trip. They stayed at Solingen not far from the River Rhine. The English boys paid an agreed sum for the visit. When over, a party of German youths made the equivalent return visit to England. John's 'opposite number' was a boy named Arnaud. Because Dorothy's mother was unable to sleep the additional boy in the house, Dorothy and I agreed to take both John and Arnaud for the duration of the visit. Solingen is an industrial town producing cutlery. Arnaud brought with him a quantity of cutlery which he gave to Dorothy and I for recompense for his stay in England. Actually we were not looking for payment in cash, but the German method of exporting some of their products in payment was rather different from the English method of payment in cash! Although Arnaud was quite a pleasant boy, he was obviously a 'Hitler Youth'. He invariably addressed me as "my friend who is my enemy". This did not strike me as amusing! In addition he was always wanting to stage pillow fights in the bedroom that he and John were sharing. In these he was most aggressive. I was glad when Arnaud returned to Germany. He was so obviously infected with the 'Nazi' doctrine.

In June 1935 just before I took up my appointment to Tilbury Dock, Dorothy and I went to Stowmarket in Suffolk to visit Mr & Mrs Gibbons, whom we had met in Southampton when I was assisting in Romsey Station. He was now suffering badly from the onset of Multiple Sclerosis which was finally to cause his death. Mrs Gibbons was, with official permission, assisting her husband to carry out his Excise duties in the Stowmarket area, driving him round his Station to visit Old Age Pensioners and carry out other Excise duties.

We afterwards went on to another small town, Needham Market, where Dorothy had relatives from her grandmother, whose maiden name was Mortimer. Her grandfather, Frederick Brown, had hailed from Ipswich, fairly near. From Needham Market we went to stay at the Civil Service Holiday Camp at Corton in Suffolk. We had visited this holiday resort previously when we 'escaped' from Blackpool following the Federation Council held at Southport. The Holiday Camp was run by Civil Service Associations for members and was a very high class venue. A Committee of Civil Servants controlled all the activities. The Committee was chosen each week by the 'campers'. Accommodation was in first class chalets with communal feeding arrangements.

On our arrival at Corton this time, Dorothy and I were met by a gentleman who told us that he was Chairman of the Camp Committee. He then said his name was 'Sheppard'. I told him this was strange because my name was also Sheppard! He then said but mine is spelt SHEPPARD. I said 'so is mine'. He asked what Government Department I was serving in. I told him, Customs and Excise. He asked what rank. I said "Officer of Customs and Excise". He said so am I. He then said "Where?" I said I was due to take up an appointment in London Port from Rochester. He then said, "I am stationed in London Port". I said "I am due to go to Tilbury at the conclusion of this holiday." It transpired that he was an Officer serving in King George Vth Dock, by the name of 'Freddy' Sheppard! Quite a coincidence. I have since found out that he was a prominent Mason. I have never seen him since that meeting at Corton. I now reside in a Residential Home owned by the Royal Masonic Benevolent Institution at Chislehurst, Kent. 'Freddy' Sheppard also resided here and was well known for his organising abilities, being Chairman of the Residents' Association, as I am now!! A long arm of coincidence! 'Freddy' who was

134

considerably older than I, has passed on 'but his memory lives on at the R.M.B.I. Residential Home.

In October 1936, Dorothy gave birth to our first son, Colin, in St Bartholomew's Hospital, Rochester. In 1937 we again visited Corton, taking with us Colin's full equipment of a fancy cot lined with pink satin! This caused quite a sensation to the other "campers". Dorothy easily won the Ladies' race by many yards leaving the rest of the field yards behind. I came nowhere in the mens' race. We had a 'comic' cricket match, ladies against the men, but we were "crossed dressed", men as women, and women as men. Dorothy excelled at cricket, but I did not. But I did win the tennis competition! Only because my partner in the 'doubles' was a Wimbledon competitor. She told me to stand aside on the edge of the court, playing the ball only when it came my way! While she played our opponents single handed! Such was the C.S. Holiday Camp, now owned by 'Warners'. No longer run efficiently by Civil Servants in the grounds of Colman's Mustard.

Dorothy and I named our baby son, Colin, after the famous Kent cricketer, Colin Blythe, who was killed in Ypres, on 8th November 1917.

In September 1939 we were again visiting the Civil Service Holiday Camp at Corton. This time with my parents. A bowls green had been laid out and my mother, playing bowls for the first time found that she had a natural aptitude for the game. She won the bowls competition. Dorothy won the ladies' race once again. I did not win the mens' race as usual. Neither did I win the tennis because I failed to draw a Wimbledon player this time as a partner! When my mother returned home she straight away joined the Rainham Bowls Club. The players there were not up to her standard so she joined the Civil Service Bowls Club to become a champion there. She was a 'natural' at the game. My father also played but not with the expertise of my mother. She ultimately became the 'runner up' in the Kent County Championships, and played at Wimbledon in the English Championships for Kent. She represented Kent twice when Kent won the John's Trophy. (The Johns' Trophy being the County Championship for all English Counties). She was appointed Hon. Secretary of the Civil Service Ladies Bowls Club at Gillingham and later Chairman. She became a selector for the Kent County Bowls team and played for Kent against every other county in England having a Ladies Bowls team. When she passed away at the age of 88 she was still playing bowls for her Club. Such was the result of a chance game of bowls on the green at Corton in 1939.

My parents, with Dorothy and I were at Corton when war was declared in 1939. We had Colin with us as a small boy of 3 years. At a moment's notice we were ordered out of the camp. It was taken over by the Navy for housing naval personnel. A hurried return home to Rainham and Gillingham!! At first, no sign of hostilities or of enemy action. This was to come later since we resided in what became 'bomb alley' for the German Air Force.

CHAPTER TWELVE
Employment at Tilbury Dock
on Customs work.

Under the Fixed Relief Officer Scheme that I had proposed to the Board via the Customs and Excise Federation, three vacancies were announced for Tilbury Dock. As I have already recorded this was the nearest I could get for a Fixed appointment without having to move my residence. To have delayed might have involved me in a compulsory appointment to anywhere in the country when I became near the top of the appointments list. I therefore accepted that I would have to go to Tilbury Dock until a more acceptable vacancy occurred elsewhere.

Of the three vacancies announced, two were quickly taken by 1914/18 ex-service men. One lived in the Southend-on-Sea area. Another was an Officer in a Doncaster Excise Station, by the name of Joseph Richards. He was an ex-Mathematical School boy and very anxious to return to the Medway Towns area. I was the third to be appointed. Tilbury Dock consisted of a main basin in which vessels from Belgium arrived daily with cargo. Off the main basin were three arms for other dock berths. Additionally there was the Landing Stage where vessels berthed, at first to land passengers and cars before proceeding into the dock area. On the River Thames side there was also a Jetty where various boats could berth to discharge cargo.

Inside the main dock area there was also a berthing quay for vessels of the P & O Line. Of the three arms of the dock area, the 'Far Eastern', took vessels of the City and the Shire Lines. The 'Near Eastern' berthed the Clan Line. The 'Far Central' dealt with the Orient Line. The other berths in the Central and Western areas were occupied by miscellaneous vessels as necessary.

There were eight Officers employed with back-up clerical staff on the 'Ostende' Station. Two more Officers at the Jetty, two more at the P & O berth, two at the Orient berth and two at the Clan Station. At the 'City' and 'Shire' berths, there were three Officers, with back up clerical staff.

The Fixed Relief Officer, from Southend chose to officiate for the Jetty, P & O and Orient Officers. Six in all, with liability to assist elsewhere if necessary. Mr Richards still at Doncaster had yet to make his choice when he took up his appointment. He was senior to me. On my arrival therefore I was sent to the Ostende Station where miscellaneous cargo arriving daily was examined. I was there a few weeks until Richards arrived. He chose the Ostende Group. This left me to take over the City, Shire and Clan lines group. The sixth Station in this Group was at the Baggage Warehouse where all cargo in the form of baggage was dealt with awaiting the time when the owners were able to produce the necessary evidence to establish entitlement to ownership and so take possession, if importation was in order.

While I was at the Ostende Station I was very popular, simply because I announced that I was not interested in working 'overtime'. The hours of attendance there were 8.00 am to 4.00 pm or 10.00 am to 6.00 pm. Early arrival of a vessel from Belgium meant that sometimes the 8.00 am start was brought forward to suit the arrival and Officers involved worked overtime. Similarly if cargo was still required to be examined after 6.00 pm the necessary number of Officers to do the examinations worked overtime after 6.00 pm. A 'rota' was maintained to ensure that the overtime was evenly shared out among the total staff of Officers. By choice I was excluded from the 'rota'. Overtime was very much sought after by the Officers. Occasionally a ship was still being dealt with with either imports or exports throughout the night. So 'all night' attendances were even more appreciated. During the week this meant even more overtime, particularly if the night attendance was on a Friday or week end, when the normal 4 hour spell of duty on a Saturday was extended even more so. 'Overtime' was a very popular item of attendance at most of the Stations in Tilbury Dock, but none more so than at the Ostende Berth!

Eventually Richards arrived from Doncaster and I departed from the Ostende Station, which he had chosen. I went to officiate in turn for the six Officers at the Shire, City, Clan and Baggage warehouse Stations.

By becoming a Fixed Officer at Tilbury Dock I had to surrender my 'seat' as an Unattached Officer on the Federation Executive. It was some years later when attending a Federation Council held at Western-Super-Mare, as a Fixed Officer delegate from Dover Branch, that I was again elected to the Federation Executive Committee and to a number of Whitley Council posts to negotiate with the Board on matters affecting the Officer Grade.

At the City Line I officiated for two Officers, Clarke and Scott. For the Shire Line it was a Mr Mullins. He also dealt with cars discharged from any vessel at Tilbury Landing Stage. At the Clan Line Station, the Officers were Herwig and Judd. City Line vessels brought cargoes from India, Shire Line from Burma, Clan Line from New Zealand and Australia, while the Baggage Warehouse 'cleared' baggage. All the Officers gave me advice when requested. I found that my Customs training in Alexandra Dock, Liverpool, stood me in good stead. I never had once to use the knowledge of gauging casks, I had obtained at the Albert Dock, Liverpool! None of the duties I had to carry out at Tilbury were nearly as complicated as the work in the Long Room at Rochester when officiating for Mr Ottaway.

To get to Tilbury Dock I first cycled to Gillingham Railway Station. I had an arrangement with the caretaker for the Masonic Hall nearby, to leave my bicycle in the passage to the Hall. Next to travel by train at varying times to suit either an 8.00 am or 10.00 am start at the Dock. A short walk to the ferry to cross the River Thames and another walk to enter into the Dock area. Returning to Gillingham in the reverse order. Crossing the Thames was the problem, particularly when, as often happened, fog prevented the ferry boat from crossing. Those wishing to cross had then to use a small motor boat, operating independently which could take only six or so passengers. This required climbing down or up the side of the jetty into or out of the small boat. Quite a hazardous procedure. It sometimes happened that when one or more of the Customs staff left early to ensure getting home by small boat when there were fog problems, the Surveyor, named Service, had also made the same decision and was already in the motor boat! A quick decision had then to be made whether to await the next crossing by motor boat, in the fog, or to accept the crossing in the company of the Surveyor! He was free to come and go as he pleased, but sometimes overtime working could be involved if the Officer had left before the time recorded in the attendance register on the Station! 'Overtime' played an important part in the life of an Officer at Tilbury Dock! But for me, overtime was not, by choice, one of my priorities. Only Officers on the Kent side of the river needed to cross by ferry. Those on the Essex side, mainly living in the Southend-on-Sea area had a good rail service into Tilbury railway station adjoining the dock. In my group, Mr Herwig and Mr Judd, both ex-service men from the 1914 war lived in Gravesend. Mr Scott and Mr Smith, pre-war entrants, came from Southend. Mr Mullins another ex-service man lived at Meopham in Kent and Mr Clarke also ex-service at nearby Grays in Essex.

On the combined City and Shire Lines office and for the separate Clan Line office there was clerical staff who dealt with the clerical work involved in recording 'entries' for cargo, comparing these with the descriptions in the Ship's 'Report'. Entries were then passed to the appropriate Officer to examine the goods described on the 'Entry' who if satisfied, released the various items of cargo to the merchant or agent acting for him. Sometimes items of cargo had to be sent under a 'bond', entered into by the owner, or under seal or lock, to another wharf in London Port, such as Butler's Wharf or Canary Wharf for examination there by Customs staff. This conveyance was by 'lighter', a much used method of transferring cargoes within London Port. Also goods could be sent by rail or road under 'bond' to the premises of the owner, to be examined there by an Excise Officer.

Each vessel arriving from foreign for the City Line and the Clan Line was dealt with alternately by one of the Officers for that particular shipping line. He was responsible for the entire cargo carried by the vessel. In this way work was shared out evenly. Mr Mullins dealt solely with the Shire Line ships. These arrived less frequently than did the City Line vessels. The clerical staff dealt with all the clerical work for all the ships. Mr Smith at the Baggage Warehouse did all the clerical work himself. The Surveyor paid a visit once or twice each day to supervise.

The only time I found goods not in agreement with the merchant's entry was for some machinery imported from Belgium when I was at the Ostende Station. The drawings for the machinery did not agree in any way with the actual goods. I declined to release the goods. In response, the merchant entered into a 'bond' to have the machinery conveyed to his premises, there to be examined by the

140

Excise Officer whom he insisted was more conversant with what was imported than I was! I did not agree, using my previous engineering knowledge as proof. The Surveyor sanctioned the transfer to the merchant's premises and I heard no more on the matter. On another occasion I discovered some suspicious looking items, possibly, drugs hidden in sacks of corn or wheat meal, from India. These became forfeit to the Crown. I sent the suspicious items to the Government Laboratory for confirmation. The outcome I did not learn. Mr Smith at the Baggage warehouse did not tell me!

All the ships arriving at Tilbury Dock were regularly boarded by the uniformed Preventive Staff, searching for contraband. I soon became conversant with Customs procedure but I avoided working overtime as far as possible. Mr Mullins, however, dealt with all arrivals of motor cars which were discharged at the Tilbury Dock Landing Stage. Such arrivals were at all hours so when officiating for him and the Shire Line I had no alternative but to attend for duty at any time, involving working overtime when necessary.

At the Landing Stage I had the opportunity to see 'Dusty' Doust and his wife embark for their emigration journey to Australia. The next time I was to see him was a chance encounter several years later in Holborn, London. He had returned to the UK, a disappointed man from his treatment 'down under' by native 'Aussies' who had resented his employment there; being a 'pommy' likely to prejudice their own chances of promotion. 'Dusty's' wife died from an incurable disease. He was subsequently found dead in bed, in Gillingham when a neighbour observed milk bottles unopened accumulating at his front door. A sad end to a clever man, a great companion and good friend from the time we were apprentices together.

In August 1939 the Board announced that applications could be made by members of the staff of Customs and Excise to join the Royal Navy Volunteer Reserve. It was obvious that a war with Germany was imminent. I applied for permission, as also did the Clerical Officer on the Clan Station. I had in mind that my knowledge of electrical engineering might be of value although this was becoming somewhat 'rusty'. In addition I knew that Mr Ottaway, Officer at Rochester Custom House, for whom I had officiated on a number of occasions, was a Commander in the R.N.V.R. because of his position as Registrar of the Reserve at the Custom House. He had never been called up for active service. My application to join the R.N.V.R. was refused but that of the Clerical Officer at the Clan Station was granted. At the outbreak of war he was called up and became a Naval Writer. I have no knowledge of his career in the navy or whether he survived the war. Being in a vulnerable area of Chatham and Gillingham, I applied for transfer at my own expense to a number of Excise Stations in the South including Bexley, Canterbury and Tunbridge Wells which had advertised as vacant. Also as far away as Wallingford in the Thames Valley. All my applications were unsuccessful, the vacancies being filled by senior applicants.

I was employed at Tilbury Dock for approximately 5 years, from July 1935 until November 1940. The war had broken out in 1939 but for a while it had little effect on the shipping we were dealing with, except that fewer ships arrived from foreign. A solid looking air raid shelter was built near the Clan Line Office to protect, if necessary, the C & E staff. An official from Head Office came to inspect it. His verdict was that it would secure us from shrapnel but if a bomb dropped nearby, we would all be crushed to death by the solid concrete roof to the shelter when the walls gave way from the bomb blast!!

By 1940 the German Air Force commenced bombing in earnest. Ships from foreign ceased to arrive and the staff was at a standstill.

With the imposition of rationing, in 1940 I commenced keeping a few chickens. With meat becoming in short supply I started also to keep a few domestic rabbits to augment our meat ration. The nearby local school where Colin would be due to attend was required to surrender its playing field for allotments to be substituted. I applied for one and started to grow vegetables for our consumption. The Borough Council started a "Dig for Victory" campaign and I became a member of the Committee to help promote the project. Dorothy and I who had been members of Rainham Tennis Club when we returned to live in Gillingham, joined instead the Civil Service Tennis Club which had nine courts. I became Hon. Secretary. The Rainham Club closed down soon after the outbreak of war. Dorothy was a very good player as also was her sister Marjory, both individually, and as a 'pair' for matches. At first all was quiet on the war front but in 1941 bombing by the German Air Force by night and by day became severe. Many air contests in the "Battle of Britain" took place in the sky above us, but Dorothy still played tennis on the courts near our residence. She took Colin in his perambulator and when the German planes were overhead, she and the other players, all ladies, crouched in the hedge surrounding the courts to watch the contests. I was at first travelling to Tilbury Dock, but soon I was travelling to London when Purchase Tax came into force. Great laxity was allowed for attendances due to enemy action preventing rail travel.

More intense bombing by the German air force began. Gillingham was directly in 'Bomb Alley', with Chatham Dockyard as a prime target. I had already dug an air raid shelter at the end of my garden before the bombing started, lined it with timber from the local timber yard and reinforced it with old railway sleepers obtained from the railway sidings at Gillingham. Dorothy's mother came to stay with us, her father having been sent to the Plymouth area to train naval artificer apprentices. Her sister had married and was living in Century Road near to my parents. My father had constructed his air raid shelter in 1938 before war was declared, so neither my father nor I had need to apply for an Anderson Air Raid Shelter when these were distributed by the Council. Dorothy's elder brother Fred, had been called up for the army and was in the Hampshire Regiment bound for North Africa. Her younger brother, John had joined the volunteer defence force, later called the Home Guard, as soon as it commenced to operate. He then volunteered for the Air Force and was sent to Canada on a training course. He returned as a 'bomb aimer' on a Wellington bomber, with the rank of Flight Sergeant.

My neighbour next door who was a school teacher had been appointed 'Air Raid Precautions Officer' for the Borough. While I was digging the soil and chalk out for the shelter my neighbour by the name of Banham, put his head over the fence and enquired whether it would ever be required. The bombing had not yet started! I installed electric light and arrangements for heating the shelter. All was ready for eventualities. When the first air raid occurred, the first person to seek shelter was Mr Banham!! A bomb had fallen in a residential area. Banham later went to inspect the damage. Fortunately no casualities had resulted. Banham said to me "It had been a good exercise" for the air raid staff!! I was not amused. The Anderson Shelters had not been distributed at the start of hostilities but my shelter was in regular use at times by the post woman delivering in the road and by two collectors of household rubbish on one occasion when the air raid warning was sounded.

CHAPTER THIRTEEN
Purchase Tax work in
London Central Collection.

In 1940 the Government announced that a new taxation policy was to be instituted for the duration of the war! (It remained in force until after 1973 and was called Purchase Tax. It was only discontinued when another new tax, known as Value Added Tax, (VAT) took its place!!). The new Purchase Tax (PT) was to be levied on a specific range of goods at varying rates. Practically every industry and commercial business was affected. Many Officers in London Port and other ports were idle with no Customs work to perform. Those in Tilbury Dock were ordered to go on 'Detached Duty' in London, first to instruct traders on the application of the new tax and then to check and verify 'returns' to be made by the traders collecting the tax from their customers. Special PT Districts were set up in charge of Unattached Surveyors, who themselves had to learn the procedures for obtaining the revenue from the new tax. Officers on 'detached duty' were each allocated an area of control after first instructing the traders therein how to apply the Purchase Tax to their sales and how to remit receipts to the Collector who then transmitted the 'returns' made, to Officers to verify and check. It was a gigantic exercise throughout the country. Ordinary Excise Officers had to apply the regulations to traders in their individual stations. But it was carried through by the Department successfully. I was one of the Officers from Tilbury Dock sent on 'detached duty' to London Central Collection. My days as a Customs Officer were over! Strangely enough, while at Tilbury I had made a suggestion to the Board for a revision of forms used, known as 'Bills of Store', to enable goods of British origin, returned to the UK, to be admitted free of duty. My suggestion was accepted by the Board and my personal record 'noted'. By the time the Board's decision reached me, I was no longer a Customs Officer, being now a Purchase Tax Officer - British Returned goods were not being received at the docks!!

I was allocated an area of the City of London, centred round the Mansion House plus an additional area in the East End. First Officers had to instruct 'traders' on the tax procedure. Rates of tax charged varied with the type of goods sold and so attracting a tax charge. My area around the Mansion House contained most of the fur traders in the City including the large Hudson Bay Company. There were many Jewish traders dealing in fur skins, dressed, undressed or made up into garments. It was not an easy area to control. Furs were charged at the highest rate of tax. One small trader in furs, when I asked him to show me his business records, produced a small booklet about three inches square in which he said he kept all the records he needed to conduct his business of buying and selling furs! He added that he kept his records "in his head". I had to persuade him that in future he would have to keep full records of all purchases and sales and would have to pay purchase tax on sales unless they were to another 'trader' registered with the Customs and Excise when they could be delivered without a tax charge, but even for these sales, a full record was required. Eventually all the businesses visited accepted the purchase tax regulations. They soon settled down to making the required 'returns' to the Collector of tax charged to the customer whether or not it had actually been received.

In my area for control of purchase tax I gained considerable knowledge of the fur trade both of expensive skins and of the more prosaic skins such as rabbit. These could be treated to resemble expensive furs. At home I was keeping rabbits for their flesh. For fur purposes I needed 'chinchillas'. Some 'fox-like' rabbit skins could be used for gloves and fur collars. I obtained chinchillas from an advertisement. When the chinchillas were killed and the carcasses skinned, I dried the skins, stretching them on the wooden boards I was using for black-out purposes. The dried skins I took to a fur trader who 'cured' them ready for further manufacture into garments. Some were first dyed, others sheared to the necessary short length. The final process was to have skins manufactured into garments. I was therefore a manufacturer, but not buying or selling any goods. My processors also were not selling any goods, only charging me for the 'services' carried out on my goods. Purchase tax had to be charged on the selling price to a buyer. This was not a 'loophole' in the law. It was simply that tax was not chargeable on 'services'. The same consideration arose over 'joint' activities by associations such as the Womens' Institutes where the members combined to produce articles jointly from cloth and indeed from rabbit skins for making gloves. Fur articles were subject to the highest rate of purchase tax of 100% making such expensive. Discussions were taking place on the matter at C & E Head Office. By invitation I took one of my garments processed throughout manufacture, for inspection. As a result processing was ruled non-chargeable to Purchase Tax. It is interesting to note that when after 1973 the Value Added Tax (VAT) replaced Purchase Tax (PT) all processing and 'services' were subject to VAT.

One morning when going to catch a train at Chatham Railway Station I passed the Rochester Custom House which was situated above the Tailor and Outfitting shop, Laveys, in Chatham High Street. The Customs House was entered from a doorway in Hammond Hill. I observed smoke billowing from Laveys Shop. I was concerned for the Customs records in the Long Room above the shop, so I immediately telephoned Mr Jewett, the Surveyor who summoned the fire brigade. As a result the fire was arrested before the Custom House became involved. The irreplaceable Registry of Shipping records and other documents suffered no damage. The facts were reported to the Board and I received thanks for my prompt action! It was pure chance that I happened to be passing Lavey's shop premises at a vital time.

CHAPTER FOURTEEN
Employment as Special Constable in Police.

At the outbreak of the war in 1939, I had applied to the Board for permission to join the police force in Gillingham as a Special Constable. The Chief Inspector for the 'specials' was a tailor in the town and a friend of my father-in-law. He was also the Secretary of the Masonic Lodge I had joined in 1933. The Board granted my request so I became a 'part time' policeman. Duties were generally at week-ends giving the regular police some respite. But when war actually started we were required to go on patrol, making specified 'points' where we had to meet the Special Constable Inspector. We were given police uniforms and we patrolled in pairs. My companion for these patrols was a school teacher in Gillingham, also a mason but in a different Lodge to the one I had joined. His name was Ball and we became good 'pals' on our walks around our area to make the required 'points' where sometimes our Inspector would be waiting for us. His name was Rockcliffe, a bank official. One 'point' we were always required to make was at the Central Hotel very near to my residence. It was newly built and very popular. I had attended Masonic Ladies Nights there. The licensee was a Mr Cox, a Borough Councillor, who later became Mayor of Gillingham. At one period during the early years of the war, some Canadian soldiers were in camp nearby. The Canadians had become rowdy on one occasion and had got into dispute with local residents using the hotel. When we approached them they took off their army belts and threatened Ball and I with them. Fortunately the licensee came on the scene and was able to introduce a calmer atmosphere.

Often when on our 'beat' Ball and I would find time to go via my allotment where I could observe how my produce was faring! Even sometimes to spend a quarter of an hour with a hoe! At weekends, as policemen we were on duty at the railway station checking on arrivals, Gillingham being in a restricted area. Also on a few occasions acting on traffic control in the town. The presence of the special constables in the town was a relief to the regular police in many ways.

The police staged a horticultural show with prizes for best produce, open to members of the Police Force and to Special Constables. At the vital time I was ill with an attack of influenza and confined to bed. To meet the situation I asked Dorothy to go to my allotment and obtain some of the produce I was growing there. Beetroot, carrots, potatoes, leeks, etc. etc. This she did so well despite being a 'non-gardener'. She prepared the produce for the show and with Colin in his perambulator, pushed him with the produce for the show being held at the police station where it was set up. I won quite a few classes including that for the best collection of vegetables! Also the Council instituted a scheme of prizes for the best allotments in the town. Judging was carried out by the Park Superintendent at times unbeknown to those cultivating allotments. I won the third prize for my allotment on the former school playing field. The first two winners were two pensioners, from allotments in the town which they had cultivated for many years, before the onset of the war, so were in good condition. My third prize was therefore quite an achievement against seasoned competitors. Eventually due to demand, a further section of the school playing field was opened up for more allotments. I decided to take a second piece of the playing field quite close to my first plot. My neighbour on the allotment next to mine also decided on a second plot next to my second. But whereas he employed a man to dig the hard soil, previously the school playing field, I dug my own. It was tough going! We had both prepared our new plots ready for sowing. A few days (nights) later there was an air raid by the Germans. Two houses around the square of Vinall Park which our house faced had a delayed action bomb in the front gardens. The inhabitants were evacuated in time. Dorothy and I were watching when the bomb exploded completely demolishing the two houses. They were less than 100 yards from our house on another side of the square park. I set out in the morning to cycle to the Station to go to London as usual, passing the Civil Service Sports ground I saw that part of the Pavilion had been hit by a bomb that night so I turned round and went home for some tools and nails etc. to carry out emergency repairs to the sports pavilion which was a wooden structure. I was then Secretary of the Tennis Club. Afterwards I went on to London. Attendances there were always subject to enemy action! That evening I went round to my allotment only to find that another bomb had been dropped directly between my newly dug second plot and that of my neighbour who had paid for his second plot to be dug. Instead of my newly dug plot I had a large chalk crater while my neighbour had a huge heap of chalk thrown up from my crater!! These two plots remained in this condition until the end of hostilities when the playing field regained its proper function. As for the sports pavilion, the end that had been damaged was boarded up thus reducing its capacity. Much later after the war, a new brick-built pavilion was erected on the Sports ground.

CHAPTER FIFTEEN
Effect of war on purchase tax work.

Early in 1941 bombing by the Germans became so intense that I decided to send Dorothy and Colin to North Wales for safety. Her mother went to stay with my parents and was able to share my father's air raid shelter. The village to which I evacuated Dorothy and Colin was, if my memory is correct and I can reproduce the Welsh name, was called 'Mais a ghyrkin' which I was informed meant 'place in a cornfield'. A friend I had in Gillingham had evacuated his wife and daughter to the same area near to Bangor. I secured rooms with a local quarryman, but Dorothy was unhappy being away from her home. After three months she insisted on returning to Gillingham and I went up to North Wales to get her and Colin. By the irony of fate the next week a German bomber on its way to bomb Liverpool, apparently lost its way and dropped its bombs, striking the area where Dorothy had been staying, killing one inhabitant. Up to that time the inhabitants of the village had not know that a war was in progress!

The severe aerial bombing that took place from about May 1941 caused many problems for the Purchase Tax staff. Businesses that were in existence one day had disappeared into rubble the next and with them all the records on which the collected tax were kept, no longer available. Officers were instructed to visit premises damaged by enemy action to endeavour to salvage as much as possible of the accounts, in many cases a forlorn hope. In my particular area of control including part of Upper Thames Street a large printing firm was demolished and with it all records destroyed. I visited as instructed. The only item I saw was a large electric clock lying in the rubble. The proprietor was present. I enquired whether he would allow me to purchase the clock which appeared not to have been damaged, simply thrown on the printing works floor by the blast.

The printer offered to give it to me! I insisted on paying and he eventually accepted one pound! I took the clock home, it was too big for a household. Instead I took it to the Civil Service Sports Club pavilion and erected it, connecting it to the electric mains. It worked perfectly. It even survived the bomb which struck the Sports Pavilion, although this was at the other end of the building. Later when the new brick pavilion was built, the clock was transferred. I visited the new Pavilion many years later, the clock was still in position over the bar, still working! No one knows now where the bar clock came from! I asked the barman. He did not know. My mother knew but she has passed on. The secret of the bar clock is safe, unless I now write and tell the Sports Council Secretary of what occurred 55 years ago and how the Sports club obtained an electric clock for £1.00, erected free, which is still working perfectly.

Other bombing incidents occurred almost daily. Walking up Moorgate to the C & E Office a window frame from a bank, loosened by a bomb, fell in front of me and I almost gained a metal necklace!! It became even worse when the 'flying bomb' campaign commenced and later when the V2 rocket bombs fell but that needs to be told later.

In August 1941 Dorothy gave birth to our second son. Colin had been born by Caesarean section in St Bartholomew's Hospital in Rochester, but Brian was born naturally although his birth took place inside a Morrison Shelter erected in the back room of our residence! The doctor had been sent for and was ready to convey Dorothy again to hospital for another 'Caesarean'. Brian, as we named the new arrival, decided to take up residence in Cecil Avenue, Gillingham without any formalities! The Morrison Shelter had been supplied to residents who were without the earlier Anderson Shelter, so we now had two shelters, neither of which would have survived a direct hit, but at least they gave protection from 'blast' and the shrapnel that regularly fell from our anti-aircraft guns situated in the nearby field. In the 'Morrison' Dorothy could shelter with her mother and with Colin who was an infant 5 years old. He regularly sat on the crossbar of my bicycle to accompany me to my allotment. As a Special Constable, and later the Assistant Adjutant of a Royal Engineers cadet force, plus 'digging for victory' on my allotment, as well as being a 'Fire Watcher' on any spare night I had; ensuring that incendiary bombs had not been dropped in our area, and then travelling daily to

London with all the hassle that involved; supplying meat in the form of rabbit to neighbours free of charge, all additional to my official duties, I felt that I was doing more in the war effort than a friend we had in a house a few houses away. He was an Air Force Officer in Coastal Command located in the dockyard area. He was in charge of funds for paying the men of the Command. He rode off on his bicycle every morning about 8.00 am and returned regularly each evening about 6.00 pm, his war effort for the day completed!! In private life he was a banking official from the Croydon area. He never saw a shot fired in anger but for all that was a very nice man. Dorothy and I became good friends with him and his wife; Cliff, and Gwen Martin. They had two children, girls, approximately the same ages as our two boys and we all got on famously together. Dorothy and Gwen played tennis together. At the end of the war, Cliff Martin received an award, by being mentioned in despatches!! For his war effort! He deserved it!!

Other purchase tax problems were arising on the liability of some goods which alone were subject to tax but which could be incorporated into goods which were not so subject. A Special Verification unit was set up to visit premises involved. Some 10 Officers were selected for this work, of which I was one. With the Surveyor in charge, I visited railway workshops and an aircraft factory , as well as other premises. At the railway workshops it was agreed that items such as cushions, cloth etc. which by themselves were chargeable, could be rendered non-chargeable when incorporated into an article which was non-chargeable such as railway carriage under construction. Similarly on aircraft, which used staples for fastening panels together. Such staples individually were chargeable; when incorporated into an aeroplane became non-chargeable. There were numerous examples of this sort, where chargeable goods were incorporated into non-chargeable goods during the course of manufacture. But where chargeable goods were supplied as 'replacements' into a non-chargeable item already completed, such as an electric lamp for a carriage where a lamp had failed, the replacement lamp was chargeable on being supplied to the Railway Company. It became very complicated involving maintaining separate stocks. The special verification staff (known as the S.V.S.) carried out numerous enquiries throughout the country without regard to Collection boundaries, until a uniform procedure was established. The S.V.S. also undertook enquiries into minor suspicion of fraud. For one of these I had to visit a trader in cosmetics. This was in South London area. The man I saw had a withered arm and a deformed ear. I cleared up the problem with him, it was not very serious. He then told me that he had a son who was a very talented pianist. The son's name was Peter Katin (if my memory is not a fault). The father said that one day I would see his son's name displayed at the leading orchestral concerts. And I did!! What a strange reversal of fortune for a handicapped father to have such a talented son.

While employed on the Special Verification Staff I had to investigate the accounts for a large multiple chemist selling cosmetics. The firm was Mumfords having branches in London and on the South Coast. My main enquiries were centred in Hove, Sussex. Having cleared up my enquiries and reported to the Board, I received notification in 1941 of the Board's appreciation of my work and that my personal file at Head Office had been noted.

At home one evening the phone rang and I received instructions from C & E Head Office that I was to present myself the next day at Millbank at the Offices of the Ministry of Aircraft Production. I had no knowledge of what the instruction was about but I duly attended. There I found that I had been nominated by the Board for transfer along with two other nominees from Customs and Excise for appointment as a Secretary to Lord Beaverbrook, the Cabinet Secretary for that Ministry. I enquired what my duties would be and it became clear that I would be on call from his Lordship and on duty at all times, often overnight. Also to go with Lord Beaverbrook whenever necessary to various parts of the country. I had no wish to be appointed to this position, since it would leave Dorothy and my two young sons alone when I was away. I told the interviewers of my decision. So I was not appointed. Neither of the other two nominees from C & E were appointed. One was already holding a responsible position in C & E Head Office. Other nominations had been made for the vacancy by other Government Departments. Who was ultimately appointed I do not know. I have no regrets at declining the possible appointment but it was an honour to have been selected by the Board for what should have proved an important appointment leading to further advancement in the Civil Service.

In London Central Collection again, I was taken off Purchase Tax controls for a while to investigate suspected frauds over Clothing

Coupons. The issue of replacement coupons was allowed to seamen and others who had lost their clothing from enemy action. Clothing could only be purchased using the necessary number of coupons for a garment. Those persons considered eligible for replacement coupons could apply at Collector's offices. In London there were four main Collector's offices situated in London South, London West, London North and London Central. The appropriate form was stamped with the issue number etc. of coupons and returned to the applicant. Some applicants had discovered a method of erasing the official stamp and then presenting the form at another Collector's office. By this means extra coupons could be obtained. Coupons represented 'cash' when sold on the 'black market'. At one office the Clerical Officer dealing with applicants was suspicious and retained the form. On receipt by me for enquiry I had the form examined under special lighting at the Government's Chemist's laboratory. The previous issues were clearly visible. The applicant had used an address in Cable Street in the east end of London, not a very salubrious area for me to visit. The door was opened to me by a very large black woman. The man I wanted to interview, a seaman, had 'fled'. But the black woman was naked from the waist upwards. My look of surprise encouraged her to explain that she was a model for the sculptor, Epstein, and that she was off shortly to 'sit' for him. Such were the vagaries of Customs and Excise work. Just another experience of an Excise Officer.

154

CHAPTER SIXTEEN
Commissioned into Royal Engineers Army Cadet Force as Assistant Adjutant.

On my journeys to London I often travelled with an ex-soldier who had been a Regimental Sergeant Major in the 7th Dragoon Guards. He was a real regular soldier having served abroad in India. He had been approached to be the Adjutant to the Colonel commanding a training battalion of cadets in the Medway Towns. These cadets were in varying schools. The Adjutant's name was Stanley Hales. He asked me if I would care to serve under him as Assistant Adjutant. To do so would involve leaving the police force as a special constable. I discussed at length with Dorothy and decided to apply to the Board for permission to accept an army commission in the Royal Engineers Cadet Force. This was granted. So I became a second lieutenant and was duly gazetted. I was no soldier! The first time I walked along Chatham High Street in a new trench coat which hid my rank, I was saluted by two Royal Marines, but I did not know whether I was to salute back in acknowledgement! I soon realised that Stanley Hales whose rank was Captain had many jobs for me to fulfil. I was to be Transport Officer, Sports Officer, also to take over the band among other things. As Sports Officer I had to referee football matches between different companies in the cadet force. Also to ensure the Chatham team arrived at different football grounds to play against other cadet forces in the county. I also organised a cross country running competition, persuading the licensee of the Central Hotel to provide a trophy for the winner. At one stage I had to take the salute of the band outside Chatham Town Hall at a march past. It was a new experience. My downfall came, however, when an inspection by 'regulars' from the Royal Engineers was decided to check the efficiency of the cadet force Officers. All Officers apart from the Colonel who was a school master in Chatham but had been an Army Officer, were required to parade on the Royal Engineers parade ground. We stood in order of rank, the Major who was second in command, then the several Captains of the different units plus my friend Stanley Hales. I was last on the line being of the lowest rank. The Regimental Sergeant Major of the Royal Engineers gave the order to slope arms. I had never held a rifle before, so promptly got my rifle on to my right shoulder. All the rest had theirs on the left shoulder! The drilling sergeant crooked his first finger towards me and asked if I had ever done this drill action before! My reply being "No" he called another sergeant and instructed him to take this Officer to another portion of the parade ground and instruct him how to slope arms. He persisted in calling me "SUR" in his best tones!! Eventually I managed to slope arms and returned to the line with the other Officers of the Cadet Force. The Regimental Sergeant Major then gave the order "Present Arms". My rifle was hoisted on my left shoulder, but all the others had theirs 'erect' in front with the barrels before their eyes!! Again the wagging finger and another spate of instruction. We then all had to perform various drill by marching, "about turn", "right turn", "left turn" etc. I was all at sea! Eventually the session was concluded but we all had to do a spot of map reading with written answers. I came out of this easily top of the class so my reputation was saved.

Author in uniform as 2nd Lieut.
In Royal Engineers Cadet Regiment,
as Assistant Adjutant 1942/4

CHAPTER SEVENTEEN
Employed in London North
Collection on Purchase Tax Work.

At the Civil Service Sports Club an audit had discovered a serious misappropriation of funds. As Secretary of the Tennis Club I was asked to help with the investigation. I sought the advice of a firm of accountants in London that I had contact with on my official duties. Their advice was to sack the club steward and appoint a new Chairman. It was obvious that the steward and Chairman had been 'milking' the bar of whisky and other assets. The sacking being accomplished I was invited to take over the position of General Secretary of the Sports Club. This I did for a very short period until developments in my London Office brought another change to my life in the Customs and Excise.

Having served on Purchase Tax work generally from November 1940 until August 1941 and then for a year on Special Verification enquiries, I spent approximately another year assisting or officiating in the Excise Stations in the Stepney area of London. One was a tobacco factory manufacturing cigarettes. London Central Collection, now that the Purchase Tax controls were running smoothly, apart from the problems of enemy action destroying businesses and with it loss of records, was obviously becoming over staffed. In September 1942 I was transferred on detached duty to London North Collection. I believe that 'Joe' Richards from Tilbury had been sent to East Anglia on detached duty so he was worse off than I was regarding his residence in the Medway Towns. At this time also under Government directions Officers with previous engineering knowledge were compulsorily directed to other Government Departments. Those with Dockyard experience as former apprentices, were sent, some to the Air Ministry, others into the Army with R.E.M.E. (Royal Electrical and Mechanical Engineers), others to Aircraft Production, but so far as I was aware none into the Admiralty now centred in Bath in Somerset. Many former dockyard apprentices employed in the C & E were so directed. I had to register under the direction scheme but I was declared 'exempt'. Why so I do not know.

I recommenced on Purchase Tax control this time in London North Collection and was allocated an area around Shaftsbury Avenue. In this area was a very large electrical components firm, also a firm manufacturing and renovating musical instruments. Another was the man who claimed that he had invented the 'Zip' fastener! So many more. There is nowhere or no Government Department more involved than the C & E in being in contact with industry or commerce now that purchase tax, (followed by Value Added Tax) has been imposed to raise revenue, in place of old fashioned taxes on licensed premises, pawn brokers, refreshment houses, carriages, tobacco dealers etc. In former days taxes on gloves, candles, loads of hay and straw, hops, larks eggs, etc. On windows or chimneys indicating where the occupants were well able to contribute to the Revenue. Now there is tax on practically everything bought or sold or processed. Plus the continuing tax levied on intoxicating liquors, tobacco and betting duty to boost the gross yield from all and sundry!

I was able at the premises of the musical instrument renovator to secure reasonable terms for renovating the drums of the band attached to the R E Cadet Force Regiment, of which I was still the Assistant Adjutant!

One interesting point to me in London North Collection was that the purchase tax office and the Collector's Office were located in Faraday House. Michael Faraday in the nineteenth century was one of the greatest scientific geniuses. He it was who discovered the relationship how to use magnetism to produce electricity. A wit at the time composed a small couplet I recalled from my student days:-

> Around the magnet Faraday
> Was sure that Volta's lightings play
> But how to draw them from the wire?
> He took a lesson from the heart;
> 'tis when we meet, 'tis when we part,
> Breaks forth the electric fire.

Faraday House was the Headquarters of the Institution of Electrical Engineers. I had in the 1920's received my National Certificates of my competency in Electrical Engineering from the Principal of Gillingham Technical Institute endorsed by the Institution of Electrical Engineers. So long ago and I had nearly forgotten all I learned of electrical engineering!

CHAPTER EIGHTEEN
John Brown and war events.

Dorothy's parents received the sad news that their younger son John who was in the Royal Air Force and engaged in Bomber Command had been declared 'missing' from bombing attacks. He was flying from airfields in East Anglia to bomb railway targets in Northern France. It caused great sadness in the family. The only other casually my family had suffered was of my cousin, Horace Ayears, second son of Aunt 'Lil' who was still living at Cliffe-at-Hoo. Horace Ayears lost his life in the evacuation from France in 1940. We heard no more from the Air Ministry about John Brown. One day late in 1944 Dorothy's mother opened the front door in response to a knock and there stood John Brown! His Wellington bomber had, in fact, been brought down in Northern France by German aircraft fighters which flew beneath the English bombing planes and fired upwards. Of the crew of 7 in the Wellington, three lost their lives. John Brown and three others landed by parachute. One was captured by the Germans to become a prisoner. John hid his parachute and met up with another member of the crew, Bill Johnson, from Liverpool. They found a church in which to hide. When the priest arrived he hid them and sent a message to the 'alleged' French carpenter who was shielding other British airmen. The whole incident is described in a book by T.D.G. Teare, who himself was a British airman hiding from the Germans in Occupied France having been brought down in September 1943. The book is most interesting. It is called 'Evader' published by Hodder and Stoughton in 1954.

John Brown and Bill Johnson remained with the French Resistance movement under guidance of T.D.G. Teare in the Revigny-Sur-Orain area until the Americans, advancing from the South ultimately ensured their release. They had many escapes from Germans and witnessed many atrocities by German troops and the Gestapo. John

Brown is described in the book as the "Bright spark of the party" and known as 'Ginger' Brown. John Brown is also mentioned in another book entitled "Massacre over the Marne" by Oliver Clutton-Brock, published in 1975 by Patrick Stephens. There is an amusing incident described in both books when the 'escapees' acquired the head of a dead horse and T.D.G. Teare, acting as the butcher decided to cut it up to prepare a meal when meat had become a memory. Bill Johnson enquired what it was and Teare, to allay suspicion replied that it was a cow's head. John Brown was suspicious of the reply and asked where were the horns, while Bill Johnson said that he had never seen a cow with such big front teeth, so they walked off to discuss with other 'escapees'. The horse's head was turned into nourishing soup without further questioning, although some of the consumers at the third boiling described it as ninety-nine per cent 'potato water' and hoped that another horse would die soon!

John Brown was fortunate to have survived the war. On being released by the American forces he was taken to Paris and then on to London. Subsequently after interview, he walked up Canterbury Street in Gillingham. A knock on the door for it to be opened by his mother with great joy to find her son was alive and well! He later married an Air Force girl with the name Dorothy. A second Dorothy Brown entered the family! Married, they had a daughter who attended Bristol University and became a schoolmistress. John ultimately returned to civilian employment with the Electricity Board. He now resides at Hove in Sussex. He makes frequent return visits to Revigny to see the friends there who sheltered him from the German army. He has walked up the Champs Elysees with members of the Allied forces celebrating various Allied successes in the war.

John Brown and Bill Johnson on one of their frequent return visits to Revigny to see see their friends in the French resistance, went to visit the farm of Paul Thomas about five miles from Revigny and the field and the field where their Lancaster had crashed after being blown up in mid-air by the German fighters, killing three of the crew. Paul Thomas had found the injured Navigator, Eric Brownhall, lying on the ground nearby, due to his parachute failing to open in time to prevent a heavy landing. The Germans arrived and took Eric prisoner. As it was Paul Thomas's 81st. Birthday when John Brown and Bill Johnson revisited the site, they were invited to celebrate with champagne. Paul Thomas then revealed that after the crash of the

160

Wellington bomber, he had found a pair of airman's boots in the field. He produced the boots to to John and Bill and they recognised them as belonging to Eric Brownhill, bearing his identifying number. With Paul Thomas's agreement they brought the boots back to England and advertised for Eric's present whereabouts in the local press of Watford, where Eric had lived with his parents. It transpires that Eric had married, had two daughters and now lives in Reading although working in Abu Dhabi. One daughter had a friend still in Watford, who spotted the advertisement and got in touch with Eric's family. On Eric's next leave from Abu Dhabi, John and Bill went to Reading and presented Eric Brownhill with his boots lost on the night of 18th/19th July 1944, just over 37 years earlier! The 'ceremony of presentation' was duly reported in the local press and appeared on radio and television.

The "Ceremony of presentation" of the boots to Eric Brownhall

Dorothy's elder brother, Fred, survived the war after being enrolled as a despatch rider with the Hampshire Regiment. He was involved in the invasion of North Africa in the 5th Army, the invasion of Sicily, of Salerno in Italy, finally into Austria before returning home. He suffered badly from shell shock. He was a commercial artist and married the lady secretary of a commercial firm producing posters and the like. A very gentle person who should never have been involved in warlike activities. He lives on a new estate in Chatham.

When the German Air Force ceased their ordinary bombing next came the 'flying bomb' campaign to be followed by the 'rocket' bombs. We had watched the first flying bombs from our bedroom window and thought at first that what we saw was a plane on fire. Soon the flying bombs were coming over regularly. Barrage balloons were erected near to us with the object of intercepting the bombs as far as possible. Some were shot down as they crossed the coast but

161

many reached the London Area. If travelling on a train, when one heard the sound stop, it was time to lie on the floor of the carriage in case it fell near the railway line. The same whenever one heard the end of the 'buzz'. There was no knowing where the bomb would fall. Take cover!! But the rocket bombs were impossible to deal with. They fell without any warning. On one occasion I was travelling on a tramcar to North London along the Balls Pond Road. Suddenly the tram shuddered to a standstill. I thought it had left the tram railtrack. A shower of paint came over the nearby houses and covered the tramcar. Some even descended on to the tram conductor. What had occurred was that a rocket bomb had struck a paint factory immediately behind the houses. The paint was from the factory demolished by the bomb, descending on to our tramcar. The passengers including myself had been within yards of where the rocket fell! I continued my journey of investigation on foot! The incident of this bomb falling without any warning and against which there was no possible protection was repeated in many parts of London. Working in London was grim.

CHAPTER NINETEEN
Appointed to Special Investigation Branch of Customs and Excise.

I was employed on Purchase Tax in London North Collection until May 1944. Earlier in 1944 a vacancy had been announced for the Special Investigation Branch of the C & E. This was a very important Department of the C & E under the control of the Head Office via the Chief Investigating Officer. The Branch had no boundaries. It carried out complex and even secret investigations generally too complicated for ordinary Station Officers to undertake. Station Officers could supply information about a suspected fraud or illegal action to the S.I.B., for that staff to investigate and pursue to finality, with a lawsuit or prosecution to follow if necessary and appropriate. The S.I.B. staff at the time of the announcement consisted of 30 'hand picked' Officers capable of carrying out enquiries anywhere in the whole of the United Kingdom and Northern Ireland. The S.I.B. staff was recruited from Officers and from the Waterguard Service (who were used to dealing with 'smuggling'). Waterguard staff selected were immediately promoted to the Officer grade. All appointments were usually of young men willing to go anywhere at any time, but all were based in London. There was a language test for applicants to the Investigation Branch, so necessary for dealing with possible foreign miscreants. A considerably monetary allowance was paid to cover extra attendances. Appointment to the S.I.B. was a much sort after career in the C & E. I applied but did not consider my chance of selection very high due to my age. I was now 38 years old. In addition I had not been in London North very long for the Collector there to assess my 'skills'. But I applied and secured an interview. One of the interviewing panel was in fact from Head Office and had been interviewed with me for appointment to the post of Secretary to Lord Beaverbrook in the Ministry of Aircraft Production!! He had since been promoted within the C & E Head Office. My foreign language knowledge was rather below the required standard in French. There was only one vacancy and this was secured by a detached Officer from London Port who had been in London North Collection since 1940 and was the Staff side representative on the Local Whitley Council. However, I was offered a vacancy for an Investigating Officer in the Ministry of Supply. The Head of this section of the Supply Ministry was a former member of the S.I.B. I duly attended another interview and could have been appointed. There were many other applicants for the vacancy in the S.I.B. but only two, from London North were interviewed. I declined the vacancy in the Investigation Branch of the Ministry of Supply and informed the Board. Then the unexpected happened. A member of the S.I.B. took the post. I was sent for again and this time was offered the vacancy created by the transfer of the S.I.B. Officer to the Ministry of Supply. So in May 1944 I became an Investigator in the C & E. The Chief Investigating Officer was a Mr Horace Kimber. Maybe the similarity of our names had produced an advantage at my interview!! 'Horace' is not a common name in the 20th century! My father received his name in 1886, I expect Horace Kimber received his also in the late 19th century. Just a thought! I was allocated to a group of Investigators headed by a former Waterguard Officer and was then a Senior Investigator by the name of Charles Simison. He certainly knew his job and I learned much from him during my tenure on the S.I.B. Charles Simison later became the Chief Investigating Officer and well deserved his appointment to that important position. He received the award of an O.B.E. on his retirement. My investigation career commenced!

Because of my appointment to the Special Investigation Branch I had to resign my appointment as Assistant Adjutant in the Royal Engineers Cadet Force. Also I gave up the position as General Secretary to the Civil Service Sports Council at Gillingham. I was going to be far too busy with my official duties in future on the S.I.B. I was able to continue as a member of the Tennis Club on the Sports ground and of course I continued to cultivate my allotment which was not damaged by enemy action. My large crater nearby, continued to remind me of the bomb that destroyed my plan for a second allotment!

One of the first enquiries I undertook was concerned with the discovery at the docks of a strange inclusion of birds in consignments of wood pigeons to be delivered to Smithfield Market. The pigeons had been imported from Southern Ireland, all described as 'pigeons'

164

on the invoices to the merchants in Smithfield. But records there showed deliveries of earlier consignments which included a description of 'Nedlogs' and 'Epins' to such customers as Harrods the large store in West London. Other customers were restaurants in London. Pigeons from Southern Ireland could be imported and were welcome as an additional item of food for gourmets in the period of rationing during the war. But what were Nedlogs and Elpins purchased by restaurants in London to satisfy the palates of their customers? Suddenly 'the penny dropped'. 'Nedlog' was in fact 'Golden' in reverse and Epins was 'Snipe' And the Nedlogs were Golden Plovers! Plovers and Snipe were prohibited importations. Those still at the dock were seized. No more were allowed for importation. Consignments of pigeons had to be pigeons!

On another investigation with Charles Simison, I went to Old Compton Street in Soho. Bottles of Napoleon Brandy were on display in the window at twelve pounds a bottle. Quite a high price at that time but members of the American forces were buying it without question. Charles and I inspected the bottles. They were clearly labelled Napoleon Brandy and covered with dust, to be expected on a bottle possibly 150 years old. If in a bottle for so long, the brandy would in 1944 be priceless and worth much more than £12.00. If recently bottled from a cask of Napoleon brandy, the contents of the cask would have all evaporated or nearly so. We visited the cellar of the shop. There was a full scale operation in progress of bottling from a cask. Having been filled, the bottles were corked with a cork marked 'Napoleon'. The bottle was labelled 'Napoleon Brandy'. It was then immersed in a bath of "gluey" water for dust to be blown from a blowing apparatus to cover the bottle. A suitable cap was placed over the cork and the bottle was then ready to be displayed in the shop window at £12.00. Next to discover the origin of the brandy. It was certainly not Napoleon Brandy. The proprietor produced his invoice. The brandy was in fact Portuguese Brandy, purchased from the King's Warehouse and duty paid! Originally it was a consignment seized from a vessel bound for Germany, intercepted by the Navy at the beginning of the war and held in the King's Warehouse for three years until due for sale by auction! The Customs and Excise Department could do nothing about a bona fide sale it had made itself. But the Food and Drugs section of the Ministry of Food could! The shop keeper's offence was for selling goods purporting to be something else, and was duly reported for action. Sales of Napoleon Brandy at £12 a bottle were discontinued! The Americans who had purchased brandy were possibly quite satisfied.

I was involved in investigating the condition of some large drums of white rum sent under bond and sealed, from Liverpool to East London for further manufacture. On receipt at the refinery, the drums were found to be heavier than when despatched from Liverpool. The seals appeared to be in order. A very close examination, however, revealed that they had been tampered with. Somewhere en route a quantity of white rum had been extracted and replaced with water. Checking on the strength confirmed that water had replaced some of the spirit. But water being heavier than spirit revealed that extraction had taken place by someone who had not realised that weighing the drums would show the attempted fraud. Naturally the lorry driver was suspect. This proved to be the case. He had stopped overnight in Northampton, trying carefully to remove the seals, extracting spirit and replacing it with water, before putting back the seals. As a result the bond entered into by the sender became forfeit and the lorry driver prosecuted.

I had the investigation of a man who had decamped from Chester owing a considerable sum of purchase tax from a business there making and selling toy lead soldiers. My enquiries in Chester showed he had probably gone to Bedford. So off to Bedford. First call was the police who knew nothing of him. Next call, the local press where a young lady knew of the man who, she said, drove a red car. She had been a passenger in it and remembered the registration number!! Back to the police station to ascertain where the car was now. I was extremely lucky. Mentioning the registration number another policeman spoke up. He was at that very moment dealing with a case of careless driving by a man in a car with the identical registration number who in Hastings had driven his car over the top of workmen in a trench who had had to 'duck' to avoid being struck by the chassis of the car! So off to Hastings. Again to the police. One policeman had seen a red car parked outside a house on his 'beat'. Next to the house where the lady I saw said her 'lodger' was making toy soldiers in a small factory in a nearby lane! The car, she said, had gone to be sold in London. Next to the factory in the "nearby lane." There was my man busily producing toy lead soldiers! He told me that his car was to be sold from a garage in London. He even told me the whereabouts of the garage. I made a quick call to the S.I.B. office. Another Officer went to the garage and formerly seized the car in lieu of purchase tax due in Chester. One investigation full of lucky coincidences.

Charles Simison was investigating a strange case of American soldiers camped near Dunmow in Essex. I went with him on his enquiries. Two American soldiers had died presumably due to drinking wine at a local public house. Other Americans had become blind at the same place. It was clear that the deaths and blindness were due to a particular red wine sold at the public house, wine which must have contained industrial alcohol which is poisonous. The publican had obtained the wine from the proverbial man "with two eyes and a nose". But our enquiries eventually established that the wine in question had come from the east end of London. By chance, I knew, from my short period of assisting and officiating in the Stepney area prior to my transfer to London North Collection, that a small winery existed in Stepney. Charles Simison and I decided to visit it. We were able to establish that this was where the wine sold in Dunmow had come from. The winery was run by two Jewish Rabbis. They received special consignments of raisins and other fruit from Israel for the purpose of making wines for Jewish religious ceremonies. Nearby there was a paint manufacturing establishment receiving industrial alcohol. Eventually we established the Rabbis had 'laced' some of their wine with the industrial alcohol from the paint factory and sold it to another man "with two eyes and a nose"! A chain of sales of the wine was uncovered. Eventually a court case took place. Each seller of the wine needed to establish that he was unaware of the composition of the wine. They all briefed celebrated Counsel. One was the K.C., Christmas Humphreys if my memory is correct. The matter was serious because of the deaths of the Americans from drinking the wine. Eventually the Rabbis were convicted and went to prison.

Another case I investigated was of the sale of mirrors in retail shops where tax charged had never been accounted for by the seller. I found that two men operating in North London were making mirrors, selling them, charging tax to the buyers and never accounting for the tax. I eventually found the address from where the men were operating. Strangely, one had fallen down in the lavatory and fractured his leg. I interviewed him in the London Hospital in the East End. He was unable to avoid me! These two men also went to prison. I received the commendation of the Board for this case and had my personal record noted.

Officers on the S.I.B. operated where necessary in pairs for confirmation purposes. Consignments of imitation jewellery had been discovered in army trucks returning from Czechoslovakia. Previous consignments may have escaped detection. Ken Bowes, another S.I.B. Officer and I were on the look out for such in the West End of London. We found a jeweller's shop in Regent Street displaying such imitation jewellery. Ken and I interviewed the shop owner, he too had bought from the proverbial man with "two eyes and a nose". The shop owner suggested to us that if we were to go away for about half an hour he would give us £400 and his window would be cleared!! Ken and I took possession of the imitation jewellery as being suspected goods smuggled into the country. The shop owner who was of North African origin, in his defence to the Board, when charged, made the assertion that Ken Bowes and I had asked for a bribe of £400 to go away and forget the whole incident! The owner was heavily fined for possession of uncustomed goods. It was highly important on the S.I.B. staff to avoid a possibility for a compromising situation to develop. My experience was that persons hailing from North Africa had to be dealt with very carefully.

Once however, when investigating unlicensed sales of spirits, possibly smuggled, in the London area, with an S.I.B. Officer named John Henderson, we took the suspect to lunch hoping that he would disclose the origin of his sales. He was too wily. He disclosed nothing at that interview but when we returned to the office, he had already phoned to say that he had had an interview with two officials who had tried to intimidate him on the provision of a free lunch! Eventually we were able to establish the origin of the spirits, smuggled from Canada and the man was convicted and fined. On another occasion an Englishman living in Worthing reported me to his M.P. A question was asked in Parliament on the matter. Unlicensed sales had taken place to a Club in Baker Street which I was able to establish to the satisfaction of the Chief Inquiry Officer.

Investigations took place concerning a large quantity of champagne in cases left under cover in a front garden of a house in Colchester. It was established that the American forces who had over-run Reims had 'commandeered' a large quantity of champagne which their air force flew to England leaving it in the front garden of a house they were occupying. No one came forward to claim the champagne so the S.I.B. removed it to the King's warehouse, eventually to be sold in the absence of a legal owner, to benefit the Crown.

Another member of the S.I.B. had to investigate the suspicion that a race card 'tipster' was under-declaring the number of cards he was selling on racecourses. These sales of cards, tipping horses likely to win, were subject to purchase tax. The only method of verifying sales was to watch and observe how many cards he sold on the average for each race on a particular day. It was a wearisome task, but in among the crowds at a race meeting it was probable that we would not be noticed 'ticking off' the sales the tipster made. Our first attempt was at Ascot where a 'tipster' would stand in the space approaching the Silver Ring and Tattersalls. John Rogers who was the S.I.B. member investigating the suspected P.T. fraud took 'turns' with me in counting. It was decided to conduct another count, this time at Hurst Park racecourse where we followed the same procedure. Ultimately we forwarded the results of our 'counts' to the Station Officer to compare with the figures submitted by the 'tipster'. Our investigation proved positive and a prosecution followed. John and I had had two days at the races without seeing a race!!

John Rogers and I were returning from some enquiries John had been making in the Coventry area. We chose to take the road via Banbury to London. We stopped in the Market Square for lunch and noticed in a high class jewellers shop window, a quantity of watches obviously of foreign origin. We decided to make enquires as to the origin of the watches. Two very charming oldish ladies, who were the proprietors, said that they had purchased the watches from a man they did not know. They had no documentary evidence to prove the watches were duty paid. The law provides that any person possessing dutiable goods is required to prove payment of the duty, not that the Customs authorities have to prove goods have not paid duty. The onus of proof is on the person possessing dutiable goods. John and I took possession of the watches and the proprietors were prosecuted. Such is the law. The two ladies were very apologetic about the whole matter. But for a chance decision to return to London via Banbury the offence would not have been discovered.

My most disappointing case concerned a purchase tax fraud by a firm manufacturing cosmetics in the Paddington area. Failure to account for the tax charged to large retail stores had been found by the local Officer. The case was referred to the S.I.B. The firm called "Radium Vita" was supplying cosmetics reputed to use a radium substance in manufacture to a number of large stores. There was a chemist supposedly knowledgeable in radium, plus clerical staff, not one of whom had anything to do with submitting the purchase tax account. It was prepared solely by the proprietor. I assembled all the evidence from many stores and was ready to put it to the proprietor for his explanation. He was killed by a flying bomb which dropped on Tulse Hill Railway Station! My efforts and all the enquiries involved were nullified. I never understood how radium could be used in manufacturing cosmetics for the purpose of enhancing the appearance of a lady. My chemistry knowledge did not reach that conclusion.

I had an interesting case concerning Indian Carpets for sale in Worthing. The shop was Bentalls. Such carpets were in very short supply during the war and their display in quantity in Bentalls Store was open to suspicion. The carpets had been supplied to them by an Army Officer living in Scotland. The chain of events was that this Officer had been in command of a company in India. Under a special provision by the Army command and authorised by the Board, each member of the force serving in India was allowed to purchase one carpet and take it home, free of duty for his own use. The Officer in question conceived the idea of getting each member of his company to purchase a carpet, take it home to England where he would reimburse the soldier and then to sell to a store in England. By this means he obtained many carpets and sold them to Bentalls who were only too pleased to have goods in short supply. My enquiries took me off to Scotland to the small town of Dallbeattie in Galloway, near to Dumfries where Robert Burns the Scottish poet had been the Excise Officer from 1789 until his death in 1796. I was able to see the statue erected to his memory. But this was not the object of my visit! I had travelled to Dumfries by train and now had to get to Dallbeattie by a bus. This accomplished, I visited the Officer's residence on a lonely hillside. He must have heard that Customs enquiries were afoot. He had departed to an army psychiatric hospital in Birmingham! Here his rank plus his illness (?) would prevent interrogation!! I went to Birmingham in an endeavour to see the Army Officer but the hospital authority declined to let me interview him. I could do no more than return to London to report the situation to the Chief Investigation Officer. He in turn took the matter up with the Army Council. It was a clear case of 'closing ranks'. I heard no more and the file was closed as far as I was concerned.

CHAPTER TWENTY
History of former Excise Officers, Robert Burns and Tom Paine.

But my enquiries had given me an opportunity to visit Dumfries en route to Dallbeattie. In Dumfries I had my first chance of seeing the Burns' statue. It commemorates the man considered by nearly every member of the C & E Department to have been the most famous Exciseman. He had, in Dumfries, as the Officer for the "First Floor Walk" (not the 'Ride') responsibility for a brewery, 9 victuallers, 6 tanners, 3 tawers (makers of white leather), a maltster and 50 dealers in Exciseable goods, namely 7 wine dealers, 22 spirit dealers and 21 tea dealers, the whole considered to be one of the most important and one of the most difficult in the whole Collection. Recommended for promotion, Burns died of heart disease before a vacancy arose. But poetry, the wine and Scottish Mary had swayed him away from official matters.

It is appropriate here, to mention that on the way to Dallbeattie I could see the area of the Solway Firth where Robert Burns patrolled to intercept smugglers, besides carrying out his normal Excise duties. The Isle of Man was nearby which gave smugglers a considerable advantage to 'run' their cargoes. Burns superior Official reported that "although he was a bustling, active gauger, he does pretty well". Once when a lugger was stranded on the sands nearby, Burns was posted to keep watch while help was sent for. Waiting, Burns composed a rhyme

> We'll mak' our maut an' bre' our drink,
> We'll dance, and sing, and rejoice, man
> An monie thanks to the muckle black De'll
> That danced awa' wi' the Exciseman!.
>
> (For or against?)

The smugglers' ship was broken up and Burns bought 4 brass cannons and sent them to France as a token of sympathy with the French revolutionaries. This act earned him disfavour when the cannons were impounded at Dover. Burns was not therefore entirely free of criticism. Burns salary was £50 a year but he did not have to maintain a horse as did another Exciseman, equally famous, who had £18 deducted from his salary of £50 for the horse he needed to travel round his 'Ride' fulfilling his duties!

It was alleged also that Burns was not entirely against small Excise misdemeanours by the populace in his Station and, in fact, would overlook them. He was therefore a popular Exciseman. It is said that on one occasion when he heard that his Surveyor was likely to pay a visit to check on the controls being exercised, Burns warned likely breakers of the law! It was then that he composed the rhyme,

> "The De'il cam fiddling thro' the town,
> an' danced away with the Exciseman,
> an' ilka wife cried "Auld Mahoun",
> We wish you luck o' your prize man".

He also composed the following, mentioning the wish for the fate of the Excise man!

> "There's threesome reels, and foursome reels,
> there's hornpipes and strathspeys, man,
> But the best dance as e'er cam to our lan'
> Was .. the De'ils awa' wi' the Exciseman".

Now, another Exciseman, equally famous, but an Englishman who served on the East and South Coasts where smuggling was also rife in the eighteenth century. What has to be remembered is that naval vessels were engaged in wars with France so that prevention of smuggling was of secondary consideration. Wool was smuggled from England in exchange for brandy and tea from France. The wool to be manufactured into cloth, then came back to England for further manufacture. Customs and Excise were separate services but the Exciseman had continually to be on the lookout for smugglers once they had landed their contraband.

172

Thomas Pain, later to be known at Tom Paine was born in 1737 at Thetford in Norfolk, the son of a small time farmer and staymaker, who was a Quaker. He attended a local grammar school and was later apprenticed as a staymaker (in modern terms a maker of women's corsets). He twice ran away in an endeavour to be a seaman, the second time successfully, enlisting as a seaman on board the privateer, "The King of Prussia". But not for long, he returned to staymaking in London where he also attended 'philosophical lectures'. He next went to Dover, again as a staymaker, but then set up his own business in Sandwich (the Cinque Port I controlled as Excise Officer in 1933)! There he married his first wife but the business failed and his wife died within a year. However, her father was or had been an Exciseman or a Customs official which inspired Paine to enter the Excise. This he did by returning to Thetford in 1761 to prepare for admission to the Excise. He was in 1762 appointed a supernumerary officer (? U.O) with the task of examining brewer's casks at Grantham in the Collection of that name. In August 1764 he was promoted to be a regular officer patrolling a section of the Lincolnshire coast, on horseback to intercept smugglers, a dangerous task. It was in this area that he committed the misdemeanour of 'stamping', i.e. certifying a consignment of goods that he had not examined. This offence was quite common due to the fact that Excisemen were expected to carry out more duties than they could conscientiously perform. Paine was dismissed by the Excise Board. He wrote a humble letter of apology which in 1766 secured his reinstatement. There was, however, no immediate vacancy, so Paine commenced teaching English in a London elementary school.. He was offered a post in the Excise in Cornwall which he declined. He was then appointed Officer of Excise in Lewes in Sussex, another dangerous post on account of smuggling considered in Lewes to be a recognised profession! Excise Officers were far from being popular. Paine carried a heavy load of responsibility for a salary of £50 which he claimed was reduced to £32 due to having to maintain a horse to carry out his duties. He led agitation for improvement in Officer's conditions of service, publishing his "Case of the Officers of Excise" on behalf of the Officers who were protesting to Parliament on the insufficiency of their present salary. The protest failed and the Officers in frustration turned on Paine accusing him of absconding with the campaign funds. Paine was again dismissed. Later he was tried for treason, and sentenced to death. He escaped to France where he sat as a Deputy for Calais in the Assembly. Opposing the guillotining of Louis XVI he was thrown into prison by Robespierre. Sentenced to death again, this time in France, he escaped by what has been described as 'the skin of his teeth' because he was a member of the French Assembly. He then did what another Exciseman (Robert Burns) had contemplated doing, he emigrated once more to America. He became friendly with Benjamin Franklin and Thomas Jefferson and is reputed to have assisted in composing the "Declaration of Independence". Back in Europe in 1787 he promoted the first design for an iron bridge. Paine's first pamphlet, "Age of Reason" crystallised the argument for Independence, fuelling the American Revolution. His book "Rights of Man" sold 200,000 copies in Britain alone. It was written in defence of the French Revolution, but caused Paine to be tried for seditious libel and his effigy to be hanged, shot and burned as a threat to the powers that be. The desk on which Paine wrote "The Right of Man" in Islington is now in the proud possession of the National Museum of Labour History in Manchester. In America he was at one time, Clerk to the Pennsylvania legislature. Paine is said to have been the first person to have used the phrase "United States of America". Tom Paine died in 1809 and was buried on his farm at New Rochelle in New Jersey, but was only in his grave for four months when William Cobbett, the author and political activist opened it and stole the contents with the idea of exhibiting Paine's remains to attract crowds to a campaign to force reformation of the British government and the Church of England! How Paine's remains would have helped the proposed campaign was not clear. Cobbett willed Paine's bones to his son but he went bankrupt. For the bankruptcy it was ruled that the bones were not an "asset". they vanished and have never been recovered. So ended the history of a remarkable Exciseman. It was said that he was more detested than loved during his lifetime. No book in English was so often banned as Paine's "Rights of Man" and no author so shamefully defamed. Napoleon is said to have slept with a copy of Paine's "Rights of Man" under his pillow. Of course the claim was untrue, at least it was never confirmed by Josephine!. The only monument to Tom Paine that I am aware of in England stands in the main street of Thetford opposite the licensed premises of "The Bell", which I specially went to see. There is a Paine monument at

New Rochelle and a statute at Morriston, in New Jersey. Both in the U.S.A.

Robert Burns wrote "Auld Lang Syne" possibly the song most sung throughout the Western world, certainly in Great Britain, and also many famous poems, some of which cannot be understood by mere Sassenachs!!

Burns can quite rightly be held to be the most famous Exciseman, Scotland has produced. Equally Tom Paine, despite being dismissed twice, can equally be considered the most famous English Exciseman. Together, who deserves the "British" title? Scotsmen, the world over hold a Burns' Night" on January 25th to celebrate his birth. The Haggis is piped in to accompany a 'dram' of whisky. There is no "Paine's Night" on January 29th. There is, however, a "Thomas Paine Society" of which the Rt. Hon. Michael Foot is the President.

CHAPTER TWENTY ONE
Further account of
service in Investigation Branch.

The importation of many goods was prohibited during the 1939/45 war, but prohibition invariably brings in its train, a desire to secure articles which are in short supply. Nylons for the ladies were a great attraction especially when friendly Americans could meet the demand! I had a 'contact' who sometimes gave me 'information' that was useful in investigation. Possibly he could have been described as a 'nark'. But in the Investigation Branch one had always to be ready to listen! Even to reward! This man once told me that a taxi would arrive outside Aldgate Underground Railway Station to unload nylons. How he knew he did not say. With another member of the staff I waited. A taxi drew up and my informer gave the signal. Three large suitcases were unloaded on to the pavement. We approached the driver to enquire the contents. He made off at speed! So did the informer with one of the suitcases! The contents of the two remaining suitcases were nylons of high quality. Who was to receive them I did not discover. The informer had received his reward - a case of nylons! So did the Crown when in due course the contents of the two remaining suit cases were sold by auction from the King's Warehouse.

Watches had been seen for sale in a jeweller's shop in the East End of London. To establish their origin it was decided to keep a 24 hour watch on the premises because it was suspected that the watches were coming from a ship in the nearby dock. I was one of the band of watchers and was actually there when three women went into the shop. They were obviously stewardesses. We followed them in. They were asked the purpose of their visit. There was no sign of a single watch. It was decided to take the women to Leman Street Police Station where female staff would be able to search them. At the police station a body search was carried out. A number of watches were found concealed in a very personal item of women's clothing. But for the body search we would have been unable to prove a case of smuggling.

Another case of suspected smuggling of watches occurred for inquiry. Charles Simison received a file reporting that watches were available from an address in West London. We went to the address where it was alleged watches could be obtained. It was that of a dance band leader who freely admitted us. We searched the premises but found nothing to incriminate the person we had seen. Back then to the office, when later the phone rang. It was from a Solicitor to say that his client wished to make a full statement about disposal of watches. It was to the effect that he had received some watches from Canadian friends and had supplied them to other acquaintances. There were some in his pocket when we interviewed him. In due course a 'confession' was made and on the strength of this the 'culprit' was prosecuted at the London Sessions and a fine of £1,100 imposed. It was a very simple case and possibly no more would have happened had not the Solicitor recommended disclosure. After the hearing, the offender approached both Charles Simison and I and thanked us for dealing with the matter so well and easily. He was a perfect gentleman and displayed no rancour. It was the easiest enquiry I was ever engaged upon! Some years later with Dorothy, I was attending a Dinner/Dance in Maidstone at the Star Hotel in aid of the St. John Ambulance Service. Our host was later to be appointed Mayor of Gillingham. The dance band was led by the person Charles Simison and I had investigated over watches. He instantly recognised me and during the interval came and sat at our table, much to the astonishment of others attending the Dinner/Dance. He had seen Dorothy and I dancing and suggested that he arrange for us to attend a "Come Dancing" session in London for the B.B.C. programme. We were honoured! But we did not accept although our dancing was apparently up to the required standard. (Memories of being chosen by the judge, Santos Casani, to dance in the finals for the Columbia Dance Championships, when I failed to arrive in time from distant Ormskirk!). Another happening a year or so later similar to that at the Star Hotel, Maidstone. Dorothy and I were attending the Annual Dinner/Dance held by Bearsted Golf Club of which I was then a member. This was at the Tudor Hotel near Bearsted where we then resided. The same band as before and the same recognition. Other members of the golf club wondered why the dance band leader chose to sit at our table during an interval, but our connection was not disclosed. He was still a gentleman and displayed no ill feeling. In fact the opposite. The nicest man I ever interviewed!!

I could relate other occurrences while serving on the S.I.B. It was easily the most interesting period of my C & E service up to that time.

Early in the war period, transfers to vacant Stations due to retirements or death were suspended. Hence a backlog of vacancies was building up until the time transfers or appointments of U.O.s or F.O.s. to Fixed Stations would recommence. Many Fixed Officers were still on 'detached duty' elsewhere and anxious to get back as soon as possible. Some had moved their residences and were content to stay in their 'adopted' Collections. I gained information from the Establishment Division at Head Office that when transfers recommenced, Officers on 'detached duty' in a Collection would be allowed first choice for vacancies in that Collection. Those wishing to return to their old Stations would be permitted to do so provided that services were required there. Otherwise they would remain on 'detached duty' as long as was practical. The solution seemed reasonable to me. But I had no desire to return to Tilbury Dock should my tenure on the S.I.B. come to an end. The Board I was aware, had a wish to employ only young men on the S.I.B. staff. The Board had in mind a maximum period, for an appointee to the S.I.B. would be 10 years. He would then be appointed elsewhere in the Service. By this means, keen young men would be appointed although the Senior Investigating Officers would continue to serve on the S.I.B., guiding and training new staff. It was in fact a reasonable plan. Officers serving on the S.I.B. could be promoted to being a Senior Investigator in any case, if suitable. I made very discreet enquiries!! Tilbury Dock at the end of hostilities would not require so many Fixed Officers because of changes in shipping over which the C & E had no control. So I would be the last to be returned of the staff that had been moved on detached duty, since I was still the junior. Two others had been appointed after me, but one was still in the forces having volunteered and the other was now an Unattached Surveyor. Under the Board's plan to give Officers on detached duty first choice for vacancies in their 'detached' Collection I needed to become 'detached' not in London, but in Dover where there were several Excise Station vacancies due to retirements. I was aware that by so doing I would forfeit the higher salary I was receiving as a member of the S.I.B. My elder son, Colin, was now over 10 years of age and attending the local school adjoining my allotment! I had plans to seek to send him to the King's School at Rochester which was a Public School of ancient foundation, second in age only to King's School in Canterbury. I had sat the examination for Surveyorship earlier and qualified but did not succeed at the interview. I was not disappointed because I had no desire to become an Unattached Surveyor required to officiate in any part of the country, possibly eventually necessitating changing one's residence when fixity as a Surveyor became required. I still had my eyes fixed on a Fixed Excise Station in Dover Collection. Despite the loss of salary it would entail, I decided to apply for employment in Dover Collection on Detached Duty. My discreet enquiries had established that this would be possible. A return to Tilbury dock was unlikely and continued employment on the S.I.B. problematical. I applied. Horace Kimber, the Chief Investigation Officer was not amused! He did not take kindly to members of his staff leaving voluntarily.

CHAPTER TWENTY TWO
Transferred to Dover Collection and appointed to Maidstone 5th Station.

I left the S.I.B. for Dover Collection on Detached Duty in June 1947. The war was over. I became the senior in the Collection for appointment. There were a number of options. Cranbrook Station in the Weald of Kent has been closed, the controls for that area having been transferred to a new Station in Maidstone. This was the very area I desired. Other stations in Chatham, Ashford and Hythe were vacant awaiting appointments. At first I was employed for five months officiating in Rochester, Chatham, Gillingham, Maidstone and Sittingbourne, once again on Excise but with Purchase Tax included, of which I was very familiar! An enjoyable period commenced. I was free of the railway journeys to London and much more the visits nation-wide on Investigations. Old Age Pension work had ceased.

The new Maidstone 5th Station was advertised. I applied and was appointed. At last I had secured what I had always wanted, a country Excise Station. There was a very small brewery by the name of Masons close to the River Medway in the town and also a small area leading out of the town to a vast countryside as far as the Kent-Sussex border in the South. To the West almost to Tonbridge and to the East to Ashford. Many of my assistants, who from time to time came to Maidstone described it as the finest Station in the Country! I thought so too! I soon settled in and was travelling on Excise duties to such villages as Biddenden, Benenden, Marden, Smarden, Goudhurst, Hawkhurst, Horsmonden, Brenchley, Paddock Wood, East Farleigh, West Farleigh, Linton, East Sutton, Edgecombe, Pluckley (of Darling Buds of May fame), Yalding, East Peckham, West Peckham, Bearsted and Harrietsham etc. The list is endless and the work was to me, child's play. I never thought I would be so lucky, to have such a country to travel over at my own discretion.

At this time I was invited to join the "Riverites". This was an 'unofficial association' for any member of the Customs and Excise who had served 'within sight or smell' of Olde Father Thames! The 'Riverites' held an annual dinner in London which was an uproarious gathering of all ranks. The 'Motto' over the entrance to the dining room simply said 'Abandon rank all ye who enter here'. The Chairman for the evening could be of any rank, but generally well known throughout the Service. He was ceremoniously presented with a "flogger". A type of large mallet used for hammering the staves of a cask to make the bung jump out to make the contents available, whether for testing or other purposes! To become a 'Riverite' applicants for membership had to pass an initiation ceremony. This consisted of being able to shout "Hooie" loud enough to be heard from one side of the River Thames near Tower Bridge, for hailing a 'lighterman' on the opposite side of the river. 'Hooie' had to be shouted before the whole assembly, who would roar their approval or disapproval. Final adjudication was given by the Chairman for the gathering. Those failing the test had to repeat it until acceptance was given by the Chairman raising his thumb. When I took the test my 'companion of the stage' was the Chief Inspector, who was a friend of mine. Whereas I passed at the first shout, he had to do it several times, being the Chief Inspector! A regulation 'toast' was given to 'Olde Father Thames' always by someone considered acquainted with the vagaries of the river. Some years after my initiation I was invited to give this 'toast' but declined the honour. The dinner was followed by an entertainment by talented members of the C & E staff, and was directed at 'taking the Mickey' out of all those of higher rank, by sketches and songs (generally parodies),. It was always one great lively gathering. All members were given a number, indicating their order of joining. I expect by now, I am probably the oldest living member, holding the lowest number. The membership runs into several hundred, increased now by the appointment of many female staff. I have not attended for many years after moving to Poole in Dorset. I would not now know many, if any, of the present members of the Riverites.

I continued to live in Gillingham, but intended to move to the Maidstone area as soon as I could find a suitable residence. At the time there was a severe shortage of properties available for purchase. I knew, even if others were not so aware, that there was a Treasury provision under which a Civil Servant having to change residence for official reasons could claim recompense for mortgage repayments due to having to purchase a property at a higher figure than the one he was selling. It was obvious to me that the best policy was to purchase a property at the highest figure one could reasonably afford and to place the difference in mortgage repayments above the selling price for the property to be vacated, upon the Treasury! One did not receive the whole difference but a figure making it worth while. I was only going to move from Gillingham to Maidstone a distance of 8 miles, but Excise Officers were required to live within their Stations. I was at first given permission to continue to live in Gillingham travelling daily to Maidstone. Eventually I secured a house in Bearsted 3 miles outside of Maidstone, but within my Station. It was also approximately 8 miles from Gillingham. The acquisition was rather dramatic. The house which was detached with a nice garden, fruit trees, lawns etc. was for sale at £4,000. My house in Gillingham in which I had lived for about 12 years I had purchased for £700 but it was now advertised for sale at £2,600. Viewing the proposed new house the agent told me that the local doctor was keen to purchase it and would probably go to Ashford the next day, where the agent's premises were situated, to conclude the purchase. I therefore wrote a cheque for the required deposit of 10%, £400. and posted it to arrive before the village doctor appeared to complete his deal. Sharp practice perhaps, but then "all's fair in love and war!" My 'ploy' was successful. Dorothy and I became the proud owners of a beautiful detached house in Bearsted, renowned as a picture postcard village with a large village green, a pond, a cricket team that played on the village green, two licensed premises at the corners of the village green, in fact all that one could desire for living in comfort after the trials and tribulations of the recent war. The village doctor was not amused! My elder son Colin now 12 years old could travel to King's School Rochester by bus. I had secured his admission to the senior school. Brian started at the village school opposite the Green.

The house was called "Orchard Gate" from the 5-barred gate entrance to the drive to the house. It was in a private road, Manor Way, a short distance from the Green and the ancient village church. Opposite was the Memorial Hall built to commemorate King George V. Here were held village functions including a Womens' Institute, meetings of the Bearsted Dramatic Society, Missions to Seamen etc. None likely to cause annoyance. We were in heaven!! The house had a large through sitting/dining room 28 feet long with a beautiful

182

'Claygate' open fireplace. An enormous kitchen with a 'walk-in' pantry. Three bedrooms, the master bedroom being over the dining/sitting room, again 28 feet long with views north and south. The usual facilities upstairs and downstairs. An integral garage capable of taking the largest car. We sold our Gillingham house for the asking price of £2,600, so the Treasury was due to foot the bill for the mortgage repayments on the balance of £1,400. This lasted for 7 years when the scheme was discontinued, by which time my mortgage repayments had ceased. The house was 'mock Tudor' with elm wood facings. The dining/lounge room had oak beams possibly recovered from an ancient vessel! Very impressive. My parents and Dorothy's were pleased with our acquisition. So were we!!. There was room at the end of the garden for a tool shed and room to keep fowls. Also in due course the erection of a greenhouse. Our only neighbours were Mr and Mrs Peach. He was a former Kent County cricketer, she, the daughter of one of the 'Barker' family of Kensington, London. We became good friends and with the other few residents in Manor Rise.

Author's residence at 'Orchard Gate',
Bearsted, Maidstone. Kent. 1948-1974

Shortly before we moved to Bearsted, Dorothy lost her father from a sudden heart attack when sitting on a tramcar on his way home from work in the Royal Naval Barracks where he was employed instructing Naval Artificer Apprentices. It was a sad blow to the

183

entire family now all re-united after the war. More tragedy to Dorothy and I was the death of our third child, a little girl we named Heather. Dorothy had become pregnant but was ill through the later stages She finally had to enter the Medway Hospital for observation and on restricted diets. The baby was born prematurely in September 1946 but was immediately placed in an incubator. Dorothy eventually returned home with the baby. It thrived for a while but I was seriously disturbed because I noticed that the baby seemed not to be able to see. The incubator was one that uses oxygen for assisting breathing difficulties but I learned later that it can cause blindness. The little baby survived some three months but succumbed to pneumonia to our great sorrow. We had so longed for a daughter to complete our little family.

We sold our Gillingham house to a Naval Officer who immediately went on a cruise in his naval vessel causing us some concern until he returned to complete the purchase. Colin started to attend as a pupil at King's School, Rochester. The school was attached to Rochester Cathedral where assembly was held each morning. It was a fee paying educational establishment considered rather superior by most inhabitants in the Medway Towns. School uniforms consisted of a special grey suit, white shirt etc. with a distinctive straw hat of black and white design. There was a boarding section with fees I was quite unable to meet but most of the pupils were day boys from residents in the area. Colin was well able to attend school from our house at Gillingham and when we moved to Bearsted, from there too. There were quite a few boys reaching the school without trouble from the Maidstone and surrounding area. "King's" was easily considered to be the best educational establishment in the district. I had long ago decided to give my sons the best education that I could afford taking the view that a "Public School" was essential in this day and age. My struggles through Council School, Technical School and Dockyard School had convinced me that progress via a Public School was the easier road to a better life provided the pupil was able to take advantage of the opportunities available. Dorothy played her part too, sending Colin off each morning well up to the standard required by pupils at 'Kings'. Brian settled in to attending the village school at Bearsted opposite the Green although for a short while he had to attend first Thurnham Village School and then Hollingbourne Village School due to accommodation problems at Bearsted. These solved, he returned to Bearsted School and proved quite a clever youngster.

When I eventually secured his entry into the junior school at King's' at the age of 10, the Bearsted Headmaster was quite annoyed on the grounds that Brian was a 'certainty' for the 11-plus exam then in vogue, for admission to Maidstone Grammar School. Another boy from Bearsted living close by also became a pupil at King's so Colin and Brian had a companion for the journey to Rochester daily. King's had been evacuated to Taunton College during the war.

In Rochester in 1951, a 'Dickensian Fair' was held. Part of the celebrations included a cricket match played on the grounds of Rochester Castle. The teams were dressed in old fashioned clothes, tail coats, top hats etc. Colin was in one team. They played as of olden times with only two stumps, no bails, and with a 'crooked bat' plus bowling under arm, as at the commencement of cricket as a contest. Also at this time, Brian had won a prize in an 'I Spy' competition in a national newspaper where edifices of any sort that were thatched had to be reported. We, in our travels at the time, had spied a thatched bus shelter near Redhill. Brian had to attend the television studio near Islington to receive his prize, it was not of great value. Dorothy took him, I was at a Federation branch meeting in Canterbury, where the reception was so poor I could not pick out Brain among the other winners.

I commenced my Excise control in my Maidstone Station visiting villages as far away as Hawkhurst and Goudhurst on the Sussex border. Apart from control of Masons brewery which was almost a daily visit at varying hours, my main control was at a firm called Plant Protection Ltd. This was a branch of Imperial Chemicals who had taken over a small firm producing nicotine sprays for control of fungus problems in the many hop gardens existing in my Station area. Nicotine had, of course, been superseded by chemicals imported by I.C.I. Further to this though, I.C.I. imported many other chemicals for manufacture into sprays for many purposes world wide. The import and the subsequent re-export of manufactured sprays involved considerable amount of control since the chemicals were allowed a concession for entry free of duty provided the subsequent export of the finished sprays was established. I also had control of many manufacturing businesses for purchase tax. A celluloid collar manufacturer removed from Hackney in London during the war to the village of Horsmonden, renowned in the distant past for iron works producing cast iron metal guns for war. A sidelight on the collar manufacturer. He was very religious. He always greeted me when I called, usually quarterly, to verify his P.T. account with an enquiry as to whether I was at peace with God! But he could not do plain arithmetic! Mistakes occurred in the totalling of the account, but always on his side! And never in the pence column. Always in the '£s' and then not in the single pound column, always in the hundreds or thousands column. So if a total of say £9,000 had a mistake in adding up of 1, it became £8,000, never £10,000! He was always so apologetic, promising to be more careful!!

There were two specialist manufacturers under the Craft Centre Scheme approved by Government ordinance to promote manufacturing by craftsmen of products normally subject to tax but for which the buyer was exempt from paying the tax. This was something I had never had to deal with in all my extensive control work in London. The first was a maker in a small workshop behind his cottage residence in Hawkhurst. He made violin bows! They were inlaid with gold, or silver, or pearl, tortoiseshell or even platinum and entirely "hand made". The maker who worked alone had been a bow maker for a London firm, but retired to Hawkhurst. His small cottage residence, he found, was opposite a small wood yard. There he acquired a supply of the very specialist wood which did not break when honed down to the size required for a violin bow and then bent to the standard curve for a bow. It was a chapter of coincidences, for in nearby Cranbrook Town he discovered a jeweller who could supply the necessary precious metals for inlaying the end of the bows. He acquired pearl material, as well as tortoiseshell from second hand shops, on hairbrushes and the like. It was a fascinating story of a craftsman who had retired, finding the opportunity to secure materials to carry on his craftsmanship solo, in his own time at his own speed, literally in his back garden! But for the tax charge, stranger still. He endorsed the invoice to the purchaser with the tax due but with a statement saying "which I am not charging you". He included the tax in his P.T. account and paid it in the normal way to the Collector, who then sent the tax return to me to verify. I certified the amount. The manufacturer submitted this to the Craft Centre of Great Britain who re-imbursed the manufacturer with the tax he had *not* charged to his customers but had paid to H M Customs and Excise!! The Craft Centre in turn received recompense from a special fund set up to foster the work of genuine craftsmen approved by the

Craft Centre. The same system applied to the other craftsman in my Station in the village of Brenchley. This man made specialised furniture to a customer's order. It was all hand made. He employed a workforce under training. Furniture was supplied to many in the theatrical profession and to concert artists. Returning to the bow maker, I once observed an account in the magazine 'The Stradivarius' or the 'Strad' reporting the sale of a 'Bultitude' bow for over £1,000. I showed it to Mr Bultitude since that was the name of my trader making bows at Hawkhurst under the Craft Centre scheme. He remarked "Yes, I made that bow when I was an apprentice for one shilling and sixpence" The bow was now on a par for value with a Stradivarius violin. The same could apply to the furniture manufactured by craftsman, Mr Joyce in Brenchley Village. To have met two such craftsmen in one Station was to me remarkable! I believe, however, that the whole system employed by the Craft Centre to foster craftsmanship was discontinued some time after I retired from the C. & E. Department. In any case V.A.T. now rules in the C. & E!!

In Brenchley I once had to clear a load of furniture for Customs purposes for a Bishop returning to the UK from India to take up an appointment as a parish priest! Brenchley is a small village, where once the author Siegfried Sassoon resided to play for and watch Matfield Cricket team. He wrote there "Memoirs of a Fox Hunting Man". He hunted over the Kent and nearby Sussex countryside, all well described in his book. He later wrote "Memoirs of an Infantry Officer" describing life in the Army in the first world war. His pacific views brought him into conflict with Army control causing much distress to his associates. Also in Matfield, part of Brenchley parish, lived Alan Watt, former Kent County cricketer who was a great bowler but remembered more for his enormous hitting of 'sixes'. He once hit 42 runs from 8 balls, 5 sixes and 3 fours, a feat never likely to be repeated. Alan Watt was the licensee of a public house in the village and could be relied upon to tell me a few stories of Kent cricket when I called to see him to 'survey' the premises. Other cricketers I met were Les Ames, Godfrey Evans, and most interesting of all, 'Tich' Freeman the diminutive former Kent and England 'Test' player. I had many interesting 'chats' with 'Tich' at his residence on the Ashford Road. All these these Kent 'stalwarts' lived near me in the village of Bearsted. Additionally 'Plum' Warner had lived in a house overlooking the village green before his death.

Also in my Station were two manufacturers of mineral waters subject to a duty charge, to add to the Revenue received from the duty on beer, wines and spirits. These mineral water manufacturers also produced cider which was not subject to tax although had been so at one time. The tax on cider was abandoned as too difficult to manage! When I commenced my period of service in Maidstone little did I realise how the manufacture of cider was going to cause me problems in the future!

I had under control a variety of traders, for Purchase Tax. Two tailors, four printers, a silversmith, at least six photographers entitled to obtain films for producing photographs not subject to P.T., a manufacturer of stone garden ornaments, a manufacturer of plastics, a large manufacturer of hand made paper, makers of garden sheds and a whole host of others difficult now to recall. The largest manufacturer of all, subject to P.T. was Marley Tiles an almost world wide organisation. There was a 'bill board' manufacturer in Hawkhurst who had inside knowledge of the progress of the search for oil beneath the North Sea, long before it was common knowledge. He had been actively involved in the Middle East in production of oil but was now pursuing a much more mundane occupation. But a large oil company intending to import apparatus for the search of oil, needed an agent in the UK to maintain the required records of material imported, solely to be exported to use outside the three mile limit when exploration commenced. There was a special provision in the Finance Act to deal with the matter but records had to be kept, especially when as happened, some items were lost at sea during explorations. The Hawkhurst man became the agent, although the explorations were taking place hundreds of miles away. I became the Officer to deal with the records required to be maintained, and these in a small village on the border between Kent and Sussex!! Another experience for an ordinary Exciseman!

The manufacturer of hand made paper was a very interesting firm to control for purchase tax. A small stream , called the River Len rising near Lenham had the correct consistency. The paper was made from cloth, mainly cotton and wool reduced to a pulp to be drained through wire mesh, clearly leaving what became the 'watermark'. This firm had for many years manufactured the paper for the old style £5 notes and those of higher value. But a member of the Government at the time who had a paper making factory near the Wookey Hole caves in Somerset decided to award the contract for making bank note paper to the Somerset firm. This was old history of long before the advent of P.T., but still interesting! The firm located just outside Maidstone continued to manufacture hand made paper of very high quality. But subject to purchase tax, although most of the production was exported. I expect the Wookey Hole firm lost their contract when the 'white' old style bank notes were discontinued.

Another celebrated author I once visited on a small enquiry was Richard Church, who compiled the book on Kent in the 'County Books' Series. He wrote many books of which perhaps the Trilogy of "The Porch", "The Stronghold" and "The Room Within" are the best known together with his autobiographical essay under the title "Over the Bridge". He lived in a converted Oasthouse at Curtisden Green not far from Goudhurst. I knew that he was once employed in a clerical capacity in the Government Laboratory. We talked of the 'lab' which he knew so well and of Billingsgate Fish Market next door. It brought back memories to me of my period on the fifth floor of the Custom House which was completely occupied by the laboratory of the Government Chemist. Richard Church was transferred from the 'lab' to the Treasury where he had more scope for pursuing his poetry and literary tastes far better than he had had in the 'lab'. He became a member of the "Bloomsbury Set" led by Vita Sackville-West. Richard Church was neither a 'Man of Kent' nor a 'Kentishman', having been born a Cockney. Nevertheless he had conceived a great love of Kent. During the 1939/45 war he served with the Goudhurst Home Guard detachment on the tower of Goudhurst's famous church where the Goudhurst men defeated the Hawkhurst Gang of smugglers led by Kingsmill in 1747. Entering Richard Church's oast-house residence with its iron stairway to his study was like being in a Kentish hop garden again, overpowering with the smell of hops, particularly when it was wet outside, causing the walls of the oast to surrender their long held distinctive odour.

Vita Sackville-West, of the 'Bloomsbury Set' later lived at Sissinghurst Castle near Sissinghurst, part of Cranbrook parish, and where she established the extensive Sissinghurst gardens now under the control of the National Trust. It was from Sissinghurst Castle that the prisoners of war in Napoleonic times were allowed to walk as far as where three roads met on the way to Biddenden. The prisoners were told to go as far as "trois routiére". There now stands there a licensed house under survey called 'The Three Ways'.

One day, 'out of the blue' I received an invitation to a party at Glassenbury, home of the Roberts family for more than 300 years. The party to be held, not in the moated castle-like building about 3 miles from Goudhurst, but in the fine building on the drive leading to the moat. The invitation was from the Cranbrook Pony Club about which I knew nothing. I have never owned a pony neither do I wish to. Nevertheless with two friends from Gillingham, I attended with Dorothy. There was a large assembly with a London dance band playing. No one asked our credentials for being there. Couples were sitting about everywhere, on the stairs, in corners, the whole episode was a mystery to me. But the outstanding factor was the food that was supplied. Fish pie and nothing else! It was totally uneatable. Every one present seemed to be searching for a hiding place to dispose of the fish pie! Behind curtains, under chairs and settees, the place was full of uneaten fish pie! My little party made an exit as quickly and as unobtrusively as possible. I never heard from the Pony Club again or the reason I had been invited to attend. A complete mystery. Maybe someone thought that the newly appointed Excise Officer for the area was sufficiently important to meet pony lovers. Or, because as in past times the Excise Officers had a horse (or pony) to perform the duties of their 'Ride'. One thing I did learn about Glassenbury was that Napoleon Bonaparte's famous white horse, Jaffa, was brought home by a member of the family to Glassenbury, after the Battle of Waterloo. It lies buried in the grounds there. Maybe that is why the Pony Club meets at Glassenbury!

Within my Station was the famous Leeds Castle, then owned by Lady Baillie. The estate was divided by the main Maidstone to Ashford Road. This fact created a problem due to the use of diesel fuel in the motor vehicles necessary to maintain the extensive estate. Entrance to various parts involved the vehicles travelling on sections of the main road. Vehicles used solely within a farm or estate were entitled to use fuel free of tax. This, in the case of Leeds Castle was not allowed because the vehicles had necessarily to travel on the road to get from one part to another of the estate. The estate vehicles were not using the public highway for any other purpose. I submitted the facts to the Board of C & E which gave a concession to the owner, Lady Baillie, entitling her to use duty free fuel in the vehicles maintaining the estate provided they were not being used for any other purpose. The Estate Manager was grateful for my action in securing official approval. He gave me permission to bring my young son, Colin, to fish in the moat surrounding Leeds Castle, a privilege Colin took advantage of a few times. Leeds Castle has a small 9 hole golf course surrounding the castle and moat, with several holes on the other side of a road to Broomfield Village. Play took place by going twice round the 9 hole course. I was given permission to use the course with colleagues from the Excise Office in Maidstone. On one occasion, playing there and reaching the stage of putting on the green of the 9th hole, a car drew up. Two ladies and several children alighted and proceeded to spread the materials for a picnic. It was Lady Baillie, who had driven down from her residence in London, simply to have a picnic in the grounds of Leeds Castle! Fortunately we had just completed our game of golf.

Another control to be applied was the checking of Club returns. All Clubs had to submit an annual return of purchases of intoxicating liquors. The total arrived at was subject to a percentage charge for tax. The reason was to ensure revenue from club sales to members equated as far as possible to the revenue from premises operating under a licence charge. It was a wearisome task for an Officer to total all the various invoices. Some Club secretaries, however, adopted an approved method of having their total purchases submitted by a Chartered Accountant thus relieving themselves of reaching a total and the Excise Officer of verifying it as correct! One parish in my Station had the distinctive name of Loose. The local Womens' Institute was the butt of many remarks with its proud notice over the door of the Institute's Hall, "The Loose Womens' Institute". I did not have to visit the premises for any revenue purpose!

Maidstone Station included many of the old type traders still under survey because of the possibility of receiving smuggled goods such as could have happened in the last century! Officers were still visiting licensed premises, (public houses) to inspect the Spirit Book into which the licensee was still required to enter every receipt of spirits which had to be accompanied by a spirit certificate from the supplier. What protection that was against receipt of smuggled spirits I fail to understand, or that of looking into casks to see if 'grogging' to extract spirit from the wood of the cask was being undertaken. Visiting small village shops selling methylated spirits, quite unpotable, to enquire if a customer was consuming it in some form or other; calling on schools and hospitals which possessed a still, in case it was being used for distilling to produce a concoction capable of consumption. It was all woefully out of date. But however, it did give the Excise Officer the chance to listen sometimes to what was happening in his area. But there were other controls to exercise. Diesel oil particularly. Used by farmers and haulage firms especially. One man I visited assured me he was using vast quantities of oil to heat his swimming pool and warm his residence. But he was using very little to fuel his vehicles travelling the length and breadth of the country!! The vehicles were required to use fuel on which the duty had been paid whereas he could use an identical fuel for his swimming pool, duty free. I had to call in the Special Investigation Branch staff to observe the journeys made by his vehicles to prove that false records were being produced to me. But most 'dual' users were honest and their records trustworthy. Eventually, because of the dangers that the taxing of fuel had produced, the Department brought in the 'colouring' of dutiable fuel, so to identify duty free oil being used in vehicles. A staff of mobile inspectors was created to stop and check vehicles on the road and to sample contents of fuel tanks. This control took some time to bring into use but eventually proved effective in the control of oil supplied genuinely for non-dutiable use. But much oil was used by horticulturists, in their greenhouses or in mushroom beds, by egg producers for keeping their battery chickens warm, by growers under glass of roses, carnations, chrysanthemums and other pot plants and especially of tomatoes. All came under Excise control for their use of duty free oil for heating purposes. Up to this time I had considered myself to be fairly knowledgeable horticulturally, but I learned much from visiting a vast array of market gardeners using glass. I even had two growers of exotic orchids under control exporting them to various destinations. I learned how to grow tomatoes and cucumbers in the greenhouse I erected at "Orchard Gate", using 'ring culture', something I had never heard of previously. Visitors to "Orchard Gate" invariably made straight for my greenhouse to inspect the produce and take home a sample! Chrysanthemums I also grew successfully as well as raising plants from seeds to stock my garden. I was well able to combine work with pleasure! At two hospitals, one at Benenden and the other at Linton I visited the laboratories where immature spirit was received to ensure that with the stills available, a potable spirit was not being produced. At both of these hospitals I was to become a patient in years to come! At the two semi-public schools at Sutton Valance and Cranbrook against whom Colin would play cricket for King's, Rochester in future years, I inspected the stills in their laboratories to ensure no mis-use. There was also the renowned Benenden School in the parish of that name. For visiting Benenden during the time Princess Anne was a pupil there, I had special permission to enter the grounds. I never found any evidence of misuse of the immature spirit (alcohol) or of their stills for production of potable spirits at any of the schools or hospitals I surveyed in accordance with the Board's instructions. At Benenden Hospital I was invariably greeted when I 'turned up' with the words "He's here again". It was all so pleasant performing this type of work from the more difficult controls I had to exercise at Plant Protection Ltd., at Yalding on the Medway or at Marley Tiles for purchase tax and other enquiries as well as at Hawkhurst for the control of materials for oil exploration. I also had the standard Excise control of Mason's brewery, including when required, the calibration of the 'collecting vessels' or vats, for assessing the duty due on the 'worts' (Beer, before fermentation commences). I had really become an Excise Officer in the most pleasant part of the country. And enjoying it!! I once had to visit a large barn like building built from the celebrated Kentish ragstone, in the small parish of Boughton Monchelsea. Around were genuine Tudor houses with their wood beam frontages. I visited the ragstone building to dip two large oil tanks in the roof area. This accomplished I learned that the building had once been a 'Malting' i.e. used for the production of malt from barley to make beer. It had last been 'surveyed' by an Excise Officer in the years before 1880 when the tax on malt was replaced by the tax on beer before it had reached the fermentation stage (worts)!!. Also near Bedgebury the site of the extensive pinetum, an extension of Kew Gardens, where I surveyed a licensed premises, (a public house), I think it was called the 'Rainbow' and stood in an isolated part of Kilndown village, part of Goudhurst parish. When asked to produce his spirit certificate book, I found it was one going back to 1880, beautifully kept and endorsed with the signatures of past Excise Officers inspecting it. In the early days this had been quarterly, then half yearly, finally annually. There was no indication that any Officer from 1880 onwards had found anything to indicate an Excise offence. The post

1880 system was still in force but whereas past Officers surveyed their 'rides' on a horse costing them of £18 per annum, I was surveying using a motor car for which I received a mileage allowance at a figure agreed from time to time between the Board and the Staff side of the Departmental Whitley Council!

One day at Maidstone I received a visit from two gentlemen from Czechoslovakia sent by the Board to visit Maidstone to enquire about the possibility of producing 'slivovitz', a brandy made from plums. Someone in Head Office thought that Maidstone was an area for growing plums and that maybe a disused oast house would serve to set up the distillery for producing the spirit. I took the two men towards the village of Lenham on the Ashford Road where I was aware of a disused oasthouse, formerly used for drying hops. I had to explain to them as best I could because of language difficulties, that the regulations in Great Britain for distilleries were very strict. The premises would have to be completely secure and under lock; that the procedure within would be under very strict Revenue control with access to whatever was produced, restricted, until account of it had been taken by the revenue staff. I do not think that they fully appreciated the problems that would arise to bring a disused oasthouse up to the standard required in the UK for premises manufacturing any spirits including "slivovitz". In any case I told them that Kent, and particularly the area of Maidstone was not a prime plum growing district. That, I told them, was in Worcestershire. They departed, I think convinced that the advice from Head Office to seek premises near Maidstone was not sound. I learned afterwards that they did in fact go to Worcestershire but did not find there what they were seeking. Later still I learned that despite Government hopes that a 'slivovitz' factory would be an asset to the British economy, the Czechoslovakians departed for the USA in the hope that there they would not find the revenue protecting conditions so involved as in the UK.

I had two cinemas within my Station. One was on "certified returns" of admissions on which the charge for entertainment's duty was reasonably secure. The other was quite different. It was an itinerant exhibitor of films in various halls in different villages one night in each week. In fact a travelling showman. Under the regulations I was required to inspect the tickets issued to patrons. These were numbered. Entertainment's tax was paid on the number of tickets

194

issued. Each ticket had to be torn into two, one portion going to the patron and the other retained for inspection by an Officer making a routine check. This exhibitor had evolved a clever method of reducing detection of fraud by 50%. Assuming an admission of 50 patrons. He issued 50 tickets properly, at the first village hall. At the next hall in another village on the next night he would first issue 25 tickets properly. Then to the next 25 patrons he would issue 25 tickets from the halves retained from the previous night in another village. He still had the half tickets from the admissions to the first hall. And so on. Each night he was issuing 50% new tickets and 50% halves of old tickets. When an Officer went into the hall to examine the half tickets in the possession of patrons, some would have a half corresponding to a half in the exhibitor's possession at the entrance, but some would only have a half with no corresponding half outside. It would be a half from those retained by the exhibitor from the previous night! So he reduced the chance of detection by 50% from the examination of halves in the possession of patrons. I detected the fraud and reported to the Board. The exhibitor was prosecuted and fined at Cranbrook Police Court. How long the system had been worked before I took over the Station I do not know. The exhibitor operated in a different village each night of the week. Under the rules for surveying I had to visit at least one village hall each week, involving me in going out one night in each week. A drawback to my complete freedom but then I often had to visit Masons brewery on a "control" in the evening. I received another commendation from the Board for my detection of the entertainment's duty fraud, my personal record again being noted.

I received a note from Head Office, that one of the staff there, who lived in the Maidstone area, had observed watches obviously of foreign origin, being on show in the "Beehive Stores" in Maidstone. I knew the proprietors well, two brothers who were friends of mine. Nevertheless I had to visit to ascertain the origin of the watches. They had been purchased from the Queen's Warehouse by auction!! They were duty paid so were properly exhibited for sale. I hoped that the Head Office employee was satisfied! Memories to me of the Napoleon Brandy on sale in Old Compton Street in London, that I had investigated when a member of the Special Investigation Branch with Charles Simison and which was found to be Portuguese Brandy bought at a King's Warehouse sale and duty paid!

CHAPTER TWENTY THREE
Family and foreign guests.

My father retired as he always said he would, exactly on his 60th birthday, 25th June 1946, receiving a pension from the Admiralty. He was awarded the Imperial Service Medal for his work in the Electrical Department of Chatham dockyard. My mother was still operating the credit sales business started so long ago but now with many more customers and retail shops for supplying goods. Father was now able to assist in the collecting of instalments using his car to travel around the area. Since I was but 8 miles away I was able to use my weekly visits to see them, to assist in keeping the accounts. Dorothy's younger brother now back from his spell with the French Resistance returned to his former employment with the Electricity Board in Rochester. For a time he lived with his wife with his mother until he was promoted and went to live in Hove for his employment in Brighton. Dorothy's sister after a marriage break-up then went taking her baby son to live with her mother, so that Mrs Brown did not have to live alone, after Dorothy's father died so tragically. Marjorie was first employed with a bank, then with the mineral water manufacturers in Rochester and finally became the Secretary to a large firm of Estate Agents and Valuers named Rogers, Son and Stevens. This was the firm in which Paul Rogers was a partner. Paul's twin brother was Peter Rogers the producer of the 'Carry On' films, who had gone, first into journalism, then into the film business. They were both former pupils of King's School. She remained there until she retired. Dorothy's elder brother Fred, was also back from the war, again employed as a commercial artist. He was, unfortunately suffering from shell shock from his wartime experiences. Sad for a very quiet unassuming man.

Dorothy and I took another short holiday at the Civil Service Holiday Camp at Corton as soon as it opened after the war. Both boys came with us. I think we could almost claim to be first 'in' after being 'last' out in 1939. Conditions had not yet returned to normal. There were rumours that the holiday centre might be sold off to Warners Holidays but that did not materialise until some years later. We went again about 1953 but this time had a full family gathering with my parents, Dorothy's mother and her brother John plus her grandfather. Also my sister and her husband with his mother. It was quite a family gathering. It was now quite clear that the holiday centre would soon be taken over by Warners. The next family holiday was to a similar holiday centre at Brixham in Devon on the hill overlooking the town. This time we took the son of a colleague in Rochester named Shave as a companion for Brian. They were both at King's School. It was a change from Corton. We all enjoyed the holiday especially Brian and Shave's son. They had found some girlfriends! There was a competition for 'cross sex' dressing. Brian and I entered. I was able to borrow from Dorothy but Brian did much better by borrowing a modern young lady's outfit. He won the first prize.

Dorothy's brother Fred married the Secretary to the firm of commercial artists in Rochester. He was a first class artist and designed excellent posters for cinemas and theatres in the Medway towns. Unfortunately Dorothy's mother developed leukaemia from which she eventually died. She had been a wonderful mother, bringing up four children on the low wages of an engine fitter in the dockyard at Chatham She was full of quaint sayings which kept her listeners amused. I recall that on one occasion she saw a brown and white horse go past the house. She said "That means good luck, a 'five balled horse' has just gone by!" She was cheerful to the end. Dorothy went to see her every day during her illness, to get her meals; Marjory being at business. After her mother's death, Marjory went to live in Rainham in a bungalow offered to her by a school friend, both former members of the defunct Rainham Tennis Club, when her friend married a second time, to the local bank manager.

As soon as I took up my appointment to Maidstone I was appointed Hon. Secretary of Dover Branch of the Customs and Excise Federation. The previous Hon. Secretary, Bert Fry, was the Officer for Herne Bay and a friend I had known for many years. He was anxious to give up the post and welcomed my arrival in the Collection and Branch. I also became Chairman of the Dover Staff

Whitley Committee and Vice Chairman of the Joint Committee. I was really back into Federation affairs. I attended several annual Councils of the Federation in towns such as Manchester and Birmingham. At a later Council I was once again elected a member of the Federation Executive. This was held at Western-Super-Mare at the invitation of Bristol Branch, I now began to attend Councils regularly in my Executive member capacity.

In 1950 now that both our sons were scholars at King's Rochester and away from home all day, Dorothy decided to seek employment again. She was extremely keen on Market Research. From an advertisement she secured an interview with the largest research firm of all, J Walter Thompson Ltd operating from Berkeley Square, London. She was appointed immediately and assigned to market research in Kent. It was not the familiar type of market researcher one meets in the street with a folder and file in which she, (usually a female) records your answers to specific questions. The system Dorothy operated was in retail shops or outlets where she carefully counted the stock of specific items on sale. Cosmetics, cigarettes, rubber goods, foodstuffs, stocks in chemists, the list was endless. A month later she would again check, count stock, compare it with receipts and eventually arrive at a figure for sales. Dorothy was in her element. The purpose of the market research was to assess the impact of advertising particularly by television. Eventually the project was hived off to an associated firm called Retail Audits Ltd. Dorothy became Controller for the South East and a "trouble shooter" for the whole country. Dorothy had found her meteor. She was a 'natural' and revelled in the work.

When problems arose, she travelled the country, Devon, the Potteries, Liverpool, Manchester, Birmingham, in fact most of the big towns, sometimes even the Metropolis. Also she attended conferences where decisions were made regarding the research business. She was offered the managership of South Wales when television opened up in that part of the country. She declined knowing that she had a husband not likely to agree moving to South Wales and with two sons at school. As an alternative she agreed to go to South Wales for a fortnight in each month to superintend the staff she had engaged there, as well as training them in the first place. She controlled quite a large staff and they all liked her. Our phone was ringing continuously for advice. It was fortunate that I was at home when her employment commenced. Later when both sons were at

University she was ale to spend longer spells away from home. I was very happy to see her enjoying her career and of course her salary was of great value in maintaining our sons at King's School, Rochester where the fees were always having to be increased to meet the higher costs of education. Also for assisting them at Universities.

She suffered a serious 'set-back' when she developed a gall bladder complaint. After a short spell in Maidstone Hospital she was admitted to Westminster Hospital, London for an operation. It was a very worrying time but I visited her daily. After her operation she remained in the hospital for a period awaiting discharge. She had a more than disconcerting experience when she found another patient had "passed away" behind a lavatory door! Eventually she was deemed well enough to return home, Dorothy for her part was not so sure but had to accept the medical decision. On the day for discharge when she was prepared for the journey home, I was to collect her. That day I was attending a Federation Executive meeting in Holborn. At the time arranged, mid-day, I was unable to go to Westminster Hospital but it was agreed that I would call as soon as my meeting concluded, expected to be about 4.00 pm. From noon onwards Dorothy sat waiting, with her bed allocated to another patient. The inevitable happened. The stitches opened, not having healed sufficiently for her to return home as she had all along suspected. When I called around 4.00 pm I found that Dorothy had been rushed back to the operating theatre for attention caused by the neglect in proposing to discharge her before she was ready. It was a case of 'panic stations'. There was a possibility that Dorothy would not survive. It was proposed that I should remain at the hospital overnight in case her condition deteriorated. Fortunately it did not, but Dorothy had to spend a few more weeks in hospital. I had a serious talk to the Consultant who had carried out Dorothy's operation, being far from satisfied with what had occurred. Eventually the hospital arranged for Dorothy to have a lengthy spell of convalescence in a nursing home in Brighton where she ultimately recovered from the trauma of her experience in Westminster Hospital. What I pointed out to the Consultant was that had I called to collect Dorothy at around noon as suggested, the opening of the stitches could easily have occurred in my car on our way home. As it was, my later arrival at 4.00 pm had ensured that the problem arose while Dorothy was still in the hospital. Apologies received did not absolve the hospital staff from blame for what had happened.

I too had a spell in hospital caused by a painful abscess that declined to heal after attention in Maidstone Hospital. I decided to seek admission to the Royal Masonic Hospital in West London. This hospital retained a panel of Consultants to cover every type of medical problem. It involved admission on a fee paying basis which I was prepared to meet. Eventually I was seen by a Consultant with knowledge of my problem. After a series of injections and drugs he effected a cure, but it took three weeks to solve. It was obvious that Dorothy and I were passing through a period of our lives in which medical attention was becoming necessary. My gall bladder problem, however, arose much later, after I had retired from the C & E. Bu. that too, after a much more serious spell in hospital the telling of which is lengthy and will be described in due course with other medical incidents.

Colin at the King's School proved to be quite a useful cricketer and gained a place in the First XI when he was twelve years old. The captain was a youth named Kingston, older but a first class cricketer who later played for Kent County team 2nd XI. There were also two brothers in the First XI named Reader, the sons of the cricket ball manufacturer at Teston, a village outside of Maidstone. They were also the grandsons of Jack Hubble the former Kent County wicket keeper so were well versed in cricket. Colin was in the King's First XI for five years up to the time he left to go to University. He played against most of the other school teams in Kent - Sutton Valence, Cranbrook, St Edmunds at Sandwich, Dover and others, but King's Rochester never played against King's Canterbury whose team was in a different class. I usually managed to be in the area if he was playing locally, such as at Sutton Valence where I saw him make his team's top score with 75 runs. There is little doubt that he inherited his cricketing skill from Dorothy's father and not from my side of the family!

Brian on the other hand, when he reached the upper school at King's, had no interest in cricket or in sporting activities in general. He was much more studious although he proved an excellent 'shot' in the rifle team of the Cadet Force attached to the school. I recall taking the boys to Canterbury to see Kent playing a county game. Colin sat and watched every ball that was bowled. Brian sat with his back to the match, reading a book!!

200

At the end of the war, when petrol was still in short supply we went on two brief holidays to Herne Bay in Kent, staying at a boarding house. Colin was very keen on fishing which he was able to do on the long Herne Bay pier. I had obtained a fishing rod and line. He spent some of his time waiting for a 'bite'. He enjoyed, however, walking along the pier to where seasoned anglers, were fishing. He enjoyed putting the bait for the other fishermen on to their hooks. On one occasion while he was so occupied, I went into the town quickly and bought a kipper from a fish shop. I took it back and hooked it on to Colin's line when he wasn't looking! He eventually came back to see if he had caught anything and was surprised to find a kipper on his hook. He was not amused. It was a horrible trick to play on him. The next year while at Herne Bay I learned that the Kent team was playing a friendly match at Canterbury, so I took both boys to watch. To my surprise I found that Frank Woolley was playing cricket for the last time for Kent. It was not a County Championship match, but never-the-less it was such a pleasure to see Frank Woolley once more playing at Canterbury. Since he was born in 1887 it is obvious that when I and my sons saw him that day in Canterbury he was nearing his 60th birthday. Still as upright as ever, stroking the ball to the boundary.

We also stayed one year for a short holiday at Goudhurst when the 'hopping' season was in full swing. It was here that we first met Laurie Latter, the hop factor staying at the same hotel and a number of men from the firm of Urquahart installing alternative heating arrangements by oil, to dry the hops, instead of the coal fires which had been in use for centuries! The hotel proprietor arranged for the two boys to ride on the footplate of the rail branch line that ran from Paddock Wood to Hawkhurst via Goudhurst. The 'hoppers' were busy all day picking the hops into their bins but at night and at the week-ends the hotel yard was full to overflowing. Goudhurst railway station was quiet for 11 months of the year, but at 'hopping' time, literally thousands used it as the inhabitants from the east end of London and elsewhere flooded in for 'hopping'. At week ends the husbands arrived to swell the numbers. They all slept together in the 'hop huts' provided by the hop growing farmers in fields adjoining the hop gardens. Some 'hoppers' even brought items of furniture, but mostly, it was a case of 'putting up' with the bare necessities for about a month, meeting with other 'hoppers' from previous years. With the children on school holidays, whole families came to enjoy a holiday in the country away from life in the East End of London. Also to earn a few pounds from their 'picking'! All has now changed with the system of machine cutting the hop bines which are then carried to a central depot for the machines to operate stripping the hops off the bines, thus doing the work of hundreds of pickers in the hop gardens.

Hop gardens caused me a little trouble because local tradesmen arranged for small shops to be set up within the hop gardens to supply the pickers with foodstuff etc.. The 'etc..' covered cigarettes for which a licence of five shillings and three pence was required! A small matter, but it necessitated a check up each year to ensure each hop garden shop had the required licence. One 'bright' farmer had the idea also, to have beer on sale by a local publican. This was quite outside the law because sales of intoxicating liquors have to have a Justice's Certificate for the premises from which the sales are to take place. I had to point this out to the farmer concerned and to warn the publican.

One shopkeeper arrived one morning to find his small shop in a hut in the hop garden completely empty. The thieves had taken the roof off!! It will not happen again because hop picking, as residents in Kent have witnessed at least from the 17th century has ceased. The hordes from London come no more to enjoy a working holiday in the fresh air amid the smell of hops. And the Excise Officer no longer required to ensure that all hop huts in a hop garden being used as a temporary shop, selling cigarettes, have the required five shillings and three pence licence!!

I had a colleague stationed at Margate who had, in the final stages of the war met some Dutch inhabitants, one family of which had asked him to allow their daughter to come to England when hostilities ceased, to learn English language. His name was Jack Cox (no relation!). But he did not have any children so he approached me to ask if Dorothy and I would accept the young girl for a month or two. We agreed and she duly arrived. She was very happy to be in the company of our two sons, but she was unable to attend school with them because King's at that time was not co-educational. She was no trouble to have living with our family. At the same time I had been in contact with an organisation arranging mutual exchanges of boys with French families. I was anxious for Brian to visit France to learn the French language. It was duly arranged for a French boy to visit us first, then, for Brian to go to a French home. At the last moment we were informed that the French boy due to visit us, had misbehaved and so his visit was cancelled. In his place, however, a substitute had been secured and would arrive the day before the Dutch girl would be leaving. We made arrangements to have the Dutch girl and the French boy at the same time for one night and then to take the girl to the airport for her return. But when she found herself in the company of not two, but three boys she did not want to go home! She had to depart. When she learned that Phillipe, the French boy, was from an extremely wealthy family and would soon be flying his own helicopter she was even more loathe to go home. Phillipe for his part promised he would fly his 'copter' to Hilversom in Holland to see her!! Whether he did so I do not know.

Our new guest was Phillipe de Montrichard, eldest grandson of Count de Montrichard of the Chateau de la Chasseigne, St. Parize La Chatel, Nevers, Nievre, France. Phillipe's father had been a diplomat, a victim of the war, so that Phillipe was now the heir to his grandfather, with numerous farms and estates. The family had a residence on the French Riviera, access to the French Alps and an apartment in Paris. Phillipe's grandfather was also involved with the ownership of the French newspaper 'Figaro' which Phillipe was instructed to purchase while in England. He was a most charming boy, who made himself thoroughly at home living with an ordinary English family. But for the misdemeanour of the first 'exchange' we would never have enjoyed the company of so pleasant and adaptable young man. He attended King's School with Brian but found the French master's pronunciation excruciating! He was intrigued with our boys 'funny' straw hats and Colin's walking stick he was entitled to carry as a prefect. But he gained a knowledge of English very quickly. His instruction to purchase his grandfather's newspaper he 'amended' to the purchase of ice cream. Phillipe had to keep a precise account of his expenditure in England. Hence the purchase of an ice cream became purchase of a newspaper! Phillipe's uncle was also a diplomat at the French Embassy in London. Phillipe was required to visit him. He did so one day but came back immediately to play tennis with our boys. He had no wish to linger in London. In due course Brian went for the return exchange visit. He had to conform to procedure in the de Montrichard chateau, 'dressing' for meals etc.. It was vastly different to our home life. But he enjoyed his stay visiting the Riviera and Paris. We kept up the association with Phillipe, meeting him in Paris some years later, after he was married.

From the visit of the Dutch girl we had more applications from Holland to have young boys to live with us. We accepted two at different times but their presence threw a strain on Dorothy especially when she was employed on her market researching work. One boy we took to Dymchurch Bay where we usually played cricket on the sands. He preferred to 'field' on the edge of the water so he could dash into the sea to retrieve the ball. His remarks were "cricket, it is always the cricket". Visitors from abroad can never understand our English game! Another French boy came as a result of the reputation we gained for accommodating visitors. He was though, much older. When with us he sat continuously listening to the French radio, sighing for the girl friend he had left behind in France! Colin had one exchange visit to Holland. I took him to Harwich for the sea trip but he did not enjoy the visit to Holland and had no wish to learn the language there.

I was approached by a senior Masonic member in Maidstone to allow my two sons to attend the Church Service for all Kentish masons due to be held in Canterbury Cathedral, for them to carry the Masonic "Volume of the Sacred Law", used in their normal lodge ceremonies. Both my sons were 'Lewises', that is born to a mason after their father had become a mason, and so qualified as such. They would be expected to carry the 'volume' at the head of the procession in front of the Provincial Grand master for Kent, who was Lord Cornwallis. I agreed and they duly performed their allotted task. Lord Cornwallis afterwards rewarded them with a gift of a five shilling piece (a Crown) each!! I was in the procession of many masons from all parts of Kent attending the church service. The following year the annual service was to be held in St. Peter's Church at Maidstone and I was again approached for Colin and Brian who were both pupils at King's School, Rochester, to lead the procession into the church. This time, not only Lord Cornwallis heading the many masons in the procession, but he was accompanied by Prince George, Duke of Kent, who was the Grand Master of the United Grand Lodge of England. Again I agreed for the two boys to carry the Volume of the Sacred Law at the head of the procession. A problem then arose. On the day of the church service, King's School was playing a cricket match against another Kentish Public School and Colin was a member of the King's First Eleven. I had agreed for the boys to attend the service so I explained this to the Sports master named Newman. He was not a mason and in fact I soon realised that he was 'anti-masonry'. Colin was dropped from the King's cricket team for two or three matches by Newman who picked the team. A 'small minded' action by a sports master who was not very popular with the team. As Colin was soon due to leave King's to go to Leicester University, he was not very upset, although he missed playing for a while. But another "Crown" each from Lord Cornwallis!

One day a caravan drew up at Orchard Gate. It was the parents of our first Dutch girl visitor. She was now in Canada, but her parents were touring in England with two younger children, boys. They were very pleasant and spent the night bedded down on the floor of our lounge in preference to sleeping in their caravan parked in our drive. Years later Dorothy and I met them in Arnhem, Holland, and they took us on the River Rhine in a motor boat they had on hire.

At the age of 17 Colin was awarded a Kent County Education Authority Exhibition. He obtained admission to Leicester University studying Economics, Business Management and related subjects. He also secured a diploma in Education. He was at Leicester for five years. On arrival at Leicester in residence, he immediately became Captain of the University Cricket team and of the Hockey team, positions he held until he graduated. Brian too was progressing at King's School but he never achieved any sporting awards. Except he was a member of the rifle shooting team.

At Leicester University Colin as Captain of the University Hockey team was chosen to play hockey for the Combined English Universities team. He really preferred Hockey to Cricket. When Kent County Cricket team was playing Leicester at Leicester, the Kent Captain, Colin Cowdrey, asked Colin to go for an interview. It was possibly for inviting Colin to join the Kent ground staff which might lead to playing for Kent, either in the 1st or 2nd teams. Colin had no wish to become a professional cricketer so the interview lapsed. He did, however, play hockey for Cambridge Nomads, a first class hockey team. Also later in London for Blackheath, another first class hockey team.

Brian did not like organised sport as had Colin. They were completely different. In fact whereas Colin had enjoyed his school days at King's Brian disliked King's School although he was in the upper stream scholastically, finding no difficulty in learning. No doubt he would have succeeded whichever school he attended but I felt as a policy I had to give both my sons the same opportunities to progress. One boy at school with Brian and a co-prefect when in the top form was John Gummer later to become a member of the Conservative Party Cabinet under Mrs Thatcher and John Major.

Author's wife Dorothy 1957

Author's son, Brian; Author,wife Dorothy: and Author's son Colin 1957

206

When the Federation Council was held in Cardiff, it happened that Dorothy was on a visit for market research in South Wales and was staying in Cardiff but at a different hotel to that where the council delegates were staying. When the Council was over, I arranged with Dorothy to move into her hotel and take her in my car to her remaining research visits. When Dorothy asked the hotel management to transfer her from her single room to a double to accommodate her husband, she was looked at with some scepticism by the hotel staff!! Much the same happened on another occasion when I was attending a Federation meeting in London, when Dorothy phoned to say she was staying overnight, and inviting me to take dinner with her at her hotel in West London. I went there and to her bedroom, where I went into her bathroom to 'freshen up'. While in there with my shirt off, the chamber-maid came in, not knowing I was there and expressed surprise later, to Dorothy that she had found a strange man in her bathroom, washing, and wanted to know what he was there for! After our dinner, I returned to Bearsted, but Dorothy remained at the hotel having explained that the man using the bathroom was her husband! Some incidents can invite suspicion especially in a hotel.

CHAPTER TWENTY FOUR
Further experiences in Maidstone.

In the early 1950's a new Collector, a Mr Raymond was appointed. I had known him for many years, back to the days when he was an Unattached Surveyor and I was employed at Tilbury Dock. This appointment was welcomed by me since Dorothy and Mrs Raymond were good friends as well. Soon afterwards a 'rescheming' of Excise Stations was ordered to bring the work loads in the Stations within the Collection more equal. From this 'rescheming' I shed a number of parishes to the West, including Plant Protection Ltd, in Yalding Parish. I was not sorry to see my association with the I.C.I. associated company severed. In place of the parishes westwards towards Tonbridge, I took over control of a whole area of parishes to the East including the town of Tenterden, but extending also over the border into Sussex to Robertsbridge, Bodium and Northiam near Rye, in fact almost to the border with the town of Battle. I retained control of Masons Brewery, but the new area meant I would have much more travelling to do to carry out the required surveys. Tenterden town had a medium size manufacturer of cosmetics, but Robertsbridge in Sussex had several large firms, manufacturers paying purchase tax. One was Gray Nicholls the manufacturers of cricket bats and related sports goods. Also a large timber merchant and a printer. Plus several more users of duty free oil. In due course I was able to purchase from Gray Nicholls a new cricket bat from a special collection they reserved of test match standard. Colin used this bat as Captain of Leicester University team and still has it. I was pleased with the transfer of parishes in the West of my former area and the change to parishes in the East. But the change brought me much additional control work in years ahead.

In 1954, the Government realised that the sales of gin were falling and with the fall, a drop in revenue receipts from this alcoholic beverage.

There was however, a change in drinking habits, particularly by the ladies, to what was known as "Babycham". This was a cider or perry made from fermented pear juice. It became very popular. It was produced in the West country mainly from pear juice imported from the continent. In the 1954 budget the Chancellor of the Exchequer imposed a duty on Cider with a strength of 15% proof or over.

Kent is of course, referred to as the Garden of England, mainly because of the growing of fruit of which apples are the main crop. These too are grown in the Weald of Kent which constituted practically the whole of my Excise Station. Many farmers and a few licensees of public houses, made cider from the apples on their farms or obtainable nearby. The advent of the new tax on cider caused me a considerable amount of extra work. I soon established that there were five main cider makers in my area. These were at Marden, Staplehurst, Smarden, Benenden and Biddenden. It was necessary to concentrate on these makers first. The two at Staplehurst and Marden decided to cease making cider. They were both under survey as mineral water manufacturers. The cider maker at Biddenden, under the trade name of Bodyguard decided to cease manufacture. This left the two largest firms, Church Farm Cider at Smarden and Bob Luck's cider at Benenden both with extensive sales of strong cider to bring under Revenue control. For the remaining small cider makers it was agreed that farmers making cider for their farm workers and not selling it would be exempt from the new tax. Additionally a few publicans making cider for sale on their premises would be outside of the tax charge provided the strength was below 15% proof spirit. I had no method of testing for strength but was generally satisfied that what was sold was under the dutiable strength. In any case publicans did not openly display their cider because brewers and tied houses were averse to sales of home made cider. Church Farm Cider owned by a Colonel White was easily the simplest to control for duty purposes because a responsible clerical staff was maintained showing details of all sales. Bob Luck's cider on the other hand was the most difficult. A whole large field existed on his farm premises, with dozens, in fact hundreds of casks strewn about with fermentation 'bubbling' away. He had a large apple press from which he could obtain apple juice to fill any casks that had been emptied previously. It was a most haphazard system but was a profitable business. Casks were emptied to have their contents transferred to a shed where a workman filtered the cider into small casks and jars but no bottles. The proprietor's sons distributed to publicans, mainly by the 'back door' method, so not to arouse the suspicion of brewers owning tied houses. Fermentation in the casks in the field was obtained simply by introducing a quantity of demerara sugar into the cask, fill it with juice straight from the press where apples, good, bad or indifferent came under the press and then to ferment. Bob Luck was a very likeable person, rough and ready, unused to any control over his thriving business. Bob Luck's cider was reputed to be the strongest in the county, possibly in the country. He obtained his casks from Scottish distilleries, usually used sherry casks, but he considered that a burgundy cask produced the best cider. There was nothing in Luck's establishment to prevent him taking jars or small casks way without accounting for such removal. I reported the matter to the Board and as a result an Inspector from Head Office was sent to see the 'set-up' and to evolve if possible, the safeguards needed. Bob Luck was a 'character'. On the front of his delivery lorry, driven by one of his sons, were the words "Here's Luck" and on the tailboard , "Bob's your Uncle"!! A most unconventional character. Eventually it was agreed that all casks fermenting in the fields were to be numbered. A record kept of transfers to the filter shed and for the workman's wife to keep a record of all deliveries and sales.

Bob Luck also pressed apples for any person who delivered them to his premises. A farmer would deliver a whole crop of apples, ripe or bad, 'drops' included. Twice a week a tanker would arrive at the farm and take away 3,000 gallons of apple juice to Somerset, for producing Somerset cider from Kentish apples! I am sure that Officers in Somerset and Hereford where cider was also produced had problems with the new cider duty equal to those I had encountered with Bob Luck's cider.

Author with Bob Luck at Luck's cider farm Benenden 1956

About this time, with others from Federation Head Quarters, I attended a meeting of the Trade Union Congress held in the Church Hall near the Houses of Parliament. The Federation delegation was very small compared with those from the larger trade unions. I was asked and appointed as a 'teller' to collect the votes from the various delegations. Quite a simple task when they held up the cards to indicate their strength. At the time George Woodcock was the General Secretary of the TUC and struck me as being very efficient. Among other speakers was George Brown, later "Lord George" and Foreign Secretary. I knew that at one time he had been a 'partner' in the John Lewis Partnership but had left that gathering of distinguished members which had included Miss Audrey Hepburn to enter politics. George Brown had plenty to say to the conference members, but to me, nothing of moment to impress. Maybe I was prejudiced. The Federation delegation did not add anything to the debates that took place, but for me it was an interesting episode in my life, although only a 'teller'.

In Goudhurst I had under Excise control, a manufacturer of concrete garden ornaments. These were of various sizes and very expertly made. Besides the ornaments, the manufacturer also made concrete paving stones and kerbstones but these were not subject to purchase tax, but the ornaments were. The manufacturer, in fact the director of the company, was also the licensee of the 'Star and Eagle' public house standing next to the famous Goudhurst Church, where the battle between the Hawkhurst Gang of smugglers and the hastily formed Goudhurst Militia took place in 1747. Meeting resistance and suffering casualties, the Gang retired leaving Goudhurst villagers victorious. I was in the Star and Eagle on one occasion when a film company was filming in the interior of the house. As a consequence I became one of the 'extras' gathered around the bar! What the film was about I did not discover so I never saw myself on the 'silver screen' as George Sanders aptly described the cinema! Besides being the proprietor of the Star and Eagle public house, Peter Holt, was a director of the garden ornament firm, employing a staff. The other director was The Hon. Fienes Cornwallis who lived in the adjoining parish of Hormonden, also in my Station. He was the son of Lord Cornwallis, a leading Freemason who incidentally sponsored the building of my present residence, Duke of Kent Court, in 1926. Peter Holt invited myself and Dorothy to have lunch with him and the Hon. Fienes at his residence opposite the licensed premises, once the home of cloth weavers in Elizabethan times.

Next to the premises where the ornaments were produced, I discovered a small cider maker that I had been unaware of. The cider made was not very strong, so did not attract the recently imposed duty, but it eventually closed down.

Eventually the new cider duty settled down but I had extra visits to add to my quota of work for total Station Units, plus the additional travelling to visit the cider makers to verify the tax receipts. Whether the revenue receipts from sales of gin recovered or whether 'Babycham' was made to a strength under 15% proof spirit I did not learn. VAT is now chargeable in any case.

I subsequently heard of another cider maker in Biddenden. His name was Hall and he sold small quantities to licensed houses in the area. He had an apple pressing plant and it was fairly obvious that the cider would exceed the 15% figure for proof spirit. He wasn't too pleased to receive my first visit but finally agreed to reduce the strength to below the limit for being subject to duty. He proposed to do this by dilution. I pointed out that he would need to give official notice of carrying out the dilution. He did so by timing it for 6.00 am so as to make it very inconvenient for the dilution to be witnessed. I had at the time a young Unattached Officer assisting in the Station and he volunteered to attend. Mr Hall did not give such "notice" again, since he too, had to arise early to carry out the dilution process. Eventually he kept his cider strength below the 15% limit. However, I received information that a garage owner in Biddenden had died under strange circumstances. It was found to be from lead poisoning. The cause was found to be drinking the cider received from Mr Hall. When pressing his apples, the juice ran over and through lead pipes where it became contaminated. I took samples from the cask of cider at the garage and submitted to the Government Chemist. Also reported to the Board. The incident was not considered a revenue matter. Mr Hall discontinued making cider except for his own consumption. Whether he discontinued the practice of using lead pipes I do not know.

I had another case of lead being the cause of illness. A small maker of cider in the village of Egerton near Pluckley was admitted to hospital in Tenterden, being very anaemic. In hospital he recovered his normal pallor. He had been drinking his own cider using some lead utensils when fermenting his apple juice. These small incidents only came to my notice from the imposition of the new tax on strong cider. In Pluckley, however, I discovered a small manufacturer of fur skins using fox skins sent to him from time to time. He managed to keep his sales of finished garments to below the limit for requiring registration for purchase tax as a manufacturer for sale. Such small manufactures of all types had to be visited annually to ensure that they had not exceeded the limit for total sales, which could, if exceeded, render them subject to purchase tax registration and control. There was a photographer in Pluckley who obtained his films free of tax for the purpose of photographing paintings in the National Gallery and elsewhere to be incorporated in high class books and magazines. He set his photographic apparatus up in the galleries overnight when closed and worked through the night to obtain his specialised pictures. He also made tapes of sounds of minute marine life from the fish pond in his garden. He won prizes for these in B.B.C. competitions. A most interesting 'trader' to visit for control of his negative films obtained free of purchase tax.

Another photographer, residing in Smarden obtained his films free of tax for the purpose of photographing wild life in Africa. This type of 'trader' had to be visited to check his stock and his output to ensure that films obtained tax free were not being mis-applied.

An Exciseman's life in the country, as at Maidstone apart from the large 'traders' such as Plant Petrotection Ltd., or Marley Tiles, was most varied and interesting. With production of cider now also under control it became even more so. One day I received a 'file' concerning a man named G. Sanders, giving an address at a farm-house in Egerton. I knew that the address was that of a Colonel. The importation of motor vehicles from abroad was allowed free of duty for one year by which time the vehicle had to be re-exported. The "file" concerned a motor cycle from Japan. I called at the farm-house. I saw a lady and explained that I had to interview Mr Sanders. "Oh" she said, "you mean George". "He's down the garden". She called out for 'George'. I looked round to see a tall gentleman who said "you want to see me". I replied "I've seen ;you before somewhere". He said "I expect it was on the silver screen", in a very deep husky voice! It was George Sanders the film star! I asked about the motor cycle and he told me that he had given it to his brother-in-law! I explained that he had exceeded the year's grace for free importation. He was prepared to pay any import duty due.

He voluntarily explained the circumstance of having the motor cycle. He had been filming in Japan, "The sinking of the Titanic" and found it convenient to travel from his hotel there, to the film set by motor cycle. His domicile was in Switzerland and he was in England with his wife to await the arrival of his wife's daughter from America. All very interesting but little to do with the motor cycle except that he would be required to account for the duty. We then went outside into a large barn that was being cleared for a party when the daughter arrived. Here I saw a most pretty lady. It was, I believe, (Billy Burke), George Sanders wife, also a film star. She offered me a bright red apple in the style of Venus! I was in strange company! In the barn were two motor cars, both with foreign registration plates. One, a Rolls Royce and the other, a Mercedes Benz. George Sanders explained they were his and that he would be taking them back shortly to Switzerland. I was invited to join the party when the daughter of 'Billy' Burke arrived! I did not do so. The 'File' went back with the comment that the 'importer' was prepared to pay the duty due.

I had a similar file concerning a motor car, imported from Canada by a Mr John Gregson who was residing at Benenden. He was, in my opinion, most objectionable, in answering my enquiries. I realised that he was the radio and television 'personality' who sometimes gave answers to questions from listeners or viewers. His answers to me appeared to suggest that I was being 'officious' and he declined to accept that he was liable for the duty on a motor car that had exceeded the time allowed for duty free use in this country. On the other hand, his wife, who I recognised as Pat Kirkwood an actress I had seen in a theatre show in London, was most pleasant. I left to make my report to the Board. By the time I arrived back in my office, Mr Gregson had phoned to say that he had been subjected to an unpleasant interview by an objectionable 'customs man'. The Surveyor had received the phone call from Mr Gregson. I gave him my account of the interview. The Head Office 'file' went back with my report. The matter was then one for settlement between the Customs staff who had reported the non-re-exportation of the car and Mr Gregson.

What a difference between the discussions I had with George Sanders and that with John Gregson. I think that Mr. Gregson's reaction bears out the adage "The lady doth protest too much, methinks", from Hamlet. Substitute 'gentleman' for 'lady' first!!

214

I had a 'trader' in Headcorn, who was a large dealer in seeds. He used diesel oil in his vehicles hence I had to check his account occasionally. He owned a windmill at the back of the village where he ground corn. The mill was surrounded by a flock of Muscovy ducks. When I expressed an interest in them he offered to give me two young ones. I accepted and took them home where they wandered in my garden. Eventually they grew to maturity. They proved to be a drake and a duck. Next the duck laid clutch of eggs. Thinking that she would not sit to hatch them, I placed the eggs under a broody hen from my chickens. The hen hatched 13 ducklings! But the Muscovy duck promptly laid another clutch. They too hatched this time under the duck! I then had 26 ducklings! They needed water so I obtained a large bath and placed a wooden plank on it to allow the ducklings to climb in. Much to the amazement of the 'mother ' hen, but not to the mother duck. I had meanwhile purchased four small geese at Maidstone market. I then had 26 baby Muscovy ducks plus their father and mother and four small geese wandering about in my garden. The hen was returned to the chicken run! The geese fed on the grass from the lawn. The effect of all these birds on my garden was catastrophic! It was difficult to walk anywhere without problems from so many birds around. Dorothy threatened to leave home! She said "it's either me or the birds". I had no option but to dispose of them. The geese I took back to Maidstone market and sold them at a profit. All the Muscovies I persuaded my colleague at Ashford to accept them saying I was going on holiday, which was true! He took them away. He had a large pond in his garden so the ducks were quite at home. When he offered to bring them back, I suggested that he retained them. He did! He told me afterwards that the Muscovy ducks flew about the village, where he lived outside of Ashford, much to the consternation of other residents in the area. He subsequently transferred to Yeovil Station in Somerset. Whether he took the ducks with him I never found out. But Dorothy stayed with me minus the flock of birds! I did, however, receive a present of a Muscovy duck from Sid Gorringe, then the Officer for Ashford at the Christmas following his acceptance of my 'flock'. As it arrived dead and ready for 'plucking' we had duck for Christmas that year.

I had a 'trader' on the outskirts of Cranbrook who was a small time 'potter'. He came under control for purchase tax. On a control visit to his premises I noticed a flock of hens all sitting down in his garden. He explained that that morning a lorry had gone by his premises and a crate containing chickens had dropped off without the driver noticing. The lorry went on. My 'trader' went out to find that the crate had broken open and all the birds were sitting down in the road. The were 'battery' hens at the end of their economic life as layers but they did not know how to walk about! The lorry had been taking them to market. My 'trader' picked up all the birds and conveyed them to his garden where they all sat down again. The next time I called, the birds were housed in a proper chicken house and run. They were still laying eggs for my 'trader' as a gift from their unknown owner.

On one occasion Her Majesty, the Queen, and the two young Princesses were attending the Post Office and Civil Service Sanatorium Hospital at Benenden. (The 'Queen' is now the Queen Mother). Before opening a new wing of the Hospital there was a ceremony on Benenden village green which I was permitted to attend. There was strict security on all the roads leading into the village. The Royal party had travelled by Royal train to the small railway station outside of Cranbrook on the branch line, since closed by Dr. Beeching, that ran from Paddock Wood to Hawkhurst. Cranbrook Station had been very suitably decorated for this special occasion with flags and bunting. The small windows and doorway were suitably draped. The Royal party went on by a fleet of cars awaiting them from Cranbrook railway station to Benenden village green. They were due to return to London by car. After the ceremony was over, I went back via Cranbrook and took the opportunity to call to see another small 'potter' who operated in the outhouses attached to the railway station. The flags and bunting and all the decorations had been removed. The window frames and doorway not previously covered by the decorations had been freshly painted for the Queen's visit. But the portions under the decorations had not! So there was the strange sight of the door and the windows partly painted and the remainder still in their dirty condition! I am sure that the Queen was impressed by the decorations that had been put up for her visit to Cranbrook Railway Station. The first ever Royal visit, and the last! It is now closed permanently.

Hawkhurst was a most interesting parish for producing enquiries and situations necessitating Custom and Excise attention. I had a special file from Headquarters involving some ancient documents and records discovered in a bricked-up fireplace in the village. A resident

216

in the village having re-construction to his house, found documents behind a fireplace being removed. The papers were records of 'surveys' carried out by Excise Officers in the early eighteenth century. I was instructed to examine the records and then to transmit them to the Departmental Information and Records Unit. The documents I saw were very fragile after being hidden for so many years. In the end I agreed with the finder that he would take them personally to C & E Headquarters, where they duly arrived.

There was a bookmaker in Soho, London, who had failed to produce his records. He told the Excise Officer for Soho that the records were kept at Sandhurst on the outskirts of Hawkhurst. The man's name was Humphries. When I went to the address I found that it was the location of premises for training and keeping many greyhounds. The man Humphries was already under enquiry by the police for offences connected with being a bookmaker and owner of greyhounds which were then running where he operated also as a bookmaker. My task, however, was to gain access to the bookmaking records. The gate was barred and with a notice instructing callers to ring for admission. There were two Rottweiler dogs at large in the grounds. Eventually I was admitted when the dogs were tethered. The books I wished to see were not available but I was assured that they would be if I called again. On the next visit I asked the Surveyor to accompany me. Again the problem of admission. Again the dogs barring entry. Eventually when the dogs were under control, some records were produced. It was fairly obvious that 'delay' was the 'order of the day'. I sent a report back to London West Collection for the information of the Officer for Soho. The outcome was then a matter for action in London. I had no further requests to go to the premises at Sandhurst. Neither did I want to!! It was obvious a very suspicious 'set-up' was being operated by a bookmaker running his dogs where 'punters' were placing bets.

I had to call to see Mr John Millais, a nephew of Sir John Millais who painted the well known picture of "Bubbles" which is used by Pears to advertise its soap. My visit to see Mr Millais concerned a Bugatti car awaiting re-importation from South Africa. In the normal way such an importation would attract payment of Customs duty. The car was of foreign manufacture. But this was a 'vintage' car of high value which it was alleged had originally been exported from England to South Africa. I was shown a number of other vintage cars kept at the Hawkhurst premises and to which my interviewee wished to add, with the Bugatti. No evidence was available at Hawkhurst to support the claim although I was satisfied with the genuiness of what I was told. A new Bugatti car on importation would certainly be subject to a duty charge, but this was clearly a vintage car, so the story of its passage to South Africa and return was probably true. I reported accordingly. It was a matter for the Import Officer to decide.

In Hawkhurst was a very reliable Antique dealer with a shop, where I regularly visited on my visits to the parish. There, on one occasion, I saw two small pictures, one of Fort Amhurst and the other of Fort Pitt, two of the guarding forts from Napoleonic days, for Chatham Dockyard. These I purchased for a modest sum and hung them eventually in the corridor leading to our flat in Poole. There they were seen by a dealer who had come from Maidstone to examine some antique books I was willing to sell. He offered me a figure for the two pictures that I could hardly refuse. I replaced them with two pictures of young ladies in ballet costumes purchased in Spain, which Dorothy appreciated more that I did! I regret now disposing of the pictures of the two Forts.

In the same antique shop in Hawkhurst I purchased an antique map of Kent by Blaeu, the Dutch cartographer and dated 1650, for the sum of £5. I have had it examined and it has been declared genuine. It is now framed and hangs in my present residence in Chislehurst. It is in colour and is engraved with the arms of Odo Bishop of Bayen, Wilt Impress E of Flan, Hubert de Burgh, Edmond Woodstock, Thomas Holland, William Neville and Edmond Gray. It also bears the Royal Coat of Arms. It is shown as "CANTIVM, VERNACULE, KENT", while to the north is shown as ESSEXIÆ. The lathes of Aylesford, Sutton, Scraye, Saincte Augustine, and Shepway are all delineated with all the various 'hundreds' in each lathe. The North Sea is shown as Oceanus Germanicus. At the bottom is a large engraving of a female, seated holding a basket containing what appears to be the ears of corn (wheat) some hops, and fruit, apples and nuts. Alongside is an engraving of a sheep. All the 'U's' in the wording are 'V's'. All the letter 'S's, in the names of towns and of villages are in the old fashion 'f' unless at the end, to denote a plural when a normal 's' is used. I have been told that the map I purchased for £5 and had framed is now worth several hundred pounds.

I also purchased later a second antique map, but not in colour, of Kent by "Eman. Bowen, George. To his late Majesty", (published in 1762 - presumably to George II). This map shows a picture of the South Prospect of Christ Church Cathedral of Canterbury, and another of the North Prospect of St. Andrew Cathedral Church of Rochester. There is another picture of ropes, anchors, buoys and fish undoubtedly representing the maritime connection. Also trees showing fruit hanging and falling to the ground. A further section of the picture shows a female picking what must be hops from bines climbing poles. The whole map is covered with minute writing in beautiful 'copper plate'. Descriptions of all the main towns are given. Maidstone, for instance is said to be "a place of great antiquity" as also is Canterbury, Rochester, and so on. A full list of the Earls of Kent, of the seats of nobility and the lists of the Deaneries in the two diocese of Canterbury and Rochester. Kent is stated to be 56 miles in length, and 30 in breadth. Cranbrook is said to be the first place that worked at cloth. Kent is 162 miles in circumference, and covers 1,550 square miles. It has 39,245 houses, 124,800 acres, 408 parishes and 162 miles in circumference. The 5 Lathes contain 62 'hundreds', 31 market towns, and sends 7 members to Parliament. The list is endless!, as stated, in the most excellent 'copper plate'. One outstanding feature of the "Eman. Bowen map" is that it shows the minute area north of the River Thames opposite to Woolwich, as a 'part of Kent'. Something that the 'Blaeu map' omits.

Photograph of Blaeu's map of Kent 1650

I have bequeathed the Bowen map to my elder son, Colin and the Blaeu to Brian the younger one.

Hawkhurst was renowned for its gang of smugglers in the eighteenth century. It was probably the most notorious band of smugglers in the country, but it earned its notoriety as much for its terrorising of the population in general, as for its smuggling activities. But the murder of the elderly Excise Officer, Galley and of the informer Chater, at Rake in Sussex brought such revulsion that seven of the gang were eventually apprehended and hanged. It is an interesting facet to this gang that although they operated from "Oak and Ivy" premises in Hawkhurst, they used the mansion at 'Seacox' (an altered spelling of 'Sea Cocks') on the Hawkhurst Road to Ticehurst, as the repository for their ill-gotten goods. "Seacox" became later the home of Lord Goschen, one time Chancellor of the Exchequer!!

There was a large wood turning manufacturer in Hawkhurst manufacturing the 'stocks' for all types of brooms, brushes and sweepers of all sizes and shapes. Small household brushes for the housewife. Brooms for the floor or the gutters. Large or small, the firm made the wooden portion into which the hairs, bristles or artificial brushing parts could be inserted. These were 'turned' out. 'Turn' being the operative word. The firm was under revenue control for fuel for the lorries used to carry the alder, birch, willow and other soft woods, cut from plantations in the surrounding countryside. The trees were cut into whatever length required for brooms and brushes. Large or long lengths for large or long brooms. The smaller portions of the trees for brushes. As was to be expected there were parts of trees could not used due to knots or disease. These pieces were thrown aside and piled in heaps outside. These could be collected at five shillings or so for as much as could be carried away. I sometimes collected five shillings worth, filling my car boot to use the fuel for our open fire at our home! One of the advantages of living in and being the Officer of Excise for the Weald (wood). I also made official visits to the premises of the manufacturer of the wooden parts of brushes and brooms!!

One day in Headcorn I was surveying a Spirit Dealer who was also the sub-postmaster. He was well known in the village for using rather colourful language to 'all and sundry' no matter who was in the shop, which was also the largest general store in the village. His

220

name was Hubble and he was related to Hubble the former Kent County Cricket wicket-keeper. This Mr Hubble had played county cricket for Norfolk in the Minor Counties League, before retiring to his native county Kent to take the village store in Headcorn. Standing beside him behind the counter in what was his office, he observed two smartly dressed people passing down the main street dressed ready to attend a meeting of the Ashford Valley Fox Hounds. Mr Hubble's comments to me were "See that bu..... on the brown horse, that horse belongs to me. And the bl...... woman on the white horse, that horse belongs to the butcher. They never pay their bills but strut around on those bl..... horses as through they own the place. This comment in a loud voice for all the customers to hear. Mr Hubble did not mince his words!

One day I had a police telephone call to tell me a plane had crash landed in a field on the borders between Goudhurst and Hormonden parishes. I went off straight away and found that the pilot was from Australia on his way to Argentina. A Waterguard officer also arrived but I told him that he was not required! He had come from Gravesend, the Headquarters of the Waterguard for my area of Kent. The plane was so badly damaged that there was no possibility of it 'taking off' from where it had crashed. It would have to be dismantled. The pilot told me he had a quantity of presents he was taking to Argentina. These were not very bulky so I took possession of them. The pilot's immigration documents were in order so he was free to depart, leaving the plane to be dealt with in due course as he wished. I had the parcels of 'presents' conveyed to the Queen's Warehouse in London where the pilot could regain possession whenever he wished to proceed on his journey. It was a strange event for this single engine plane to have travelled from Australia, via Singapore, India, and the Persian Gulf, across Europe and then decided to crash land in my Station! I made a report to the Board via my Surveyor which was the end of my involvement.

There was in Headcorn parish a small airfield that had been used during the war as an emergency landing site for British planes. For all such small airfields the owner or occupier had to maintain records of all 'comings' and 'goings' by planes. I regularly received notification of private planes leaving a small airfield near Chobham in Surrey particularly, and from other inland airfields of planes leaving, indicating that they intended to put down at the Headcorn airfield. It was a convenient site for private planes to use for journeys across the Channel. As such, a vulnerable spot for smuggling. This was some years before the current problem existed for smuggling of drugs. Nevertheless I had to convince the farmer owning the Headcorn airfield that he was required to keep a record of all arrivals and departures. There was still at the airfield, a 'hanger' for planes to use should they not travel on to the next 'landing' straight away. The whole business of control of private departures and arrivals from a site so close to the continent was a continuous problem for me as the nearest Customs and Excise official. I was not helped by the owner of the airfield being very loath to keep the required records. The airfield was 'wide open' to abuse but I could only continue to press for the records to be maintained, for what they were worth! Control of air traffic by small planes using landing 'strips' was a problem not peculiar to me but for the whole country and the Department. It could only get worse!

These small incidents make for variety in an Exciseman's daily life. Some of the work is difficult, the rest as compensation, simple, so it all averages out over the year.

In Gillingham I had cultivated an allotment, which was surrendered once the war ended and the site became once more the school playing field. On moving to Bearsted, in addition to my large garden at "Orchard Gate, Bearsted" I endeavoured to secure an allotment there on which to grow vegetables etc.., for the house. The plot I was offered was on a ridge of the track of sand and "Fuller's Earth" that runs from near Redhill in Surrey to beyond Lenham in Kent. It was utterly impossible to grow anything there. No wonder the plot was vacant as were all the others nearby! The council was required to provide allotments so they did so where nothing would grow! Eventually the whole area was disposed of to a builder for a housing estate.

However I did become a member of the Royal Horticultural Society and found much advice in cultivating my garden. I commenced playing golf at the Bearsted golf club, I found, however, that when on the fourth tee, I could look across the village green to my garden in the distance! It made me think, "what am I doing here, chasing a little ball to get it into a hole in the ground, when I could be much better employed cultivating my garden!" The garden won and I was content to restrict my golfing to occasional visits to the course at Leeds Castle.

At Robertsbridge I had Excise control of the grower under glass of orchids which he exported by air to all parts of the globe. He used oil for heating although being a very competent engineer he installed supplementary heating should for any reason the oil heating fail. He was a member of the Royal Horticultural Society, so we had that in common. With him I visited the Spring shows of the R.H.S. in Westminster. It was a very friendly association.

I was also able to visit the Chelsea Flower Show on member's day. Dorothy not being available, I took with me my younger daughter-in-law, Brian's wife who is a keen gardener. She grows all the vegetables and some fruit for their consumption, from the kitchen garden on their 2 acre site at Worplesdon. For her visits to the Chelsea show, I had to insist that she wore a hat to be in the fashion with all the other ladies at the Chelsea Flower Show, many of whom take a delight in wearing headgear attracting attention in competition with the exhibits. Both June and Brian are now members of the Royal Horticultural Society. Living at Worplesdon they are conveniently near to Wisley the Head quarters of the R.H.S. which they often visit. My elder son, Colin is following in my footsteps by cultivating an allotment near to his listed cottage at Chislehurst. This he does, because he enjoys doing it and for the exercise involved as well a providing fresh produce for the table. His small garden attached to his cottage is a riot of colour throughout the year.

At Poole I had no opportunity to practice my skills at gardening, although I frequently felt that I could do some things much better that the gardener employed at Sunset Lodge in The Avenue to keep the grounds in perfect condition. However, our apartment had a large balcony facing south on which I grew plants in pots and tubs to make a brave show throughout the year. With our garden chairs we could imagine we were once again in the lovely garden we had left behind in Bearsted. In any case we could always enjoy sitting in the extensive grounds surrounding the Sunset Lodge apartments.

As Secretary and later President of the Dover Branch of the Federation, I was involved in a number of "extramural" activities. One General Meeting was held at the Sun Hotel in Chatham with a concert to follow. One of my colleagues at Maidstone gave a grand rendering of the Major General's song from Gilbert and Sullivan "The Pirates of Penzance" but with Customs and Excise words substituted for a few of those appropriate only to a Major General. I was persuaded to accompany my colleague from Ashford in a "parody" on the Gendarmes' song, "We run 'em in', etc.. I have now forgotten the words, so long ago! Another 'smoking concert' was held at Canterbury, where I had to act as a "know-all U.O." repeatedly correcting the officer-in-charge over the disposal of a valuable fur coat by a purchase tax trader, free of tax as a "Coronation left-over". Coronation "left overs" such as drinking mugs had been allowed by the Treasury to be disposed of without a tax charge, as a special concession. But using the concession to sell a fur coat was going a 'bit too far'. The Officer-in-charge, acting as a 'simple soul' in the 'skit' was for allowing the sale, but the 'know-all' U.O. (me) objected! Just another memory! I organised a Dinner/Dance at Bobby's, the large Departmental Store in Folkestone which went very successfully. I took a party of my friends in the Civil Service Motoring Association down by coach to swell the attendance, but it was well attended by the staff of Dover Collection. There were also Collection dances for all grades, held in Dover Town Hall. Dorothy and I attended but I was free from doing any of the arranging. This was carried out by the staff on duty in Dover.

In Maidstone the old Surveyor, Mr Releen had retired. The Surveyor when I took up my appointment was a Mr Battison. He was not easy to 'get on with'. He too lived in Bearsted but nearer the town. He was a fitness fanatic and regularly walked to the office in Maidstone through the extensive Moat Park where once the Earl of Bearsted, a Shell Oil 'magnate' had resided. He had bequeathed the park to the Borough of Maidstone. It contained a large lake on which Maidstone Sailing Club could manoeuvre their boats when there was sufficient wind! Kent County Cricket Club played County cricket there once a year during the Cricket Week. Mr Battison was rather careful in his dealings with me since I was Chairman of the Staff Side Whitley Committee and Vice Chairman of the Joint Committee of which my friend Mr Raymond was Chairman. Battison did not take kindly to staff associations. I was often away on Departmental Whitley business but managed to keep my Station duties up to date, although for protracted absences I received assistance from Unattached Officers sent from Dover. I had been appointed Secretary of the Officer Grade Committee of the Departmental Whitley Council which met the Board's representatives once a quarter. I had become, by the passage of time, a senior member of the Federation Council. I attended Councils in a number of towns, Looe in Cornwall at the invitation of Plymouth Branch, where I sampled Devonshire cider although I was not a 'drinking man', Southsea invited by Portsmouth Branch, Cardiff by Cardiff Branch, Brighton by Brighton Branch and others. At Cardiff and Brighton I saw Dorothy who was in those towns on market research but staying at a different hotel than that at which the Council delegates were staying!! Dorothy was becoming well known to delegates and familiar with Council meetings. In about 1960 Dover Branch invited the Council to meet in Folkestone. I was able to secure the Leas Cliff Hall for the meetings. The Mayor of Folkestone attended to open the proceedings. It was quite successful. Possibly my reputation as an organiser received a 'boost'. For the "out of Council activities" we played a golf match against the 'locals' but the highlight was a cricket match I arranged between the Council delegates and Dover Customs Sports Club. I do not remember who won, but we played by permission on the County Cricket Ground used by Kent. What I do recall, however, was that for the Umpires I arranged for two Scottish delegates to perform in their kilts!! Something that had never been seen before on a County ground, Umpires in kilts! I did not play but I secured a delegate who had played for Scotland to Captain the Federation team. At the usual and proverbial 'smoking concert' that accompanied the Council Dinner, I performed with two delegates from Birmingham, a parody on the Gilbert and Sullivan song out of the Mikado, "Three Little Girls from School" but instead of "Three Little Girls", we were "Three Little U.O.s are we". My colleague from Ashford Station, adjoining mine, did a parody on the popular song at that time "Oh my papa, to me he is so wonderful". Instead of "papa", the word "Surveyor" was inserted, so it became "Oh, my Surveyor, to me he is so wonderful" etc.. Fortunately Mr Battison was not present to hear his praises! Others did their 'turns' some of which I had seen before. The President, an Officer from Edinburgh, gave the soliloquy from Shakespeare's Hamlet to much applause. But some Council business was also conducted!!

Due to a shortage of staff many Officers were being required to carry out duties in excess of the normal station 'units' which was in fact having to work overtime which was not favoured in the Excise. I was particularly asked by the Federation Executive to suggest a scheme to meet the problem. Accordingly I prepared a solution which I based on what I knew was in force in other Government Departments where a Civil Servant was under 'pressure'. He could receive a payment of either 3% or 8% above his salary according to the additional work he

Meeting of Customs and Excise Federation Council
at Southsea, Hants,1959,
Author 8th from left, 3rd row from front (in dark suit).

was performing. I decided to base my proposals on the Unit system used in the Excise and which was unique. I proposed that Officers should re-assess their units each quarter, submit them for approval by the Surveyor, the figures then to go to the Collector who would authorise 'Extra Unit Allowance' (called E.U.A.) on a scale of 3%, 6%, 9% or the highest rate of 12%. The figures of 3% etc.., were based on that percentage above a mid-way average. My scheme was approved by the Executive and put to the Board who agreed without amendment. The whole became accepted Departmental policy until sufficient staff was available. Meanwhile Officers were being allowed to continue in their employment beyond the normal retiring age of 65, indeed up to 66 and 67. With my extra cider duty work, I reached the top %age of 12 for some years which was most useful in assuring my two sons were not short of funds at their respective universities.

Mr Battison, Surveyor, died from cancer, despite being a non-smoker and fitness devotee to fresh air. I assisted Mrs Battison with her application for Probate of his estate via the Principal Probate Registry in London because it was well above the limit I was authorised to deal with as the local Probate Officer. The new Surveyor was a Mr Braithwaite who had been the Officer for Gillingham when Armstrong retired. I knew him quite well. He was not a Mr Battison!! Every morning on arrival from driving from Strood, Rochester, any staff present had to endure a complete 'run down' of the previous night's television programme. He eventually transferred to a District in Southampton and his place was taken by a Mr Richardson who was a pleasant change from television!

226

CHAPTER TWENTY FIVE
Colin and Brian
at University.

Brian was nominated by King's School for a Public School scholarship to attend a University at the expense of an industrial firm. He attended a number of interviews, often remarking to his mother as he set off, "This will be the last one!" But he was successful. First he went to the Coal Board and with others spent a few weeks as a miner underground. He was not enthralled with mining as a career! All trainees for managerships had to have spent some time as an ordinary miner hewing coal! Next he went to the Steel Industry near Doncaster. This too, did not appeal to him as a career. Finally he went to Swansea where there was a British Petroleum refinery. BP offered him a scholarship at Swansea University College for which they would meet all fees, cost of books, subsistence, in fact practically every expense involved with his degree course.

He had hoped to go to Cambridge, but there was no BP refinery at Cambridge! During vacations he would spend part time as a trainee at the Swansea Refinery.

During vacations from Leicester University, Colin sought employment in a number of temporary occupations. He 'watered' beans in a bean field in Bearsted. He picked apples and plums in orchards in the next village of Otham, once nearly falling out of the tree down into a quarry, saved only by his 'picker's bag' getting caught on a branch of a tree. He worked on a building site at Reeds Paper Factory at Aylesford and also as a hop quantity booker and checker in the hop gardens at East Farleigh. But his most interesting employment was at a hotel at Camber near Rye in East Sussex. With his friend from King's School, Clive Burren who also lived in Bearsted, they went off to find employment somewhere on the South Coast. Clive was then at Manchester University. They were looking for employment in an hotel or similar. They went to Brighton on Colin's Lambretta motorcycle I had bought, then to Eastbourne and Hastings and smaller towns in between. Eventually they ended up at the King William Hotel at Camber Sands. The proprietor also owned the nearby holiday camp. Clive was to be the barman and Colin the waiter in the restaurant, with accommodation. The proprietor supplied them with white jackets but they needed black trousers. Back to Bearsted. I let Colin have a pair of my old black dress trousers. Clive got his from his father. Then back to Camber Sands where they stayed until the end of their vacations. With Mr & Mrs Burren, Dorothy and I went down to Camber to have a meal! Mr Burren was keen to try the beverages in the bar!! He was served by Clive. Colin came in with a napkin over his left forearm in real waiter style. Colin served us all our dinner very expertly, 'silver service' included! Afterwards we all went up to their room. There was a cap, full to overflowing with Clive's tips in the bar and Colin's from the restaurant. They were doing very well and sharing. Also they played golf on the adjoining course every afternoon so were having a holiday into the bargain. Eventually both boys went back to University. The Hotel proprietor invited them both back for Christmas but they were not able to go.

I discussed with Brian his prospects in a University and pointed out that he needed to engage in some type of activity additional to his studies for a degree. He was, I knew, interested in sailing. I arranged for him to 'crew' for one of the boats using the large lake in Moat Park. He enjoyed this 'sport' far more than he did at 'games' sessions at school. My arrangement to have him involved in sailing in Maidstone's Moat Park was to have far reaching repercussions when he commenced on his degree course in Chemistry at Swansea.

We had a friend we had met in a hotel in Goudhurst who was a 'hop factor', by the name of Laurie Latter. He had lived on the family farm at Wadhurst, just over the Kent/Sussex border. He now lived in a superior flat near Earls Court, West London, with his sister Eugene, both being unmarried. The Maidstone Sailing Club organised a Christmas raffle, the first prize being a sailing boat, with monetary equivalent if the boat was not wanted. I bought a book of twenty tickets and gave one to Laurie Latter. When the draw for the prize was made, my address was on the winning ticket but the name was "Laurie Latter". He happened to be at our house at the time. We were telephoned to say that Laurie Latter had won the boat. He just said "Lucky Laurie" and answered that he would prefer to have the cash instead! As a hop factor, he examined all hops grown throughout the County, on behalf of the Hop Marketing Board which assessed the figure on which payment would be made to hop growers. It was a very specialised occupation requiring a detailed technical knowledge of hop growing. Dorothy and I fully expected Laurie Latter to accept the boat and present it to Brian, but we were disappointed!

Laurie Latter had formerly lived at Earls Court Farm at Wadhurst, although the actual farm land was now let. The farm was named after Earls Court Farm in London where the present Earls Court Underground Railway Station is now situated. Laurie Latters' family had farmed there from before 1860 until the site was sold for development and the subsequent Underground Railway Station. When the family moved to a farm at Wadhurst, they named their farm Earls Court Farm and grew hops. Laurie did not farm but became an expert on hops and the Hop Factor for Kent. It was from Earls Court Farm that Earls Court Railway Station and area received its name.

Site of Earls Court Underground Station in 1860, then Earls Court Farm, farmed by the Latter family, in what is now an area of West London

Brian eventually took up residence in Swansea and found himself occupying a room "in Hall". The occupant of the next room was named Obo and was related to the royal family of Nigeria. Brian discovered that there was a University sailing club and became a member. His experience, gained crewing in Moat Park, stood him in good stead. He became a member of the University team, sailing against teams from other Universities. It was the practice of the Mumbles Yacht Club, centred in Swansea, to invite the members of the Swansea University Sailing Club to its Annual Ball. Brian attended. He noticed a nice young lady dancing, so asked for a dance. The two obviously enjoyed dancing together. Another member of the University Team remarked to Brian, "You're aiming high, that's the Commodore's daughter!" The friendship continued. The Commodore was Mr Bellingham who owned a steel works producing very thin steel plate such as used for cigarette boxes etc.. The family lived in an estate at "Wernfadog" near Clydach, formerly the residence of John Player (cigarettes). The daughter's name was June. The second daughter was Elizabeth and there was a son, also named Brian studying as a Chartered Accountant. The estate also included several farms. Mrs Bellingham was the daughter of Colonel Bevan, a former President of Glamorgan County Cricket Club and High Sheriff of Cardigan, now resident at Neath. Brian's friendship with June Bellingham continued. Her father sometimes went to pick up Brian, in his Bentley car, to take him with other undergraduates to play tennis with his daughters. Eventually I bought a small Austin car for Brian so that he could go to June's home without troubling her father to make the journey into Swansea.

Mr Bellingham was also Vice-Commodore of the Bristol Channel Yacht Club. He owned a large ocean going yacht capable of crossing the English Channel. He sometimes moored his boat at Salcombe in Devon, at other times at Lymington, Hants. Dorothy and I visited the Clydach residence staying there with June's parents. They also came to Bearsted to stay with us. It was a very friendly association.

Meanwhile Colin had graduated from Leicester University. He secured an appointment as a Personnel Officer with Yorkshire Imperial Metals, a branch of I.C.I. in Leeds. Besides his degree he was a possible asset to his firm as a cricketer for its membership of the Yorkshire Cricket League. He played a few games for Y.I.M. but was not too well received by the professionals they employed for the purposes of strengthening their team. As a Southern amateur displaying his school colours on his blazer and cap he was not popular with the tough Yorkshire 'pros'. In any case he was a member of the firm's management! He discontinued playing cricket for Y.I.M. He met a young lady studying in Leeds for qualifications as a domestic science teacher. She was the daughter of Mrs Olive Deeming who had divorced her first husband, an Air Force Officer named Martin, subsequently marrying Charles Deeming the owner of several cinemas, restaurants and dance halls in the Leicester, Loughborough and Coalville area. Charles and Olive Deeming resided at "One Ash" an extensive estate near Quorn on the Leicester to Loughborough Road. Charles Deeming was an expert keeper of bees, having many hives of bees from different parts of the world, in addition to a number of English hives. Once a year the grounds of "One Ash" were open to the public in aid of the Queen's Institute of District Nursing, organised by the National Gardens Scheme. Charles Deeming also had an open day for beekeepers to attend. He had an observation hive for viewers to see the bees at work building the combs as well as bringing in the honey. At the appropriate time of the year he took complete hives to the heather area of Derbyshire for his bees to collect the distinctive strong honey from wild heather. Dorothy and I went many times to stay at "One Ash" with Olive and Charles Deeming. Also when the grounds were open to the public and to beekeepers. We had many happy visits to Quorn and eventually when Colin married Elizabeth, Olive's daughter, all our family, grandparents, my sister and husband with their sons and daughter, Dorothy's sister and son, and her brother John with his wife and daughter attended the wedding in Quorn Church, followed by the wedding reception in the marquee in the grounds of "One Ash". I managed to get them all accommodated in various hotels in Leicester. Charles Deeming treated his step-daughter Elizabeth as though it was his own daughter. Brian was Colin's best man. Dorothy and I were very fond of Elizabeth.

Colin left the employ of Yorkshire Imperial Metals and secured a post as Education Officer for Phillips, the large radio and electronics firm with offices in Shaftesbury Avenue, London. While at Phillips he was invited to become a 'guest' lecturer at the North West Polytechnic in Camden Town area. Colin and Elizabeth were then living in the Lewisham area of London, but he purchased a holiday home at Sheringham, Norfolk, where Dorothy and I were able to take a holiday sometimes. From being a guest lecturer at the N.W. Poly, Colin was invited to become a full-time lecturer. From this appointment he rapidly progressed to Senior Lecturer, Principal Lecturer and finally to Head of Department in Business Management.

After graduating with a good degree Brian was employed by British Petroleum as a research chemist at the Research Establishment at Sunbury in Middlesex. His 'girl friend' in Swansea, June Bellingham, had been educated at Taunton Boarding College. She was Captain of cricket and a first class pianist. Her father, Gerald Bellingham had arranged for tuition for her to become a competent shorthand typist. When Brian was employed at Sunbury, June obtained a post at nearby Richmond. They wanted to marry. Mr Bellingham agreed. Colin had married Elizabeth Martin in 1963 at Quorn, Leicester. Brian married June Bellingham at Clydach, Glamorgan in May 1964. This time I took all the family and many friends to Glamorgan, booking them all in at the Dunraven Hotel in Bridgend fairly near to Clydach. My party occupied the entire hotel. Dorothy and I stayed with Mr & Mrs Bellingham at "Wernfadog". The reception was held in the Music Room. The grounds were in full bloom with rhodo-dendrons. There was a beautiful view across the Swansea Valley towards the Mumbles. The next day we made our way home via Ross-on-Wye where we stopped to see Symonds Yat before going on via the Cotswolds. It had been a very grand wedding. Colin was Brian's best man. June's sister Elizabeth was Chief Bridesmaid.

Brian by this time had been appointed to the BP Refinery at nearby Hoo-St. Werberg, on the Grain Peninsular, as Works Chemist. Brian and June bought a house at Hoo. Our first grandchild was born there. He had the distinctive red hair of Dorothy's family. He was named Adrian Marius, (Marius being the name of friends of June in Glamorgan). Brian was promoted to Development Chemist at the Refinery. June and Brian then moved to a BP house at High Halstow, still near to the Refinery. Later they purchased the house from BP. Here they had a lovely garden where June could cultivate her flowers. She was an excellent gardener. At High Halstow our second grandchild was born, a girl, and named Elaine Deborah. She arrived one day too late on 17th June, instead of on my birthday, the 16th!! Colin and Brian were both Men of Kent, as I was. Adrian, however, was a Kentishman having been born on the north side of the River Medway. Elaine like Dorothy was a Fair Maid of Kent there being no distinction as to which side they were born. Elaine did not have the distinctive red hair of the Brown family but was the image of her mother, June. She remains so!

CHAPTER TWENTY SIX
Holidays.

Now that our two sons were settled in their careers, Dorothy and I were able to think about taking holidays abroad. Dorothy was averse to travelling by air following the news of two air accidents, particularly the one where members of a Women's Institute lost their lives. So our first trip was with Lunns to Switzerland by coach staying at the far end of Lake Lucerne, in the small town of Fluelen. We visited Lucerne by boat but did not enjoy the holiday very much due to the poor accommodation at Fluelen. Our return was via Paris staying at a very low grade hotel although we were able to see briefly some of the sights. The final part of our journey home was hurried, due to a threat of a strike.

The next year we went to the Italian Riviera with Cosmos by coach via Dover to Ostend, then Brussels into Luxembourg, Germany and Switzerland, into Northern Italy. There were overnight stops with no night travel. We particularly enjoyed stopping overnight in Milan seeing the magnificent cathedral and visiting the opera house. Then on to Alassio and Diano Marina for a week's stay. Here I unfortunately had my wallet stolen with all our money. Through the good offices of the hotel manager who advanced me cash and the help of a fellow tourist, we eventually returned via Monte Carlo and Nice to Avignon, where we saw the famous bridge, halfway across the river. Then to Paris where we were able to see more of the French capital than on our previous visit. Also a visit to Versailles of historic importance. Home again to Bearsted. The following year we went to Yugoslavia, again with Cosmos. This time we had to fly from Manston in Kent, to Basle in Switzerland then to continue by coach. Arriving at Manston we were informed that the aircraft, a DC4 had been found to be faulty so a replacement would be obtained. This involved a 4 hour delay. Refreshments were served and eventually the replacement plane arrived. It was a Dutch DC6 with a Dutch crew. We eventually took our seats inside the plane. I was directed to a seat near the front. The plane took off. Then the 'accident'. Two large canisters of hot water for use in making tea for refreshments en route, overhead immediately in front of my seat, fell out because the maintenance staff at the airport had failed to fasten them in. Boiling water gushed out over my left foot. The stewardess, a Dutch girl, came to my 'rescue'. I was taken to the rear of the plane. My shoe and sock removed to reveal severe scalding of my foot. The Dutch stewardess went to look for the first aid box, only to find that all it contained were some safety pins! She then searched in her own handbag and found some cold cream, presumably a cosmetic. She put some on my ankle but it did not give any relief from the pain. I now realise that this was of no value and that the best treatment would have been a cold water bandage. Conversation with the Dutch stewardess was not easy and we were getting nearer to Basle, away from Manston every minute. The pilot was informed and he offered to put back to Manston. As there had already been a 4 hour delay, an alternative was suggested. That since the plane was already well on its way to Basle while I was receiving attention in the plane, he would continue the journey and at Basle I would be seen by a doctor with the possibility of going into hospital there. The pilot's problem was that he was due to return to Manston from Basle with another party of tourists who had already waited 4 hours from the delay over our first plane being faulty. I was given the choice. I decided to go on to Basle where a Cosmos representative would be available with the proposed doctor in attendance. I was made 'comfortable' at the rear of the plane. We duly reached Basle, the Cosmos 'rep' was there but no doctor! The 'rep' was prepared to have me taken to a Basle hospital for treatment. Because of the delay all the suitcases including Dorothy's and mine were quickly loaded on to the waiting coach. I enquired what would happen to Dorothy. The answer was that she could proceed with the other tourists on the trip to Yugoslavia! This did not appeal to me at all!! Then another suggestion, since no doctor was available at Basle airport, I would be made 'comfortable' in the rear of the coach and taken on to a small town, I think it was called Flums, where the party was due to stay overnight. There I was told Cosmos would have a doctor available to treat my blistered foot and ankle. So a further journey to see a doctor! We arrived. The courier plus the hotel manager took me to see the 'doctor'. The rest of the party sat down to their delayed evening meal!

234

I reached the 'doctor' but soon realised that he was a surgeon. He took a look at my foot and ankle and without any further examination proceeded to remove the blisters! Unfortunately he did not speak French so a conversation had to be carried on between the Cosmos courier in English to the hotel manager who then did his best to talk to the surgeon in German. Eventually the blisters were dressed with an ointment and pads with instruction that I should dress my foot twice daily with a similar ointment. I tried to explain that I was going on a journey of a thousand miles or so by coach to Dubrovnik in Yugoslavia. I gathered that the surgeon said, "Do the best you can". With that, back to the hotel where the other tourists had already gone to bed. Dorothy was waiting but I had a most uncomfortable night and wished that I had taken the option of getting the pilot of the DC6 to return to Manston in the first place. After the night in Flums, we went on to Venice to stay one night. I was limping about with my bandaged foot, but with four other tourists from South Wales we went into Venice at about 11.30 pm on a service bus. We reached St Mark's Square just as the clock struck midnight. An orchestra was playing to late night visitors in the Square. As our party of six approached the orchestra immediately struck up "Puppet on a String" which had recently won the European Song Contest with Sandy Shaw singing for England. Obviously the orchestra had recognised a party of English tourists! We had to get two taxis back from Venice to our hotel. The drivers declined to take more than four passengers and we were six! A short night's sleep and we were off next day to Trieste where the waiter serving a 'sweet' after the main meal, did so with a fork distributing pineapple slices straight out of the tin! I 'did the best I could' as the surgeon had instructed using the dressing he had provided. Next stop was Zadar for the night where I managed to have a shower with one leg hanging outside the cubicle.

We had a brief stop at the naval town of Split on the way to Dubrovnik. In Split was the palace of the former Roman Emperor, Diocletian, whose mother was a native of Dalmatia. The palace was more of a ruin, with houses built inside. We visited the market place where the natives were busy picking over the mounds of strawberries with their fingers for the best!! Late comers got what was left, all squashed and almost unfit to eat!

Next stop was our destination, Dubrovnik. By this time my ankle was getting painful and looked 'fierce'. We were accompanied by the

Cosmos courier, a different one to the one who had left us at Basle. She decided that I should go to Dubrovnik hospital for treatment. So I spent the next five days having treatment in Dubrovnik hospital! It was very primitive with beds, (mixed sexes) almost touching each other in the ward! The medical staff I saw there immediately changed the dressing from 'wet' to 'dry'. From then on my ankle felt much easier. I was ready to start to enjoy my holiday. We went to Cetinje where the population came out of the church on a Sunday with their distinctive and beautiful white headgear. Then they all danced in the square to a string orchestra. The onlookers, tourists, were invited to join in the dancing. It was all very picturesque. On another day we all went on a tour into Albania visiting the capital Tirano. We were shown a room where Queen Victoria had, reputedly stayed with the then King Zog of Albania! It was a very dirty and untidy town, maybe it was cleaner in Queen Victoria's time. On another day we went in a small boat we hired for the day to a pretty little town called Cavtat where we could bathe in the harbour and view Dubrovnik in the distance. Our boatman slept in his boat all day until we were ready for the return. Dubrovnik was a lovely city, very clean with no traffic. The marble streets and pavements were hosed down every night. Our hotel was outside the town with a tramway system to the gate in the walled city. The tramway was always full with passengers clinging to the outside; a dangerous practice. Our hotel had a large swimming pool that had been used in past years for Olympic contests. Also staying at the hotel was a party of Russian peasants, all female except for two 'gauleiters' (or whatever is the term for Russian taskmasters). The women were on a state holiday as a reward for their good work on a Collective farm. The men referred to Dorothy as "The English Rose". They drank plenty of vodka. On the day of our departure the men toasted us in vodka, so I reciprocated with a glass of English gin, although drinking spirits was not really 'me'.

There were two very quiet ladies among the party going to Dubrovnik. They sat in front of Dorothy and I in the coach. One obviously wore a wig so I, unfortunately nicknamed the two ladies "Wiggy" and "Woggy". I was being very cruel. Fortunately they were unaware of their nicknames. At the hotel Dorothy and I shared a table for four with the two ladies. They were quite easy to converse with. One day "Wiggy" went off, presumably to the 'loo'. She came back smiling, to tell us she had opened a door to find someone already in possession! She said "I know it was a gentleman because he raised his hat". "Wiggy" certainly had a sense of humour!

236

One night our little party of six (the 4 Welsh friends plus Dorothy and I) visited another hotel. There I saw the 'natives' drinking wine which they diluted with a type of mineral water. I found out that the wine was called 'Grk' or something similar. I was to hear of it much later in my career! I tasted the 'Grk'. It was very dry. To me it tasted horrible!

The six of us also visited a night-club held within the walls of the city. The cabaret was excellent given by a party of Serbians, acrobats, singers, etc.. We left Dubrovnik for Sarajevo stopping first at Mostar where we saw the famous bridge with boys ready to dive into the river beneath for coins thrown by tourists. Then on to Sarajevo for the night. We went round the Turkish Quarter to see all the copper and other work in progress. We stood on the bridge where a young Bosnian shot dead the Archduke Franz Ferdinand which precipitated the 1914/19 war, plus the end of the Austro-Hungarian Empire.

We then went on to Zagreb and Llubljana but first visited the marvellous Plitvice Lakes with their numerous waterfalls. This was a National Park. Anything that falls into the water must remain there to become solidified by the action of chemicals in the water. There were thousands of fish swimming in the lakes but they may not be taken by fishermen.

After Yugoslavia which was a grand holiday except for my scalded ankle, it was back to England via Austria, Switzerland and France. My first action was to visit my doctor who immediately told me to go home and take sick leave for a grade 1, 2 or 3 burn. I do not remember what the grade was! I had taken the precaution of securing from the hospital doctor in Dubrovnik, a certificate describing my scalds which he had treated. It was in a language that I did not understand, but it bore stamps showing its authenticity. I was able to produce this to my Department and a copy to Cosmos when negotiations over the injury commenced. But my ankle was far from better. Under Civil Service Regulations, should a Civil Servant suffer injuries due to the action of a 3rd party, he is required to report the circumstances to his department. This I did to the Board of C & E. Meanwhile I consulted my solicitor and made a claim against Cosmos Travel. Cosmos declined to accept responsibility saying it was the fault of the aircraft company. I then made a claim against the English Aircraft Company. They too, declined to accept responsibility on the grounds that it was the fault of the Dutch airline who had failed to ensure that the hot water tanks had been securely fastened before take-off. Suing a Dutch Airline in England presented many problems. My solicitor advised that I press Cosmos. In the end Cosmos offered me a payment of £100 to settle. The facts were reported to the Air Ministry Accident authority. They pointed out that when a cyclist is knocked off his bicycle or when a person is run down on a pedestrian crossing, this has occurred many times and a fair estimate of damages due, is known. But so far as could be traced there was no previous case of a person being scalded on a plane! In any case I was told, I had gone on with the holiday despite my injuries!! In the end my solicitor advised that I accept the payment of £100. I believe they paid his expenses as well but this I did not enquire into. I certainly received no charge from him. But here was the rub!! My Department pressed Cosmos for the full cost of my absence from duty, not only for the time spent on holiday but also for the additional fortnight I had been on sick leave after I returned!! The Department did quite well because my salary for over a month exceeded considerably the £100 paid to me. Dorothy and I decided to take another holiday the next year using the £100 as part payment. But not with Cosmos! We went with Wallace Arnold Coaches and to Portugal.

I was now firmly established in Bearsted and Maidstone although Dorothy and I had kept our connections with the Medway towns especially with Gillingham. There I was a member of Civil Service Motoring Association which I had joined as long ago as 1933. I organised many local rallies for the South Eastern Branch members as well as entering myself a few national ones organised by the Headquarters of the Association with offices just off Lower Regent Street in London. I gained an award in the Reliance Trial held around the Kent-Sussex border near Westerham. I was elected to the HQ's Social Committee of the C.S.M.A. One year I arranged the social activities for the Association at the conclusion of the "Curtis-Bennett" rally for members from all parts of the UK to Llandrindod Wells in mid-Wales. It was quite successful although the competitors arrived very tired after driving hundreds of miles over a gruelling course. I did not continue my membership of the HQ's Social Committee very long because it was taking up too much of my time and I was more than fully busy with Customs and Excise Federation work, with the relevant membership of Departmental Whitley

Committees. I assisted, however, in promoting fresh branches of the C.S.M.A. in Dover, Maidstone and Tunbridge Wells where there were numerous Civil Servants in post. I also was approached to assist in the formation of a Branch of the Civil Service Sports Council in Maidstone. The main movers in this were members of the Prison Officers Association who had secured a small area of ground not too far from the Maidstone prison. The Prison Officers erected a pavilion which became the centre for sporting activities nearby although the ground was too small for major sports. There was tennis and archery but no bowls, cricket or football. The Club House at the Pavilion was, however, the main attraction.

CHAPTER TWENTY SEVEN
Further activities in
Customs and Excise Federation.

I continued to attend many Federation Councils in the main towns of the UK where branches existed. I attended one at Peebles in Scotland at the invitation of Edinburgh Branch, another in London held in the Guildhall by permission of the City of London. London Port Branch sponsored this Council meeting. The Council dinner was held in the Cafe Royal in Regent Street and was a very successful function with members of the Board present. At the meeting held in Peebles I developed an eye infection caused by a germ in the left tearduct. This became so painful that I attended the local hospital. There the Consultant advised that I return home to be seen by my local doctor. I explained that I was at a conference at the Peebles Hydro. So he consented to see me there each day because he attended at the Hydro daily in any case. He did so and injected me with penicillin each morning until the Council and the following Executive meeting were both concluded.

I returned home, going to see my doctor straight away. He was on holiday so I was seen by his 'locum tenens', a lady. She arranged for my immediate admission to Maidstone Ophthalmic Hospital where I was seen by a surgeon, Mr Ormorod. Within a day or so he performed an operation on my left tearduct replacing it with an artificial duct. I had, for years been troubled by tears forming each time I bent down to sow seeds in the garden or to address a golf ball before driving off. There were a number of patients in the ward all with eye problems such as detached retina for which the patient had to lie perfectly still for some days. A Lascar was admitted after suffering an eye injury at Tilbury Dock. He had to be supplied with special food due to his religion. My operation proved successful but, unexpectedly I was recalled to the Ophthalmic Hospital some six weeks later for a similar operation to be carried out on my right tearduct. When this was completed and I was recovering I enquired of the Consultant what was the cause of the abscess in my left tearduct in the first place. The Consultant was surrounded by his 'students'. However, he told me confidentially that the germ involved was most unusual appearing in the eye but was undoubtedly the same germ that had previously caused the abscess when I had to enter the Royal Masonic Hospital some time before for a cure. I have had no further trouble with my tearducts and can now sow seeds or address a golf ball without tears flowing from my eyes.

But, when I was leaving my doctor's surgery in the first place having been seen by his 'locum tenens', she had noticed a sore spot on my forehead. I had told her that it was persistent and would not heal. She said that she would arrange for me to be seen at St William's Hospital at Rochester later. In due course I was sent for and there was told that I had a 'rodent ulcer', a form of skin cancer which would be treated by radiotherapy at the hospital. This the hospital carried out. I was extremely grateful to the 'locums' who had dealt with my eye problem and even more so for observing the 'rodent ulcer' on my forehead. I had not heard of the skin cancer problem. I have had several of these skin cancers since the one treated at Rochester. These have been treated at Rochester and Poole Hospitals. I appear to be particularly susceptible to this problem which I have been told is probably due to sunbathing when much younger. I was very fair when young which I am told rendered me vulnerable to the sun's rays.

One day in my office at Maidstone I received an enquiry from Hawkhurst from a Mr Ray who wished to sell a quantity of wine. I called to see him at a farmhouse in the parish. It was Cyril Ray who was the Wine Correspondent for the Observer Sunday Newspaper. I had read his articles from time to time. He explained that as an expert on wine he often received several bottles of different wines to test and report upon in the press. As a result of these receipts he had built up a stock of wine which he wished to dispose of. I was able to tell him that sale by retail could not be permitted without a Justices' Certificate, but that sales in wholesale quantities would be permitted. He was extremely grateful and said he would sell his 'surplus' stock in wholesale quantities of 2 gallons or more. I took the opportunity to enquire of Cyril Ray whether he had heard of the Yugoslavian wine called 'GrK'. He had and said it was a dry wine quite pleasant to the palate. This was the wine I had seen the natives drinking in the hotel in Dubrovnik. Sometime later Cyril Ray rang me up to say he had secured a supply of 'Grk' for me!! I was sorry about this because I had no use for a supply of 'Grk'! No doubt he was able to include the Grk in his sales by wholesale of his surplus wines.

Following the Customs and Excise Federation Council held at Folkestone I became to all intents and purposes a permanent member of the Executive although an election was held each year among Council delegates. I was again appointed Staff Side Secretary of the Officer Grade Whitley Committee which met the Board's representative quarterly or more often if necessary. As Secretary I had to agree the Minutes of each meeting with the Official Side Secretary. He was a pleasant man and I had no difficulty in agreeing the Minutes with him. I was sorry for him because he had the unfortunate name of Raper. He told me that the name was causing distress to his son at a public school. Eventually he decided to change his name by deed pole to Roper, so from then on the Minutes had to be agreed between Roper and Sheppard!

The Annual Councils continued to be held and I attended one held at Ayre in Scotland at the invitation of Glasgow Branch. The Scottish distillers were most generous with whisky for the Council dinner for the delegates! From Ayre I managed to visit the birthplace of Robert Burns about two miles to the south of the town. It was a clay built cottage, the original of which was blown down in a storm a few days after Burns' birth. Another town for the Council was at Leeds. I had previously visited Leeds to address the Branch. They had afterwards taken me to a village somewhere on the moors for a typical Yorkshire supper. It was "Pie and Mushy Peas"! The Treasurer of the Federation was Ken Pascoe, an Officer in Leeds and who was a close associate and friend of mine on the Federation Executive. He was a real 'Yorkshireman' and devotee of Yorkshire cricket,. He also claimed that an ancestor of his, was Lieutenant Pascoe who hoisted the signal "England Expects etc...." at Admiral Nelson's command before the Battle of Trafalgar commenced. At the Ayre Council where I shared a room with Ken Pascoe, I had a word with the chef at the hotel and arranged quietly with him for Ken to be served with Yorkshire pudding at every meal, breakfast, lunch, and dinner as well as what was on the menu. Ken invariably sang the praises of Yorkshire pudding saying that it should be served first with gravy in Yorkshire fashion before the rest of the meal. Ken took it all in good part and ate the puddings! We are still corresponding although he too, has entered a nursing home, in Leeds.

242

I attended a Federation Council held at Whitley Bay at the invitation of Newcastle Branch. There were the usual discussions on many subjects affecting the conditions under which Officers did their work. But the main consideration eventually turned on finding successors to the offices of General Secretary and Organisation Secretary of the Federation. The two current officials named Haswell and Martin had just been notified by the Board that they had been selected for promotion to Surveyor. The old system of promotion by a rigorous written examination on revenue law and practice had been abandoned. In its place was substituted an interview of Officers in the appropriate age group who applied to attend. This system was not favoured by many since it could lead to favouritism by Collectors and others in their reports to the interviewing panel. Despite objections, the new interviewing system was adopted. The former examination for Surveyorship was abandoned after many years, which had been above suspicion as a method of promotion. The Council had to decide on appointing two new Officials. No obvious younger members of the Executive Committee were available. In the end it was decided to ask Ted Buckingham who was the Staff Side Secretary of the Departmental Whitley Committee and as such had an office at King's Bean House, the HQ of C & E Department, to accept nomination as General Secretary of the Federation. I was asked to become Organising Secretary, in addition to being Units Secretary. Normally the post of Organising Secretary involved frequent attendance at Federation HQ's so that the appointment to a Station near London was a prerequisite for this post. I had no intention of leaving my Maidstone Station. I took the step of telephoning the Chief Inspector whom I knew very well. He was another ex-dockyard apprentice from Portsmouth and a year junior to me. He told me that if I accepted he would allow assistance to be given to me at Maidstone for all time involved. On this basis I agreed nomination and with Ted Buckingham, we were duly elected by the Council. It was really a case of enlisting and using the experience of two older Officers to fill the gap created by the promotion of two younger Federation officials. Ted Buckingham who was a year junior to me and was another ex-dockyard apprentice, from Plymouth remained in post until he retired at 65 by which time the Federation had amalgamated with the larger Civil Service Union. The Federation had by then ceased to exist as an Association solely in the C & E Department. I remained in post as Organising Secretary until I was age 61 but remained an Executive member for a further year. When I finally retired from the Department a year later in 1969.

CHAPTER TWENTY EIGHT
Activities in Maidstone.

In Bearsted I became a member of the local history society which held its meetings in the King George V Memorial Hall immediately opposite "Orchard Gate", but the Committee meetings were held at the Secretary's residence near the railway station. I became a member of the committee but did not take a great deal of interest in the ordinary discussions. I preferred to listen to Dr Felix Hull who was a member living in Bearsted. He was the Kent Archivist and very knowledgeable on Kent history. I was particularly interested in the Roman roads that crossed Kent. I traced the road that ran south from Rochester towards Hastings meeting up with the road from Lympne above Romney Marsh to meet the Rochester - Hastings road at Benenden, almost in the grounds of Benenden School. Lower Stone Street in Maidstone is a reminder of this road.

I was asked to give a talk to Maidstone Rotary Club on the subject of H M Customs and Excise in the Star Hotel at Maidstone. The Collector also asked me to give a talk to the Nurses Association, in Ashford, on the history of Customs and Excise and another to the Police Federation, similarly. This involved a deal of research taking up my time. I could not refuse so carried them out to the best of my ability. I was also asked by John Bridge, FSA a member of the Kent "Archaeolgia Cantiana" to assist him in the compilation of a description of "Maidstone Geneva, an Old Maidstone Industry" by giving an explanation of "proof spirit". I did this as follows:-

"The origin of Proof Spirit goes back to the Middle Ages, when Proof Spirit was that mixture of pure alcohol and water, which when mixed with gunpowder, burned with a steady flame, and did not either explode, which was overproof, or

244

extinguish, which was underproof. In turn, Excise Officers, first a Mr Clarke in the middle of the eighteenth century, and then a Mr Sikes in 1816 invented an instrument, which by means of tables, could be more scientific than the "Gunpowder Test". Both, however, used as Proof what was thought to be Proof at the time and as a result of this the original test was used.

Proof spirit is defined as such spirit as at the temperature of 51° Fahrenheit shall weigh twelve thirteenths of an equal measure of distilled water. Application of this definition shows that Spirit of Proof strength contains very nearly equal weights of pure alcohol and water.

The proportions required to give Proof spirit are:

By weight   Pure alcohol   49.28)
             Water   50.72) at 60° Fahrenheit

By volume the figures are pure alcohol 57.1 and water 46.7.

Owing to the contraction in bulk, accompanied by a rise in temperature which takes place on mixing, these figures for volume will give 100. Addition or reduction of the amounts of water as given above will give a mixture termed Under Proof or Over Proof, respectively. Thus 30 under proof means that 100 volumes contains 70 volumes of the proof spirit as defined by law. Thirty over proof means that 100 volumes of the 30 over proof liquid contain enough pure alcohol to make by the addition of more water, a quantity of 130 volumes of proof spirit. In practice, the quantity of proof spirit in any mixture of pure alcohol and water is ascertained by the hydrometer invented by Mr Sikes referred to, using specific gravity tables in conjunction with the temperature of the mixture. It is on the proof spirit that all Customs and Excise duties are based. It is interesting to see that the normal gin and whisky sold today at 70 proof contains more water than pure alcohol."

My definition obtained from official sources was duly printed.

I was nominated by my Collector, Mr Raymond for the post of Press and Information Officer for the Department. I attended for interview but I was not selected. The post went to another official, a Surveyor, who was the Editor of the Catholic Herald. I was not unduly disappointed since the appointment would have involved me in leaving my Station in Maidstone to travel daily to Customs HQs in London. I had received, as one of only two Officers in the Collection, the Coronation Medal, awarded to mark the occasion of the Queen Elizabeth's Coronation.

One evening at home I received a telephone call, the caller not indicating who he was. He asked that if I was offered the award of the MBE in the forthcoming Queen's Birthday Honours, would I accept it? I had no hesitation in saying "Yes". The caller rang off after telling me not to discuss the matter with anybody. I told Dorothy! When the Queen's Birthday Honours list was published in June 1964 my name was included. In November 1964 I received the notice to attend at Buckingham Palace. I was allowed to take two guests to watch the ceremony in the Palace. There was, however, an indication that an additional guest could be allowed in special circumstances, so I applied for permission to bring my two sons and my wife. This was accepted and so Colin and Brian with Dorothy were admitted to Buckingham Palace. I wore full morning dress. It was a very impressive ceremony attending for Her Majesty to pin the medal as a Member of the Most Excellent Order of the British Empire on my chest. Dorothy, Colin and Brian watched from the gallery inside the Palace. A military band played suitable music. By a strange quirk of fate, my daughter-in-law, Elizabeth, Colin's wife's father who was an Air Force Officer received the same award on the same day. Though we did not know this at the time. He had been divorced by Elizabeth's mother. My parents together with June, Brian's wife and Elizabeth, all travelled to London to see us emerge from the Palace after the ceremony. Also Laurie Latter, our friend, the hop factor, took us all to his flat for lunch. Afterwards we all went to dinner at a restaurant in the West End before going to see the play Kismet, at a theatre, I believe it was the Dominion. Altogether a most memorable day. The local press duly reported the award. I received many congratulatory messages and letters from the Board, the Chief Inspector of HM Customs, from the Chancellor of the Exchequer, the Chief Secretary to the Treasury, my Collector in Dover and so many more. From then on I was entitled to put the letters MBE after my name but I very seldom did so. I was the only Officer that year to receive the award, although others, of higher rank received OBE's, CBE's and CB's etc.. plus Imperial Service Orders. No-one in my office, except the assisting UO, took any interest!! But the UO contacted the local press to say that H.A.B. now had an M.B.E. to add to his name and a congratulatory announcement appeared in the local press, The Kent Messenger.

Author and Wife, Dorothy at Buckingham Palace,
November 1964 when awarded the M.B.E.

Dorothy and I went down a few times to St Margaret's Bay to stay with Mr & Mrs Raymond. They had a beautiful house on the top of the cliff overlooking Dover. He said, in a joke, that with his telescope he could see whether the staff in Dover were working!! He was then offered promotion to Higher Collector, Southampton. I had provided him with a hop plant for his garden at St Margaret's Bay. When he moved to a nice house at Bassett on the outskirts of Southampton he wanted another hop plant for his garden there. I was able to supply him again with a hop plant from one of the many hop growers in my Maidstone Station. Dorothy and I went occasionally to stay with Mr & Mrs Raymond at Bassett, Southampton.

CHAPTER TWENTY NINE
Further Federation Activities.

In 1966 I had as Organising Secretary, to visit Northern Ireland mainly to go to Newcastle, County Down, (where the Mountains of Morne roll down to the sea) to agree with the local Federation Branch, Belfast, on the suitability of the hotel for the delegates and the venue for the forthcoming Council meeting, the first that had been held in Northern Ireland. Also to visit Londonderry to address the Branch there. For this visit I had to fly from Heathrow to Belfast airport. At my own expense I took Dorothy with me to see Northern Ireland. We boarded the plane to find we were sitting behind Michael Miles and his secretary. We learned that he too was going to Derry for a TV Show, "Take Your Pick". As the Vanguard aircraft was taxi-ing for take-off the aircraft began to fill with smoke. I wrongly imagined this was due to exhaust from the engines being sucked into the plane. But the smoke was due to an engine being on fire. All the passengers had to make a hurried exit from the plane. As we stood on the runway, up rushed two fire engines and several ambulances, fortunately not needed! Next down the exit came stewardesses carrying briefcases etc., all left behind by the passengers in their hurried exit. Among the other passengers were two MPs McMaster and Clark, as well as a Short's aircraft chief. We were all taken back by coach to the airport lounge and told we could have refreshments free from the servery. So we all lined up! Michael Miles preferred liquid refreshment as did his secretary! The passenger, one ahead of me chose a whole range of food, only to be told at the check-out that this would cost him over three pounds. He remonstrated but was told that the limit for refreshments to be supplied to the aircraft passengers was three shillings and eight pence. He put all he had chosen, back! Dorothy and I were not very interested in eating and had a cup of tea. This was Dorothy's second experience of flying. This, after our earlier disastrous flight to Basle, en route to Dubrovnik!! We duly arrived at Belfast airport to be met by reporters anxious to have a story for the evening paper. This duly came out. Colin and Brian conferred and came to the conclusion that their mother would not have agreed to board another plane should she be one of the passengers on the faulty 'take-off' plane. But she did. Fortunately there was a car waiting to take us on to Derry from Belfast. I had hoped to be able to make a short detour to see the Giant's Causeway in Antrim. Time did not permit due to the delay at Heathrow. I reached my destination and presume that Michael Miles did too. Dorothy was taken off by wives of Officers attending my meeting. When this was concluded I joined her to attend a 'ceilidh' in one of the Derry Officer's house. It was quite a gathering. The Irish certainly knew how to make their own entertainment.

The next day we went back to Belfast to stay overnight with 'Ske' Martin, another member of the Executive Committee, (a bachelor) and his mother. We then went on to Newcastle, County Down, this time with Joe McReynolds another member of the Executive. All was satisfactory at Newcastle. Dorothy and I then went on to Armagh to stay the night at a hotel. McReynolds was an Officer there. His wife was the niece of De Valera, the Eire Leader. The hotel was very ill organised. No breakfast arrived. I went down into the basement to find it empty. It had been arranged by McReynolds for Dorothy and I to go by observation train to Dublin from Portadown. Eventually a hotel employee arrived on her bicycle. When I explained that we were due to catch a train at Portadown, she simply said "There'll be ane'ather"!! She boiled two eggs and with that we left. McReynolds picked us up in his car and we made for Portadown to find the railway staff there watching television! The train was due in but nobody seemed to be worrying! For our reception in Londonderry, full marks, but for Armagh and Portadown, maybe one out of ten!! Probably that's Ireland.

We reached Dublin having travelled in the Observation carriage enjoying the scenery. Mrs McReynolds met us to say she had secured tickets for us "for the match". What the "match" was we had no idea, but it turned out to be a Rugby International, Wales versus Ireland. We had seats in a very smart stand. With a match between Wales and Ireland I was in a quandary which side to cheer. My daughter-in-law was Welsh but we were guests of the Irish! So I kept quiet. Not so Mrs McReynolds. Her language when Wales secured the ball defies description. Who won? I simply do not know. Rugby football is a mystery to me!

Dorothy and I had two days in Dublin looking around and then departed for Belfast Airport and Heathrow. It had been a visit full of incidents including the aircraft engine on fire at Heathrow, the 'ceilidh' in Londonderry and the "Irishness" of the staff in Armagh and Portadown. But the facilities at Newcastle, County Down had been inspected and approved. And we had attended a Rugby International!

In due course the Council meeting in Newcastle was imminent and with it a fresh set of problems. A railway strike was declared and with it no ferry services to Ireland. I had to arrange for all the delegates from various towns in England and Scotland to be transported to Belfast by air. Two from Cardiff, one from Swansea, three from Bristol, six from Liverpool, five from Glasgow, etc.., etc.., etc.. About 60 delegates plus 12 Executive members and the back-up staff from London. The Federation telephone bill must have been enormous. But I got them all there by a fleet of Officers' cars at Belfast for the journey to Newcastle. Many delegates had booked their cars in advance hoping to use the visit to Newcastle as a start to a tour of Ireland, some with their wives and families, by car. Northern Ireland had never before staged a Council meeting. That wasn't the end of my problems. The Irish bank staff also went on strike, so arrangements had to be made for cash to be taken from England by the Federation Treasurer to re-imburse all the delegates for their expenses. Troubles sometimes come in threes, but mine came in just two! But that was sufficient!

After the Newcastle, County Down Council which pursued the normal course with deliberations on various subjects involving the Officer Grade, all the delegates were taken over the border into Eire to the town of Dundalk for the proverbial Council dinner and entertainment. This was given by artists, all from Eire except for Joe McReynolds who had an excellent voice. The highlight of the entertainment was by a troop of 'line' dancers displaying skills equal to those now being shown in London theatres. This was over 25 years ago! It has taken all that time for the skills of girls dancing in unison with their hands by their sides to become appreciated by English audiences! It was really a magnificent entertainment by singers and dancers and appreciated by all the delegates. At the conclusion of the Newcastle, County Down Council and the subsequent meeting of the Executive Committee, I took a train to Dublin, staying at the same hotel where I had stayed with Dorothy when we attended the 'match' with Joe and Mrs McReynolds earlier that year. I then hired a car and made a quick visit to Killarney to view the "Lakes and Dales" of the famous song. I witnessed a Roman Catholic procession from the church there; made a circuit of Kerry and returned to Dublin Airport via Limerick. I had not the time to visit Cork or to kiss the Blarney Stone! I did meet, however, a band of travelling gypsies, en route, who displayed some of the poverty then, of Eire. I had now seen both Northern and Southern Ireland.

The new Collector at Dover was a Mr Crellin, a Manxman. He too was very friendly. He came to our house with his wife for the parties we sometimes had there. We visited him at his house on the main road just below Dover Castle. Also I was very friendly with the Assistant Collector 'Bill' Thelfall whom I had known as an Unattached Surveyor, playing golf with him at Bearsted Golf Club where I was a member, but I was not a very good player!

In the Civil Service there is always one day in the year allowed as a holiday to celebrate the Queen's birthday. Most Government Departments worked a 5-day week. The Customs and Excise staff, however, was at that time still working a 6 day week, in the belief of supplying full service to the public! In my Maidstone Station I always attended on Saturday mornings to deal with Probate cases. For the Queen's Birthday, annually, the statutory 'day off' in the C & E Department was taken on a Saturday. In Dover Collection this had been regularly used to stage a golf tournament for all grades, on various golf courses in Kent. The favourite course was at Lord Harris's estate outside of Faversham although we also played on other courses, Bearsted, North Forland and Ashford etc.. As Secretary of the Dover Branch of the Federation, I had the task of organising the matches including a mid-day lunch. Mr Usher, the Officer for Deal whom I had met when officiating at Ash Station was possibly the best golfer. The Preventive staff was included, plus Surveyors and clerical staff.

In Dover, as Vice Chairman of the Whitley Committee and Chairman of the Staff Side I had the problem from the Waterguard staff of dealing with fumes in the examination sheds from cars en route to, but more particularly from those on returning Cross Channel ferries. The cars for examination were the responsibility of

251

the Landing Officers, being cargo. The contents, however came under the scrutiny of the Waterguard, especially the contents of suit-cases and other baggage. In addition to the fumes from cars which continued to emit exhaust when engines were kept running, during the winter months, the examination sheds were bitterly cold. For the fumes, I agreed with the Collector to have a medical check on specific staff employed for several hours in the examination sheds. Blood samples were taken before a spell of duty and again at the end, to check the 'fume' content. It proved abortive, in fact the blood samples taken were found to be more congested prior than after being in the shed for some hours! There was no answer to the problem except to have massive fans blowing warm air through the examination sheds which necessarily had to remain open so to dispel the fumes and, at the same time keep the staff warm. On the basis of the medical evidence there was little more that could be done other than to accept the solution of warm air being blown through the examination sheds.

CHAPTER THIRTY
Car problems.

I made further visits for the purpose of agreeing accommodation for Council and Executive meetings. One was to Llandudno at the invitation of Chester Branch. Also one to Liverpool. For the Council meeting I agreed with a new Secretary named George Burn who had recently been elected and whose home was then in Northumberland from where he was awaiting transfer to London to take up his appointment, to take all the Federation documents required for our meeting with me to Liverpool in his car but afterwards, when our meetings were concluded to return them in the car of my colleague, Leslie Sims, Officer at Gillingham, who was coming up to Liverpool with his wife and with Dorothy for a tour of North Wales. After their tour they would come to Liverpool to collect me and all the Federation documents so that I could call at the Federation Offices in Great Ormond Street, London. It seemed at the time to be a simple solution getting documents from London to Liverpool and back again. But like all simple solutions, they can go awry! Les and Gladys Sims with Dorothy had their tour of North Wales and returned via the Birkenhead to Liverpool tunnel. Leslie's car had a dispute with a Jaguar car at the entrance to the tunnel! As a result it had to be taken to a nearby garage for attention. The front offside wheel had been damaged. The garage said they were unable to attend to it for several days. The 'three travellers' came on to me by taxi! Les Sims was more or less prostrate and I had to bribe my hotel proprietor to allow him to rest in the room I had vacated while I went by taxi to Birkenhead to see the garage people where Leslie Sims had left his car. I saw the foreman and with the aid of a "suitable Treasury Note" persuaded him to effect temporary repairs to the car. The car brakes were 'hors de combat' so I drove the car over to Liverpool using the gears for slowing down! Leslie had recovered sufficiently so in due course when evening arrived and traffic subdued, I collected the Council documents and we set out to drive via London to Maidstone! Dorothy sat with me in the front while Leslie and Gladys relaxed on the back seats! Fortunately I knew the route from my days in Liverpool so went by the less busy road via Chester, Newport, Salop etc., down to London. It was quite late when we reached the Edgware Road. I approached all traffic lights with great care slowing down on the gears, yards before necessary. We reached Great Ormond Street in the early hours of the morning, deposited the Council documents and then set off for the last stage of our journey to Maidstone. We waited at home until Roots' Garage, the home of Leslie's Hillman car, to open. I drove there. The garage foreman looked at the car in amazement. He touched the off side wheel and it dropped off!! So ended an epic journey! Liverpool to Maidstone without brakes! In the dark!

My father also had a Hillman car. He went with my mother and two friends from the Civil Service Bowls Club, on holiday to Torquay. There, he too had an accident when another car came out of a side turning on his off side where my mother was sitting, and ran into his car. The damage was not too severe and the party reached home. Fortunately I had a car damage repair firm at Charing in my Station. My father was more concerned with the shock to my mother than he was about his damaged car. For a modest sum I had his car repaired so it was impossible to see where the damage had occurred. So another satisfied customer, my father.

From Colin, however, I 'inherited' a much more difficult car problem. I had bought him a second hand Hillman car when he was at Leicester University. With his colleague at the University, David Moscow, who later became his partner in business, they went to a hockey match for Leicester University. On the return to Leicester, he overturned his car into a ditch near Kettering. He managed to get the car to a public car park in Kettering where he left it! I did not hear about this for some weeks. With Brian who was still at King's School, we went to Kettering and found the car in the car park. I had taught Brian to drive a car, but Colin's car would not start. I had taken towing ropes with me so I decided to try to tow Colin's car back to Maidstone. Colin's car had no lights working but I had a torch. Brian and I took turns in driving my car towing Colin's car with the non-driver steering Colin's car. Also with the torch showing out of the rear window when necessary. It was another epic drive but this was before my drive from Liverpool to Maidstone. In the dark we made for the A5 road via Northampton meeting up with it at Towcester. From there I knew the road well via London and over Vauxhall Bridge past the Oval Cricket Ground and on to the A2 road over Blackheath. Thanks be to the Romans for building such straight highways!! When I eventually took Colin's car to the repairer at Charing near Ashford, the verdict was that it was too far gone to be repaired. I received £30 for the parts as scrap. I might as well left it in Kettering!

One more story needs to be told about cars, although I was not personally involved. My father regularly took my mother to her bowls matches for the Civil Service Club of which she was President, or to Kent County matches for which she was a selector for the team. Father was taking her to a match at Gravesend. Outside of Rochester road repairs were being carried out including 'tarring' of the road surfaces. He was 'busy' looking at the work going on and failed to notice that the car ahead had stopped. He ran into it but did little damage. In the normal course of events the matter could have been dealt with by ordinary exchange of insurance details. But the other driver was a driving instructor, although not instructing at the time of the collision. He insisted on calling for the police to take details. As a result my father was summoned for "driving without due care and attention". Not a very heinous offence. He was irate and wanted to attend the court to contest the charge. I counselled him to contact the AA of which he was a member, to appear on his behalf, to plead guilty and accept the nominal fine that would be imposed. But he was adamant. In the end, however, he accepted my advice. He was anxious not to be thought to be a poor driver by the members of the Civil Service Womens' Bowls Club, many of whom he took to matches from time to time. Eventually the case was reported in the local press. But it was that a Mr Sheppard age 17 had been charged and fined. My father's age was 77 and by a misprint the incorrect age had been published. Some of the lady bowlers mentioned to my parents that they had seen the report of one of their grandchildren (my sister had 3 sons, one about the age of 17) had been fined at Chatham Police Court. They did not disabuse the lady bowlers, so father was not found guilty in the eyes of the lady bowlers!!

CHAPTER THIRTY ONE
Colin's and Brian's progress.

While at the oil refinery at Grain, Brian besides being the Development Chemist after promotion from Works Chemist, was anxious to acquire other qualifications useful to BP. He therefore attended a course in Management at the Medway Technical College. This was an evening course and covered all aspects of Management. At the time, I too was free for evening studies, so I attended with him. At the end of the course, an exam was held but I was unable to take it because I was away at the time attending a Federation Council. Brian, however took the exam and was so successful that the College authority asked BP if he could have day release to attend a full-time course at the College. This was granted so Brian commenced full-time study for the award of a Diploma in Management. At the conclusion of the course another examination was held. Brian was successful and was declared "Student of the Year" receiving the monetary prize that went with it. At the subsequent Dinner that was held to present the award he was granted immediate membership of the Institute of Management. The next development was that BP transferred him back to the Research Station at Sunbury as Personnel Officer. Brian and June sold the house they had bought from BP at High Halstow and purchased one at Ottershaw, Surrey, convenient for working at Sunbury. At Sunbury they were both able to join the various activities available there, badminton, tennis and golf. June was an excellent sportswoman and quickly made the BP teams. Brian too enjoyed his spell at Sunbury as a Personnel Officer. Among other duties there he was directed to deal with the closing of a BP Sub-office near Leatherhead and the accompanying dispersal of the staff.

After a period at Sunbury, Brian was appointed to take charge of the oil pipe lines into Sullom Voe terminal in the Shetland Islands, from the oil rigs off the north coast of Scotland. He went regularly from Northolt aerodrome to Aberdeen then on by a smaller plane to Sullom Voe. From there as necessary out to an oil rig by helicopter. He was there when the Queen formally opened the oil terminal, although it had been operating before her visit for some time. He was in charge of the pipe lines for over two years before being transferred back to BP Headquarters at Britannic House in the City as Personnel Manager. He had sold his house at Ottershaw and purchased a very fine property standing in two acres close to Worplesdon Railway Station , very convenient for attendance in London. He remained in this position at British Petroleum until he retired voluntarily at age 50. He did, however, after retirement take on a few private consultancies in Management for firms such as Nestle. For BP he visited the Far East to Bangkok. Since retiring, with June he has had a tour of Australia and New Zealand as well as to the USA and to the Caribbean, the Canadian Rockies and the Continent. He and June still join in sporting activities arranged from Sunbury, June being a member of the BP Badminton team. She has won several cups at golf and is at present the Captain of the Worplesdon Ladies Golf Club, a position once filled by Joyce Wetherhead, the celebrated golfer. Brian is a member of the Chobham Golf Club where most of his friends play but he often plays at Worplesdon with June.

My two grandchildren attended school in Worplesdon. Both went to Universities. Adrian, first to his father's old University at Swansea, where he graduated in geology. He then went on to the Imperial College, London and obtained a Master's degree. He is now employed by the Post Office. He married another geology graduate from Swansea who is now employed by the River Board. They live at Egham, Surrey. My grand-daughter obtained her degree at Portsmouth in Sociology and computer studies. She obtained a Master's degree from London and is now employed by the BBC. She has a flat at Putney.

Both my grandchildren separately went on "back packing" tours of Australia after their first graduations from University before they started on their University courses for their Master degrees. Both started in the south and went north to Queensland. In the case of grandson Adrian he also went to the Fiji Islands. So far as I am aware he found there no one named Barnabas!! He did not think much of the Fijis as a holiday spot.

Colin meanwhile, decided to resign from his position as Head of Department at the North West Polytechnic and to set up his own business as a Management Consultant. In this venture he was joined by David Moscow his former colleague at Leicester who had obtained a Ph.D. from Leicester University and had been seconded to the Dutch Government. The secondment being completed, with Colin they formed the Company of Sheppard, Moscow and Associates, recruiting staff from his former contacts at the NW Polytechnic. He purchased a house at Eltham in South East London, converted the roof space to offices and went into business with David Moscow. The business prospered so well that they formed it into a limited company with the title of Sheppard, Moscow and Associates Limited. Their clients were most of the large firms in England with some in the USA and on the Continent of Europe. Fords, Shell, Hewlett Packard and others. They were recognised as among the leaders as Management Consultants.

The office was then transferred to more commodious premises at Lee Green near Lewisham when the Company went Limited Colin purchased a house in Yester Park, Chislehurst, Kent. He also purchased a second holiday house at West Runton near Cromer, Norfolk, near to Sherringham. This was a much larger property with a nice garden, a greenhouse and a bowls green.

Dorothy and I had several holidays there after I retired from HM Customs and Excise. On one occasion we went with her brother John and his wife Dorothy. On another with two friends from Poole in Dorset after I had attended a Council meeting of the Civil Service Retirement Fellowship at Churchill College in Cambridge, when I was the delegate from Bournemouth Branch.

CHAPTER THIRTY TWO
Final Federation activities.

While still a member of the Customs and Excise Federation I had proposed that the relief arrangements for Officers in groups could be simplified by allowing two or more Officers to officiate for each other for holidays, with a reduction in their overall units to compensate for the additional work each would be required to carry out. This suggestion would break the long held conception of an Officer being solely responsible for the total work in his Station. It would, however, relieve the Collector of the responsibility of sending relief staff during an Officer's absence on holiday. In the case where there were several officers in one building it could result in an additional Officer becoming 'fixed' instead of being a "Fixed Officiator" who would eventually have to move to take a Fixed Station elsewhere. The suggestion had both merits and objections but was accepted by the Board via the Whitley Committee. In Maidstone, it resulted in the appointment of a sixth Fixed Officer to cover the scheme of inter-Station relief for leave, as well as allowing each of two Officers to take their holidays by mutual agreement instead of having to adhere to the 'age old' system of choices in the order 1, 4, 7, 2, 5, 3, 6.

The time for my retirement from the C & E was approaching. I had fully decided that I would retire on my 60th birthday when I would have completed 37½ years in Customs and Excise. This with the half-time I was entitled to for the 5 years as an apprentice under the Admiralty in Chatham Dockyard, completed the required 40 years as a Civil Servant entitled to a pension at half my salary for my final years. Shortly before this, however, the Board brought in a scheme for "Allowanced Officers" in each area of appointment. He would receive an 'allowance' of £200 per year for acting as Deputy Surveyor in the absence of the Surveyor. This sum is now trivial by today's rates of pay, but in 1965 it meant for me an extra

£100 additional to my retirement pension. As Dorothy would also get an addition to the one-third rate of my pension in the event of my death, it was advantageous for me to remain in the Service until 1969 when I would have completed 3 extra years as an Allowanced Officer. I was duly appointed to the new rank. I did not find the duties of being the Deputy Surveyor very onerous and in any case it was only for a small portion of the year.

I attended my last Federation Council as Organising Secretary at Pitlochry. I had previously visited Elgin near to the birthplace of Ramsey MacDonald. At Elgin I addressed a joint meeting of Inverness and Elgin Branches of the Federation. I was taken by car from Aberdeen through the Spey Valley, the site of many Speyside distilleries. But we did not stop! For the pre-Council meeting to be held in Pitlochry Dorothy accompanied me. We stayed with Eddie Hunter, a member of the Executive, at Tayport on the other side of the River Tay from Dundee where Eddie was an Officer. The facilities at Pitlochry were ideal, with a hall for the meeting of the Council in the Atholl Place Hotel. Afterwards with Eddie Hunter and Doris, his wife, we went to a social function of a dance in Perth. Doris was employed in the laboratories of St. Andrews University. We paid a visit to St. Andrews town which was very interesting although no time to play golf! It was a most enjoyable 'last pre Council visit' for me. The Council was duly held with the discussions, as usual on all manner of subjects affecting the Officer Grade. At the conclusion I was presented with a portable typewriter by the delegates. Possibly in recognition of my atrocious handwriting? When I finally left Pitlochry to catch my train back to London and Maidstone, I was "piped" to the railway station by a lone piper, playing "Will ye no' come back again". It was rather a sad moment for me. The next Council was held at Richmond at the invitation of London West Branch. As I was still a member of the Executive, I attended but took little part in the discussions. This was my final attendance at a Federation Council. For my remaining years I became an ordinary member. I had completed my service to the Customs and Excise Federation spread over nearly 40 years. I also resigned my offices as Secretary of the Officer Grade Committee and of the Outdoor Service Sectional Committee of the Departmental Whitley Council.

I was, however, invited to serve on a joint committee of all grades in the Department that was considering in advance, the arrangements for the introduction of the Value Added Tax, to replace Purchase Tax, which would be far more comprehensive in taxing the public. I had had the earlier discussions with the Head of the Waterguard Service who wanted to transfer the examination and control of a motor car which ranked as cargo, from the Officer Grade to the Waterguard dealing with the baggage carried in the car. In effect, two different officials were dealing with a motor car and its contents. Since by law the car was cargo I could not accept on behalf of the Outdoor Service, that clearance of a motor car should be undertaken by the Waterguard. In the end, however, the matter was solved when the Outdoor Service was amalgamated with the Waterguard for the purpose of dealing with the revenue control of the Value Added Tax. One of the problems facing the Waterguard after the end of the war was that with the vast increase in tourism abroad, with the consequential return of the tourists, a greatly increased staff was required at ports such as Dover and Harwich. This additional Waterguard staff had to be brought in from other places with consequential additional cost for subsistence and disturbance, plus, of course, the interruption of the staffs' domestic life. The introduction of VAT plus the amalgamation of the Outdoor Service with the Waterguard, helped to solve the problem because staff could be employed on 'tourism' during the heavy summer period, and on VAT at other times. By the time all this occurred I was no longer involved, other than being myself a tourist!!

CHAPTER THIRTY THREE
Further journeys abroad.

Dorothy and I duly made our trip to Portugal with Wallace Arnold, using as part of the cost, the £100 received from Cosmos for the injuries received on our visit to Dubrovnik in Yugoslavia. We went to Northern Spain by coach through France to San Sebastian. On then to Burgos with its magnificent cathedral. Next to the ancient town of Salamanca, after Valladolid. Next across the border into Portugal at the hill town of Guarda. We finally reached the sea again and our hotel at the small fishing town of   We visited Lisbon and Oporto where we were 'entertained' in the cellars of the port merchants! We visited a very small fishing village where the women-folk sat crocheting all day long sitting on their doorsteps. The men hauled their fishing boats ashore with the aid of a team of bullocks. Small, indeed, very tiny fish, were leaping about in the boats, presum-ably to become whitebait in a London restaurant! Above on the cliff top was a shrine to the Virgin Mary where three small children are reputed to have witnessed her re-appearance on earth. A chapel marked the spot of the "vision". Dorothy and I visited the local dance hall in Figueira da Foz. The next night others in the party wanted us to go again this time with them. The dance hall was over the casino in the basement but we did not descend to try our luck! Another evening, we found a disco in progress but the dancing there was not exactly our style! The return was via the same route. We spent one night at Poitiers, the site of famous battles of the past; of Charles Martel over the Saracens in 732 checking the spread of the Moslems from Spain, later by the English over the French in 1346. All we heard was the din from lorry drivers coming and going. The restaurant was their favourite stopping place. We got very little rest that night. We returned home via Le Mans where our driver did a circuit of the famous race track, just to let us be able to say we had driven at Le Mans!

262

We went again to Yugoslavia with Wallace Arnold. This time to Opatija in the Istrian peninsula. We made friends with a party from Wales that included a nephew of Lord ElwynJones, the Labour Lord Chancellor. Opatija was a very small resort but we were able to visit the more popular resorts of Pula and Porec on the other side of the peninsula. There were memorials to the native population who had lost their lives opposing the German occupation forces during the war. These memorials showed the only weapons they had, just agricultural implements and tools. We also visited the Island of Krk, one of the thousand or so that extend down the Dalmation coast. A grand barbecue was arranged for our party visiting the island. Our friend from Wales who was also named ElwynJones came from Llanelli where he worked for the Admiralty. He lived with his brother and sister-in-law. Some years later after we had moved to Poole in Dorset, Dorothy and I were attending a show in the Pavilion Theatre in Bournemouth when we found ourselves sitting in the next seat to ElwynJones! He was on a holiday by himself and was glad to see us again. He told us that he regularly visited Bournemouth on holiday. Thereafter he came to see us at our apartment every year. He always brought with him, a pound of real Welsh butter as a present from Wales!! He was so glad to have found somebody to converse with during his solo holiday!

We also had a short holiday in Paris, staying at a comfortable hotel in the Montmartre area. We climbed the many steps to the Plas de Tertaire and the white church of the Sacré Coeur. There we saw the 'artists' with their brushes and palettes at work, which makes this one of the sights of Paris and a popular venue for tourists. One artist wanted Dorothy to 'sit' for him, but she suggested that he should "do" a portrait of me! He countered by saying that his sister who was drawing on the next position, should draw me while he 'did' Dorothy! So eventually we finished with two excellent drawings in black and white to bring home to have framed. They were about 15 inches by 10 inches and very good likenesses. They were hung in our hall in Poole as mementoes of a trip to Paris. We also went up the Eiffel Tower but not to the very top! There was a grand view of Paris from where we stood. We also walked up the Champs Elysees to the Arc de Triumphe. We also attended the theatre show at the Lido which was so crowded that when a spectator near us fainted, he had to be carried out over the heads of the rest of the audience. It was an excellent show. The 'ladies' almost in the nude stood still! I wonder if the bare bosoms caused him to faint!

We had let Phillipe de Montrichard, the young man we had had to stay with us some years earlier, know that we were visiting Paris. He was now the Count de Montrichard and a diplomat, as had been his father. He was awaiting his enrolment in the armed services to do his period in the army. He called at our hotel with his wife and took us to a very smart restaurant in the Champs Elysees for a fabulous meal. Afterwards we went to his apartment in the best residential part of Paris before returning to our hotel. Altogether a very lovely evening out with an expert on Paris! Phillipe kept in touch with us for many years. On one occasion when Brian went on a trip to the South of France after graduating, with two others of his period at Swansea University, they called at the Chateau de la Chasseigne, at Nievre, in France, and were all well received by Phillipe and his mother, staying overnight. The last we heard of Phillipe was when having completed his national service in the French army, he came occasionally to England to attend horticultural and farming shows to judge Charolais cattle, of which he had become an expert.

Home again we went to see the show, "Fiddler on the Roof" in London. Topol the star had gone to Israeli war but his replacement was very good. I think it was Alfie Bass. On our return to Maidstone by train, Dorothy fell over a paving stone breaking her arm, so had to go to hospital. We then went to the Isle of Wight on holiday, Dorothy having her arm in a sling! We took our car so were able to travel around to see the many attractions. The next year we went again but this time took my parents. We stayed at Sandown and again travelled to see the 'sights'. Strangely my parents did not enjoy the holiday, thinking they had 'gone abroad' when they crossed from Portsmouth to Ryde! But my mother watching a bowls match at Ryde was quick to point out the 'faults' of the competitors! At a visit to the theatre at Sandown my parents won a prize of a suitcase, for being the oldest couple in the audience!

Dorothy and I went next on a coach tour holiday to Scandinavia via Belgium, Holland and Germany to Denmark. In Holland we stayed at Arnhem where we met the parents of the Dutch girl we had had to stay with us and who did not want to return home when she found she was missing having three boys for company, Colin, Brian and Phillipe! The girl was now engaged on relief work in Eastern Europe. Her parents when they met us, took us on a trip on the River Rhine in a motor boat that they had for holidays. We also visited the sites of the many graves of our soldiers lost in the abortive attempt to secure the river crossing at Arnhem during the war. Next into Germany where we stayed a night in Hamburg and visited a night club of dubious attractions!

From Denmark we were due for a cruise in the Baltic but the seamen went on strike, so instead, the coach had to go 'island hopping' to reach Copenhagen. We made friends with a couple from Frinton in Essex and another party from Australia. We all went together to the Tivoli Gardens and had an enjoyable time at all the various entertainments and activities available for the single admission charge. In the dockside area we saw the little statue of the maid on a rock. But nearby a USA and a Russian warship "docked" in line astern!! Next on to Sweden and Stockholm, rightly named the "Venice of the North". Everywhere so clean and tidy. Next on into Norway via Norrkoping where we attended a dance. Two Scandinavians wanted to change partners with Dorothy and I to dance. They spoke perfect English, so we obliged! Up to that time the rest of our party had not realised that Dorothy and I were reasonably accomplished dancers! Finally to Oslo and another dance. This time a Norwegian gentleman insisted on Dorothy dancing with him! We visited a minor fjord and ascended in a bucket contraption through mist and rain, so not very pleasant.

We returned via Gothenburg to Aalborg in Denmark where we stayed at a most magnificent hotel, reputed to have been a Royal Palace. Dorothy had her usual bout of sea-sickness, crossing the Cattegat, but this was not unexpected. The crossing was really rough. Even some passengers of Asian origin, naturally pale, turned green! I went on to the top deck to face the wind so to combat my feeling of sickness. Once we had landed at Aalborg, Dorothy as usual regained her composure! Back home via Hamburg and Bremen into Holland with another stop at Arnhem to visit the wild life park where lions came and almost looked through the window of the vehicle.

Continuing our list of holidays abroad, we again went to Northern Italy to Diano Marina, this time taking Dorothy's sister Marjory with us. In Milan we visited the famous opera house, where Marjory 'trilled' a few notes in the balcony just to say she had sung in Milan Opera House! No-one else heard her! She was a member of the Women's Institute Choir in Rainham, Gillingham! This time I was careful not to have my wallet stolen! The Manager of the hotel was most pleased to see us again. He quickly remembered our previous visit. We went along the coast westwards to San Remo and eastwards to Genoa, Rapallo, St Margareta and Portofino. We returned to Rappallo by sea. It was a very nice trip. Home to England via Monte Carlo where we saw the changing of the guard at the palace. The soldiers of the guard were brought to near the palace by coach and returned the same way. An unkind 'wit' said that they were all taken back to resume their duties as waiters in Monte Carlo! A visit to the gaming tables was enlightening. To watch the habitués using their different 'systems' to win a fortune! Then to Nice and again to Avignon to let Marjory see the famous bridge. We later passed a sign pointing to Nevers, the district where Phillippe de Montrichard has his residence. We were unable to stop to call on him!

Charles Deeming and his wife, Elizabeth's mother, went on a world cruise via Africa, Australia, New Zealand, Far East, India etc.. On their return to Southampton, Dorothy and I with Elizabeth went to meet them. I had let my friend Raymond know of the arrival back in England and he went down to the docks also to ensure no problems occurred! He was the Higher Collector and saw them safely ashore. I too went through the customs barrier but I was carrying my camera. When I attempted to come back I was quickly stopped by a female Customs Officer and challenged about the camera I was carrying, a Japanese Nikon! I had some difficulty in explaining who I was but eventually all was in order!

It reminded me of a previous occasion when Dorothy and I were passengers in a coach arriving from France at Southampton. I had previously notified some senior colleagues in the Department, serving at Southampton, of our intended arrival. When the coach drove up the ramp, two officials came aboard. They enquired of the courier whether she had a Mr Sheppard in the party. I sat quiet! She said she had and pointed me out. The rest of the passengers in our party looked apprehensive thinking I was in trouble. They approached me and said "Welcome home, Shep". I was known then throughout the service as "Shep". They then gave the driver the signal to proceed without any further ado! No Customs check. It was only then that the rest of our party knew that they had had a Customs official travelling with them through their tour abroad. I often heard fellow travellers discussing their intended actions on our visits abroad, for when they arrived back in the U.K. Often very enlightening!

The time for my retirement arrived and finally took place on 17 June 1969. I had to serve an additional day beyond my 63rd birthday for some reason that was not clear to qualify for the average of my salary for the last three years. I held a party at Slatter's Restaurant in Canterbury where many of my friends could attend from Dover Collection. Mr Raymond and his wife came up from Southampton. His successor as Collector, Dover, Mr Crellin and Mrs Crellin also attended. No Federation officials attended because the Annual Council was being held in 1969 at the same time in Folkestone. But many friends I had made in the Customs and Excise Department did attend. Besides which I received many written messages. Mr Crellin made the presentation to me of a fine mahogany bookcase which still holds many of my collection of books on all sorts of subjects. I received later a photographic album of pictures taken at the retirement party. We all sat down to the refreshments provided by the restaurant.

CHAPTER THIRTY FOUR
Retirement and accident.

In October 1969 some 4 months after my retirement I was on my way to attend a Masonic meeting in Staplehurst, in my old Station, in the evening, when rounding a corner, a car pulled out over the clearly marked white line. It crashed into my small Morris Minor car. My car finished in the ditch and I fell out on to the road. I looked up to see a policeman standing over me. My leg was broken. I could not stand. I said to the policeman, "some 'b........' has broken my leg". He replied "Yes, it was me". He had been driving an unmarked police car, a Wolseley, much heavier than my small Morris. I then 'passed out'. The next thing I remember was waking up in hospital. (It was the West Kent General Hospital) four days later. There was a tall man standing at the end of my bed. I said to him "Are you the policeman that knocked me down?" He said "No, I'm the Consultant dealing with your injuries. My name is Sheppard". I said "So is mine." He smiled! I had been in intensive care for four days. My right leg was broken in three places above the knee and I had lost my kneecap. Further than this I had also sustained a broken nose, two broken eye sockets and two broken jaws. In other words, I was in a mess and lucky to have survived. A metal plate had been inserted on my right leg which was now in tension. The next day I was transferred to Queen Victoria Hospital at East Grinstead and my 'face' put under tension by a type of "scaffolding of Great Britain" by cementing part to my lower teeth and the rest on to the top of my head. By this means the hospital doctors were pulling my face back into shape but my jaws were closed and I was unable to eat. My leg was still under tension over the end of my bed. For six weeks I had no food apart from thin soup which I poured into my mouth by pulling open my lower lip. Dorothy came to visit me daily from wherever she had been working on her market research programme. I was unable to shave. On one occasion, a nurse said to Dorothy, "Is the old gentleman your father?" Dorothy nearly exploded! Her reply is almost unprintable! But she did say "No, He's my husband." The hospital at East Grinstead is the one where the Consultant Mr McIndoe practised during the war, tending to airmen disfigured from plane crashes from action with the German airforce.

There were a number of other patients at the East Grinstead Hospital. The man in the next bed was having a complete replacement nose graft with flesh from his chest. Another having new fingers, after damage to both hands from attempted suicide by electrocution, when he lost his job as a foreman at the Defence establishment at Woolwich. Saturday evenings and Sunday mornings were the peak times for admission of fresh cases. They were nearly all Rugby football players with broken jaws injured in play the previous afternoon. The man in the next bed had lost his nose in a scalding accident. Replacement was proving a difficult operation.

The final removing of my "scaffolding" proved very painful to my teeth and face. With my leg still under tension I was returned to the West Kent General Hospital. After another three days I was transferred to Linton Hospital where I stayed for a further five months without once getting out of bed! My leg was under constant tension and my bed at an incline by raising the bottom end higher than the top end.

I learned that both my sons had visited the scene of the accident on the morning after the previous night of the accident only to find that my car had been taken away. I never saw it again! The road had been scrubbed clean to remove all traces of what had happened. The police had been hard at work to remove any evidence likely to prejudice their defence of what had occurred. Thus the police had taken early action to protect the police driver from a charge of dangerous driving or even of a less serious charge

I remained in bed at Linton Hospital until February, a full 5 months from the date of the accident. Except for one day, when I was taken to Cranbrook Police Court by ambulance to give evidence against the police constable who was driving the car that ran into me on the Staplehurst road. He was charged with dangerous driving. There was a 'lay' bench dealing with the charge. It consisted of two farmers and one haulage contractor, all three of whom were acquainted with the police and as such possibly sympathetic to members with whom they came into contact. I was kept outside while the evidence was given by the other policeman who was in the car at the time of the accident. Eventually I was carried into the court to give my evidence of what had occurred. I could only say that I was driving towards Staplehurst when a car coming in the opposite direction had pulled out over the white line round a sharp corner and collided with me forcing my car into the ditch at the side of the road. The prosecution was conducted by an outside Solicitor who had been brought in especially to conduct it whereas the defence was conducted by the Solicitor who normally carried out all prosecutions for the Police Authority. The Solicitor who was briefed to prosecute never at any time had an interview with me before the case to ascertain what had occurred so knew nothing about the accident, except what the police had told him! I had consulted my own Solicitor but he had no standing in the Court and could not speak on my behalf. In other words the subsequent prosecution arrangements favoured the defence. I was only a witness and could not call my own Solicitor or anyone else to give evidence. The lay bench retired and on return announced "that they had every sympathy with Mr Sheppard on his predicament, but they could not prejudice the career of a young policeman so they had decided to acquit him". These are the actual words the magistrates used so there was nothing I could do except return to my bed in Linton Hospital. The case aroused comment in the local newspaper, the Kent Messenger. It was clear that as it was a police case, the magistrates had thought it best not to convict. The policeman was defended by the solicitor who normally prosecuted for the police while the prosecution was conducted by an outside solicitor. This outside Solicitor at no time consulted with me about the case or came to see me. I did not know his name or his address. Having to wait outside the courtroom when the case was presented I had no knowledge of what was said by the 'prosecuting' Solicitor. It seemed to me that everything had been done by the Policy Authority to secure an acquittal rather than performing its proper function of securing the conviction of an offender. A photograph of me in bed at Linton Hospital with my leg under tension was published in the Kent Messenger. The magistrates, of course could have reduced the charge to one of 'driving without due care and attention' but this seems to have been conveniently forgotten! In any case the comments about "not wanting to prejudice the career of a young policeman" were completely out of order. As a result of the acquittal I lost entitlement to damages. My own private Solicitor told me that

I could mount a claim for damages but should I do so and lose the case I would be responsible for costs of myself and the defendant. He took up my case with the police and eventually they offered me £1,200 without prejudice to meet the costs I had had to incur for employing a gardener for the time I was incapacitated. My solicitor advised acceptance. I never saw my small car again. I had at the time a second car, a Rover, which might have withstood the impact better.

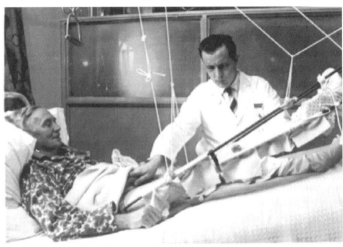

Author in bed at Linton Hospital,
Coxheath, Maidstone, Kent, 1969 after motor car accident.
Taken by Kent Messenger newspaper.

After 5 months in bed I was allowed up and was fitted with a 'calliper' iron frame fastened daily into my specially adapted shoe. I stayed at Linton undergoing therapy daily for a few more weeks. When I finally went home, Dorothy put my 'iron leg' on each morning for me to get up before she went off on her market research programme. After several more months the 'calliper' was removed and I was given a 'zimmer' frame to allow me to walk about. After a year I went back to Victoria Hospital, East Grinstead where the remainder of my bottom teeth were removed and also some of my top teeth. At East Grinstead I was fitted with false teeth to replace the whole of the bottom set and some of the top ones. So I lost what had been a fairly good set of normal teeth. Finally I was supplied with two walking sticks to replace the 'zimmer' frame. Next I dispensed with one stick and finally the other one. But it was two years before I finally came off the sick list. I asked the Consultant, Mr Sheppard, how long the plate would remain on my leg. His reply was "for ever". It is still there. Once when going through 'control' at an airport the alarm rang. It was my 'plate' detected through my clothes and my flesh.

271

My kneecap loss caused some problems when trying to kneel but has gradually become easier, although when playing bowls I have some difficulty in bending down to 'deliver' the bowls. So I use a specially adapted walking stick to maintain my balance. Another result of the accident was that my upper lip had been split open which, when it healed left me with what was the appearance of a 'hare-lip' of which I was very conscious and disliked immensely. Dorothy agreed with me that I was lucky to still be alive from such a horrendous accident. The verdict of all who knew the circumstances of the case was that "You can't win against the police".

Such is the saga of my serious accident. Had I not retired at 63 but elected to remain in the C & E Service, I would have received my pay, being on sick leave instead of the half pay I received as a retired Officer. Just my bad luck! Bu one cannot foretell the future. I am still alive at 90 years!!

After returning home from my accident we were able at last to have my grand daughter, Elaine, christened. This had to take place in Bearsted Parish church. My grandson, Adrian, had been christened in St Paul's Cathedral, under a special privilege allowed to members of the Order of the British Empire. Adrian's christening took place in the crypt of the Cathedral in the Chapel of the Order situated there. It was quite an impressive ceremony performed by the church dignitary allocated to the Order. After Adrian's christening which was attended also by June's parents who came up from Clydach near Swansea specially for the occasion, and my family, we all repaired to the Whitehall Hotel in Bloomsbury for a celebration lunch. I had secured a case of vintage champagne for the occasion from Dover for the lunch refreshments.

For Elaine's christening I had intended once again to avail myself of my privilege to have it in the crypt of the Cathedral but it was not to be since I was unfit to travel to London. I recall that Adrian was most upset because the vicar at Bearsted church had made his little sister cry! She was most vociferous in the church!

Dorothy continued her market research work travelling occasionally to distant parts of the country. When I was well enough I took her by car particularly in the south which was her particular area of control. At Christmas time we had many places to visit delivering bottles of champagne to all the clients in shops who were co-operating in market research surveys. We went as far as Torquay, Taunton, Bristol and most of the South Coast towns.

272

CHAPTER THIRTY FIVE
Civil Service Motoring Association.

I had for more than 40 years been a member of the Civil Service Motoring Association. At one time I was a member of the Headquarters Committee dealing with Social Activities. However, my official duties plus my membership of the Customs and Excise Federation as a Council delegate plus membership of meetings meant that I had little time left for active work with the Civil Service Motoring Association much as I would have liked to. I did, however, serve for a short period on its Social Committee. Meetings were held at the Headquarters offices just off Lower Regent Street, in London, before the offices were moved to Brighton. I was asked to deal with the social side of the annual contest for the Curtis Bennett trophy when teams from the various group of the C.S.M.A. competed in a gruelling motor rally from all parts of the country finishing at Llandrindod Wells in Wales. I asked my colleague Leslie Sims, the Officer for Gillingham to accompany me with Dorothy and Gladys, his wife, so that he could provide the music for the dancing to follow the rally. It proved very successful but most of the competitors had driven many miles over the difficult courses to the finishing point, and arrived too exhausted to enjoy what had been organised. Leslie and I with our wives simply had to drive straight to Llandrindod Wells where we stayed overnight. We returned via Worcester and Oxford. I asked to be relieved of my membership of the H.Q.s Social Committee since I had other activities occupying my time.

I was, however, still able to arrange for facilities to be available for members of the C.S.M.A. South Eastern Centre at various farms and other places throughout the Weald and other suitable spots in my Station. We had picnics at Bodiam Castle in Sussex, at Glassenbury near Goudhurst, at Scotney Castle near Lamberhurst on the Kent/Sussex boundary, the Bedgebury Pineton, on Hothfield

Common and Seal Common etc. At Seal we heard the radio broadcast of an interview that Vic. Fuller, one of our party, had given earlier to Wilfred Pickles in a 'Down your Way' programme at Gillingham. Vic. Fuller was the Commodore of the Gillingham Cruising Club and as such had been one of those Gillingham celebrities interviewed for the programme. Mr James Day a large scale farmer at Headcorn provided a field for the Association to hold its annual gymkhana. For the gymkhanas I was able to secure in Smarden, loud speaker apparatus to announce the result of the various competitions.

At Benenden, Bob Luck the cider maker, allowed the Civil Service Motoring Association members, the complete use of his field at the cider farm to stage a 'bonfire night' in November. He supplied all his old barrels and boxes to build the biggest bonfire in the area. Members came from all over Kent, Gillingham, Maidstone, Tunbridge Wells and even Dover to join in the fun. A barbeque was arranged with 'hot dogs', plus cider 'on tap' for those willing to risk a 'drink and drive' return home, but in moderation.

I also arranged some motor car rallies throughout the area and also treasure hunts trying to secure most outrageous articles. My most successful rally was one where competitors had to discover the most suitable place for a Russian agent to drop a bomb down the funnel of a train engine travelling from Paddock Wood to Ashford. This is a straight track where the rail goes under and over bridges to cross the roads, lanes and pathways in this part of the Weald. All competitors were supplied with an Ordnance Survey map to plan their routes throughout the area. What many forgot was that to drop the bomb it was only necessary to visit road bridges over the rail track and not bridges where roads, lanes and tracks went under the railway. It produced a successful rally.

Eventually all road rallies and treasure hunts had to be discontinued because of the increasing amount of road traffic in the area. Rally etc., cars simply out for pleasure could cause traffic problems for road traffic going about legitimate business.

The South Eastern area regularly held dances in Gillingham which we attended. Each year the local area held a fancy dress dance when every member attending entered into the spirit of the occasion. In the year that the Princess Elizabeth and Prince Phillip went to Canada on a 'good will' visit, Dorothy hired a 'royal looking outfit' from the fancy dress agency in Maidstone. I borrowed from Dorothy's cousin Ivy's husband, his Naval Officer's uniform. We had in Rainham some friends who had a business selling ironmongery and similar items. We approached them to let us borrow two enamel chamber pots! These Dorothy and I 'tried on' in the window of their shop, much to the amusement of passers by! Dorothy and I put cotton wool round the rims of the chamber pots to resemble ermine and with our costumes as royal princess and husband (I wore the naval uniform) we went to the fancy dress dance as the "Prince and Princess of Poland" with the chamber pots on our heads. Rather a rude gesture but we won the first prize! On another occasion for the fancy dress dance, Dorothy hired six fancy dresses suitable to be worn by a Queen. They were rather 'grubby' so Dorothy laundered all six, putting them on the clothes line in our garden to the amusement of our neighbours. With five other lady friends in our party, Dorothy and they went as the six wives of Henry VIII. A male member of suitable stature was Henry. We borrowed six sets of roller skates and the six wives skated round Henry in order of accession, Catherine of Aragon, Anne Boleyn, Anne of Cleves, Jane Seymour, Catherine Howard and Catherine Parr. The tableau did not win a prize but the sight of the six girls trying to skate round Henry caused amusement.

We had many friends, not all Civil Servants who attended with us. We thought it would be an innovation if, instead of going individually in fancy dress, we went as a group. This we did the first year of our plan by putting on a show as 'Olde Tyme Music Hall'. We put up a temporary curtain in the lounge of our house at Bearsted and there held rehearsals. In fact the rehearsals were as much

Author as "Harry Champion" singing "Any Old Iron" at Civil Service Motoring Association Annual Fancy Dress Dance, Franklin Rooms, Gillingham, Kent.

fun as the actual show when we finally put it on. We were very fortunate in having Leslie Sims, my colleague who was Officer for Gillingham and an excellent pianist to play all the tunes we required for our show. Colin, with Dorothy on the back seat of a tandem we borrowed from the local cyclist shop, rode round the room at the hall in Gillingham singing "Daisy, Daisy, give me your answer do" etc.. Marjory, her sister sang "Daddy wouldn't buy me a bow wow!" Another member of our 'gang' sang "Burlington Bertie". Two others did "If you were the only girl in the world". My mother and father even came on to sing "Three pots a shilling". Another did "My old man said follow the van". Another sang "Knocked 'em in the Old Kent Road". Another sang "Lily of Laguna". Another "There was I waiting at the Church", another "Where did you get that hat?"

Full cast of presentation of "Olde Tyme Musical " at C.S.M.A. Fancy Dress Annual
Dance at Franklin Rooms, Gillingham Kent. Singing "Three Pots a Shilling"
(by Author's parents as 'Costers') "Burlington Bertie", "Daisy, Daisy, give me your
answer do" (by Author's wife, Dorothy and son Colin)
"Knocked 'em down the Old Kent Road". "Waiting at the Church",
"Lily of Laguna", " If you were the only girl in the world" and
"Daddy wouldn't buy me a bow, wow". plus Author, "Any Old Iron".

There were at least 16 of us all with different songs from former days. My song was "Any old iron?", by Harry Champion. The show when we finally put it on was a sensational success. All our performers were in suitable clothes. My parents were dressed as 'Costers'. Dorothy was in 'Bloomers', Colin in knickerbockers. The deputy head master of my old school, The Tech., was marvellous as George Robey, singing "Only girl in the world", to the wife of a future Mayor of Gillingham! His wife did "Follow the van" carrying her canary in a cage! Our 'producer' was the manager and part owner of the big Departmental Store in Gillingham. 'Le Fevres', later 'Debenhams'! The whole audience joined in the choruses. What fun it was!

Author's son, Colin and wife, Dorothy, riding their tandem bicycle round the hall, singing "Daisy, Daisy, give me your answer do".

Full assembly of members at C.S.M.A.Fancy Dress Dance at Franklin Rooms.

The following year to "Olde Tyme Music Hall" we did another joint show. That of a circus. We had two 'prancing horses' in Marjory and the wife of the future Mayor of Gillingham, being driven by our pianist's wife; Dorothy as a knife thrower's "Moll" having a large board fastened to her back into which knives had been inserted, while the future Mayor was throwing rubber knives at her. I was the back end of a horse while my friend Tom Burkett was the front end. There were other characters from the circus, a make believe trapeze artist, plus a Ringmaster. Even a chocolate girl going round with her tray of sweets. Not so amusing as the previous year, although the pantomime horse was a great success. I had been to Tonbridge to hire the horse 'skin'. Our producer walked behind the 'horse' in case it 'misbehaved'. He carried a bucket, shovel and brush!! I was dropping small balls of brown wool as we pranced round the room.

Full cast in C.S.M.A. show 'Historical Hysteria' characters represented -
Adam and Eve, Nelson, Florence Nightingale, Grace Darling, Nell Gwynne,
Duke of Wellington, Cleopatra, Elizabeth 1, Noah, Lady Godiva, Lady Hamilton,
Guy Fawkes, Pepys, Dick Whittington, Beethoven, etc. etc.
and in front Nelson's Sailors!

"Historical Hysteria"
show at C.S.M.A.
Fancy Dress Dance
Colin(son)
as Charles 11,
Dorothy (wife)
as Lady Hamilton,
Author as Nelson,
Brian (son)
as Dick Whittington

The following year we did quite a different 'show' which I called "Historical Hysteria". There is a musical show where characters sing a song, "If I was not upon the stage, someone else I'd like to be" whereupon they perform a mime of what they would like to be, such as a chimney sweep pushing his brush up the chimney. Instead we each sang in turn which character out of history we would prefer to be. For example, my mother dressed as Florence Nightingale, sang "If I had lived in olden times, Florence Nightingale I'd like to be" and then added the little couplet I wrote for her "Put a rug round this old soldier, he needs peace and quiet". She practiced it for days!! I wrote little couplets for each to sing to accompany the character they wanted to be. I was Nelson, Dorothy was Lady Hamilton, Colin was Charles the Second, Brian, Dick Whittington, my father Noah, my mother Florence Nightingale. My colleague, Joe Richards was Guy Fawkes. All had a character to play, a couplet to sing and all were dressed for the character they represented. All except our pianist who played for the little couplets. This show was as successful as had been 'Olde Tyme Music Hall' especially when the last two characters appeared as Adam and Eve dressed in furskins!! It really was "Historical Hysteria"!! The show drew complementary comment and a photograph in the local press.

The next year we did 'Old Tyme Music Hall' again but this time with some different "Olde Tyme" music hall characters. We finished this show with a party of the small children from some of our friends marching on in uniforms of small soldiers to the tune of 'Soldiers of the Queen' sung by Sybil Burkett wife of my former partner in the pantomime horse. This 'finale' to the show really 'brought the house down'.

Next year a Combined Radio and Television show 'In town tonight'. For this I approached the Governor of Maidstone prison for his assistance in providing a 'black-cloth' of Piccadilly Circus to erect in the hall for our show. He had an artist in prison who was glad to oblige! This backcloth was later stored in the roof space of our pianist's bungalow and so far as I know is still there! Dorothy, her sister and Netta Trill, one of our party came on as the "Beverley Sisters" and mimed "Sisters, Sisters", while I activated a record producer behind a screen! The audience really thought the girls were singing the song. They had rehearsed so well. Tom Burkett and I did "The Western Brothers" only we were billed as the "South Eastern Brothers". Our pianist was Liberace carrying a candelabra borrowed from my mother's home. The future mayor's wife did a little show as 'Top of the Form' with two large balloons to illustrate the allusion to the play on words, wearing a suitable bra!! Tom Burkett built a realistic red telephone kiosk. His wife stood inside telephoning while a large queue formed outside to illustrate a play on words of 'Women's Hour', she was so long using the phone! There were 7 girls in our party when we did the Television Show. So the "Beverley Sisters", "Top of the Form" and "Women's Hour" all did a quick change into costumes as "Television Toppers" with tights,

short skirts, top hats, white blouses each with a walking stick (cane) for a dance together as a troupe. They had rehearsed the dance so well that they had no difficulty in getting their right leg all together over their canes in real Television Topper style, except for our pianist's wife who was 'no dancer'. But she managed it eventually. The costume change took place while Tom Burkett and I were performing as the "South Eastern Brothers". The audience of the rest of the members of the C.S.M.A. could hardly believe their eyes when the Television

Author and Tom Burkett, as
"The Western Brothers"
"South Eastern Brothers"

280

Toppers came on. We were so fortunate in our producer, from the Le Fevres Store who brought along members of his staff to assist in dressing and the make up of our 'dancers'. This show was so successful that our MP at the time for the constituency of Rochester, Julian Critchley, who was attending as a guest of the Civil Service Motoring Association, asked us to give the same show at Maidstone later in the month where he would be attending another function. We did so. That too was successful, especially the Beverley Sisters!!

Marjory, (Dorothy's sister), Netta Needham (friend) and Dorothy as The Beverly Sisters singing "Sisters, Sisters".

"The Show Girls" as "The Television Toppers", Joan, Hilda, Netta, Gladys, Dorothy and Marjory, in Television Show, at C.S.M.A. Fancy Dress Annual Dance.

*Author in 'drag' as the bride
in 'cod' opera, 'Alphonse'
at C.S.M.A. Dance*

*Full cast in 'cod' opera, 'Alphonse' at C.S.M.A. Annual Fancy Dress Dance.
Characters, left to right, Undertaker, pianist, parson, producer, villain Alphonse,
bride, mother of bride, Author of opera and second undertaker.
Front row The Chorus girls*

Our final show before Dorothy and I retired to Poole was a "cod" opera when Joe Richards, my colleague formerly of Tilbury Dock, now Officer at Rochester Customs, was a villain Spaniard murdering all in sight whosoever looked at his 'bride'. I was the 'bride'. In 'drag' so 'made up' that even my parents didn't recognise me! Two of our party were the undertakers who carried off the 'bodies'. At the finale, the villain "Alphonse", killed off the "author" (who was the deputy head master of my old school) and also killed off Tom Burkett who was the priest due to marry us. All the girls were our chorus. They sang every time a murder was committed. I had a marvellous bouquet of cabbage and rhubarb leaves, carrots, onions, a turnip and other vegetables. I had to sing the flower song from, I think, Faust, and leap over the 'dead' bodies, before the 'undertakers' carried them off. This show was another success but was our last because Dorothy and I were soon due to go off to Poole to live. For all these 'shows' the rehearsals were the enjoyable times which were always followed by a meal and a party. We were so lucky to have Leslie Sims my colleague in the Excise in Gillingham who could play the piano so well.

Dorothy and I had purchased our baby grand piano after the war. Dorothy had been a competent pianist up to the time of our marriage, over thirty years earlier. But when we got the piano home we had both forgotten how to play! I was much worse than Dorothy. But both my daughters-in-law, Elizabeth and June were excellent pianists. When they visited us at home together, they played duets. Eventually we sold the piano so we could have a picture window fitted to replace the french window that led from our lounge on to the lawn and garden. The new picture window was a great improvement to our residence. I was able to get a local builder to put it in but I was somewhat scared that the wall above it might collapse until the builder assured me that the steel beam would prevent any trouble developing. He was right. With timber covering the RSJ beam, the appearance of the house was preserved. It was a great improvement. But our piano had to go since it stood in the way of the large picture window. We then had a greatly improved access to our garden.

CHAPTER THIRTY SIX
Re-union of apprentices and Colin's problems.

In 1972 I decided to endeavour to hold a reunion of my fellow apprentices who had entered the dockyard employment in 1922 to become electrical fitters and hopefully, electrical engineers. My good friend Bill Holloway had died in Bath while in the employ of the Admiralty as a Senior Draughtsman. Les Ansell had also passed on while an Overseer similarly employed. Chris James was back in the Inland Revenue Department after his spell of being recalled during the war, for work at Bath. My 'best man' George Lawrence had retired but still living in Bath. Harold Attwood was back from Bermuda and again living in Gillingham. 'Dusty' Doust after his spell in Australia and in England at the Air Ministry was also now living in Gillingham, Frank Smallwood was, as usual, the 'odd man out', living in Wiltshire. I arranged a celebration dinner at the Queens Hotel, Wigmore, Gillingham. An Electrical Engineer from Bath attended to 'honour' the proceedings, as did Ron Hunter, one of my party that 'did the shows at the motor club dances. (He was George Roby in "Olde Tyme Music Hall", 'scared' that pupils from the Technical School would recognise him!) He was Deputy Headmaster and a former Dockyard Apprentice. Other old friends and relatives came to the celebration dinner. Attwood, Doust, James and Lawrence were present with Olive Holloway deputising for her late husband. Smallwood was unwell and could not attend. I was unable to trace Mrs Ansell. The following day Dorothy arranged a grand party at our Bearsted home when they all attended again except for Doust. Photographs were taken at the dinner and published in the local press with a nice 'write-up' of our re-union.

About this time, Colin and Elizabeth's marriage broke up for reasons we never discovered, except that they separated, later to be divorced. It was a great blow to Dorothy and I and to Elizabeth's mother in

Reunion of 1922 entry of electrical fitter apprentices, in September 1972, Harold Attwood; Chris James; George Lawrence; Olive Holloway, widow of Bill Holloway; Author; and Horace (Dusty) Doust.

Leicestershire. We had earlier attended a celebration of Charles Deeming's 80th birthday, Elizabeth's step father. This was a grand affair held in a marquee in the grounds of "One Ash" at Quorn. I was still using the 'zimmer' frame from my accident, nevertheless managed to get around on the specially laid wood floor in the marquee, so the guests could dance to the orchestra arranged for the party. To Dorothy and my great regret, this was our last visit to "One Ash", although I have been invited many times to go to Colorton near Colville in Leicestershire where Elizabeth now lives with her new husband, a Mr Gooding, who formerly resided in Yester Park, Chislehurst. Elizabeth still sends me a Christmas card annually, and calls me "Pa".

Colin's business flourished. With David Moscow and as a limited company, it became one of the leading Management Consultancies in the country. They left their offices at Lee, near to Lewisham and purchased a large house in Willow Grove in Chislehurst, employing many Associates as Consultants, plus clerical staff equipped with all the modern electronic equipment. Colin went to live at The Coach House in Timber Close, Chislehurst.

The house at Yester Park was sold.   Colin also disposed of his house at Sheringham and the one at West Runton, Norfolk.   He purchased a property at Redbrooks Wood, in Hythe in Kent for a week-end 'retreat'.   It was situated in 10 acres of woodland, grasslands, with a kitchen garden.   He later married Eileen Longley from Eltham.   They have no children.

On retirement I received a pension of one half of my salary over the final three years of service plus a lump sum also based on my salary.   I decided to allocate a portion of my pension to enhance the pension my wife would receive as my widow should I die before her.   I was anxious to ensure that Dorothy would be able to live a normal life free from financial problems in the event of my demise before her.   In any case we would both be entitled to the National Retirement Pension within two years, plus of course Dorothy would receive a widow's pension when I died.   In the event it proved a bad bargain because over the past 27 years I have received a lower pension whereas Dorothy did not benefit from my allocation.   But that is just the luck of the decision I made and I have no regrets for the action I took.

CHAPTER THIRTY SEVEN
Reconstruction of Kitchen and explosion.

As for the lump sum this I invested in three different building societies to bring in a modest addition to my pension. I did, however allocate a portion to pay for a reconstruction of our kitchen. I took considerable trouble to measure the kitchen and ordered all the necessary Hygena fitments from a reputable local firm in Maidstone. Kitchen cabinets, cupboards, etc.. I had in mind to fit these myself when they became available. I also ordered the local heating engineer to instal a Raybourne stove which would supply central heating to our residence plus cooking facilities in the kitchen additional to the gas cooker we had already. Eventually all the equipment I had ordered was received by the builders merchant and by the heating engineer, but by then I had suffered a serious motoring accident so that the project for the reconstructed kitchen had to be postponed. All the fitments ordered remained in store at the builder and the engineer's premises for over 12 months until I eventually came out of hospital and even then, the work of installing the kitchen fitments had to be carried out by the builder's merchant workmen instead of, as I had planned personally by myself.

As soon as I was able to move about sufficiently to instruct the builder's men, the kitchen fitments were delivered and work on the reconstruction of the kitchen commenced. When completed the builder congratulated me on the exactness which I had shown in measuring the space where the new kitchen fitments were to be installed. I was still with the calliper leg iron fitted to my right leg and fastened into a shoe especially adapted. At one stage, Dorothy called to me for my agreement to have the 'walk-in' pantry replaced by the many fitments being installed. I was so disappointed at not being able to carry out the work myself that I simply said "do whatever you wish". The workmen dismantled the old pantry, fitted a

R.S.J. beam to take the weight of the lavatory above on the first floor immediately over what had been the pantry. The change over proved a great success so that Dorothy's idea had been the correct one.

When completed we had a party inviting our many friends from the Medway Towns to come and view the new kitchen. It is difficult to describe the next episode of the new kitchen!

The workmen at the local gas works together with their fellow workmen throughout the country, decided to go on strike. As part of the procedure for nullifying the reduction in the supply of gas for domestic use, it was decided to lower the gas pressure available. We were unaware of what was happening. Dorothy and I retired to bed one night as usual. I was awakened by Dorothy shouting that there had been an explosion. I told her to go to sleep and stop dreaming. But she was right. Fumes were coming up the stairs. There had been an explosion from the new Raybourne stove fitted in our new kitchen. All the cupboards had been blown apart and the contents thrown on to the floor by the repercussion of the blast. Glassware and crockery were all broken. The kitchen door with its plate glass inset was forced off its hinges and the glass broken. Our new kitchen was a wreck. As soon as it was light I summoned the heating engineer who had installed the stove. He summoned the gas company manager and the builder who had installed the various fitments. A conference was held to which the Insurance company representative was invited. The verdict on the cause of the explosion was that the lowering by the gas company of the pressure had caused the pilot light to be extinguished so that when the pressure was restored, gas had escaped into the kitchen and an explosion was the result. The gas company was keen to reduce any publicity over the explosion that had taken place. Eventually the gas company and my insurers reached an agreement to meet the cost of restoring the kitchen. It was agreed that the heating engineer was in no way to blame for the explosion that had taken place. The builder who had installed the fitments to the kitchen returned and restored the kitchen to its pristine condition. The cost of replacing the broken glassware and crockery was also met by the insurers.

Dorothy returned to her work as Controller for the Market Research Company and eventually I was able to take her on occasions visiting locations where market research was required. One such was a visit to Torquay, Newton Abbott, Exeter, Bristol and Taunton. She was, however, complaining that her eyes were beginning to give her some concern.

I had now recovered from my accident apart from the loss of my kneecap which could never be replaced. My father for some years had problems with his 'water-works' and shown a great preference for sweets. It is fairly obvious to me now that he was diabetic and that the sweets he was consuming were having an effect on his pancreas. He had a violent attack of vomiting and was taken to the Royal Naval Hospital in Gillingham. He passed away there in 1968 in his 82nd year. His last wishes and thoughts were for his six grandchildren; my sister's four and my two. He had been a good father and devoted to his family. My sister and her children had benefited greatly from him during their childhood with gifts of bicycles and other help financially. I think that my sister's husband had sometimes resented the attention that was being given to his three boys and the granddaughter, but that was how my father, and my mother, wished to help their daughter to bring up her family. For my part, my parents realised that my sons were well cared for and did not require additional help.

My mother continued to live alone in the house at Rainham. She declined an offer I made for her to come and live with us at Bearsted. She still wanted to stay where it was convenient for her bowls and the friends she had in the area. I regularly called to see her. She was a very capable woman, tending her garden, besides going off as often as possible to play bowls at the Civil Service Club where she was President, playing in matches and for Kent against other counties. She was asked to be President of the Kent County Club but declined, not wanting to make speeches, necessary for the President to do. Instead she suggested a much junior member for the office who was duly appointed. I was sorry she did not accept. It would have been a fitting tribute to her service to her club and to the Kent County Womens' Bowling Association.

CHAPTER THIRTY EIGHT
Masonic activities.

I joined a Masonic Lodge in Gillingham in 1933 but I took no part in the meetings or 'ceremonies'. I was far too busy with my official duties plus living for part of the time away from Gillingham. I attended a number of Masonic lodges in different parts of the country when invited by friends, Cardiff, Leicester, Robertsbridge and Maidstone, but more frequently at Cranbrook, but I took no part in 'ceremonies'. In 1967, however, I was approached by a fellow mason in Staplehurst to become what is termed a 'founder' of a new lodge to be formed in Staplehurst but which was to meet in Paddock Wood. The invitation was extended to about 12 masons who would form the nucleus of the lodge membership. Without much enthusiasm, I agreed. The lodge was formally started in 1967. I knew that I would be retiring in 1969 so thought that maybe, it would give me some interest, when retirement occurred. From the "office" I would occupy in the lodge I would in normal circumstances reach what is known as "Master of the Lodge" in 1972. So I started attending meetings and found a number of new acquaintances and friends.

The 'Founder' Master of the new Staplehurst Lodge was a former bookmaker named Mick Hayes, who had changed his business activities by purchasing a mineral water manufacturing concern known as 'Popes' in Staplehurst. Through this I had come into contact with him and so became one of the Founders of the new Staplehurst Lodge. This brought me into association with many more residents in the area some of whom I had already been visiting officially, not knowing of their Masonic connections. So many more friends, but I did not let this interfere with my official controls required as Excise Officer for the Weald of Kent. One firm I had been visiting officially was a market gardener by the name of Ledger who used considerably quantities of dutiable fuel, but because of having no vehicles, the control was academic, all the fuel was used in heating the greenhouses.

Mr and Mrs Ledger, however, had a relative in Otham, a village adjoining Bearsted, who was a fruit farmer, also growing Kentish cobnuts on the ragstone ridge renowned for producing this very tasty nut of the hazel family. He also grew prize strawberries and had appeared on a B.B.C. Television programme dealing with the cultivation of this fruit. He possessed two farms in the Otham area and another in East Malling where the Ministry of Agriculture trial grounds are situated. At all the farms he grew apples, Cox's Orange pippins, Golden Delicious and other varieties as well as pears and rhubarb for early marketing. I was invited to attend Frank Ledger's lodge at Ashford for the ceremony of Ernie Nicholls entry into masonry and from that developed a close friendship with both Ernie Nicholls and his wife Daphne, which has lasted even up to the present time. Also in Otham with two more residents, I met Bill and Belle Hardy. He was the press representative for a number of London newspapers. From this I then became acquainted with the proprietor of a large wholesale newspaper business in Hastings and surrounding country. His name was Charles Jenyon living in St. Leonard's with his wife Mary. So my circle of friends grew, having no connection with official Excise duties. With the Hardys, the Nicholls and the Jenyons, Dorothy and I attended a number of Press Association functions in London which were rather prestigious meetings.

Dorothy's firm, Retail Audits Ltd., held a number of Dinner/Dances for the employees, in the Hilton Hotel in Park Lane, to which husbands and wives of the employees were also invited. With Dorothy, I also attended a few Gentlemen's Nights at the Rembrant Hotel in West Kensington where Lady Masons entertained their men folk. Dorothy had a proprietor of a large chemist shop who was on her panel for Market Research and was also a Lady Mason in London. She invited us to attend. The lady masons were just as adept at staging a 'Gentlemen's night' as were the men with 'Ladies' Nights'!! The concept of 'Lady Masons' was frowned upon by Masonic Head Quarters of 'Male' Masonry. Dorothy although invited to, did not join although she had friends in Gillingham who were lady masons. Colin also arranged two fabulous parties for his clients in his business, which had prospered and had become one of the leading organisations in advising on Management. These two parties were held at the Waldorf Hotel just off the Strand.

We had some grand parties at Charles and Mary's beautiful house in St. Leonard's, Sussex. He was quite a wealthy man driving a Rolls Royce car. When we attended his Masonic Ladies Night, held at the Grand Hotel, Eastbourne, (although his lodge was centred in Hastings), he always received preferential treatment when parking at the Grand Hotel! On one occasion a raffle was being held in aid of a charity. The ticket sellers were young girls from the hotel. It was at the time of what were known as "Hot Pants", very very short shorts! Charles Jeynon kept buying tickets for the raffle from the "Hot Pants" girls until Mary became suspicious and told him to stop. I cannot recall whether Charles won any prizes with the numerous tickets he had purchased just to get a closer look at the "Hot Pants". Eventually he and Mary went to live at Bexhill-on-Sea when he retired. Dorothy and I went to visit them there and they came over to see us at Bournemouth when we retired to that area. Prior to our move we had built up an extensive circle of friends in Bearsted, Staplehurst and surrounding area besides continuing with those we had in Gillingham and Rainham. It was quite a wrench to leave them all behind but most of them visited us in Poole once we had settled there. We soon began to secure even more friends and acquaintances in the Bournemouth district.

Then my accident occurred and I was unable to take part in Masonic lodge business from October 1969 until early in 1971 when I was able to attend using my two walking sticks. My position in the new lodge had been reserved for me. In 1972 I became "Master" of the Lodge which was transferred from Paddock Wood Masonic Hall to a new building converted from a former Church mission hall for hop pickers but now unused. This building when reconstructed into a Masonic Hall was much more convenient for members to attend. It was situated on the main road from Cranbrook to Hawkhurst at the hamlet of Hartley and became the meeting place of a number of other Lodges in the area of Cranbrook and Tenterden. The formation of the new lodge known as Staplehurst Lodge was very successful. My immediate predecessor as Master was a Police Inspector I had known for many years who lived in Rochester. The Secretary was another retired Inspector of Police living in Sutton Valance. The Lodge was very successful in attracting members from the surrounding area.

In 1973 towards the end of my year as Master, I held the customary "Ladies Night" when the ladies and friends are invited to attend with the members of the lodge, their ladies and friends. This I held at the Great Danes Hotel very near to Leeds Castle. Normally such a gathering attracts about 150 to 200 members and guests. For my Ladies Night the attendance reached 320 a record for any such gathering in the area. It is customary for the Master of the Lodge to present all the ladies with a gift. Dorothy and I decided to give them all a handbag holder that can be affixed to the table when dining out. We visited all the big stores in the area, Gillingham, Rochester, Maidstone, Brighton, Eastbourne, Folkestone, Canterbury and Ashford, buying up the entire stocks of the article we wished to present to each lady attending. With an attendance of 320 I needed over 180 gifts because there are more ladies attending than men. I could not find sufficient. In the end I made up a few 'false' packages for my immediate family and guests with a promise to supply the 'real thing' when more articles arrived to replenish stocks. This subterfuge worked! Within a few weeks I was able to replace the false packages with the real article! It is customary also for the Master to present his Lady with a personal gift. I gave Dorothy a pearl necklace plus a set of silver table mats we secured from a jeweller in Brighton. My Ladies Night was held on Trafalgar Day in 1973. It was very appropriate seeing that my name is Horace and Lord Nelson's name was Horatio! The table mats I purchased in Brighton for part of Dorothy's present were all inscribed with scenes from the Battle of Trafalgar, so it really was a Trafalgar Day 'Ladies Night'! Instead of the normal Menu cards for the dinner, I made about 150 'scrolls' of imitation parchment with details of the menu; the names of the Lodge organising committee, a couplet welcoming the Ladies etc.. The scrolls I wrapped round a blue wooden stick in the fashion of olden times announcements. The imitation parchment was decorated with a picture of Trafalgar Square with Nelson's Column and with two old fashioned ships of the battle of Trafalgar depicted. The evening was a great success, blue being the Masonic colour. I wrapped the scrolls, and tied them with red tape, and sealed with sealing wax, as a mark of my Civil Service career! My immediate predecessor, the Police Inspector, by the name of Bob Green, made the speech to the Ladies, customary for such occasions. He had obtained from Dorothy's sister, Marjory, details of Dorothy's life especially her prowess as a runner. His theme was that she had run so fast that I was unable to escape!! I had engaged two London artistes to entertain the guests with songs from the 'The Shows' and a dance band for the dancing. Due to the large attendance, the hotel had to open up the full length of the ballroom for the dancing. This was something not often necessary, so we were all able to dance in comfort. The 'Tombola' held as part of the proceedings raised several hundred pounds which I bequeathed to a building fund for a new meeting venue. It was a grand evening. My mother, my sons and two daughters-in-law and Dorothy's sister, also the friends we had made from South Wales, on our visit to Dubrovnik when I sustained the accident to my leg, all attended swelling the numbers to record proportions. The hotel authority was first class in catering for such a large gathering even when at the last minute, on the day of the function, friends were ringing me to ask if they could be 'fitted in'. My reply was "If the hotel can feed you, I can seat you" so all wishing to be present were accommodated. It was an evening that went down in the Lodge annals. My only regret was that my father and Dorothy's parents had not been able to be present.

CHAPTER THIRTY NINE
Removal to Bournemouth area.

We needed to look for suitable premises for our retirement to Bournemouth so we went there to start the search in the area. We first found a flat near to the Royal Bath Hotel on the East Cliff in the course of erection. We duly paid a deposit to secure. On return home we came to the conclusion that it was unsuitable in some respects, not having a separate garage for my car, only a parking space in the basement. Also there were clauses in the purchase agreement inferring that the annual maintenance charge could be increased. In the end we advised the agent of our doubts and he quickly offered us another flat in The Avenue in Poole, some 40 to 50 yards over the boundary with Bournemouth. It was what we were looking for. Additionally to the attractions of the accommodation, there were two garages included. This to me was ideal since one would house my car while the other would serve as a workshop enabling me to carry out the 'odd jobs' that go with being a householder. My garage in Bearsted had been big enough for both my car and my workshop. The house agent transferred the deposit we had already paid to one on the flat in The Avenue. Dorothy and I in the past had often driven down The Avenue some half mile from the sea at Branksome Chine and never thought that one day we might live there. The Avenue residences originally consisted of large houses each standing in at least one acre. The houses were systematically being demolished for a block of flats to be erected on each site as it became available. It was often said that the finest road to live in in Bournemouth was The Avenue in Poole! The flat we eventually bought was on the third floor of a block with 5 floors excluding the ground level. The address was No 8 Sunset Lodge, 30/32 The Avenue, Poole. The numbers 30/32 was because, whereas houses in The Avenue each stood in one acre, our block stood in two acres, two houses having been demolished for one block of flats

to be erected. We had, therefore extensive grounds with lawns, cultivated gardens and a putting green. It looked towards the sea half a
mile down The Avenue. 1¹/₄ miles from the centre of Bournemouth
and 3¹/₄ miles from the centre of Poole. Both towns had parks and
other attractions drawing visitors regularly for holidays.

We sold Orchard Gate in Bearsted to a doctor who was retiring for
£26,000. I had paid £4,000 for it some 26 years earlier. The flat cost
£22,500 but from the excess, we were due for agents' costs and legal
fees but there still remained some funds for purchase of furniture.

Brian had purchased a house at Brockenhurst in the New Forest for
holidays. We were able to use this house to live in while we were
dealing with the negotiations involved in searching for a residence in
Bournemouth and for the eventual successful 'buy'. Also for
purchasing the new furniture we required. During this time our
friends who had lived near us in Cecil Avenue, Gillingham during the
war, Gwen and Cliff Martin, who had now returned to their peace-
time home at Shirley near Croydon, came to spend a holiday with us
at Brockenhurst. He was the Air Force Officer who had been
'mentioned in despatches' I have mentioned earlier in these Memoirs!
We were very good friends still. Their two girls had now married,
the elder to a scientist, with a Ph.D. and the younger to a schoolmaster. We had often visited them at Shirley and also attended the
wedding of the younger girl.

Gwen Martin did not approve of her younger daughter's choice of a
husband. She was a Cornish woman and probably had Spanish
blood in her (from the wreckage of ships at the time of the Spanish
Armada). That is my opinion! She was so vehement when 'roused'.
But for all that a very good friend and we all got on well in each
other's company. For her younger daughter's wedding, at first she
declined to attend until Dorothy persuaded her otherwise. At the
reception she steadfastly declined to speak to or acknowledge her new
son-in-law's parents. It was a rather cold reception. On one occasion when visiting Gwen and Cliff for lunch I secreted a tape recorder
under the dining table with Cliff's permission! We subsequently
played back Gwen and Dorothy's conversation. It was quite enlightening but not revealing!! Just amusing! Cliff became a bank
manager at a bank in Kingsway, London. Gwen fell when playing
golf and broke her leg. In hospital the attention went sadly wrong.

A 'pin' inserted for repairs became dislodged. She became a cripple and was never able to play golf again. She died a very sad and dejected woman. Cliff went to live in Streatham in a house left to him by an elderly aunt.

A few months before we were due to remove our residence to Poole, my mother died at the age of 88. She had been playing bowls a few days earlier. A good friendly neighbour called regularly every morning to see that she was well. This neighbour found my mother had fallen out of bed and was on the floor unconscious. The doctor who was called diagnosed that she had had a brain haemorrhage. She died a few days later. She was buried in the family grave at Chatham cemetery where my father and my two grandparents lie at rest. I had the task of disposing of the bungalow and contents where my parents had lived for 54 years. It was a very sad task for me to carry out. My sister was spared. The proceeds had to be shared but I had no enthusiasm for it. In dealing with the deeds for the property I had to contact the elder of the two Thompson boys who had lived next door, the son of the former owner. This son had emigrated to Canada. Eventually the problem was solved but with the usual fees by solicitors who had to be employed for the legal problems thrown up by the private mortgage arranged by Mr Thompson and my father in 1920. The final probate for the estate presented no problems to me as a former Probate Officer.

CHAPTER FORTY
Bearsted House and cars.

During the long period from living at Barnehurst near Bexleyheath, I had owned a number of motor cars. Following the demise of the Ariel motorcycle and sidecar that had served me so well, I first had the Clyno car with the fabric body, now an almost unknown type of car. Next came a very 'classy' Fiat Swallow, quite speedy except that it was sadly in need of a rebore. Dorothy and I went to Scotland on holiday to visit a fellow U.O. from the Government Laboratory. It left a trail of smoke across England as we proceeded north. This car was succeeded by a Morris Oxford, very stylish in red and black. Next came a Wolseley which was obviously, when we started to drive it, nearly on its "last legs". Our visitor from France, Phillipe de Montrichard, was sitting in it when the battery fell through the rusted bottom of the car. We managed to get it home. After this a new car, a Ford "Classic" which was very economical. The Ford "Classic" was followed by two Ford Consuls in succession. Driving the first one, one night, into Maidstone in a heavy rainstorm and having to pull up, the car was struck in the rear by a foreign car from France driven by a Belgian. I managed to get the number before the driver drove off in haste. From the number of the car, I traced its origin via the Customs at Dover, where the motorist had arrived from France. Also his destination. It was a Mews address in the Lancaster Gate area of London. I went there only to find that he had departed! There was no way that I could claim for the damage caused. So only recourse to my own insurance and the loss of my no claim bonus.

On another occasion, I was making enquiries in Cranbrook regarding sales of wine. I parked my car in the road opposite. This was my second Ford Consul. The local rubbish collecting vehicle was nearby. A workman came into the house to find me and say "had I left my car in the road?" He went on to say that another car had run into it. There was a policeman on a bicycle cycling up the road and he stopped the car causing the damage. Two 'scruffy' looking youths driving the car were questioned. They had purchased an old car at an auction, and were taking it to London. They had no insurance or car licence. Eventually they were charged for their offences, pleaded guilty so I was not called to give evidence. My car had to have a complete new rear welded on to the front end. It was never again satisfactory. Once more recourse to my insurance and loss of no claim bonus.

My next car was a Rover 2000, the most expensive car I purchased. At the same time I had a small Morris Minor which I used for travelling in my Station. This small car was the one that was smashed by the police car, causing the injuries to me that resulted in hospitalisation in West Kent General, East Grinstead and Linton Hospitals.

When I retired to Poole in Dorset, the Rover 2000 took Dorothy and I there and we had it for a number of years, going on holidays, re-visiting Maidstone and the Medway Towns until it had to be replaced. Next was a very racy looking Opel which was very smart and efficient. I eventually gave this Opel to my grand-daughter, Elaine, and purchased another Rover car in Guildford on son Brian's recommendation. This car was excellent except that it did not have power steering, so eventually I later traded it in for a Honda with automatic gears and power steering. This car I still have and use for visits to Bournemouth, Gillingham, etc.. as well as locally.

Having been a driver, first of a motor cycle from the age of 19 and then of a car from the age of 27 I have been a driver for over 70 years, I have been granted life membership of the Civil Service Motoring Association. Having reached the age of 90 years it is probable that I will have difficulty soon of obtaining a car insurance as a driver. To stop driving will be a great blow to my life style to date but it has to be faced. Fortunately from my present residence within the London area I am entitled to free public transport, both by rail and bus which will go far towards meeting my transport requirements, but this will not give me the convenience that having a motor car available provides.

Dorothy and I lived in our beautiful house in Manor Rise, Bearsted for 26 years. Although named "Orchard Gate" from the five-bar gate that opened to the drive, capable of accommodating four or five cars, it was later given the number 29. The road was a private one kept in good condition by the inhabitants, jointly, of Manor Rise. The road led to a field growing runner beans in profusion. But subsequently this was acquired by a development company which erected a number of bungalows so that this portion of the road became subject, when made up, to further maintenance by the Rural Council, whereas our portion was maintained by the owners of properties there.

The erection of the bungalows resulted in the Rural Council renumbering all the houses in the road. From No. 29 we were given the new number of 35 but retained our name "Orchard Gate". Originally the "Gate" had led to an orchard of which a number of fruit trees remained within my garden as well as two very large ornamental "Cedars of Lebanon" trees which gave the garden great distinction. There were two large lawns one near to the house and the other beyond a flower garden. Beyond these was a further area where I erected first a small greenhouse and later a much larger one in which I was able to grow tomatoes, cucumbers as well as raising seeds to stock the flower garden. On each side of the lawns I erected stone walling to give the appearance of a sunken garden. The stone walls were built of Kentish ragstone which I gathered from my many journeys around Kent, on official and private journeys. The stone walls were supplemented with various rock-stone gathered in the Cotswolds, Devon and other parts of the country which I visited from time to time. I planted a cherry tree in the centre of the central flower bed, but annually the fruit was devoured by birds who chose the day before I was due to harvest the cherries by descending to have a feast! I planted three Morello cherry trees against the outside wall of the house, but here too, the fruit was taken by the birds before harvest commenced!. Outside the kitchen and dining room windows was a large flower bed in which spring bulbs of daffodils and tulips made a brave display, followed by summer and autumn bedding plants. In the front of the house were two large lawns either side of the drive. One contained a large rose bed, always a picture when the roses bloomed. The edges had flower beds. One was a continuation of stone walling and filled with rock plants spilling over throughout the flowering season.

300

There was another large ornamental Cedar of Lebanon tree on the corner of one front lawn partially masking the side entrance to the house. I built there a brick wall to match the brick structure of the house and erected a wrought iron gate to the side entrance.

Outside the two front lawns was a trim hedge and adjoining the road outside I maintained two narrow flower beds and lawns abutting the road. This was in keeping with other properties in Manor Rise, where the owners kept their gardens in fine condition or employed a gardener. I was particularly proud of my garden and the front aspect often drew praise from visitors to the road.

My elder son, Colin, instructed a local artist to come down to Bearsted and paint a picture of "Orchard Gate" from the front, when the roses and other flowers were in bloom. The lady did so by putting her easel and other painting apparatus up on the front lawn of house No. 29. My good friend Gerald Goodman came out to enquire what she was doing. He had to explain that due to the renumbering of the houses in the road, his was now number 29 whereas my house was now number 35!!. Gerald Goodman's house had a garden meeting mine at the end of my plot. The road took a right angled turn beyond the new number 31. The lady artist did not call to see me at number 35, but maybe I was not at home. She went off and did a fine painting of the ancient parish church of Bearsted, a short distance down the Church path opposite my house. This painting now hangs in my residence at Chislehurst along with another painting of "Orchard Gate" by a lady who was an excellent artist living in the same block of flats as the one Dorothy and I purchased in Poole. It was a great stroke of good fortune to find such an artist. She used the advertising 'blurb' describing our house in Bearsted to would-be purchasers. This contained a full size photograph of "Orchard Gate" and was authentic for her to copy.

Looking up the back garden from the house on the right hand side, the ragstone wall and flower bed, had behind it a narrow path way which I covered with turf. This was next to the privet hedge dividing my garden from the long garden of the house in Yeoman Lane at the top of Manor Rise, leading to the village green. On this pathway next to the privet hedge, Adrian, my grandson used to ride his three wheel cycle, so I named it 'Adrian's Walk' although he seldom walked anywhere. He was always riding the cycle or running. To gain access to 'Adrian's Walk', I built steps up the rag stone wall and these were called 'Elaine's Way'. The wall curved round on each side to form an entrance to the vegetable garden. greenhouse and tool shed beyond the lawns. I was able to keep a few fowls in the small shed there to provide eggs for the house. There was a large underground water tank to the side of the house with a pump to supply all water needed for the garden. Hence I was free of all water shortages when droughts occurred. Altogether it was an idealistic residence and all our friends and neighbours were astounded when we told them that we were retiring to live in the Bournemouth area.

We had made many friends in the Maidstone and Bearsted area. Two very close friends named Mr. and Mrs. Frank Manning were particularly close. He was the owner of a large tailor and outfitting shop in Maidstone. Mr. and Mrs. Peach, next door were very kind and thought the world of Dorothy. They had no family and tended to treat her as a daughter. Often Charlie Peach, the former Kent County Cricketer would give us a fish (generally a pike) he had caught, or a pheasant. He was a pest control officer for the Kent County Council. Down the road at No. 7 lived Harry and Doris Bishop, also no family. He was a director of Walsall Conduits Limited the electrical components company. They often held parties in their house which was somewhat similar to Orchard Gate and to which we were invited.

In Maidstone I made many friends, generally as a result of official duties bringing me into contact. Particularly Charles and Leonard Tye, two brothers who owned the largest general store selling everything from clothing to cameras, jewellery, watches, furniture etc.. I met them frequently when invited to Masonic functions although I did not join a Masonic lodge in Maidstone. My membership of Staplehurst Lodge which I helped to found brought me into contact with numerous people in the Weald of Kent, where I became well known simply as 'Horace' to all and sundry.

CHAPTER FORTY ONE
Dorothy's retirement and life in Poole.

Dorothy's eyesight was beginning to fail. What she did not tell me was that in fact, she had lost the sight of one eye. It was later diagnosed as a haemorrhage behind the eye which has destroyed the sight. I was completely unaware of what had occurred. We decided to retire to Bournemouth as we had always predicted we would. We first looked round all the suitable areas to which we might retire, Brighton, Folkestone, Seaford, Eastbourne but eventually agreed that it must be Bournemouth.

Dorothy tendered her notice to the Market Research firm. A large farewell party was held at the Spar Hotel in Tunbridge Wells. All the staff from the Southern Area attended to pay tribute to her as well as did the Managing Director. She had been with the firm for 23 years and would have liked to have completed 25 but it was not to be. I went to her farewell party and listened to all the tributes that were paid to her skills, her easy manner of dealing with her staff and her devotion to the company she had worked for for so long. She could easily have become the manager had not her devotion to me and our two sons and her home not been her prime consideration at all times. She was known in her firm as 'The Golden Girl', a title well deserved. She was presented with a beautiful glass decanter, an antique silver tray towards which her staff had contributed as well as the Management as a mark of respect with which she had been held by all in the Market Research organisation. They are now with my sons and will become family heirlooms.

Dorothy's eyes were the real cause of our decision to retire to the Bournemouth area. We had always said we would do so, so eventually after 26 years in Bearsted we moved to No. 8 Sunset Lodge, 30/32 The Avenue, Poole. Dorothy was disappointed it was not in

Bournemouth, but as I pointed out we were living in what was generally regarded as the 'finest road in Bournemouth' although it was about 50 yards over the boundary between the two towns and incidentally, originally the boundary between Hampshire and Dorsetshire, until local government changes transferred the whole of Bournemouth, Christchurch, Highcliffe and surrounding areas to Dorset from Hampshire. The Avenue had once been a private road leading to Branksome Chine and the sea. Poole was by far the most interesting town, historically and architecturally. Bournemouth was the modern town, formerly the place to see bath chairs but now a busy commercial centre as well as the favourite seaside resort for many holiday makers. It is reputed to have more hotels than any town in Great Britain, even London. Poole on the other hand, once the haunt of smugglers was now a busy port with frequent sailings to the continents, Channel Islands, Spain and beyond. Once it was the home of the large fishing fleets operating off the coast of Newfoundland which brought prosperity to the Poole fishing barons. It claimed to have the second largest harbour in the world although much is now silted up. Poole had broken out of its area bounded by the harbour and was fast becoming a busy industrial town, particularly in engineering and for the automobile industry.

Sunset Lodge consisted of three separate blocks A, B, and C. Block A had 12 flats on six floors including the ground floor. Blocks B and C each had 10 flats each plus a penthouse on each top floor. All flats had a garage allocated, some being double garages. My flat, No. 8 had two garages allocated because at the time of allocation, a double garage was not available, though required. So a second single garage was allocated to Flat No. 8 by the request of the purchaser at the time. Hence I acquired two garages when purchasing Flat No 8. The two garages were in different portions of the rows of garages but eventually I persuaded the owner of a garage next to one of mine to exchange when she sold her flat, so I then became the owner of two garages next to one another, a much better arrangement for me.

We soon became acquainted with a number of the other flat owners, but flats were continually becoming subject to change as owners left for various reasons, occasionally by death of an owner. The flats were in great demand as being the most desirable in the area. The extensive gardens were a great attraction with flower beds, a large lawn including a putting green. There was a fish pond almost opposite the window to our lounge, with a fountain playing. A gardener who was also the caretaker with his wife maintained the grounds and they lived in a separate bungalow at the end of one row of garages. Each flat had a lounge connected to a large dining room through an archway from the lounge. Each had two bedrooms, two lavatories with a bathroom or a shower. We had one bathroom plus a second shower whereas No. 7 flat with a different layout had two bathrooms. There was a large kitchen, with gas or electric cooking facilities. Each block of flats had a lift to each floor. There was additional cupboard space adjoining the lift entrances for storage of suitcases etc.. In fact all the flats had all the facilities for comfortable living. We were all fortunate that one flat in Block C was owned by an accountant who maintained all the financial records, relieving the other owners of employing a professional house agent to deal with all costs. As a result Sunset Lodge was among the most economical in costs for many flats in the area, particularly for those in the whole of The Avenue.

Dorothy had been a member of the Maidstone Luncheon Club but had not attended very frequently because of her work on Market Research. On arrival in Poole she joined the Dorset Ladies Luncheon Club and from that membership she made many friends. Several of the members of the Luncheon Club, which met in the East Cliff Court Hotel were members of the Royal Overseas League, so Dorothy and I were proposed and accepted for membership of what was possibly the most prestigious club in the whole of the Bournemouth area. The R.O.L. as it was generally known had headquarters in St. James Street, London. There was another office in Edinburgh and many branches throughout the Commonwealth. It was considered a privilege to be a member. Organised outings were arranged to various parts of the country. Bournemouth was the largest branch outside of London. Dorothy and I remained members for the whole of our time living in the Bournemouth area. At one time the proposed Chairman of the Branch asked me to act as his Vice Chairman and I consented. However, for some reason (he was a retired Wing Commander of the Air Force), he decided not to take on the Chairmanship for a year as was customary, and the retiring Chairman had at the last minute to agree to serve for a second year. It is likely that should the W.Comm. not declined I would have become Chairman for a year, but it was not to be. I did, however, commence to act as M.C. for the occasional

Dinner/Dances, the R.O.L. organised. I was not sorry my possible chairmanship did not materialise since I too became involved in numerous activities in the area.

I organised a coach outing through the Meon Valley reputedly the most picturesque in Hampshire, for members of the Royal Overseas League. Our destination was Portsmouth but we went via Hambledon, which claims to have been the home of the origin of cricket in the eighteenth century. Cricket had, however, been played in Kent before Hambledon rose to fame. There is a record of a match between the West part of Kent and Chatham in 1706 and another, of the first County match, between Kent and Surrey at Dartford in 1709. Hambledon remains fixed in most adherents minds from connection with the nobility who took to the game indulging in gambling for high stakes on their team's success. It is interesting to recall that Tom Paine the former Exciseman is recorded as one of the club members present at a meeting of the Hambledon Club in 1773. Since Tom Paine was then living in France, having published his book 'The Rights of Man' and was engaged in producing his second book 'The Age of Reason' in 1793, I have strong doubts of the correctness of the Hambledon Club records.

From Hambledon our party went on to Wickham near Fareham for lunch there, in the hotel of a friend of mine who had previously been at the East Cliff Court Hotel in Bournemouth and before that had been the manager of the Tudor Hotel in Bearsted, my former residential area. Next, on to Portsmouth to view the celebrated H.M.S. Victory, which incidentally was built at Chatham, although now on view at Portsmouth. The return then to Bournemouth was by a more direct route, after an interesting tour of southern Hampshire.

I had for a number of years been a member of the Association of Men of Kent and Kentish Men in the Maidstone Branch. On telling the Secretary that I was moving to the Bournemouth area he told me that in Bournemouth there was a small society affiliated to the M.K.K.M. known as the "Bournemouth and District Association of Kentish Folk". I contacted the Secretary, a Miss Le Fevre and in due course, Dorothy and I joined. It was a very quiet society with a few members, all of whom were expected to have some connection with Kent by birth, ancestry, residence for a period or similar. Associated members also belonged to attend with their friends.

There were about 40 members. Dorothy and I joined and I was soon invited to become a member of the Committee. Monthly whist drives and an occasional dance were held. Also an annual Dinner Dance when the Mayor of Maidstone was invited as a guest. I was asked to act a M.C. for the dances and the annual Dinner Dance. Bournemouth was well known for its many county societies. The "Midlanders" catered for counties in that area of the country. There were "Somerset Folk", "Lincolnshires", "Devonians", "Londoners", "The Welsh", "The Scots", "The Yorkshires", "Lancashires" etc.. Occasionally they inter-met but once a year a large gathering took place in the Pavilion, at Bournemouth, known as the "Exiles Ball", when all the different county societies joined forces for a large scale gathering of "exiles" from all over the U.K. Civic dignitaries were invited, some often themselves were "exiles" from somewhere, other than Hampshire or Dorset. This gathering was a Dinner/Dance at which a large 'Tombola' was arranged, the proceeds from which were donated to a charity of the Chairman of the "3-P's" choice. "3-P's" ——stood for "Presidents and Past Presidents" and covered as it said, all Presidents and Past Presidents of all the various county and similar societies in the district. Dorothy and I attended a number of these gatherings. My main concern was to increase the membership of the Kentish Society.

After a year or so I was invited to become Vice President of the 'Bournemouth and District Association of Kentish Folk. The following year I became President and attended meetings of the "3-P's". It was said of me that I used to wait at the entrances to the Bournemouth area to watch for pantechnicons possibly hailing from Kent with retirees from that county, to ascertain the destination and then to enrol the new arrivals into the Kent Society. Quite wrong of course but a good story. Actually with the many friends made in the area, some from Kent, and others not so blessed, I increased the membership to over 200 and the Kent Society became well known. At a meeting of the committee of the "3-P's" I was asked to act as Press Secretary so I commenced writing articles for the Bournemouth Echo newspaper covering not only the "3-P's" but also Kentish Society gatherings. Securing space in the "Echo" was not easy and I had many interviews with the Editor pleading for publication of copy.

During my first year as President of the Kent Society, I was taken ill, a subject I will refer to later, I had a spell in the Royal Masonic

Hospital near Hammersmith in London. On return to Bournemouth area I was invited to serve a second year as President. This coincided with the 25th Anniversary of the Queen's accession to the throne, so we staged a special Dinner/Dance to mark the occasion and I invited the Secretary of the "Association of Men of Kent and Kentish Men" to attend from Maidstone as a guest. He did so and we all had a enjoyable time together. The Mayor and Mayoress were also guests of the Kent Society. From the function the Society was able to contribute to the fund set up nationally to mark the occasion of the 25th anniversary of the accession to the throne.

I read a report in the press circulating in the Medway Towns that the pianist who regularly entertained the members of a local club had retired to live in Bournemouth. He was a member of a well known family of farmers in the Hempstead area of Gillingham. I wrote to him and received a reply from the Redhill district of Bournemouth where he was living with his brother-in-law named Jim Gorf, formerly a farmer in Lenham, Kent. I was able to enrol them all into the Kent Society in Bournemouth. Jim Gorf was a real 'Man of Kent' and I was soon able to ensure that he took part in the Bournemouth Kentish Society and eventually he became President, relieving me of keeping the membership growing as well as making the Kent Society a force within the "3-P's". Jim Gorf remains a sincere friend and a great colleague in other activities with which I became involved in the Bournemouth area.

CHAPTER FORTY TWO
More journeys abroad and further accident.

Dorothy and I took a holiday by coach to the Tyrol area of Austria staying at Seewen, one of the prettiest little towns in Austria. We made friends with two other holiday makers from Gravesend in Kent. Together we went up to the top of the highest mountains by chair lift and cable car for the magnificent views amid the permanent snow. One evening, when I had left Dorothy in the local hostelry with our friends while I went along the main road to ascertain where the local bank was situated, I was surprised to see my son Brian and June walking towards me. I could hardly believe my eyes because as far as I was aware, they were on holiday camping in Switzerland. It seemed that the weather there was so bad with persistent rain, they had decided to leave and come to Seewen to find us! So instead of a four-some we became a party of six. Brian and June found a suitable spot to continue camping in Seewen, but we were able to visit them daily. In the evening we all went together to the local hostelry for the dancing, 'Austrian style' with much slapping of thighs and sterns! We were invited by the Austrian performers to take part in their perfor-mances. One 'well built' Austrian picked up Dorothy as though she was a feather and twirled her around. I found a very nice little girl dancer with whom to perform! She came from the nearby village of Zirl and I had great difficulty subsequently to live down the enquiries as to whether I was going back to find "the girl from Zirl". We also went to the top of a very high mountain outside of Innsbruck. I believe it was called 'Igls'. We went up via a frightening cable car, but at the top amid the snow we enjoyed the finest apple strudel I had ever tasted. When we finally returned to ground level we were met with an announcement in headlines in the local press that four holiday makers had been killed in a cable car accident, when a cable broke! We did not make any more ascents by a cable car although the acci-dent had not been at Iggls but at another Austrian resort.

The next holiday that Dorothy and I took was a tour of Spanish Andalucia. By this time Dorothy had agreed to accept air travel to reach some of the resorts we wished to visit. For the Andalucian visit we flew to Malaga and from there went to a hotel on the outskirts of Torremolinos. The most unsatisfactory hotel we ever encountered. The food was uneatable and the accommodation more than impossible. With most of the other travellers we complained to the courier for Saga Holidays, and on return to England notified Saga HQs. I was glad to see that this particular hotel never again appeared in the company's brochure. The holiday route was in two sections. One section went westwards towards Gibraltar and one northwards to Granada. We eventually crossed routes at Seville. First via Cadiz to Jerez to visit the vaults of the sherry barons. Then to Seville, a marvellous city full of interest. The grand Easter fiesta had just taken place which we missed, but the other party were lucky to be in Seville for the celebrations. At the hotel Dorothy suffered a serious accident when she fell down a full flight of stairs leading from the lounge to the dining room which was on the lower ground floor. She struck her head on a concrete pedestal at the foot of the stairs. I was in the lounge and heard the shouts. Dorothy suffered concussion to her head and damage to her arms and legs. A very strong Welshman from North Wales, one of our party, picked up Dorothy and she was put to bed, a doctor being summoned. This happened on the first day of our arrival in Seville. The doctor when he arrived was a surgeon from North Africa but very knowledgeable, speaking six languages including perfect English. No bones were broken but the concussion was serious. A large swelling the size of a hen's egg arose on Dorothy's head. The physician regarded this as a good sign, since, as he explained to me, had the damage to Dorothy's skull gone inwards, her brain would have been damaged with serious consequences. We were in Seville for three days, Dorothy remaining in bed throughout. I was able to see some of the sights of the city but my whole concern was for Dorothy's well being.

The physician called daily to observe progress. He suggested that I obtain a 'crutch' for Dorothy to use once she became mobile. Having no idea where to secure such an article, I drew a picture of a 'crutch' and set out to walk into the centre of Seville to buy one! I called at pharmacies, druggists and any shop that might possess such, with no success. Suddenly in a side street I observed a queue outside a building that had a 'crutch' in the window!! It was pure chance.

It was some sort of clinic. I entered the building, ignoring the queue, went to the counter, and showed the picture of the crutch to the attendant. I had no knowledge of Spanish language. A crutch was produced and in some manner the price was explained to be about five pounds in English money. Strangely though, the attendant retired and came back with a quite different article, an 'arm crutch' which was used by the length being adjusted to the length of the patient's arm with a projecting handle to grip and an arm rest for the upper arm. It was the ideal article I required. I will never know what led me to the building where I obtained the 'arm crutch'. It was much more suitable than the picture of a crutch I had drawn, which was the type that goes under the patient's arm-pit. The attendant told me as far as I could understand, that the price for the new article was the same, and I paid from the Spanish currency I was carrying. The attendant then explained that I also needed a 'baton' for the patient's other arm. What a 'baton' was I did not know, so he drew a picture of an ordinary walking stick! He explained that I could obtain this at the large Departmental Store in the centre of Seville. I think that the Good Lord was looking down on me with favour on the journey from the hotel with a picture of a 'crutch' in an endeavour to secure one.

With "signs and nods" I found my way to the centre of Seville. The traffic was quite equal to that of Piccadilly Circus and I was on the wrong side of the street. A policeman was directing the cars etc.. coming from all directions. He was on a sort of platform. I put the crutch I had just purchased on my arm and feigned a poor cripple trying to cross the road!! It must have been a good performance because the policeman stopped the traffic and beckoned me to cross the road!! I did so and disappeared into the Departmental Store. That policeman will never know what a service he had performed! In the store I soon found where walking sticks were on sale. The walking stick cost me more than had the 'crutch' I had obtained from the clinic! Outside the store I hailed a taxi to take me back to the hotel, where I returned in triumph with my purchases.

It is obvious to me now that Dorothy's fall down the stairs at the hotel had been due to her poor eyesight, she having lost the sight of one eye, of which I was then unaware. She was quite unable to judge steps, a fact which later in her life caused further accidents and damage to her frame.

After the three days in Seville, the coach left for Cordoba. Dorothy was made comfortable on the back seat but was still unable to join the others in our party when they set out to view the celebrated Arab Mosque with the cathedral erected within it by the conquering Spaniards under Ferdinand and Isabella who ended the occupation of Andalucia by the Moors. Dorothy implored me to go with the others in our party but I was not at ease. The same thing happened when we went on to Granada, first to visit the Alhambra and later to go by coach to the slopes of the Sierra Nevada where the snow lay thick on the ground. In Granada we witnessed a magnificent display of flamenco dancing at a theatre. For the visit to the Alhambra, Dorothy came with the party but had to stay in the coach while the rest of the party toured to see the sights. We also took a long walk to visit the 'gypsies' living in cave dwellings outside of Granada. In one cave we were entertained by the gypsies to authentic 'flamenco' dancing and 'chanting'. Dorothy had to miss all this, the coach returning with her to our hotel.

After Granada we returned to Torremolinos but not to the hotel we had earlier occupied. Saga had changed the venue to a much better hotel. This time, from Torremolinos we visited the picture book white village of Mijas in the hills overlooking Fuengirola the next town to Torremolinos. We went by taxi so that Dorothy could enjoy the trip with friends we had made on the tour from Cheshire. We also went by taxi to Aloha, beyond Marbella to see the apartment Colin had purchased for a holiday home in Spain. It was up in the hills beneath the high mountain and overlooking the Aloha golf course to which Colin and Eileen had become members. On later visits to Andalucia Dorothy and I stayed in a similar apartment and had super holidays there. Dorothy eventually returned from this tragic trip to Seville in a wheelchair which had to be carried with her in it up the gangway by three strong aircraft employees. Saga paid all the expenses for medical expenses incurred from the insurance we had taken out. But not for the purchase of the special crutch or the 'baton'. When our doctor saw the 'crutch' costing me five pounds he said I had secured a bargain!! That's not the way I looked at the incident. I still have the 'crutch' in case I might need it!!

CHAPTER FORTY THREE
Bournemouth Associations.

Arriving in the Bournemouth area from Bearsted I made contact with the Civil Service Pensioners Alliance and the Civil Service Retirement Fellowship, both of which I had been a life member before I retired. The former was involved solely in improving the lot of Civil Servants after retirement particularly with regard to pensions, and had been in existence for many years. With other organisations such as teachers, police and nurses etc., pressure had been exerted on the Government to secure index linking of pensions to salaries paid in industry annually. Indexing was finally secured from the Government under the premiership of Mr Edward Heath and proved a great boon to all public service pensioners. The Civil Service Retirement Fellowship was a much younger organisation and had the support of the Government and the National Whitley Council covering all Civil Service Departments whereas the C.S.P. Alliance was independent of Government and in some respects was opposed officially, for many of its aims to improve the conditions of retired Civil Servants. The C.S.R. Fellowship was strongly supported by the Government. The weakness as I saw it was that the Government in effect retained the right to appoint the President of the C.S.R. Fellowship, thus ensuring that its aims were restricted to what was considered suitable and appropriate by the Government. The C.S.R. Fellowship maintained a close relationship with the Civil Service Benevolent Fund whose main aim was to relieve distress in any way which was occurring to Civil Servants both in office or retired. The result was that whereas the Alliance was intent, even by political means, of improving the conditions for retired Civil Servants along with other organisations catering for retirees from the public service, the Fellowship was solely concerned with social type events to serve Civil Servants and was not involved with any other organisations catering for public servants.

I was invited to join the Committee of both organisations. For the Alliance the lady who was Social Secretary wanted to give up the post and under pressure I took on the office. My first effort as Social Secretary was to organise a coach tour of an area of the New Forest, which proved successful. However a dispute arose immediately with the Vice-Chairman who was "ex-Post Office". He insisted that all activities proposed by me as Social Secretary had to be approved personally by him. For my part I saw no reason why I should have to get his approval if the Committee had approved my plans. This Vice Chairman was not a person I "took to" and I objected to his dictatorial manner. I think some of his action was due to jealousy of a new member of the Committee. I had no hesitation in sending back to the Hon. Secretary of the Alliance all the documents I had received from the previous Social Secretary and I ceased to be a member of the Committee. I had at the time many other activities in Bournemouth occupying my time, and I had not retired there to take orders from an "ex-Post Office employee" when carrying out a voluntary job. So my tenure with the Alliance in Bournemouth was short lived. I had no regrets on that score.

For my membership if the Committee of the Fellowship the position was just the opposite. At my first meeting a lady who had been a Mayor of a London Borough, after I had made a few comments immediately proposed me for the office of Vice-Chairman which was vacant. The Chairman was a Mr Fred Thistleton, an ex Admiralty employee from Bath formerly of Bournemouth, in the Naval Store Department at Holton Heath, near Wareham. With other members of the Committee I was invited with Dorothy to visit his flat in Canford Cliffs quite close to my flat in the Avenue. At this time I was about 68 years old. Thistleton was 10 years older but remarkably alert. He had retired from Bath at age 60 and first lived in the Queen's Park area of Bournemouth, cultivating a large garden to his bungalow there. His wife who had been a school mistress died at Queen's Park. Fred remarried within a matter of a few weeks to Margaret, who was completely different to Fred's first wife. Fred had a son, named Paul a graduate from the Imperial College, London, who had emigrated to the U.S.A. and was employed as a scientist by the Dupont firm in West Virginia. Fred never called his second wife by her real name, Margaret, but always by the name 'Serenity' which was the exact opposite of her nature! But for all that, she got on very well with Dorothy and came to rely on her for practically everything she was expected to do as wife of the Chairman. We all became very firm friends visiting each other to play cards etc..

Quite different from the C.S. Alliance which was one big Branch, the Fellowship which was the largest Branch in the country with its thousands of retired Civil Servants living in the area, was organised into many groups within the counties of Hampshire and Dorsetshire. There were groups at Fordingbridge, Swanage, Poole, Christchurch, Wimborne, Ringwood, Highcliffe, West Moors, New Milton, Lymington as well as those closer to Bournemouth at Northbourne, Southbourne and Boscombe, besides the largest group in Bournemouth. All the groups ran their own activities, sometimes combining. Each, however, held a 'coffee morning' once a month in a suitable local hall. For all these 'coffee mornings' Fred was expected to put in an appearance and say a few words to the assembled members! On becoming Vice Chairman, I too went with Fred to many of the coffee mornings so I found myself attending all over the area of the Branch to visit group meetings once or twice a week. It became quite a tie but Dorothy seemed to enjoy it and 'stood in' for Margaret, collecting entrance fees at the doors and chatting to members, seeing that they all received their coffee, and counselling when necessary. We really got to know the whole area and made many friends. Once a year there was an A.G.M. when a 'notable' from Fellowship HQs usually attended and a Branch lunch followed.

CHAPTER FORTY FOUR
Bowls.

We made friends with a Mr & Mrs Ken Rees, living in Block C of Sunset Lodge. He was a member of the Argyll Bowls Club, which had a bowling green on the West Cliff quite near to the Avenue. He invited me to join and play bowls, something I had steadfastly declined to do in Gillingham and Bearsted despite my mother's invitation. Tennis had been my game but during my short tenure as General Secretary of the Civil Service Sports Council in Gillingham I had been responsible for dealing with the green keeper in Gillingham. My mother and father had left behind sets of bowls (woods). I had already given my father's woods to my cousin Edith Morgan, later Tutt, who had succeeded my mother as Secretary. On moving to Bournemouth I had brought with me my mother's woods, a very fine set bearing her initials. I purchased the required equipment, shoes, trousers, white cardigans etc., and made application to join the Argyll Club and was accepted. Another applicant to join the same day was a Mr Ray Wilson, who later was appointed the match secretary for the club and became an expert bowler. I did not play very well, mainly due to my difficulty in bending my knee to 'deliver'.

Bournemouth and the whole area was a 'hot bed' of bowls, with many 'greens' in various parts of the town and in Poole, Swanage, Christchurch, New Milton and beyond. Competitiveness was rife with leagues organised by the Bournemouth and District Bowling Association. League matches took place every Saturday in the season for points awarded for a win. Promotions and relegations throughout the 5 leagues later took place at the end of each season. The teams in the first division were very expert, with players who competed in National Bowls competitions. There was also a bowls festival each year when National champions attended to compete for the trophies awarded. Bournemouth Council organised a supper dance in the Town Hall when the prizes were given out. Dorothy and I attended to dance.

I commenced playing with my mother's woods. My sister asked me if she could borrow them to start playing. Reluctantly I lent them to her and purchased a second-hand set for myself advertised in the Argyll Club's pavilion. My sister never returned my mother's woods to me although I sent her a second second-hand set I also purchased. I never forgave her for keeping my mother's woods and I know that she did not play much. I think the woods "descended" to be used by her grand-children in the garden, a sad end to what had been my mother's prize possession for playing for Kent in National competitions.

I continued playing at the Argyll Club and was selected on occasions to play in the league for the Argyll second team, indeed once for the first team! With two expert partners drawn 'out of the hat', I even won the Club Triples competition. With a suitable partner also 'out of the hat' I won quite a number of 'spoons' awarded in a club competition held each Tuesday when visitors from all over the country joined in. I thoroughly enjoyed my membership although never a top class player.

In the Pavilion I noticed an announcement inviting members to join the West Hampshire Masonic Bowling Association which played on a green on the outside of the town. I contacted the Secretary and was duly elected a member. It was with the Masonic Bowling Association that I most enjoyed bowling. I was soon playing in the team selected to play against bowling clubs in the area on a friendly basis, but even more so against Masonic Bowling Associations in other parts of the country. The Masonic Bowling Association team went by coach, with our wives to play against Sussex, Somerset, North Hampshire, Portsmouth, Southampton, Bath, Bristol, Surrey and even Kent Masonic Bowling Association whom we played at Brighton, each side travelling 'half way'. This was a happy match for me because I met some of my 'old' 'Masonic' friends who were bowlers on the green attached to the Franklin Masonic Rooms in Gillingham. My old friend, Raymond, formerly Collector, Dover and Higher Collector, Southampton since retired, came to watch. Dear Mrs Raymond had died returning from a holiday in South Africa, by sea, and was buried at sea. 'Ray' had since left his lovely house at Bassett and had taken a nice flat overlooking the Sussex County Cricket ground. For this grand position, to watch county cricket he had to pay extra on his flat charges. We went to see him there and to watch a county game.

My best friend on the bowling green was Basil Papadopoulos. He had spent much of his time in Nigeria on behalf of the Government, for which he was awarded the M.B.E. so we had that in common. He was one year older than I but an expert bowler. He played regularly for the Bournemouth First team, but also belonged to the Argyll Club where I played, as well as being one of the best bowlers for the Masonic Bowling Association. He really taught me how to play bowls. I proposed him and he was accepted as a member of Bournemouth Probus Club, regularly playing for Probus in the matches against other Probus clubs. He was appointed Captain. His wife Wendy joined the Ladies Probus Club and became the President immediately after Dorothy. She was a South African and they had a daughter, married, living in South Africa who they visited frequently after they retired to live in England. Dorothy and I had a very friendly association with Basil and Wendy.

When we retired to Bournemouth area 'Ray' my former collector in Dover could not believe we would give up our house in Bearsted. He later visited us at Sunset Lodge and was agreeably surprised at what was a beautiful flat. I believe it was this visit that persuaded him to take a flat residence, once Mrs Raymond had died. When inviting him to visit us in The Avenue, his remarks were that it was a dangerous thing to do for a widower, since Bournemouth was full of widows seeking a second husband, so he would have to travel by the 'back road' to avoid them!! He was a 'character'.

On the Masonic Bowling Association's visit to play Bath Masonic, I notified George Lawrence, my 'best man' and Chris James, former apprentices, of our match and they both came to watch, so it was also a happy re-union. By this time I had first been appointed 'Competitions' Secretary and then 'Match and Competitions Secretary' so I was displaying my abilities in getting our team on the green for the match as well as playing. George Lawrence was by this time a competent violinist using a violin he had made himself copying a book on 'Stradivarius' violins and how they were made. With his wife, Triss, he was a member of a string quartet which gave musical shows in Bath. Quite an achievement for someone who had no musical knowledge when I knew him as an electrical apprentice. Chris James, was continuing his hobby of growing sweet peas and had produced one from cross seeding which he had named "Batheasten" after his address and

318

which had been accepted by the Sweet Pea Society as a new variety. He was very proud of this achievement.

The President of the West Hants Masonic Bowling Association at the time was John Groves a very capable organiser. He organised and I assisted him in a bowls tour of Cornwall where we stayed at Newquay. The Cornish Masonic Bowling Association organised matches for us, both indoor and outdoor in Newquay, Truro, Redruth, Falmouth and St Austell. In the evening there was entertainment in the hotel. It was a most successful tour.

Hampshire Masonic Bowling Associations.
Finalists 1980, West Hampshire M.B.A. v North Hampshire M.B.A.
Author is shown holding cup in front row, exteme right of photograph.
Winner of Pairs competition with partner, Bill Simmonds, (next to Author)

CHAPTER FORTY FIVE
Probus.

I heard that an old friend and colleague from my purchase tax days in London Central who had retired to the Ferndown area near Bournemouth had passed away. I was invited to the funeral. His name was Don Stanley and I had served with him on the Special Verification Staff set up to deal with purchase tax by large concerns such as the British Railways, Air Ministry etc.. At the funeral I met up with a number of ex-colleagues mostly all now former higher officials. The Chief Inspector was there, named Le Fevre whom I knew of old as an Officer. He told me that he was unable to stay long after the funeral because he had to get back to Brentwood to attend a Probus Club meeting. Not knowing what a Probus Club was I enquired, and he told me that it was a club organised for retired or semi-retired professional or business men. He said that Probus Clubs were springing up all over the country. With that, another at the funeral of Don Stanley formerly a Collector at London Airport, said that he belonged to the Probus Club of Ringwood which met in nearby Ferndown. He invited me to attend as his guest, the next Probus Club meeting in Ferndown. I did so and found it was very interesting. After various formal club business there was a luncheon followed by a speaker. The meetings took place monthly on the first Monday. It struck me that this was an excellent organisation bringing together the retired men in the area for friendly discourse. I resolved to attempt to form a similar organisation in Bournemouth which was a town attracting numerous 'retirees' in which to reside. I discussed the project with my friend John Groves who was that year President of the West Hampshire Masonic Bowling Association. He agreed also to canvas for prospective members while I made enquiries in the area, for a likely meeting place. John Groves was also a Past President of the Somerset Society, one of the strongest county societies in the area while I was a Past President of the Bournemouth and

District Kent Association., so we had a nucleus of possible members of a Bournemouth Probus Club. I approached the authority for the Pavilion Theatre in Bournemouth which had several rooms where a meeting could be held as well as facilities for serving a meal. I received a favourable response and advised John Groves accordingly. I found out subsequently that Ringwood Probus Club held coffee mornings which the members' wives also attended.

At this time Dorothy and I went to stay at Colin's weekend house at Hythe in Kent for a few days. On arrival there we found that he had suffered a third 'break-in'. As a 'weekend only' residence, the house was vulnerable to burglaries. At the first one he had lost a number of valuable antiques which he never recovered. From the second 'break-in' the thieves had taken still more valuables plus the food from the kitchen cupboards. By chance a policeman had stopped a suspicious looking motorist and went with him to his residence where he found the proceeds of the second burglary! When Dorothy and I arrived we could see the evidence of a break-in from a broken window. The burglar had taken the precaution of placing the front door mat on the soil outside the window to prevent identification of foot prints. More articles had been stolen. From this third burglary, Colin decided to sell the house which was a very desirable residence with four bedrooms, a beautiful fitted kitchen, lounge and dining room, as well as the extensive garden, woods and land.

From this visit we were due to attend a Masonic Ladies Night near Maidstone. On the night before the Ladies Night I was taken ill with violent pains in my chest. After midnight Dorothy had to call the emergency service by phone and eventually a doctor arrived. He prescribed pain killing tablets with instructions to attend if possible, his surgery the next morning. Dorothy thought at first that I was suffering from a heart attack. I managed to reach the surgery, when the doctor asked me whether I had looked at myself in the mirror. I was a violent yellow colour and he told me that I was suffering from gall stones. His advice was that I return home immediately to see my own doctor with a view to admission to hospital. He supplied me with pain killing tablets. His further advice was that I get someone to drive me home in my car. Instead, I set out myself and with Dorothy drove as far as Worpleson in Surrey to see our younger son and then to drive on to Poole. Taking further "pain killers" for the night, the next day I saw my doctor explaining my symptoms. He suggested I enter a private hospital immediately. I declined. He asked Dorothy "Is your husband stupid?" This caused Dorothy to protest. The doctor then suggested that he secure my admission to Poole Hospital as soon as was possible. I then told him I would go into the Royal Masonic Hospital, so he telephoned that establishment and received instructions that I was to go at once for admission. By train and taxi, Dorothy and I went, and I was admitted. X-rays and other examinations confirmed that gall stones were the cause of my illness. Eventually I had an operation and learned that my spleen was also affected. After the operation I was sent to the Royal Free Hospital for further checks. My treatment lasted for a number of weeks but eventually I returned home and have experienced no further trouble.

Because of my stay in the Masonic Hospital I had made no progress with the proposal to start a Probus Club in the Bournemouth area. Strangely though, I heard from a friend named Houlston who we often visited for private coffee mornings with others, and who also was a Past President of the Somerset Society, that the Bournemouth Rotary Club was interested in promoting the formation of a Probus Club for Bournemouth. A meeting was to be held in the Bournemouth Pavilion by three representatives of the Rotary Club, with eight persons known to be interested in the proposal. My friend Houlston suggested that I also should attend. Which I did.

Prior to my discussions with John Groves before I was taken ill, I had contacted a number of Probus Clubs and obtained from them copies of their constitutions, rules and general procedures. These came from Ringwood Club and Farnborough Club where a retired Air Force Officer and his wife who were friends of Dorothy in the Bournemouth Ladies Luncheon Club, had lived. I had also contacted the Probus Information Centre at Bromsgrove, Worcestershire. The Chairman of the Rotary Club panel was a local bank manager. After he had opened the meeting in the Pavilion, I explained what I knew of the formation and history of the Probus Club movement. No one else seemed to have any knowledge of Probus. The Chairman said that Rotary had decided to foster the movement throughout the country but that he had little knowledge of what was involved. After I had spoken the Chairman said that it was obvious that I already had sufficient knowledge so he suggested that I be charged with setting up a formation committee to form a Probus Club for Bournemouth. With that the meeting with Rotary concluded.

I contacted John Groves, Melvern Dawbarn who was the previous year's President of the West Hants Masonic Bowling Association, Stanley Dobbins, whom I had known many years earlier as Supplies Manager for Plant Protection Ltd., in my former Excise Station, now living in Bournemouth. The other member of the formation committee was a man named Baldwin whom I did not know. He had attended the meeting with the Rotary Club members but he did not prove much of an asset to the formation committee and in fact did not become a member eventually of Bournemouth Probus Club when it was formed. The formation committee met at Melvern Dawbarn's residence in Poole. I had prepared a set of rules and constitution which the committee accepted without amendment. We decided to recommend that the proposed Club meet in the Pavilion at Bournemouth on the second Tuesday in each month. This would insure that the new club did not clash with the meetings of the Ringwood Probus Club which met on the first Monday in each month. I had already secured accommodation at the Pavilion in Bournemouth for the meeting to be held there and a lunch provided. We decided to limit the membership to 60. I contacted a number of my friends in the Kent Society, the Argyll Bowls Club and the Royal Overseas League, and with them and a few that John Groves had secured in the Somerset Society we had a nucleus of some 30 prospective members. The first formal meeting of the Bournemouth and District Probus Club was held in March in 1979 when David Dallimore, the bank manager, on behalf of the Rotary Club took the chair. The proposed rules were adopted in full, Bernard Phillips a retired Postmaster of Bournemouth also attended on behalf of the Rotary Club. I was unanimously elected as Chairman of the new club, John Groves, who was away on holiday in Malta was appointed Hon. Secretary and my neighbour in Flat No. 7, named Ron Ward as Hon. Treasurer. A Mr Cotton, a retired Probation Officer agreed to act as Speaker's Secretary, with Norman Baldwin and Alex Dewar as committee members. Mervern Dawbarn was elected as Vice-Chairman. With the two Rotary members we all then took lunch together after what had been a successful launch of the new club. A second meeting was held in May when about 50 members attended. Norman Baldwin did not attend any subsequent meetings.

I subsequently wrote an article on the Probus movement and on the formation of such a club in Bournemouth, which was published in the Bournemouth Echo newspaper. Applications for membership were invited and from this I received a flood of applications. The number of 60 was soon reached. David Dallimore called to see me at my flat and told Dorothy that the Rotary Club had realised that I had all the information that was required for the Club. He also told me that the Rotary Club had decided to present the Probus Club with a Presidential Collar and Medallion. At the next meeting of the Club in June 1979 David Dallimore again attended. The meeting decided to change the title of Chairman and of Vice Chairman to President and Vice President respectively. Mr. Dallimore presented the Club with the Presidential Collar and Medallion and I was formally installed.

One notable exception to the procedures in force at most Probus Club; the Bournemouth Club decided to have guest speakers address the members before the lunch took place. I had found that with speakers after the lunch, they often went on talking much longer than the agreed spell of one hour. As a result of this I had observed at Ringwood Club that often the meeting concluded long after the normal time of 3.00 p.m. With a commencement of a meeting a 11.00 a.m., club business for about half an hour, a speaker for about one hour and then a short break for a visit to the bar, lunch could be timed for 1.00 p.m. and all could be over well before 3.00 p.m. In 1980 John Groves resigned as Hon. Secretary but agreed to act as Speaker's Secretary. Melvern Dawbarn became the second President and I took over as Hon. Secretary. The limit of 60 members had been reached.

In December 1979 a Christmas lunch was held to which members could invite their wives or lady friends as guests. I secured the attendance of the Mayor or Bournemouth and his lady as guests of the Club. Due to the application for membership it was decided in 1981 to increase the membership number to 70 and again in 1983 to 75. Soon after this a second Probus Club known as Bournemouth No. 2 was formed with a nucleus of members from the original club plus many applicants from the Bournemouth No. 1 list who had been waiting a considerable time for a vacancy . Probus Clubs had also been formed in Poole, in Parkstone (part of Poole), in Northbourne (part of Bournemouth), and later in Southbourne (part of Bournemouth). Christchurch already had a Probus Club and soon a second Club was started there. The Probus Club movement had undoubtedly filled 'a long felt want' in the Bournemouth, Poole, Christchurch and surrounding area so I felt justified in my early efforts to bring the movement to Bournemouth in the first place. The whole area which is full of "retirees" from all walks of life needed such a movement. Probus Clubs now exist almost world wide, in Canada, Australia, New Zealand and South Africa especially. They far exceed the number of Rotary Clubs in Great Britain. After 7 years as Secretary I gave up the post having ensured that I had an efficient successor to take over. I then reverted to being an ordinary member but was elected an Honorary Member for my services to the Club.

Probus is reputed to have been started in Welwyn Garden City, sponsored there by the Rotary Club and taken up nationally by them, with the intention of promoting good fellowship and social activities among retired or semi-retired business and professional men. Hence the name PRO-BUS. Each club frames its own rules and constitution and is entirely a law unto itself. There is no central organisation although the Information Centre at Bromsgrove supplies advice if requested and also badges, emblems, car stickers, ties etc..

In 1982 at the Bournemouth Christmas lunch, the Mayoress who was sitting next to Dorothy, enquired of her, why there was not a Ladies Probus Club! Dorothy consulted Christine Groves, John's wife, and they decided to start one! Membership was restricted to the wives of Probus members of any mens' club or their widows. Dorothy was the first President for two years, and then became Secretary. The Ladies Club became quite successful and is independent of the male version! The mens' Probus Club presented the Ladies with a Presidential Collar and Medallion, which Dorothy was proud to wear as its first President.

In 1980 I received an enquiry from the Secretary of Aylesbury Probus Club as to whether Bournemouth Probus had a bowls team, since Aylesbury was visiting Bournemouth for week's stay and would like to have a match. Such was easy, since Bournemouth had many members in the Argyll Bowls Club. So commenced a series of annual matches - Aylesbury versus Bournemouth. Aylesbury continued to visit Bournemouth with their ladies for many years. Dorothy and I became very friendly with the Aylesbury Secretary and his wife, Fred and Ellen Timbury, and also with one of the members, Jack and Ethel Robinson who had a holiday flat in Poole overlooking the harbour. We spent many happy hours with them there when they visited Poole to stay at their flat.

From my initial visit to Ringwood Probus Club meeting I was subsequently invited to further meetings there as a guest and made many friends. Particularly with the Social Secretary named Bill Vaughan. He moved from the Ashley Heath area of Ringwood to a flat in The Avenue at Poole, opposite to Sunset Lodge, but remaining a member of Ringwood Probus. Ringwood had a rule that stipulated the members should live not more than 6 miles from the town, but if moving away they retained their membership. There was a clause though, that allowed the rule for membership to be 'broken' in exceptional circumstances. I was invited to become a member of the Ringwood Club and readily accepted. Ringwood Club held some dinner/dances in the Pavilion an Bournemouth. Also the club arranged a long week-end stay at a very smart hotel in Torquay each autumn. When this hotel changed to 'Time-Share' the venue for the autumn stays was changed to the Belmont Hotel in Sidmouth. Dorothy and I went on these 'autumn breaks' with the Ringwood Club. We had previously visited Sidmouth in August on several occasions to witness and enjoy the Festival of Folk dancing organised by the town. Dance teams from various parts of the globe in colourful costumes entertained the large audience in an open air setting.

The dancers came from France with their 'stilt' dancing, Norway, Columbia, Ukraine, West Africa, South America and many other foreign countries. There were of course, clog dancers from Lancashire, Morris dancers and other country dancers from England. These were very 'tame' compared with those from abroad. This display of folk dancing took place each year and was a great attraction to the town. Often during the day the dancers would be giving free exhibitions of their skills on the esplanade when practising. In addition to the dancers, the town was full of 'groups', singers, instrumentalists, and it must be admitted, many long haired "weirdies". Many looked as if they needed a wash. I think most of the local population remained at home, surrendering their town to the visitors of all sorts, good, bad and 'weird'. This was only during the first week of August. In the autumn, Sidmouth returned to its quiet existence with not a supermarket in which to hire a trolley!!

I was able to arrange for a bowls match to be played against the local Sidmouth bowls team by Bournemouth Probus club bowlers. These matches took place during the summer unconnected with the autumn visits by Ringwood. A nice lunch was put on by the proprietor of the Riviera Hotel where the Sidmouth Probus Club held its meetings. At one meeting of Sidmouth Probus Club when the Ringwood club was holding its autumn break, I was invited to attend as a guest of the club, and was well received. I also arranged for a bowls match by the Bournemouth club against the bowls club of Seaton near to Sidmouth. For this match we had a lunch well presented at the Alexandra Hotel in Lyme Regis. We invited the captain and the secretary of the Seaton club to be our guests. For all these visits to Seaton and Sidmouth our ladies accompanied us, either to watch the bowls or to use our coach for a tour of the district.

For Dorothy's and my visits to Sidmouth in the autumn with Ringwood club we were able to visit old friends from Gillingham who had retired to Tipton St. Johns near to Sidmouth. They were Doris and Vic Fuller and had been members of our 'group' that staged the entertainments presented at the Civil Service Motoring dances. He had been one of the 'undertakers' who carried off the bodies murdered by the villain Spaniard in the 'cod' opera we staged, while Doris was one of the Television Toppers in the radio/television show we did, as well as one of the chorus girls in the opera. Before retiring to near Sidmouth, Vic Fuller had been Commodore of the Gillingham cruising club based at the Strand in Gillingham. This was close to St. Mary Magdalene church and from where the 'chain' was thrown across the River Medway to prevent the Dutch fleet from sailing up the Medway to sink the British Fleet anchored at Chatham, but the chain failed in its purpose. Vic Fuller was interviewed by the B.B.C. in a 'Down Your Way' programme. It happened that the following weekend our 'gang' was picnicking at Seal Common near Sevenoaks when the programme was broadcast, so we were all able to hear Vic Fuller being interviewed!!

I was also able to visit at Salcome Regis near to Sidmouth, the photographer from Pluckley in Kent who I visited officially in the past. He was the photographer who took pictures of the paintings in the National Gallery and elsewhere for the inclusion in books and magazines for world wide distribution. His wife was formerly the headmistress of Pluckley village school, before that area became famous for the television programme 'Darling Buds of May'. They had retired possibly to the quietest village in the country occupying the former post office, since discontinued.

From my membership of both Ringwood and Bournemouth Probus Clubs I was able to organise a bowls match between the two. This developed into matches with Christchurch Probus, Northbourne Probus and Barton on Sea Probus. In the end a full scale series of matches, home and away, were being played between them all on a league basis.

After a number of visits by Aylesbury Probus, it was suggested that Bournemouth should visit Aylesbury in Buckinghamshire for a return match. This was not easy because of the distance involved; to go there and back in one day besides playing bowls. Whereas Aylesbury came to Bournemouth for a week's stay, we would visit for one day only. However, by an early start we accomplished the trip on two occasions. First we stopped at the Potters Heron Hotel near Romsey. For me a place of many memories when assisting Mr Skelt there on Widows Pension work. On the way there for coffee, I had secured each one of our parties' choices for the evening meal on our return, these being made from the menus obtained in advance. At Aylesbury we were entertained to a sumptuous lunch before the match and to tea before we set out for our return journey. All went according to plan. Our dinner at Potters Heron was ready and we all got back after a grand day out. The ladies had been taken to Waddesdon Manor, the home of the Rothschilds to see the fabulous treasures housed there. It really was a most successful outing for all.

A Ladies Probus Club had been started in Littlehampton in Sussex. The members wanted to pay a visit to the Bournemouth Probus Ladies and this was easily arranged quite successfully. Bournemouth Ladies did not want to make a return visit, so Dorothy and I went as guests of the Littlehampton Club and were well looked after.

Soon after taking up our residence in Poole, I contacted the Secretary of the Bournemouth Branch of the Civil Service Motoring Association and I was invited to join the Committee. I found that practically all the members of the committee and in fact, later, of the Branch, were at that time employees of the Post Office and the Telephone Service, (before the advent of British Telecom). Never-the less the branch was active in promoting visits to beauty spots, places of industry such as motor manufacturers, a brewery, and even to the broadcasting studios in Bournemouth. In addition they organised 'walks' in the New Forest and elsewhere. An Annual Dinner/Dance was also held which attracted members of the C.S.M.A. from surrounding areas, Portsmouth, Salisbury and Dorchester. After a while I was invited to M.C the Annual Dinner/Dance. With Dorothy I went on a few visits to places of industry. One was to the Headquarters of Barclays Bank International in Poole. I never met up with any other what I term 'real' Civil Servants, as I had done in the Medway Towns. It was all post office and telephones, members of which were fully entitled to be members of the C.S.M.A. I remained a member of the Committee until I left the Bournemouth area, but did not participate in any activities after the illness and passing of Dorothy.

CHAPTER FORTY SIX
More journeys abroad.

Dorothy had accepted once we took up residence in Poole that she would fly abroad, although our first trip was to Italy by coach visiting Milan, Florence, Pisa, Rome, with an optional extension to Capri which we took and enjoyed, visiting the island where Gracie Fields was then living. On the tour with us was a young couple named Frank and Vera Matthews with their small son, Kirk. Also a solo passenger named Ralph Creasey from Hastings. The Matthews did not take the extension to Capri staying in Rome for a few extra days. Creasey, on the other hand, was making a senti-mental return to Monte Cassino to visit the graves of his colleagues killed in assault on that German and Italian stronghold during the war. He alighted and returned to the coach on our way back from Capri. The coach then went on to Assisi where we were fortunate to witness an Italian wedding in this celebrated home of St. Francis. Next back to Rome and then on to Venice and for Dorothy and I, another chance to look at this gem of the Adriatic.

Frank Matthews was a press photographer and was travelling with cameras of all types strung round his neck! He obviously drew atten-tion to himself at every border we crossed, into Switzerland, Italy, Austria etc.. and was invariably selected for interrogation by frontier guards! There were two 'youngish' girls on the trip. When we crossed into Italy the Customs Control selected the girls to be taken into the control post to be searched!! Instead, they appealed to me as their 'father' and I declined to let them alight from the coach! The 'ploy' was successful and the frontier guards gave up their intentions to have them inside the control hut for a search!
We stopped in the Tyrol to view the beautiful coloured mountains. Frank Matthews proved a great organiser of party games among our coach travellers for the night we spent in the Tyrol. When passing

through Germany, our coach broke down on the motorway. Frank Matthews 'climbed' under the coach and located the trouble. Something to do with 'toggles' on the clutch. He effected temporary repairs and we finally reached Ostende on reduced 'toggles'!!

On the trip with us was also an Italian and his wife who had emigrated to South Wales where they had an ice cream business. He was an extremely mean man, never giving his wife any money for purchases. When the ladies of the party went to "pay a penny" the wife never had the required "penny", so she always asked one of the other ladies, often Dorothy, to keep the door open when they emerged, so that she could go in without paying! We visited Naples and Vesuvious to see the ruins that resulted from the great eruption. Somewhere on the trip the Italian/Welshman had purchased a diamond ring which he confided to all and sundry, he was going to sell hoping to make a profit when he got back to South Wales. He made his wife wear the ring as her property for passing through Customs, but it was not for her to keep. On all our journeys abroad I steadfastly never disclosed my connection with the Customs and Excise, so the Italian/Welshman did not know he was talking to someone who could easily have caused him embarrassment when he returned to Great Britain, but I did not.

In Venice I observed a lady artist painting a lovely picture of the Grand Canal taken from the steps of the renowned Rialto Bridge. I was so taken with the painting that I offered to buy it. Despite difficulties in conversation, the artist explained that it was not quite finished. I agreed to return in an hour when she said it would be completed. This I did and purchased the painting, still wet, for a number of liras which I think amounted to about £10. I then went to a nearby shop where the proprietor wrapped the painting in padding and paper to ensure it did not come to harm. It was then placed under my seat in the coach and caused no trouble at frontier posts until we passed from Germany into Holland. There it was spotted and the customs man said 'Vot is dat'. I said a painting and nothing further occurred. I had no difficulty in passing through Dover Customs but I was aware that a work of art was not subject to control in any case. The last I saw of Frank Matthews in Dover was of him being closely questioned by the Customs there! He looked a suspicious character but was not, quite the reverse! Dorothy and I continued to correspond with the Matthews and with

Ralph Creasey. I still do so each year at Christmas. We once staged a reunion of all five of us in Hastings when we travelled there from Poole and the Matthews from Burgess Hill in Sussex. For this journey abroad neither Dorothy nor I had an accident such as had plagued us on other journeys!! The Matthews' son is now a Metropolitan policeman and they are grandparents! Ralph Creasey is still alive although his wife has passed on. She would not travel abroad so Ralph had always to go solo. The picture I purchased in Venice is about 16 inches by 20. It has been framed and varnished. It is one of my proudest possessions and is admired by all who see it. It hung in our flat in Poole, but is now the "piece de resistance" in my present abode.

Photograph of oil painting in Author's possession, showing view of Grand Canal, Venice from Rialto Bridge

Dorothy and I now had so many interests in the Bournemouth area that we had difficulty in fitting them all in. I had the Mens' Probus, Dorothy the Ladies'. We both had the Kent Society, and the Royal Overseas League. I was Vice Chairman of the Civil Service Retirement Fellowship and a committee member of the C.S.M.A., also match and competitions Secretary of the West Hampshire Masonic Bowling Association, having been President in 1980. I played bowls a good deal. My successor as President of the Masonic Bowling Association was also Treasurer of the Northbourne

332

Bowling Club. He invited me to play regularly for the Northbourne Club in the Bournemouth and District Bowls Association League, so I was regularly involved in a league game each Saturday as well as playing friendly matches at my original club, the Argyll near to our residence. So life was very full and we had made numerous friends throughout the area.

Despite this, Dorothy thought she should learn Spanish, now that Colin had a second home in the Costa del Sol near the Aloha Golf Club, about 4 miles from Marbella. The Education Committee held classes for adults in a building near the centre of Bournemouth. Dorothy attended to enrol for Spanish. She joined what she thought was the right queue but found it was for 'Judo'!! Her next choice was for dressmaking and she was enrolled. I took her for each session, intending to return to pick her up after each session. Coming down the stairs I saw "cards" being played in another room.

I went in and made enquiries to be told it was a beginners' class in Bridge. I was told to make enquiries from the Principal and he said that I was free to join if I wished. So I started to play Bridge although I was quite familiar with the game. The class coincided with Dorothy's dressmaking class so we were able to attend together once a week in the mornings. I found that I was in demand by a number of the other players who were beginners. The teacher was quite good at telling each player what to 'call' but she had the advantage of seeing each player's hand first!! Meanwhile Dorothy was having problems with her instructor since Dorothy had never displayed any interest before in dressmaking so was starting from 'scratch'. I think that she was a 'problem child' for the teacher, but she struggled on. Eventually she produced a very nondescript costume which she gave away to another lady at the Argyll Bowls club. I was invited by an elderly lady playing in the Bridge Class, to visit her at her residence, with Dorothy, to play bridge in the evening. Dorothy had no interest in playing so was supplied with some magazines to read while I played with the elderly ladies!! The whole episode was a farce so was not repeated. Due to the imposition of economies by the Education Committee, the fees were increased so that instead of one fee for the whole of two sessions, September to March, an equal fee was charge for one session September to December and another for the second session from January to March. Although my Bridge teacher invited me to join the advanced class for the next set of sessions, I declined. Dorothy also gave up her efforts to make clothing she had no intention of ever wearing. She never started her Spanish language course, although I must say that on our many trips abroad I found that she was much more adept at picking up phrases in foreign languages that ever I was. Instead of Bridge we both played solo whist once a week with Fred and Margaret Thistleton, (Chairman of the Civil Service Fellowship and his wife).

During the years at Poole, Dorothy and I went on a number of holidays abroad. One of the earlier ones was to Majorca with Thomson Holidays, staying at Palma Nova. The cost was £50 per week each but because we were both pensioners we received a £5 reduction per week each so only had to pay £45! The hotel was near the front but some of the holiday makers were German who invariably went down early each morning and placed their towels on the best seats for sunbathing. Other than that it was an enjoyable stay for our first visit to Majorca. Later we stayed at the Coral Playa Hotel on the outskirts of Magaluf. This was an improvement being right on the sea front with the restaurant on the top floor and all the bedrooms lower down to sea level. There was a nice dance floor where Dorothy and I could enjoy ourselves. The hotel held a competition to choose "Miss Coral Player". With a Norwegian and a Frenchman I made up the judging committee of three, for which we each received a bottle of champagne. One of the guests, (I believe he was a police detective hoping to locate some English criminals taking refuge in a Spanish area) did an excellent male 'striptease' almost down to his pants and socks amusing all the other residents. On another visit, we booked in to quite a nice hotel in Palma Nova but on the flight over we were plagued with a crowds of football supporters, destined for our hotel. They were equally obnoxious in the hotel with their singing and shouting plus their drinking, so I asked the travel company representative to move us to another hotel. This was to the Trinidad Hotel which was a great improvement. There Dorothy and I won a dancing competition dancing the Tango. We could easily have won the subsequent dances but dancers were restricted to one prize. We did, however, come second in the Mr & Mrs Trinidad competition. The winner was a man with a long flowing beard and his partner which made him distinctive. We met there a French Canadian couple who declined to converse in English in the hotel. We changed partners to dance with them and later they came to our bedroom for a drink where they conversed in perfect English! From some of the other hotel residents I learned that they had had a very enjoyable trip to the north of Majorca by coach. There was no further similar visit arranged from the hotel by the travel company. So I spoke to a number of other residents and received enough support to organise for ourselves a similar trip. I contacted the local coach firm and was able to fill a coach from residents at the Trinidad Hotel. We were very lucky to have as one of the 'passengers' a man who could play a mouth organ very expertly. He kept the party amused throughout the trip. We were able to visit a monastery in the mountains and hear the choir singing. We finally reached Cape Formentor in the north of Majorca. Altogether it was a very enjoyable visit to the north coast. I received the thanks from the other residents at the Hotel Trinidad for arranging the outing. We had stopped en route at one of two 'bodegas' which pleased my 'passengers'. The 'mouth organist' was a great help in making the trip a success.

Dorothy and I also took a holiday to Tenerife in the Canary Islands in the late winter to enjoy the sunshine. At that visit we stayed in the north of the island at Santa Cruz, although we took a tour to the south which was then mostly undeveloped. The authorities were busy carting lorry loads of soil from the north to the south, which was mostly barren, so to be able to cultivate the area and make it more attractive to visitors.

We stayed at the Tenerife Playa Hotel on the front at Santa Cruz opposite the new Marina under construction. Sometimes camels passed along the front but it was easy to smell them approaching!! A short walk took us to the market area. The shops appeared to carry two prices, one the normal price without disputing, but the other, the lowest if one was prepared to 'haggle'. We went up through the clouds to Mount Tiede where one could always find the sun shining on to the extinct volcano. But the weather down below was first class during our visit in February. We visited a warehouse where the bananas, still green, were being packed for export. En route we saw the original Spanish residences and their distinctive wrought iron balconies. It was a most enjoyable holiday with no untoward incidents.

We later changed by visiting the Algarve area of southern Portugal on the recommendation of friends we had made in the Bournemouth area, and of one of Dorothy's former staff in Rochester. Visits there in February, were very pleasant with lots of sunshine. Our first visit was to Albufeira staying at the 'Sol e Mar Hotel' immediately on the front. We used the Travel Club of Upminster for all our visits to the Algarve. On our first visit we travelled from Faro airport by taxi with another couple, the man having business interests in building in Saudi Arabia. On arrival at the hotel our companions put their cases and a large bag containing perfume, liquor, cigarettes, chocolate etc.. they had bought duty free on the plane, down on the pavement, then going inside to secure a porter to carry their bags etc.. into the hotel. On return they found that the bag with all the "duty free's" had disappeared. A fine start to their holiday!! We visited most of the main towns of the Algarve, Faro, Portamao, Albufeira and Loule. Also the beauty spots such as Monchique in the mountain area passing through the masses of Acacia trees, Cork trees and orchards growing oranges and lemons. On subsequent visits we stayed at the 'do Garbe' Hotel at Armacao de Pera, which became our favourite venue. On a visit to Faro passing a hotel looking over the harbour we were hailed by Olive Deeming, the mother of Elizabeth, Colin's former wife. She had heard our voices down below her bedroom and hailed us. I had a car on hire so was able to take her and her sister with whom she was holidaying on some trips into the countryside. It was just lucky coincidence that we met.

Dorothy and I also went out to the very tip of Portugal, to Cape St. Vincent, the nearest point to America! Nearby was Sagres where Henry the Navigator, son of John of Gaunt, planned the journeys of Portuguese seafarers, down the West African coast, to round the Cape of Good Hope, across to India and beyond and so established the early Portuguese Empire. Dorothy and I sat on the bank and I gave her a history lesson, so she told our friends! We climbed the lighthouse tower at Cape St. Vincent but could not see America! The Atlantic waves were very heavy but some fishermen were perched on the rugged rocks trying for a 'bite'.

Soon Colin's apartment in the Costa del Sol was available and we enjoyed holidays there. On one such we were contacted by a member of the Bournemouth Probus Club named Richardson who was a millionaire and a 'name' at Lloyds. He had entered the army as a private for the war but rose to the rank of colonel. We were good friends in the Probus Club and visited each other's apartments. I had proposed him for membership. He had made his fortune at the end

336

of the war when stationed at the War Office. While there he planned to enter the publishing business and also the Health Shop trade, making a fortune. On a cruise in the Mediterranean the ship put in at Malaga. There he hired a car and went for a trip along the coast to Marbella and beyond. At Puerto Banus, the celebrated venue for the big yachts just beyond Marbella, he visited some luxurious apartments being constructed for those able to afford such residences. Puerto Banus is well known for being the haunt of all types, good, bad and reputedly criminal!! Only such can afford the yachts that are anchored there, never seeming to venture out to sea. 'Jimmy' Richardson, as I called him, finished up by buying the show apartment and all its fittings and furniture! He then went back to the cruise liner! Such is wealth! It was later that he went out to Puerto Banus for a holiday, when we too were on holiday near Colin's apartment at Aloha, nestling under the Sierra Blanca. Jimmy Richardson found Colin's site in the fresh air a welcome change from his at sea level with the yachts. Never-the-less when we visited him there, it was truly magnificent with all the facilities one could wish for. He had also purchased for his daughter an apartment at Lanzerote in the Canaries. Poor Jimmy died of cancer at his magnificent penthouse overlooking Poole Harbour. Dorothy and I were with him the day before he was taken into hospital.

CHAPTER FORTY SEVEN
Poole Workshop.

When I left Gillingham to live in Bearsted I took with me the Morrison shelter in which Brian had been born. I re-erected it in my garage to serve as a work bench for the numerous jobs that crop up from time to time as a householder and for which my training as an apprentice in the dockyard was an enormous help. I also took my two tool boxes with all the tools I had accumulated during my five year apprenticeship. One tool box had been issued by the Admiralty and was very large. The other was presented to me by my fellow apprentice, Cyril Cox, who was an apprentice as a Joiner and Carpenter. He made it in the workshop of the joinery department of the best wood available. It was one of the tests of his abilities. I valued it immensely. Moving from Bearsted to Poole, the Morrison Shelter, converted to a workbench was too heavy to transfer, so I had to leave it behind for the new owner of Orchard Gate when he took up residence. I was, though, able to take my two tool boxes and all my tools to Poole. I purchased a very heavy wooden desk at an auction with large drawers either side and converted this to a work bench and installed it in my second garage. I also purchased a number of electrical tools, such as a saw, a drill and a small rotating lathe with which I could turn out various articles required for our apartment. Having retired, I now had time to practice again my former skills at a work bench. This was apart from the numerous calls on my time from the various Offices in which I soon became involved with Associations I joined as a member or renewed.

One of the first articles I made was a portable cabinet to house the Masonic Banner for the Staplehurst Lodge. When in due course I reached the stage of being promoted in the Masonic Province of East Kent, I was given the rank of a "Superintendent of Works", no doubt as a reflection on my previous experience as an electrical fitter, and my presentation to the Lodge of the portable cabinet in which to keep the Banner when not on display within the Lodge room. The cabinet was about 40 inches square and eight inches deep! Painted light blue, (the Masonic colour), it now stands in the Masonic Temple at Hartley, near Cranbrook.

I made also a small portable lectern for the use of the President, Secretary or guest speaker at meetings of the Probus Club. This proved very useful. The Club needed a Gavel and sounding block, so I visited the timber merchant in Boscombe to secure the wood for the articles. Making the gavel was not easy to accomplish since it had to be 'turned' to shape. The sounding 'base' was much easier to make. About this time we were on one of our visits to Majorca and made the acquaintance of a Welshman who was an artist in wood. He regularly visited Majorca on holiday, and while there he scoured the countryside in search of pieces of olive wood to take home for use in his artistic work. I told him of my efforts to make a gavel and block for use by the Probus Club President. I thought no more about it. One day a small parcel was delivered to me at Poole from Wales. Inside was a miniature gavel and block made of olive wood. It was sent with the compliments of the Welsh friend I had made in Majorca. The gavel is a little less than four inches long and the block just under three inches in diameter with a recess in which to rest the gavel in an upright position. Beautifully made of olive wood from Majorca. It really was a miniature work of art, very small, for controlling a large audience, but nevertheless quite suitable for a committee meeting or very small audience.

I located a sign writing firm in Ringwood that produced 'Honours Boards' suitable for displaying the names of winners of trophies etc.. in bowls club pavilions and also for the names of Presidents etc.. on boards on view in meeting places of Associations. I had two such boards prepared showing the names to date of the President each year for the mens' Probus Club of Bournemouth and for the Ladies Probus similarly. These I presented with my compliments to each. That for the mens' club is now on display in the entrance to the Durley Hall Hotel in Westbourne, Bournemouth, and for the ladies, in the Mirama Hotel on the East Cliff, Bournemouth. Both clubs have changed their meeting places due to privatisation of part of the Pavilion in Bournemouth and withdrawal of facilities there. For the Bournemouth Probus list my name is recorded as the first President in 1979 and Dorothy's twice as first and then a second time for 1983 and 1984.

Presentation by Author, Founder President, of the Honours Board to the
current President, Rodney Maunder, of the Bournemouth & District Probus Club.
Of the 14 Past Presidents, 10 were able to be present.
Author is standing to right of Rodney Maunder.

Author with the current President of the
Bournemouth & District Ladies Probus Club, Lorraine Pardy,
when the author presented the Ladies with The Honours Board.
Lorraine is number 10 in the list of Presidents

Dorothy's Probus Club each year staged a 'bring and buy' sale at their Spring coffee morning to which the gentlemen were invited. The proceeds of the 'bring and buy' were donated to a Charity of the President's choosing. Dorothy invariably searched our apartment for 'odds and ends' to contribute to the 'bring and buy' counter. I always attended. At one of these gatherings I was amazed to see my miniature gavel and block on display with a price 'tag' of 10p. It was difficult to believe my eyes!! Dorothy, in her search for articles to contribute to the 'bring and buy' display, had gathered up my gavel and block among her contributions. Fortunately I had arrived early enough to retrieve my gavel and block but I had to pay the asking price of 10p to do so! Half an hour later I might never have seen it again. I was not amused, but the Probus Ladies were!! My 'tiny' gavel and block are now in use at this Retirement Home when I am presiding at meetings of the Residents' Association or the General Committee, as did Freddie Sheppard, one of my predecessors whom I met at Corton Civil Service Holiday Camp as described earlier in these memoirs.

In my garages, I stored my set of bowls, all my tools, a quantity of wines and spirits for Colin, much tinned food, bowling equipment in the bowls bag, deck chairs and many other articles to relieve the pressure on storage space in our apartment. Both garages were locked and with an additional padlock securing the garage lock. Also I was holding for Colin a valuable piece of Venetian glass he had purchased there and shipped home to me to hold until his return from a holiday in Italy. It was worth several hundreds of pounds. My two garages were broken into by thieves who took everything they could lay their hands on including Colin's glass, and his wines and spirits. Fortunately my car was locked, otherwise that may have been stolen too. At the time, a spate of break-ins was occurring up and down The Avenue without the miscreants ever being apprehended. Fortunately all was covered by insurance when my garages were broken open, to a figure of over £1,300. On another occasion my car was forcibly broken open and removed from the garage. The thieves were unable to start it but the ignition system was destroyed in their attempts to get it away. Bournemouth area was a fruitful district for burglaries of all sorts, but in this respect was not much different from the rest of the country. For Colin's glassware, he fortunately was able to produce the purchase invoice from Venice to substantiate my insurance claim.

CHAPTER FORTY EIGHT
Another accident,
Golden Wedding,
Neighbours and
Chance Meeting.

Soon after this, another tragedy struck us. Dorothy was on a shopping expedition with her friend Winnie Arnold when she fell again, down a full flight of stairs in Debenham's Bournemouth store. I had arranged to meet them outside the store with my car when a shop assistant came out to enquire if I was Mr Sheppard. I was told that Dorothy had been taken to Boscombe Hospital by ambulance. I went there only to find the information was incorrect and that it was Poole Hospital on the other side of Bournemouth. I saw Dorothy there. She had badly gashed her leg. It was then that I learned that she had lost the sight of one eye, and that this was causing her to misjudge stairs. After some days she was transferred to Boscombe and later allowed home. Her leg was badly damaged and would not heal. Our doctor explained that Dorothy was seriously diabetic and that this was why her skin would not heal. Eventually she was re-admitted to Poole Hospital where skin grafting was carried out. I had previously sought the advice of a Consultant specialising in diabetic problems affecting the healing of skin damage. The skin grafting proved successful and we were able to resume our normal life except that I tested Dorothy daily for blood 'sugar' and the District Nurse called regularly for a check-up. My checking was reported to our doctor, but from then onwards Dorothy's diet was paramount. Her diabetes was not of the type requiring injections of insulin although our doctor explained that she was of an age not suitable for such. Instead she had to take certain tablets regularly each day while I had to take a blood test from her finger each morning and record the result for our doctor's periodic visits to see her. Her normal diet naturally had to be changed to meet her diabetic condition.

Colin had by this time purchased a plot of land not far from his apartment in Aloha, Near Marbella. On his land he designed and had erected a magnificent bungalow villa with four bedrooms, each with 'en suite' bathroom, an internal patio in the real Spanish style, kitchen, dining room and lounge. Outside was a veranda for holiday barbecues, a large swimming pool, orange and lemon trees. Down a flight of steps to a double garage, with accommodation for a 'live-in' maid complete with own bathroom. Altogether a luxury accommodation which Dorothy and I were able to share on several occasions. The lounge and dining room were on slightly different levels with three steps. To deal with Dorothy's problems of walking, Colin had prepared a sloping access for her to use. When staying at the villa I regularly hired a small car for us to use for shopping and trips to surrounding beauty spots, such as Mijas, Ronda and Nerja, as well as to Gibraltar. With Colin we made a circuit of the "Rock", and were fortunate to secure as our guide, the President of the Gibraltar History Society who was also a taxi driver specialising in taking tourists round the "Rock". With Colin and Eileen, we made another visit to Seville to stay at the Melia Hotel where much of the 'exposition' to take place was being planned. Once again we visited the famous park where the hundreds, although it seemed more like thousands, of the white pigeons existed, for visitors to feed. Colin kept a car at Aloha permanently for use there. He and Eileen had become prominent members of the Aloha Golf Club. Eventually he was elected President which required more frequent visits to the Costa del Sol, although he still retained his residence in Chislehurst.

Residence of Author's son, Colin at Aloha, near Marbella, Spain

In 1980 Dorothy and I reached the date of our 'Golden Wedding'. For this our two sons, Colin and Brian arranged for a family celebration at the Grand Hotel in Eastbourne, easily the most prestigious venue in the town. Four suites were secured in the front of the hotel where we

343

celebrated in style. We stayed there four days with meals served privately in our suite of rooms. Photographs, telegrams, and all the other activities made this a memorable occasion.

Author and wife Dorothy, cutting their
Golden Wedding Cake 1980

Back in Poole Dorothy and I had a number of parties for our many friends we had made since moving to Poole from Bearsted.

June, Brian's wife's father had purchased a new ocean going yacht. He sailed it round to Lymington, where Brian and June could join him from Brockenhurst, their holiday house in the New Forest. Gerald and 'Toots' Bellingham (as June's mother was known to the family) also came over to Brockenhurst and we all played cricket on the common facing Meerut Road where the holiday house was situated. June was easily the best cricketer, probably inheriting her skills from her grandfather, Colonel Bevan, who had been president of Glamorgan County Cricket Club. June had been captain of cricket at Taunton School when she was a boarder there.

Gerald Bellingham had been appointed High Sheriff of West Glamorgan in which capacity he was required to attend on Her Majesty the Queen when she visited West Glamorgan. Mrs Bellingham's brother, who was a Director of Steel Company of Wales had at the same time become High Sheriff of Mid-Glamorgan, the old County of Glamorgan having been divided into three parts, in the reorganisation of Welsh counties. The new areas of Dyfed, Neath, Powys, Gwynedd, etc. were the result of this renaming of Welsh areas.

While at Lymington, June's father took the opportunity of coming over to Poole to show us his official uniform to be worn when operating in his capacity of Sheriff. Knee breeches, buckle shoes, cravat and sword etc.. all very imposing. He held a little competition for the name of his new yacht . Brian was successful in suggesting "Harvest Maid", as one outcome of their farms at Clydach.

Our neighbour in No. 7 Sunset Lodge when we first took up residence was Mrs King, the widow of a former barrister, and the mother of Judge King, a circuit judge for Bournemouth, Dorchester etc.. She was a dear old lady and soon became very fond of Dorothy. Living alone with a 'daily', she was very glad to have some one to converse with. Judge King lived at Brockenhurst so was able to call in to see his mother whenever he was 'on circuit' at Bournemouth. Unfortunately, Mrs King slipped when emerging from the lift to our flats. She was bending down to pick up some flowers she had dropped. The lift closed and she was trapped in a bending position when her coat caught in the lift as it was closing. She was trapped there until we heard her calling for help. On another occasion she fell out of bed and broke some bones and had to go first to hospital and then later to a nursing home where we visited her. Above us in Flat No. 10, was the widow of a retired Brigadier from the army. She was a rather eccentric old lady who often called on me to deal with some problem in her flat. For all that quite pleasant. She regularly rode a 'sit up and beg' type of bicycle round the Westbourne area of Bournemouth for shopping. On one occasion she left her bicycle outside a shop but when emerging it had disappeared. The loss was reported, but next day when again in the area, the bicycle had been returned and was again propped up outside the shop she had visited the day before, no longer wanted by the thief! Eventually both these ladies passed on and their flats were occupied by younger tenants with whom we became equally friendly. That of Mrs King was purchased by a railway official, retired, who accepted the post of Treasurer to the Bournemouth Probus Club which made for ease in dealing with the organisation of the Club.

Above us, No. 10 became the residence of a former graduate from Exeter University who was engaged in the insurance business. Eventually he married so we had, in Sunset Lodge the first wedding and eventually the first birth!

One day when walking round a supermarket in Bournemouth with Dorothy, we "ran into" Bertram Mitchell and his wife. He had retired from H M Customs and Excise as Chief Inspector, the highest post in the Outdoor Service of the Department. He had been Assistant Collector at Dover when I was at Maidstone. He, eventually, after being promoted to Higher Collector, Manchester, became Chief Inspector. Up to that time all Chief Inspectors had regularly received a knighthood before retiring. He fully expected to receive the same honour, so he would have been Sir Bertram Mitchell and his wife, Lady Dora Mitchell. At the time of his appointment, and then his retirement, there were moves afoot in political circles drastically to reduce the number of honours awarded to Civil Servants of all ranks. As a result Bertram Mitchell became the first Chief Inspector not to receive a knighthood. Instead he was awarded the honour of Commander of the Order of the Bath. This political move aroused intense resentment in the Department. Protests were made by the Association representing the highest officials in the Customs and Excise. These were to no avail. Since Bertram Mitchell's period as Chief Inspector, no knighthoods have been awarded, so that each occupant of this high office now usually becomes a C.B.

From this chance meeting in the supermarket, Dorothy and I developed a close friendship with 'Bert' Mitchell and Dora. I had heard that he had retired to the Bournemouth area. They lived in a rented apartment called Mildenhall on the Western Road leading from Westbourne to Bournemouth centre. Due to their continual moves resulting from the ascending of the promotion ladder, Officer, Surveyor, Second Class Inspector, Assistant Collector, First Class Inspector, Collector, Higher Collector, Deputy Chief Inspector and finally Chief Inspector, the Mitchells had never stayed anywhere long enough to purchase a residence. By the time of retirement a rented accommodation was all that was necessary. They had no children.

I must add that their apartment in Mildenhall was in no way superior to ours in Sunset Lodge, although we did not comment on it! When the Mitchells came to see us at Sunset Lodge it was obvious they were somewhat surprised, but no comment! Bert Mitchell told me that he had frequently stopped on the West Cliff Overdrive to watch the bowls being played there by the Argyll Club members. In the year I won with Bill Simmonds, the 'Pairs' competition at the West Hampshire Masonic Bowling Association, Bert and Dora

Mitchell came as my guests to the Annual Lunch when the trophies were presented. We also made the acquaintance of Dora Cobbing, who was Dora Mitchell's niece, a very cheerful girl living in the Winton area of Bournemouth and employed by the local travel agents Excelsior Coaches. She was a widow having lost her husband at an early age and with no family. Before Bert Mitchell passed on from cancer, he had, knowing, the end was near, asked me to 'look after' Dora, his wife, and then when Dora died in a nursing home, Dora Cobbing was a great help in assisting Dorothy and I to deal with the contents of their apartment. Dora Mitchell for some time prior to her death, lived in a nursing home in Westbourne where Dorothy and I visited her regularly. The estates of Bert Mitchell and then Dora, was dealt with by solicitors in Bournemouth. The Mitchells had a nephew, John Mitchell living in Woking and also a niece of Dora named Audrey Pengelley living at Twickenham. There was also a couple living in Westminster (the lady's maiden name, strangely, being Mitchell), who Dora regarded as an adopted daughter, plus Dora Cobbing. All these shared in the Mitchells' considerable estate. I still keep in touch with them all, except the Westminster couple, particularly at Christmas time, when we exchange greetings.

CHAPTER FORTY NINE
Spain, Aloha and Bowls.

Dorothy and I went out several times to the Costa del Sol, first at the hotel in Fuengirola with Saga holidays. From there it was an easy journey by rail into Malaga for sight seeing and to visit the large department store of Cortes Ingles. At the hotel there were two dance floors, one for what is termed 'Old Time' or 'Sequence' and the other more modern, including 'Latin American', which was more to our liking. On the subsequent visit when we stayed at Aloha beyond Marbella, Dorothy and I regularly made the visit to Fuengirola, over 20 miles away, in the evenings to dance at the hotel there. Eventually Colin's bungalow residence was available for our use. On one occasion we were there at Easter time and witnessed the procession of religious fanatics dragging themselves along with chains with weighty balls attached, to the church. Brian and June, with grandchildren, Adrian and Elaine, also came out for a large party together, organised by Colin at the Marbella Club, the top venue in the district. We were also able to see exhibitions of Flamenco dancing in the street plus the men in their traditional Spanish costumes some with their ladies sitting side saddle, also in Flamenco costumes, in front. Others in Spanish vehicles drawn by horses gaily bedecked; the vehicles carrying Flamenco dancers ready to perform. A really gay scene in true Andalucian style.

At Aloha I regularly played bowls, outdoor, but on an artificial 'green' with the local bowls club of Aloha Super Bowl, one of the leading clubs on the Costa del Sol. I played there so often that I was treated almost as a club member, playing sometimes against touring English teams. The Super Bowl Club held a "Bowls and Barbecue" tournament once a week for teams of four players drawn "from the hat" with a club member acting as 'Skip'. Visitors to the club were invited to join in, many of whom were not regular bowlers; some indeed had not played before! It happened that on the occasion when the local press, printed in English in Marbella, and the local radio station broadcasting in

English, 'ran' accounts on bowls, being played in the Costa del Sol, I was successful in winning the competition for the cup presented by the club. I had in my team, a young boy of 14, a young lady of around 20 who had not played before, plus an older man who had played occasionally in England. On this type of bowling green it is necessary to 'delivery' each 'bowl' at a considerable angle away from the 'jack' so that it will curl in eventually to reach the 'jack'. To assist my team, I stood 'way out' on the next green instructing my team to bowl towards my legs. My instructions proved successful and my team won that week's competition. Each member received a small cup as a memento of success. Mine now stands alongside my replicas of success in the 'Pairs' competition at the West Hants Masonic Club; the 'Tripples' competition at Argyll Bowls Club and the award received many years earlier in the Alliance Motor Rally, for the Civil Service Motoring Association. These have now also been joined by the 'runners-up' cup at the Swanley Indoor Bowls Club, awarded at Christmas and given by Colin.

At Aloha, when the newspaper came out after success at the "Bowls and Barbecue" competition and when the Radio was giving out the news, a feature was made that at bowls all could play, since in the previous week the competition at the 'Super Bowl Club' had been won by a man of 81 years with a team including a boy of 14, a girl who had not played before and a man with little experience of bowls. I was the 81 year old!

At home in Poole I was still acting as Vice chairman of the Civil Service Retirement Fellowship but my involvement with the Probus Club as Secretary; with bowling in friendly games with the Argyll Club, with league matches for Northbourne Bowls Club and more frequently, with the West Hampshire Masonic Bowling Association, all were making heavy calls on my time. Fortunately bowling only took place during the summer. Although I did for a short period join the East Dorset Indoor Bowls Club which had opened in Christchurch for winter bowling. This for me proved difficult when the playing arrangements were published. Friendly games were restricted to one or two mornings per week, very early. Because of heavy business traffic causing delays, I found it difficult to arrive on time. I soon abandoned efforts to play and resigned from the club. My initial membership fee of £50 was returned! Outdoor bowls was a summer game. The Probus Club did not meet during July and August due to pressure from holiday makers on the accommodation in the Pavilion and on alternative facilities in hotels for meetings, hence I had some time left for assisting Fred Thistleton with the C.S. Retirement Fellowship, particularly during the winter.

CHAPTER FIFTY
Holidays in Scotland.

With Fred I arranged two holiday visits to Scotland for the Fellowship The first was to Pitlochry where we stayed at the Atholl Palace Hotel which I remembered well from my Council meeting there with the Customs and Excise Federation. Since that visit the hotel had erected chalets in the grounds to give additional accommodation, so our party was comfortably housed in the chalets. All except Fred and Margaret Thistleton, who insisted on being put into the hotel; Margaret's doing! We stayed at Scarborough overnight on the journey towards Scotland. There a retired Chief Inspector of Taxes, one of our party, required me to carry his cases up to his room. Apparently, in his view, one of the duties of an organiser! I secured a porter! From Pitlochry we visited Blair Atholl, the seat of the Earl (or is it Duke?). Also the Pass of Killiecrankie, the scene of the battle between the troops loyal to King William III and the Highland Jacobites. Altogether we had a very enjoyable holiday and in good weather.

The next visit to Scotland, again with the Bournemouth Travel firm of Excelsior Coaches was to Oban on the west coast. It was almost a complete failure due to the most atrocious weather imaginable. We stopped overnight en route, at Hawick, not the best venue, if on a Saturday night with rowdy Scots crowding the bar for what was nearly an all night drinking session! But worse was to follow. In Oban it rained and rained and rained throughout the week we were there. Our hotel was set back from the sea front, never-the-less the sea washed over the promenade into the hotel entrance. The hotel management were obviously anti English. They and their staff were dressed in kilts throughout our stay and we were treated almost as foreigners! Always the last to be served! We took a trip in our coach to Fort William but because of the wind and rain were unable to get out of the coach when we got there! So we set out to return to Oban via Ben Nevis and Glencoe neither of which we could see because of the weather.

Dorothy was keen to say that she had visited the island of Mull and Tobermory but the ferry did not run for 5 days because of the weather. On Friday, before our departure, it sailed but only as far as Craigmure the nearest port of call to Oban. So we went and just had time to set foot on Mull before boarding again for the return journey. We had been to Mull but not to Tobermory. If we had done so on a coach, we would have been stranded there and missed our coach back to England! In Oban town centre we found a butcher with a cooked meat shop that prepared and sold cooked chickens. Fred and I ordered two each, to be picked up on Saturday morning as we left for home. One each for a meal en route and the other for our evening meal once we reached Bournemouth. Saturday a.m. arrived, everyone boarded the coach. The rain was still descending and the sea crashing over the promenade. Our driver decided to seek an alternative exit from the town to avoid the sea front. So no visit to the shop to pick up the chickens we had ordered but fortunately not yet paid for! I often wonder whether the butcher found another customer wanting to purchase four cooked chickens ready to eat, or whether he still has them in his fridge waiting for us to call!

Next off back to England via Loch Lomond and Glasgow. First to Gretna Green where we visited the smithy but did not require the services of the smith! Then on to the Lake District where we stayed at Windermere. Fine weather at last. Our driver organised a local coach firm to take us and some of our party on a long trip to Blackpool. Never again! The traffic was so bad, with, it seemed, the whole population of Northern England, on a similar course. It was so bad that at midnight we still had not reached the lights. Our driver turned tail and we went back to Windermere. No Blackpool. No Lights, but a welcome bed!

As Vice Chairman I occasionally found time to accompany Fred on coffee mornings. One I remember well, to Ringwood, where the venue was 'Greyfriars' where many organisations in Ringwood met. Having parked our cars I noticed that Fred was wearing shoes of two different colours. One black and one brown! I drew his attention to his shoes and advised him to keep his feet under the table in the hall.

He explained that he had started to dress when Margaret called for some assistance and for some obscure reason. He went to her with one shoe on and then returned to put on the second shoe. He picked up the wrong colour and so started out with odd shoes on. The fact that Fred never called her Margaret, but only 'Serenity' was a travesty of her real nature. On another occasion she had been a patient in the Lansdown Private Hospital in Bournemouth for some minor problem. Fred stayed at the hospital with her in a double room; a most expensive arrangement. Leaving the hospital together she slipped on a step, dragging Fred with her. Fred suffered a broken leg while 'Serenity' got up unhurt. Fred had to go into Poole Hospital for his broken leg while 'Serenity' took refuge in the Civil Service Benevolent Home in Westbourne, Bournemouth!

Eventually Fred gave up the office of Chairman and I was invited to take his place since I was Vice Chairman. I declined the invitation and gave up my office as Vice Chairman. The Honorary Secretary named John Rix, living at Ashley Heath, Ringwood, became Chairman, much to my relief. He was a member of Ringwood Probus Club and ambitious. Fred was eventually elected as the first President of the Fellowship which involved no duties other than an occasional appearance at Annual meetings. Fred recovered from his broken leg. He is still walking round Canford Cliffs (known as The Village), at the age of 100 years and declines to give up the Presidency! Margaret passed away, so Fred now lives alone with a caring helper who comes in each day to prepare his meals and on weekends, in advance. She takes him shopping once a week and also looks after the apartment and the plants etc., on his balcony. She is in fact a 'treasure' and he is a lucky man.

CHAPTER FIFTY ONE
Concorde
and East Anglia.

Colin's wife, Eileen was successful in a competition by one of the oil companies in winning one of the prizes offered; a flight on Concorde. It was for two but she had no wish to accept the prize. So Colin offered it to me to accompany him. The flight was from Heathrow and expected to be over the Mediterranean. We presented ourselves along with about 50 or so other 'winners'. After some delay not explained, we duly took our seats after champagne had been served in the airport lounge. A further delay commenced until we were informed there was a fault in the Concorde aircraft. All had to disembark! So back to the lounge for more champagne but no food. Work was taking place on the Concorde until once more we received the invitation to take our seats. We did so, more champagne was served 'ad lib'. Again a delay and an announcement that another fault had developed which we were assured would be attended to promptly. Lunch had been promised but this did not materialise. Instead again more champagne, Colin and I were not interested. After a further lengthy delay the plane finally took off but because of the time schedule, we only went over the Bay of Biscay and soon returned to Heathrow. By this time it was late afternoon. Lunch had been forgotten but we were given an excellent tea (with more champagne for those able to accept!). We received many mementoes of the flight; a certificate, a model of Concorde and photographs. Just to prove we had actually had a flight even if it was only over the Bay of Biscay! Colin and I had had an opportunity to visit the cockpit, where we had a photograph taken with the pilot. As to the flight, it was rather uneventful apart from the complete steadiness so that one did not know the plane was in motion. Nothing could be seen through the tiny windows. But we had had the flight; realised that even Concordes can develop faults and had the opportunity to consume as much champagne throughout the whole episode as one could wish for, but this last advantage did not, for Colin and myself, compensate us for the flight in Concorde having been reduced in duration, due to the faults that had occurred before 'take off'.

Author with son Colin and pilot in cockpit of Concorde over Bay of Biscay, 1994

Dorothy and I had two friends in Gillingham named Cyril and Winifred Gibbs who were amateur artists. Cyril was a member of my Gillingham Masonic lodge and a retired Civil Servant from Whitehall. They told us of a holiday they had had at Wolterton Hall in Norfolk the seat of Lord and Lady Walpole. He was a descendant of Sir Robert Walpole, often referred to as the first Prime Minister. At Wolterton Hall, flats were available for holidays by selected and approved occupants. The Gibbs had rented one for a session of painting in the Norfolk area. I wrote to Lady Walpole for permission to rent a holiday flat. The reply I received said "Any friends of Mr and Mrs Gibbs are very welcome"! Now that Colin's properties were no longer available in the Norfolk area, Dorothy and I set off for a holiday for a fortnight in Norfolk countryside. We arrived at Wolterton Hall on a Saturday. We were met by a gentleman who simply said "I'm Walpole". He explained that he and Lady Walpole were just off to spend the week-end in Gloucestershire at a 'Game Fair'. He gave me the keys to Wolterton Hall leaving

Dorothy and I in charge! Nothing else occurred to check our credentials. We climbed the stairs to our flat, passing valuable paintings, silverware, ceramics and all the treasures of the Walpole family. Later that day the estate manager arrived. He had been playing cricket but was aware of our intended stay. With that he left. Dorothy and I were in possession of Wolterton Hall until his Lordship and Lady Walpole returned from their weekend at the Game Fair. We had a delightful fortnight in the Norfolk countryside . Amid the cornfields where we picnicked 'truly rural' the larks were singing overhead reminding me of my boyhood listening to them on the Coney Banks near to our home in Luton, Chatham.

We made visits to local places of interest such as Blakeney where seals may be seen, Sandringham, one residence of the Royal family; into Norwich with its extensive market and to the Cathedral. Also to the National Trust properties of Blickling Hall and Felbrigg Hall, both very interesting. On Lord and Lady Walpole's return we were invited to a late supper with them in their portion of Wolterton Hall. On the Sunday in the middle of our stay we were invited to attend the tiny church, part of the estate. The total congregation was 14 including Lord and Lady Walpole and ourselves. I looked up during the service to see Lord Walpole taking the 'collection' so made a respectable contribution on behalf of Dorothy and myself. We had a most interesting holiday in Norfolk enjoying fine weather and much fresh air.

On a previous visit to Sheringham when staying at Colin's house there, I visited as a guest, the Probus Club of Holt, a small market town a few miles from Cromer and Sheringham, also to the Yare Probus Club in Norwich. At both of these I was able to observe the differing ways in which Probus Clubs organise their meetings. I had found at Bournemouth members were inclined to become 'cliquish' in other words to arrange to sit together with selected friends, when the general purpose should have been to mingle, so getting to know all the members. I had tried at Bournemouth to institute a system of drawing members from a container and to number the seats at the dining tables, to which a member would sit, thus mixing up members at the tables. It did not work successfully because members searched around in the container to find a matching number to hand to a selected friend. At the Holt Probus Club the solution was to hand a number to each member on arrival at which he was to sit. Searching for a matching number in the container was not permitted.

This procedure did not find favour among members at Bournemouth. They preferred to sit with selected acquaintances, so this became the "norm'.

Holt was for some time the home of Fuller Pilch the famous Kent and England cricketer. With his two brothers he played for Norfolk against the M.C.C. and Fuller Pilch against England. For £100 a year he was persuaded to leave Norfolk and come to Kent where, with Alfred Mynn, the two became the most famous cricketers in the early history of Kentish cricket.

CHAPTER FIFTY TWO
Diamond Wedding.

Back again to the Bournemouth area I was diagnosed by my doctor that I was suffering from the serious eye complaint of glaucoma which if untreated would result in blindness. Fortunately it had been discovered early. I was examined at the Eye Hospital in Westbourne and instructed to administer drops of Timoptol into each eye twice a day. I have to have an eye examination every six months and am still doing so at a hospital where ever I am residing. Fortunately the eye drops are keeping my glaucoma condition under control. I was also found to have further minor attacks of skin cancer to parts of my face. There were treated at Poole Hospital as was necessary, according to the position of the cancer. These have again been on my forehead where Radiotherapy was used; on my cheek where it was cauterised and one on my ear where cauterising ointment was used. I am still being examined periodically at the nearest local hospital. Further to my eye and skin troubles, I had started to develop painful ulcers on my right ankle, possibly due to poor circulation arising from the metal plate still fastened to my right leg, broken in the serious accident in 1969. I am still having treatment for the painful ulcers which affect my ability to walk normally and to play bowls comfortably.

In Ringwood Probus Club there were five married couples who were celebrating their golden weddings in 1990. They decided to hold a party at the Coach House Hotel for the five couples. Since Dorothy and I were celebrating our Diamond wedding the same year, we were specially included to attend the party. It consisted of a dinner with suitable decorations. The dinner party was a great success. At it I suggested that each couple should explain how they had met. It was very enlightening. One couple had met on a bus when the lady was journeying to an office for interview for employment. She had sat next to a young man, only to find that he was one of a panel of two conducting the interview! She was successful and eventually married the young man. Two other couples, as did Dorothy and I, had met at a dance, but not in quite such dramatic circumstances. Of the others, one at tennis and another through an introduction by a friend. A most happy and interesting evening was had by all those married in 1940 and by Dorothy and I in 1930.

Dorothy and I had celebrated our Diamond Wedding with a family party at the Cumberland Hotel in Eastbourne. The hotel management was first class in arranging the celebrations, producing a beautiful 'wedding cake', allocating us a separate room in which to have our 'party'. My two sons, their wives, Dorothy's sister and brother with his wife, plus our two grandchildren attended. In the midst of the celebrations, the hotel manager appeared with a very important looking telegram and marked 'Buckingham Palace'. It was from the Queen, sending us her congratulations. This rounded off a most important day in our lives. We received many presents. Frank Owen from Goudhurst put in an appearance and it was then that I showed him the photographs of the horses at Ramsgate, pulling the 'bathing huts' into and out of the sea, and he recognised them as his father's horses normally used for coal deliveries in the Lewisham district, but in the summer on holiday in Ramsgate.

At home in Poole we had a number of parties at our apartment for us to celebrate with them, our good fortune at having had 60 years of happy married life. The Queen's telegram has been framed and is displayed in my present residence.

In 1986 when he had reached the age of 50, Colin with his Co-Director, David Moscow, had the opportunity to accept a 'Management Buy-out' from the members of their firm, Sheppard, Moscow and Associates Ltd. So Colin and David were able to retire on very advantageous terms, receiving contributory pensions from the Insurance Company into which they and their firm had been paying over the years. The firm of Sheppard, Moscow and Associates Limited, is still in business under the same name from the premises in Chislehurst, being one of the leading Management Consultants in the U.K. Colin still has a few private consultancies unconnected with his previous firm which he deals with as necessary, sometimes on the continent of Europe. He now drives a Rolls Royce car as well as a Range Rover. In Spain he maintains a Peugeot for his frequent visits there. He has been elected President of the Aloha Golf Club, an appointment which requires frequent visits to Spain.

A "belated report" here of the demise of my parents' "credit clothing etc.." business. Early in the '60s', due to political pressure, the Government brought in legislation requiring all 'money lenders' to be licensed. It is a 'mute point' whether the business my parents had carried on for so long and which had proved financially successful was in fact 'money lending'. But in any case they were both prepared to accept that it was time to retire completely. So they let the business slowly 'run down', accepting no more customers, issuing no more 'tickets' and recovering as much as possible in cash from the 'customers'. They missed meeting their 'customers', all of whom were on such, a friendly basis. In any case the economic climate was changing. People were ready and willing to pay for goods they purchased. My parents had no wish to be licensed as 'money lenders' so took no steps to secure a licence for their business.

CHAPTER FIFTY THREE
Another accident
and passing of Dorothy.

Early in 1991, Dorothy suffered another fall, emerging from our lift at our apartment. Her health had for some time been giving me cause for concern, both with her eyesight and her diabetic condition. She fell heavily and it was obvious that something serious had occurred. I rang 999 emergency for medical help. The ambulance service was quickly on the spot and conveyed Dorothy to Poole Hospital where a broken hip was diagnosed. This was attended to but hospitalisation was lengthy. Eventually Dorothy was conveyed to Christchurch Hospital for a long spell of therapy. I visited her each day, all day, leaving only to have my meals. Her diabetic condition was a serious factor in her recovery, besides which she was now suffering from a very high blood pressure. When she eventually returned home, our doctor called daily to test for blood pressure. On one occasion the pressure rose so high as to go above the highest point on his instrument. He phoned a Consultant for advice who arranged for Dorothy's immediate admission to Boscombe Hospital Once more after a spell in hospital, Dorothy returned home but I was truly apprehensive as to the eventual outcome. I devoted my entire energies to caring for her at home.

Dorothy finally passed away in September 1991 when she was 81 years old. I was holding her hand.

The cremation took place at Bournemouth crematorium where the chapel was full to overflowing with our numerous friends throughout the area. It was a simple service conducted by the vicar of St. Clement's Church and generally accepted as the correct clergyman to officiate at a Masonic funeral. With my two sons we agreed the hymns for the ceremony.

For the music played by the organist when the congregation was filing out of the chapel, I had him play the tune "Ramona". This was the tune to which Dorothy and I had danced when we were chosen at Rochester by Santos Casani to dance in the final of the Columbia Dance Championship, nearly 63 years earlier.

> "Ramona, I hear the mission bells above",
> "Ramona, they're calling out our song of love",
> "I bless you, caress you and bless the day you taught me to care",
> "I'll always remember the rambling rose you wore in your hair",
> "Ramona, when day is done I'll hear your call",
> "Ramona, we'll meet beside the waterfall",
> "I dread the day when I'll awake to find you gone",
> "Ramona, I need you, my own".

This was always our tune and our song!! We sang it to each other, sometimes dancing round the kitchen, humming it!!

My last tribute to a wonderful girl and wife and mother.

Dorothy's ashes were placed in a small casket and conveyed to Chatham Cemetery to be interred alongside the remains of my parents and grandparents. Colin and Brian attended with me for the simple ceremony at the graveside by a clergyman. The account of Dorothy's death is preserved in the Memorial Book maintained at Bournemouth Crematorium in the Chapel, which is opened each day at the appropriate date but can be inspected at any time on request.

CHAPTER FIFTY FOUR
Aftermath.

Dorothy had necessarily given up her Secretaryship of the Ladies Probus Club due to her ill health. She had had, as an Assistant Secretary, a lady named Edith Reader, the second wife of Harold Reader, one of the members of Bournemouth Probus who joined early on as a result of my article on Probus in the Bournemouth Echo newspaper. Mr and Mrs Reader were also members of the Royal Overseas League where Mrs Reader was well knows as a "dresser" particularly for her hats which she wore with aplomb. Dorothy and I were very friendly with them both.

Mrs Reader was, however, a Canadian, who periodically went back to Canada to visit her family there. She was in fact, the daughter of Harold Reader's second cousin. Her first husband had turned out to be a 'bad egg', leaving her with three children before being found dead in another part of Canada. She was a very capable lady, being a trained nurse and a graduate from Toronto University with a degree in Hospital Administration. She married a second time, a man named Clare but he had died from cancer after a short married life with Edith Reader. So Edith Reader had had a sad experience, but had succeeded in bringing up her children, now all married. At the time of marrying Harold, she was the Principal of a large nursing home, which position she gave up to marry Harold and come to England to live.

Edith had acquired a valuable collection of dolls, some antique, so quite valuable, also 'teddy bears', which she brought with her, sometimes giving shows and talks to organisations. Harold Reader's first wife had died soon after he retired to Ferndown. He was formerly a top Executive with the London Stock Exchange and a Freeman of the City of London. He had two daughters, both married, living in

Hertfordshire. His residence at Ferndown was quite commodious with three bedrooms. There was a nice garden to the bungalow. He had had a large electrically heated greenhouse erected, but he was not a keen gardener, so employed a part-time gardener. Edith, on arrival, improved the lay-out of the garden besides cultivating her favourite flower, fuchsias.

When Edith returned to Canada to visit her family, Harold remained at home to look after two prize winning Siamese cats they had acquired, which they showed from time to time at cat shows in England. Edith Reader's responsibility as Assistant Secretary was to keep the Minutes of the Meetings of the Ladies Probus Club which task she sometimes neglected when about to depart for a visit to Canada! So Dorothy and I had to go over to Ferndown to collect the Minutes and if necessary, complete them with Harold's assistance. There were no hard feelings about this since we were all good friends. Edith eventually resigned as Assistant Secretary, another member being appointed to the office. Edith remained a Club member.

A sad event took place. While Edith was away on a visit, Harold died suddenly. Edith returned immediately but was a widow once again. For future Canadian visits the cats went into a cattery during her absences.

Before Dorothy's death we had been offered accommodation in the Royal Masonic Institution Benevolent Retirement Home that has been opened in Westbourne, Bournemouth. With Dorothy's continual ill health, we considered it carefully. The accommodation was for a married couple. We had a good look at it and a good 'think'. The accommodation, although possibly adequate for most couples, to Dorothy and I it was woefully small compared with our commodious flat. We would have been very carefully looked after in the retirement home. In the end we decided not to accept the offer of accommodation in the R.M.B.I. Retirement Home, but to remain in our flat.

Dorothy and I advertised in the local newsagent's window for a domestic help and as a result secured the services of a young woman, a widow with three children of over school age. She was Daphne Knight living in the Northbourne area, who proved ideal for our purposes. She came twice a week in the mornings and kept our flat in good shape, especially during Dorothy's periods in hospital. She remained with me until I finally left the Bournemouth area to live at Chislehurst near to Colin.

The final years of the 1980's and early 1990's proved a very sad time for me and for Dorothy. I lost my sister, Doris. Dorothy's sister Marjorie died soon afterwards. Dorothy had had in the Ladies Probus Club and in the Dorset Ladies' Luncheon Club, three very close friends, Molly Scrivener the wife of a Wing Commander, Royal Air Force; Eileen Pratt, wife of an Insurance Executive, retired, living near Fred Thisleton in Canford Cliffs, and Winnie (later Winnie Arnold) living in a small flat at Tollard Court on the West Cliff overlooking Poole Bay. Winnie met Arthur Arnold through me at the Masonic Bowling Association. He lived at Broadstone near to Wimborne Minster, having retired from Fleet, Hampshire. Winnie was a widow and Arthur a widower. He wanted to marry her. She finally consented but with "strings" attached! She wanted a honeymoon in the Seychelles plus a larger flat in Tollard Court which was originally the Tollard Hotel, having been converted into flats of different sizes. Winnie was with Dorothy when she fell down the stairs at Debenhams Store in Bournemouth.

The wedding took place attended by sons and daughters of the couples' previous marriages. Followed by a splendid 'Wedding Breakfast' at the East Cliff Hotel before they went off on the stipulated honeymoon! Winnie secured the larger flat! Not long after their return, Arthur was taken ill and passed away. Winnie was alone in the larger flat. After a year or so, Winnie, too, was ill and had to enter a nursing home where she died. So ended an elderly romance! Winnie was Dorothy's best friend in Bournemouth.

Dorothy's friend, Molly Scrivener, was the second wife of Wing Commander Reg Scrivener, ex. R.A.F., living on the East Cliff of Bournemouth. They formerly lived at Farnborough in Surrey. It was from Reg Scrivener that I obtained details of Farnborough Probus Club's rules and constitution, when first making enquiries about forming a club in Bournemouth. Molly Scrivener was a bank manager's widow but by marrying Reg she lost her pension received from the bank. What she did not realise was that since she was Reg Scrivener's second wife, she would not receive a pension from the R.A.F. should Reg die before her. Which he did, thus leaving her comparatively 'badly off'. Reg was suffering from glaucoma in both eyes. He entered the Eye Hospital at Westbourne in Bournemouth, for an operation which was unsuccessful. He became totally blind. He struggled on with his radio as his only comfort, although Molly tended to all his needs. Becoming ill, he was taken into the new Bournemouth Hospital, where, not knowing where he was, due to blindness, getting out of bed, he fell, breaking his leg. Later he was transferred to a private nursing home where he passed away. Molly continues to live in her flat, alone, now at the age of 94. I visit her periodically when in Bournemouth.

Dorothy's third friend Eileen Pratt, lived in Canford Cliffs, near to Fred Thistleton. She was the wife of Harold Pratt, a retired Insurance Executive from the North East and with a grown up family. Harold passed away suddenly from a heart attack. The Ladies Probus Club lost four members including Dorothy, due to deaths and transport difficulties. The mens' Club had lost three but there were many more.

Mrs Ward, my neighbour in Flat No. 7, had a sister living near Guildford, who was severely handicapped with two metal leg irons. She had a son with two delightful small children, whom Dorothy and I were always pleased to see when they called to see the Wards in No. 7. Mr and Mrs Ward had no children. She was very protective of her sister. The sister's son, a small time builder, went bankrupt and removed to Wadebridge in Cornwall, taking his mother with him. Mrs Ward still very protective of her sister, decided to move to Wadebridge as well. The Probus Club lost its Treasurer and we had lost our neighbour. The sad story is that the sister passed away suddenly soon after the move. The Wards removal to Cornwall had been in vain. The property there which they had purchased had a large garden but was rather inaccessible. Ron Ward, cultivating the garden, suddenly had a heart attack and died. Mrs Ward was isolated in Wadebridge with a large garden she was unable to cultivate due to her own arthritic condition and with a house difficult to sell. It was some years before she finally returned to Dorset, to sheltered accommodation at West Moors near Ferndown, and finally to a nursing home, due to being severely troubled with her arthritis. A sorry end to our friendship with our neighbours in Flat No. 7. The young couple in Flat No. 10 above No. 8, moved away to a house in Christchurch. The wife had a second baby. We had lost another neighbour.

Ken Rees, my friend in Block C at Sunset Lodge was a former Bank Manager. It was he who introduced me to the Argyll Bowls Club and encouraged me to take up bowls, something I had avoided doing in Gillingham when my mother invited me to do so. I regret now her invitations were not acted upon, but then I was more interested in tennis. Dorothy never took up bowls either, although she regularly came to watch me playing in the Bournemouth area. Ken Rees had been a prisoner of war with the Japanese, having been captured in the Singapore area. He suffered atrociously under the Japanese, being one of those employed building the notorious bridge over the River Kwai. From his treatment by the Japanese he developed the dreadful skin complain of psoriasis which became progressively worse with advancing years. He applied to join the Probus Club and became a member at my invitation. Dorothy and I regularly visited No. 26 in Sunset Lodge to have tea with Ken and his wife Elsie, also a member of the Ladies' Club as well as playing bowls at the Argyll Club. Ken's psoriasis finally resulted in him entering a nursing home where I visited him frequently until he passed away. Another of my close friends had departed!

I had met a fellow mason named Albert Sutton at the Masonic bowls, who lived in the same block of flats in Braidley Road near to the Town Hall where Wing Commander John Pickering also lived with his wife Joan. John and Joan were close friends of Molly and her late husband Reg, also a Wing commander. Albert Sutton's wife was Peggy. They both became members of the Probus Club. He owned a large plastics firm in Cambridgeshire, managed by his son. They had at one time lived at Plaxtol near to Shipbourne and Tonbridge, in my former Excise Station, before he was enrolled into the Merchant Navy serving in great danger on vessels bound for northern Russia during the war. By formerly living at Plaxtol, we had associated memories of that part of Kent. Albert and Peggy Sutton came with Dorothy and I several times to the Algarve in Portugal and also to the Costa del Sol in Spain to visit us when staying at Colin's bungalow residence at Aloha. To both places he drove there in his car, a Honda. When in the Algarve, we all went out together visiting places of interest. They were keen dancers but mainly in the 'sequence style' as opposed to Dorothy and my preference for traditional 'ballroom' or 'Latin American'. In Portugal we stayed at the "Do Garbe Hotel" and in the Costa del Sol they stayed at the Saga Hotel in Fuengirola, but where Dorothy and I went in the evening to dance with them. Peggy eventually died of cancer in the Christchurch Hospice where Dorothy and I went to visit her many times before the end. Another member had passed on.

In Southbourne, lived Wing Commander, R.A.F. Stanley Chiswell, an early recruit to Bournemouth Probus. I could never get him to take office in the Probus Club, even to become President, but he was a loyal member. He had been a Royal Air Force apprentice, rising through the ranks to Wing Commander. I often discussed with him what I might have attained, had I accepted the apprenticeship available when I took the examination back in 1922 and secured third place in England. He said, "At least an Air Vice Marshall" but I might have been 'shot down' or 'gone missing' during the war! In any case I was too small in 1922 to be accepted, had I wished to enrol!. So just as well! Mrs. Chiswell became a member of the Ladies Probus, but she too, fell a victim to cancer, also passing away in Christchurch Hospice. Stanley Chiswell has since died from a sudden heart attack.

Another whom I lost was Melvern Dawbarn, one of the "Formation Committee" set up following the meeting with Bournemouth Rotary. He died after a brief illness. He had been my predecessor as President of the Bournemouth Masonic Bowls Association and my successor as President of the Probus Club.

Another 'departure' was Major Sidney Butt, living at Burton, near Christchurch, with his wife Mai. With him I had been engaged in compiling the history of the formation of Bournemouth Probus Club and the commencement of the Probus movement in the Bournemouth area. The project was well on its way, when, visiting Southbourne with his wife, he was taken ill outside a furniture shop, Mai being inside. He died of a massive heart attack. Poor Mai was distraught. Both were Probus Club members and she still is, besides being an active producer of social events on behalf of the Royal National Lifeboat Institution as well as a fully qualified nurse specialising in 'all night' service. She still resides at Burton tending her garden. The history project for Probus was never completed although excerpts have appeared from time to time to be filed.

In No. 16 in Block B of Sunset Lodge, lived Mr. & Mrs. Watts who were also close friends of Ken and Elsie Rees, so we also met there.

He played a little bowls but Rae Watts did not. Both belonged to the Probus Clubs. Their main interest, however, was in the Royal Overseas League where Rae Watts was a Committee member. He was not a mason, whereas Ken Rees was a prominent member as Chaplain of a Bournemouth lodge, but he did not belong to or play with the Masonic Bowling Association.. Rae's Watts husband became ill and passed away in Sunset Lodge. Another friend had gone.

In Burford Court on the East Cliff lived Wally Machin and his wife. They were neighbours of Reg and Molly Scrivener. He was a Probus member and had been an official in the Port of London dealing in the main with the transhipment of cargo by lighter between docks within the Port. So he was fully cognisant with Customs procedure, so we had that in common. They became unable to manage in their flat so moved away to live with their daughter, a schoolmistress. So another couple lost to our clubs. She had been a member of Ladies' Probus Club Committee, so was missed.

John Houlstone who had originally introduced me to the members of Bournemouth Rotary Club at the meeting in Bournemouth Pavilion, had also died, so his wife moved away from Canford Cliffs to live near her son, with consequential losses to the Probus Clubs. Fortunately there were many applicants for membership. Both Clubs still flourish although many of the newer members are completely unaware of how the Probus movement had started originally in Bournemouth.

Bill Vaughan, my friend, the Social Secretary of Ringwood Probus Club who had moved from Ashley Heath near Ringwood, to a flat in Fountain Court opposite to Sunset Lodge in the Avenue, decided to return to the Cotswolds where his two sons were carrying on his business of Estate Agents and Valuers. He moved to Stratford-on-Avon, where his wife Winifred passed away, he then moved to Moreton-in-Marsh where he met a lady named Florence in an adjoining apartment, whom he married. He purchased another flat back in Bournemouth as a holiday home and occupied it with his new wife during the summer seasons. His 'taking of a new wife' did not find favour with his former associates in the Probus Club of Ringwood! But he was quite happy with Florence. I visited him often in his holiday home. He retained his membership of the Bournemouth Probus Club until finally going back to Moreton-in-Marsh, selling his holiday flat in Bournemouth. Then again to

Stratford-on-Avon, where I visited him and Florence living happily together in a prestigious apartment overlooking the River Avon and near to the theatre. As an estate agent, he was aware of "knowing where to live and secure the best available site"!

My successor as President of the Masonic Bowling Association who was also Treasurer of the Northbound Bowling Club and who had encouraged me to join his Club to become a member of Northbourne team playing in the Bournemouth and District Bowling Association League, was then ill and passed away. I did not have any facts about his death except that from then on, I was not included in the Northbourne team because I did not attend, other than on a Saturday for the match arranged. Members of the team were expected, quite rightly, to attend during the week to practice. I did not wish to go to Northbourne during the week and so accepted the decision gracefully. I could have all the bowls I required, playing at the Argyll Club even if not in the team there. Also the Masonic Bowls Association gave me all the friendly matches I wished for. So the Northbourne venture ceased!

John Groves, my close associate in the formation of the Bournemouth Probus Club as well as a great colleague in the West Hampshire Masonic Bowling Association went on holiday to Scotland with Christine. There he was taken ill with a sudden heart attack and passed away. His death caused gloom in the Masonic Bowling Association where, besides being a Past President, he was the efficient organiser of the journeys we took to; play against other Masonic Bowlers in various parts of the country. He had been one of the 'Formation Committee' for the Probus Club and its first Secretary, later the Speaker's Secretary and fourth President. His place in the Masonic Bowling Association was practically unfillable!

CHAPTER FIFTY FIVE
Dobbins.

Another death was that of Stanley Dobbins, another member of the
original Probus 'Formation Committee'. His 'life story' almost
'demands' a chapter to itself!!

I had known Stanley since my days in the Excise in charge of the
Weald of Kent. Stanley was a Yorkshireman with all that that
description implies. He was employed by Imperial Chemical
Industries in Yorkshire, I believe as a warehouseman. A vacancy
arose for a Chief Warehouseman at Plant Protection Ltd., the small
firm manufacturing insecticides from nicotine obtained from tobacco
residues and used for spraying hops. This was at Yalding a small
village on the River Medway above Maidstone, but with connections
by rail to both Tonbridge and Maidstone. The railway siding
adjoined the factory. The manufacture of sprays from nicotine was
soon discontinued by I.C.I., when that firm acquired Plant
Protection Ltd. Sprays using chemicals from abroad became the
norm. The vacancy for the Chief Warehouseman arose during the
war when Kent was not a favourite locality in which to reside due
to the likelihood of bombing by German planes. Stanley Dobbins
applied for the vacancy and was appointed. He soon rose to be
Supplies Manager so that when hostilities ended and chemicals from
abroad became available, he was an important 'cog' in the
P.P.L.(I.C.I.) manufacturing process. It was then that I met him.
I had to control the use of imported chemicals under special conditions and their subsequent exportation. It was mainly accounting
work, although occasionally samples had to be taken for submission
to the Government chemist.

Stanley Dobbins took up residence in Bearsted, not very far from my
residence in Manor Rise. Dorothy became friendly with Stanley

370

Dobbin's wife Phyllis. They had two sons both about the ages of our two sons. But Stanley could not afford the fees for attendance at King's School, Rochester. Instead he sent them to a small private school in Maidstone. The elder Dobbins' boy subsequently became a clerk at Plant Protection Ltd., but then obtained a position in sales with I.C.I., in London in the Paint Division. The younger boy was 'mad' on golf, eventually becoming an assistant 'caddie master' (professional) in Norway to a golf club there. Stanley Dobbins finally retired from P.P.L. at Yalding. Mrs. Dobbins had acquired two holiday chalets (or mobile homes) in the Isle of Wight which brought in a modest addition to their finances. They occasionally went over there for purposes connected with changing of tenants, but not themselves on holiday.

The elder Dobbins' boy, who had his eye to business, married the daughter of a fairly large printer and owner of a stationery shop in Maidstone. He was transferred by I.C.I. to the Exeter Branch. Stanley Dobbins was keen to keep in touch with his elder son, so he sold his bungalow in Bearsted, to go to live in a tiny village between Exeter and Exmouth. Dorothy and I went to visit them there. The residence was quite nice but there was no transport, other than by private car. This was quite satisfactory for Stanley, but Mrs. Dobbins remained isolated all day when Stanley went off to play bridge with the 'Colonels' in Budleigh Salterton. (The bridge playing 'Colonels' were reputed to be a feature of Budleigh Salterton}. Mrs. Dobbins was not very happy with the situation.

Subsequently, the elder boy Dobbins was again transferred by I.C.I., this time to Bristol. He was climbing the promotion ladder. By this time, Dorothy and I had moved to Poole. The Dobbins came to visit us there. Phyllis Dobbins was keen to move to Bournemouth but Stanley wanted to go to somewhere near Bristol to be near his son. Mrs. Dobbins to Bournemouth to be near the Isle of Wight for her 'chalets' She had her way and they moved to a flat in Bournemouth. Just as well because the son had a further transfer by I.C.I. to London. He purchased a house in the "stockbroker belt." So Dorothy and I saw more of the Dobbins. He joined the Argyll Bowls Club, but he was not a mason so unable to join the Masonic Bowling Association. He was one of the Formation Committee of the Probus Club, but so far as I recall, Phyllis did not join the Ladies' Club. She was taken ill and entered Boscombe

Hospital, Dorothy and I visited her there frequently, sometimes taking her little meals we thought she could eat. But she was very ill, Stanley, if around, invariably took home food which we had taken into the hospital, to consume at his flat! It was not long before Phyllis passed away. Stanley now had the flat to himself.

He had a phobia about taxation and frequently declared that he was not going to let the Government get its hands on any of his money! This was about the time when Inheritance Tax was being applied. Assets given away during the seven years before death remained subject to Inheritance Tax. Stanley was always discussing this rule and how to get round it! It was clear that one had to dispose of assets and then live another seven years!!

One day Stanley met up with an old lady who owned a house over-looking the Argyll Bowls Club. This house was not in the best repair condition. It had been converted into flats of varying "attractions": One flat was on the ground floor but the kitchen involved, had in it, a large tank that took the water draining from the roof in wet weather. It was a very unsightly arrangement. I saw it whenever I visited Stanley. But he did not seem to mind! The flat was very cheap which to Stanley was its great attraction. He rented the flat and sold his nice "purpose built" flat in a much more desirable area. Now he had the proceeds of his sale and the necessity to live another seven years to avoid inheritance tax! I did hear, but cannot confirm, that when Stanley's younger son came over from Norway during the winter, when no golf was possible due to darkness descending, Stanley charged his son for the accommodation occupied by the son and family!! If Stanley did in fact do so it would have been in keeping with his usual views on the economics of family life! If, however, he did not require payment for the accommodation occupied, it would have been unusually generous of him, contrary to his normal and usual philosophy of life!

Now that Stanley had the proceeds of the sale of his flat, over £40,000, he was in a position to defeat any Government attempt to levy Inheritance Tax, provided he could survive for another seven years. To his elder son he gave £20,000 to build a 'granny flat' ('grandfather') annexe to the house the son had acquired in the 'stockbroker belt.' The younger son, had given up his golfing activities in Norway, and had gone into the motor business in the West country where the wife's parents resided. Unfortunately this went awry, and the young son went bankrupt. He next obtained a golfing position near Henley-on-Thames, but there was no domestic accommodation. So another £20,000 went towards the purchase of a residence for the younger son and family. Stanley had defeated the Inheritance Tax, provided he lived for 7 years! The Government later changed the Inheritance Tax laws in a subsequent Budget altering the figure on which the tax was charged! Stanley's plan had become unnecessary, but he still had his cheap flat near the Argyll Bowls Club, even if it did have a large water tank in the kitchen! Unfortunately, though, Stanley had no capital left.

There was a lady who played bowls at the Argyll Club and who was also a member of the Ladies' Probus Club. She had a very luxurious flat in Westbourne, and she was a widow. Stanley became friendly with her. Soon he proposed marriage: possibly he was in love! The lady asked my advice as to whether she should accept Stanley's proposal of marriage. Her flat was very attractive to Stanley! I was in a quandary as to what I should advise. I knew so much about Stanley and his usual meanness, but what could I say? Whether the lady was lonely I do not know. She eventually agreed to marry Stanley. He had no capital, other than enough to purchase a suit for the wedding, but not for the honeymoon, to be spent in Spain at Torremolinos. The lady, presumably, paid for the honeymoon. So off they went, duly married. Stanley had previously removed his private effects into the lady's apartment. The rest of his furniture he placed in store in an outhouse to the flat he had occupied near the Argyll Bowls Club. Furniture and effects belonging to other residents were also in this storehouse.

Stanley died on his honeymoon in Spain!! The lady had the task of getting his body home to England by air. No doubt Holiday Insurance was involved but this did not detract from the tragedy for her, from Stanley's death in Spain and on a honeymoon. I attended Stanley's cremation in Bournemouth, along with others from the Probus Club and the Argyll Bowls Club. I recognised a typical Spanish coffin. Both sons attended the funeral, the elder one in a bright light blue suit: the younger, more soberly attired.

The next episode of this sorry tale was that the elder son sent a hired van to Bournemouth to collect all of Stanley's effects and furniture from the storehouse at the house near the Argyll Bowls Club. Unwittingly the driver took every item in the store including all the furniture and effects belonging to other tenants occupying flats in the converted house. How this was ever sorted out I do not know except that everything had to be returned for identification!

One thing I learned, was that when Stanley, (when he was alive) went to stay with his elder son, in the "granny flat"; built with the £20,000 given to defeat the Inheritance Tax, he was charged rent by the elder son for the accommodation occupied! The elder son also came back to Bournemouth to secure Stanley's effects still at the lady's residence, and demanded to know what had happened to his dead mother's wedding ring which he could not find! Maybe it had gone with her at her cremation! We shall never know. Shall I add, "like father, like (elder) son !!!. So ended the saga of Stanley Dobbins whom I had known for nearly 40 years.

CHAPTER FIFTY SIX
Further developments.

In the Probus Club I encountered another problem, although "problem" is possibly not the correct word. The President for the Club's seventh year was a man named Dillon. It was the custom for a President to chose his Vice President and then this member became the President in due course. There was no rule to this effect, but just a custom that had grown up and worked successfully. It was not always easy to secure a member who would make a competent President. Every member had the right to nominate another member to be President and in the event of more than one nomination, the contest would be put to the vote. During my time as a member there had never been a contest. the serving Vice President had always been elected President. Mr. Dillon was nominated as Vice President by Dr. Taylor, the President, who had been a Medical Officer for Health. Mr. Dillon had been a Major in the army and was a former Mayor of Bournemouth. He was therefore quite a competent President during his year of office.

Bournemouth Probus Club was limited to a membership of 75. More than this made for difficulties of accommodation in seating at luncheons. There was a long waiting list for membership. There was an official list of 10 plus a further unofficial waiting list from which additions were made to the 'official' waiting list. Eventually a move was afoot to form a second Probus Club. Those on the two "waiting lists" were advised and with a small number of members from the current Club, prepared to belong to both Probus Clubs, the new Club known as Bournemouth No. 2 was formed. Mr.(Major) Dillon took an active part in this movement and became No. 2's first President. He retained his membership of the original Bournemouth Probus Club. Both Clubs continued to attract applications for membership despite the formation of Northbourne, Southborne and other Probus Clubs farther afield.

In 1993, after Dorothy's death, I was attending the Bournemouth Probus Club's Christmas luncheon. The Mayor of Bournemouth was present, with a lady Councillor acting as Mayoress. It had always been my custom when Secretary to 'brief' anyone expected to respond to the toast of "The Ladies", always proposed by the President at the Christmas Lunch. This was to ensure that the "responder" always knew what Probus was all about. This appeared not to have been done by the then holder of the office of Secretary. But Mr. Dillon, it seems had: He was acting as Master of Ceremonies or "toast-master". When the 'Mayoress' responded to the toast to "The Ladies", she made great play on the subject that Probus had been 'brought to Bournemouth' by Major Dillon in the first place for which the inhabitants of the Borough were eternally grateful for filling a "much needed want". Undoubtedly Dillon had briefed her about Probus No.2. This would not have been so bad, had he not arose from his seat and publicly acknowledged her praise for his action in starting Probus in the Bournemouth area. Many in the audience were not "au fait" with the true picture of the commence-ment of Probus in Bournemouth. Some were recently joining members. Mr. Dillon's action in rising from his seat to acknowledge the praise heaped upon him, resulted in a round of applause. I was not amused! The fault lay with the Secretary failing to brief the speaker beforehand, but Dillon's action in accepting the praise, after briefing her himself about Probus annoyed me. I decided never again to attend a Bournemouth Probus Club meeting.

This despite many appeals from members who had been present at the Christmas lunch who too, took exception to Mr. Dillon's action in rising from his seat accepting praise for bringing Probus to Bournemouth, by bowing, thus resulting in applause from those not aware of the true facts.

This, with all the unhappiness I had experienced with the death of Dorothy and the passing of so many of my friends, caused me to forget the happier times I had had in the Bournemouth area. Probably I was too sensitive and, on reflection now, unwise, to cease attending Bournemouth Probus Club meetings. But that is how I felt and so acted. I have no regrets. Mr. Dillon can keep his spurious claim, I and many others know the true facts of the commencement of Probus in the Bournemouth area.

I suppose it was a psychological reaction that prompted me to avoid functions in Bournemouth after Dorothy's death plus all the losses of friends that occurred, that I sought relief in the Ferndown, Ashley Heath and Ringwood area where I had many friends and acquaintances I could visit. There was Blanche Hardwick, a dear old lady over 90 who was the widow of a former Deputy Chief Inspector in Customs and Excise. She was still tending her garden and remarkably active. We had many chats about former days at Federation Council Meetings when her husband was a lively delegate. I met him at my first Council as a U.O. delegate to Harrogate and others, before he started to climb the promotion ladder. Next door to Blanche lived Jack Price with whom I had played golf when he was an Unattached Surveyor, officiating in Maidstone District. He too, had climbed the 'ladder' to high office. He was a member of Christchurch Probus Club, plus the prestigious Ferndown Golf Club where one had to 'play themselves in' before membership was granted. Blanche Hardwick was a close friend of Dora Mitchell before Dora's death. Blanche and Jack Price resided in Dudsbury Avenue quite near to where Edith Reader lived in her bungalow in New Road, Ferndown. Julius and Diane Borghese, friends of Doug and Alice Flutter also lived in New Road very near to Edith Reader. Julius was a Belgian/American, an ex Army Officer from the U.S.A. now living permanently in England. Doug and Alice Flutter lived at St. Ives near Ringwood. They were the couple who disclosed at the 'Golden Wedding' party that they had met on a tram or bus when Alice was going for an interview with Doug's firm. Their close friends (and mine) were Tommy and Joan Gambles, living at Ashley Heath near Ringwood. After Dorothy's death Alice had me to lunch several times. Dorothy and I had been to lovely parties at the Gambles' beautiful bungalow. What a strange combination of surnames, Flutter and Gamble ? But Edith Reader was the one who invited me to meals more often. Having lost Harold, she like me, was feeling lonely and welcomed some company. She offered to let me use the greenhouse in her garden for growing whatever I chose. She favoured her fuchsias, but I preferred to grow tomatoes and cucumbers to remind me of my greenhouse at Bearsted before Dorothy and I moved to Poole where I had no garden to cultivate!

I was getting relief from my sad state of mind following the death of Dorothy and my disillusionment with Bournemouth now so many of my friends there had passed on. Charles Heal from Ringwood

Probus Club, regularly invited members of the Club who were masons, with their wives, to lunch, one Sunday in each month at the Bulberry Golf Club between Poole and Dorchester. Some 20 or more attended for what was an excellent meal. I became one of those in the party, and subsequently invited Edith Reader to come with me for the lunch. It was a very happy meeting for us all, having Probus and Masonry in common. And I had a Sunday lunch already prepared ready to eat without effort.

Also in Ferndown lived George and Lilian Chinn who had a very nice garden who invited me to visit them. George was the Probus member at Ringwood meetings with whom I sat at the luncheons. Another couple in Ferndown were John and Winifred Goodwin. She had been a Clerical Officer in the C. & E. Collectors Office in Manchester before retiring to Ferndown. She could remind me of Officers there that I had met, one of whom had become the Assistant Collector, but was a former member of the Federation Council and Executive. John Goodwin had also been employed in the C. & E. but resigned to go into Industry. Winifred Goodwin was for a time the Assistant Secretary of the Ladies Probus Club. The Goodwin's had a son who was a Preventative Officer serving at Poole, so we all discussed Customs and Excise and the changes that had taken place.

CHAPTER FIFTY SEVEN
Ferndown.

Ringwood Probus held very well attended coffee mornings twice a month. One in the Coach House Hotel and the other at Marsham Court Hotel in Bournemouth so that the ladies could follow it up with shopping in Bournemouth. I asked Edith Reader to attend these coffee mornings because she knew many of the ladies in the Ferndown area. There was no restriction about having to be the wife of a member at Ringwood. She was very well received and invited several couples back to her home to see her collection of dolls and 'teddy bears'.

Charles Heal who was the new Social Secretary of Ringwood Probus, arranged a holiday to Austria in the vicinity of Salzburg. Edith Reader was invited to go with the Ringwood party. I went too. It was by coach by a local coach proprietor, with no overnight travelling. Charles Heal's wife, Grita, was of German nationality which was very useful to the party. She was one of those who had visited Edith Reader's home to see the dolls. Also in the party were Tommy and Joan Gambles who later became very friendly with Edith. We visited the area where the film 'Sound of Music' was reputedly made, and saw the famous 'White Horse Inn'. We went up by chair lift to some high mountains and also witnessed members of the local parachutists practising their jumps from the top, to descend to the meadows below. A highlight of the visit was to Salzburg itself, where we went up to the 'castle' with its magnificent view of the town below. The visit brought back memories for me of the many trips I had had abroad with Dorothy.

I took up Edith Reader's offer to use her greenhouse and planted tomato seedlings plus cucumber plants obtained from the local nursery, so I was having to call to attend to them although her gardener also looked in. I also planted some sweet pea seeds to provide Edith with flowers for the house should they bloom. I needed 'sticks' for the sweet peas but could not obtain any from the local nursery. So I suggested that we went into the nearby country lanes to secure some from the hedge rows. We found a few. I saw some Muscovy ducks in a field near a farmhouse. Remembering my 'Muscovies' on my lawn at Bearsted, I called at the farmhouse and purchased some eggs. These I took home to eat, being very fond of ducks eggs but Edith kept one back. Why, I never enquired. Later she confessed that she had tried to hatch one with a hot water bottle and electric blanket! It never did, so she called on the local vet who told her it had gone 'bad'. The next I heard was that she had had a 'burial at sea' by throwing it into the waves at the entrance to Poole Harbour where she went with friends to the hotel there to have afternoon tea.

I was not present for this ceremony! The eggs I consumed were delicious! Probably all those I purchased were infertile or Edith's 'hatching arrangement' unsuitable for producing a baby Muscovy duck!

One thing I discovered at this time was that Edith had a 'heart condition'. I had wondered why she had some difficulty in reaching the chair lift when we went up the mountains in Austria with the others of our party. She told me that she had had an operation in Canada before her marriage to Harold. Her local doctor at Ferndown had recommended that she enter the 'heart clinic' at Southampton Hospital to have the operation testing her circulation by passing a 'bubble' up her leg veins to check the blood flow to her heart. She agreed and awaited an appointment.

The local travel agents, Bath Travel Services advertised a 'day trip' to Venice. Edith had never been to Venice, whereas I had been several times in my trips abroad with Dorothy, but had not stayed long enough to see all the 'sights'. Edith and I took the trip, leaving our cars at Hurn airport, to board the plane. The sun was shining brilliantly when we set out. But in Venice it was raining, and rain it did, the proverbial 'cats and dogs', accompanied by thunder and lightening. It never stopped. I recalled my visit to Oban with Fred and the Civil Service Retirement Fellowship, except that this time it was even worse with thunder and lightening. On arrival in St. Mark's Square we first went to the glass factory to see the beautiful glass objects produced. We became trapped at the exit awaiting for the storm to subside. But it did not, it grew worse We ran to take shelter in a restaurant where I was charged £9 for an ice cream, each! Next we ran into St. Mark's Church for shelter. The curb-side vendors of plastic 'macs' had sold out! The proposed trip on the canal in a gondola was cancelled. It was a case of 'waiting' to go home! The whole venture had been a waste of money, but the travel agents were not to blame. They could not forecast the weather. The weather was fine when we got back to England. Edith had seen little of Venice. I had told her of seeing dust carts (boats) collecting the rubbish; of a funeral procession I had witnessed on the canal; of couples enjoying being taken along the Grand Canal in a gondola. But none of this for Edith. I have my lovely painting of the Grand Canal as seen from the Rialto Bridge, to remind me of what Venice really looks like when it doesn't rain and rain and rain.

Edith eventually went into Southampton Hospital for her tests. I took her there and visited her most days afterwards. I feared that her tests had not been satisfactory in establishing that the blood flow to her heart was in order. She was still having to use a mouth spray at times when her breath failed.

One day Edith phoned me to ask me to come over one evening, wearing a 'respectable' suit. Actually it was on my 86th birthday so I knew something was afoot. Arriving in Ferndown, Edith took me immediately to the Dormy Hotel, a very high class establishment attached to the Ferndown Golf Club and only a few yards from Edith's residence. There I found Brian and June, who had met Edith previously, but also my grandchildren, Adrian and Elaine. There was a table set for eight places. No sooner had six taken their seats when Colin and Eileen appeared. They had come straight from the Royal Meeting at Ascot. Colin was in top hat and morning dress required for admission to the Royal Enclosure. Eileen was equally suitably dressed and wore an 'Ascot' hat. So the final two places at the table were filled. Edith said it was the first time she had seen me 'lost for words". The birthday dinner was followed by a birthday cake with many candles for me to 'blow out'. So concluded my 86th birthday party, so carefully arranged by Edith without me knowing what she was 'up to'.

CHAPTER FIFTY EIGHT
Rainham Tennis Club.

In 1991, Brian retired from his position of Personnel Manager with British Petroleum at the London Headquarters. He was then age 50 so, like Colin, decided to enjoy his life without all the hassle of the journey to London each day, with crowded trains from Guildford, resulting in having to stand when he boarded at Worplesdon, in spite of travelling first class. In 1989 he had been seconded by B.P. to the National Audit Office under a scheme for exchange of personnel between Industry and Whitehall. At the Audit Office he was employed investigating the finances of the Land Registry, and of the Scottish Office. The findings had to be presented to the appropriate Committee of the House of Commons. It was quite an experience for him to prepare evidence for Members of Parliament. The year of secondment being completed, he returned to B.P. Headquarters. With retirement he was able at last to pay more attention to the upkeep of his extensive garden. He planted more fruit trees in the orchard section. He double glazed the entire house personally, a task I would never have attempted despite my early training in Chatham Dockyard.

He and June took a holiday to the British Virgin Islands, flying first to Antigua. A smaller plane took them on to the Virgin Islands where they were met by a taxi to carry them to their destination. The taxi was driven by a native of the island who decided to take them, presumably, by a 'short cut'. He went at speed passing over what are known as 'sleeping policemen', intended to restrict high speeds. As a result of speeding, Brian and June were thrown into the air, Brian came down on his back and was severely injured. June landed on her side, so she too, suffered injuries, but not as severe as did Brian. The holiday was abandoned. Brian had to go into hospital in Antigua. He was there for about 10 days when the Travel Agents flew out a special plane with a trained nurse for return to England. On arrival Brian was taken to the Royal Surrey Hospital in Guildford where he remained for several weeks. They claimed on the insurance company for injuries sustained, liability is not contested, only enquiries by the medical fraternity into the final extent of Brian's injuries is still causing delay in settlement. Brian's enjoyment of his retirement has been severely retarded. He was a keen golfer, if not in the same class as June. They also enjoyed walking in the countryside particularly in the Mendips in the West Country and in other places. Brian's injuries from the Virgin Islands accident has curtained much of his normal activities. After several years the matter is not yet settled. He is able to carry out Consultancy work on behalf of the Management Consultancy firm of Saville Holdsworth, such as for Nestles, but that is not what he retired for.

In 1981, Dorothy's sister, Marjory, had drawn my attention to an announcement in the local paper circulating in the Medway Towns, asking for anyone who had knowledge of the former Rainham Tennis Club to get into touch with a firm of Solicitors in Gillingham. It was a firm known as Redfern & Stigant. I wrote to say that I was a former member of the Club which had ceased operating at the beginning of the 1939-45 war. I was, as a result, asked to call to see the solicitors' representative when in the Gillingham area. This I did and explained that I had been a member with my wife Dorothy, since about 1934 when were returned to live in the Medway Towns, but that I had played there occasionally with my sister before 1927. Dorothy and I had played there regularly at the Rainham Tennis club until 1940.

The point at issue was that when the war started the Rainham Tennis Club had ceased to operate. I remembered this well, because it was then that Dorothy and I started to play at the Civil Service club, where I became Secretary. The Rainham Tennis Club courts were situated behind Birling Avenue, approached by an opening between two houses which was wide enough to drive a car down but was not an official 'road' There were two grass courts plus a hard court. This hard court I had personally helped to finance for putting it into operation by running dances in the Co-operative Hall in Rainham, from which I had raised the sum of £100 to help pay for it. A small sum by today's standards, but in 1934 to 1940, quite substantial. All the courts, grass and hard, were in a deplorable condition, with trees, bushes, and brambles growing out of them. The hard court had practically disappeared. I went with Colin to inspect the site.

Nearby, living in a sumptuous bungalow was a Mr Ballard. This was in Bloors Lane leading from the end of Birling Avenue to Lower Rainham. Ballard's bungalow was the last of a row of residences. Beyond was a quarry. Behind the row of residences including Ballard's bungalow was a large meadow extending up to the tennis courts. Ballard owned the meadow. There was the Corporation site of Cozenton Park also behind the meadow and the tennis courts. Ballard wished to build on the meadow. He was a fairly large scale builder for the district. He was also building houses in the Hoo and High Halstow area where Brian lived. Brian labelled them "Ballard's Better Boxes"!

Ballard, to build on the meadow but not too near his own residence, needed access. He could not secure this from the small lane leading from between two houses in Birling Avenue to the tennis courts, which was wide enough for a car to be driven down it but not wide enough to be considered a suitable access to a housing estate to be erected on Ballard's meadow. I believe that Ballard had plans that if he could acquire the tennis courts, he could secure access to a building site by acquiring a residence in Berengrave Lane, which was parallel to Bloors Lane (in which his own bungalow was situated), demolish it, establish access, with sewage and other facilities direct on to the meadow via the tennis courts. It was all very complicated but then, Ballard knew his way round the building regulations. His first step was to purchase the tennis courts, thus extending his meadow up to the garden of a residence in Berengrave Lane.

Ballard was employing solicitors to establish the owners of the tennis courts. They had found that when Rainham Tennis Club ceased to function at the beginning of the war, a general meeting had appointed three 'trustees'. I was not at that meeting and did not know it had been called. The 'trustees' were said to be Mrs Green who had been involved with the Club when it was first established behind Birling Avenue on removal from an earlier site in Century Road where my parents resided. A Mr Hales also involved in that move, and a Mr Brundle who became a member much later. He was an employee of Gillingham Borough Council. The 'minutes' of the meeting appointing them had been lost, believed to have been destroyed when Mr Hales residence in Newington, near Rainham was bombed. Mr Hales had since emigrated to South Africa, Mrs Green had removed to the Thanet area of Kent. That left Mr Brundle, appointed presumably because of his connection with Gillingham Council and possible knowledge of the legal side of being a trustee. He was a younger man, who became a member of the Club after Dorothy and

384

I joined in 1934. He was not my first choice for being a trustee but then who was I to query the appointment since I was not present when it was made?

Mr Ballard's solicitors needed to know who were the members of the Club in 1940 when it finally closed. Hence the announcement in the newspaper for knowledge of Rainham Tennis Club. I knew the names of many members and the present whereabouts of some. No one else had come forward. I submitted to the solicitors what I knew. It was clear that without the minutes of the appointment of the trustees and/or a list of former members, the matter became one for a decision via the High Court for distribution of any assets arising from the sale of the tennis courts to Ballard. I had many and long discussions with various members of the solicitors staff, in Gillingham, Chatham and Strood as they changed and altered responsibility. The final upshot was that Dorothy and I were invited to be 'plaintiffs' in a law suit in the High Court, opposed to the 'defendants'. Mrs Green and Mr Brundle. We consented but made it clear in writing that we would not be responsible for any costs involved. I swore an affidavit in Bournemouth for which I was never paid the fee charged! I was asked to nominate 'my' solicitor, who had to be at 'arms length' from the solicitors acting for Ballard and presumably for legal purposes, for Green and Brundle. I appointed a suggested firm in Gravesend, who I never met and did not know, except that I had voluminous correspondence with them. At first Ballard had offered a very large sum to purchase the tennis courts. I understood it was over £50,000 which if paid might have been quite a 'windfall' for the members of the club. But then I learnt that descendants of deceased members would be entitled to their share. The matter was getting 'out of hand' but the lawyers were the ones to benefit finally. Dorothy had died, her sister had died, my sister had died, so had many others I had known as members. Finally I was advised by 'my solicitor' in 1995 that the tennis courts had been sold to Ballard for £16,000, but that due to legal costs this sum had been used up in full, by the solicitors' and court costs. The members alive or dead got nothing!! Ballard got his tennis court land and the law got £16,000.

Had justice been done? It had taken 14 years to accomplish! The advice of never going to law is very sound, but had not been followed in the case of the ownership of the land belonging to the members of Rainham Tennis Club. But what other action could have been taken? I think now that I had been unwise to have answered the request from the Solicitors, Redfern and Stigant. Maybe I should have known better! 'Ballard's Better Boxes' had triumphed!

CHAPTER FIFTY NINE
Elections, Bournemouth C.S.M.A.

1997 being election year, I am reminded on the many occasions I served as a Presiding Officer at polling stations in the Maidstone area. Sometimes in parish halls and at other times within the borough. The Board of the Customs and Excise Department agreed such appointments. Private leave was taken to cover the full day's absence from the C & E office. One had to collect the ballot boxes overnight, take them early next day to the polling station, ready for voters to commence registering their votes. A Presiding Officer usually had two polling clerks to mark off voters as they came in to record their votes. At the end of the voting session checks had to be made on the sealing of the ballot boxes, which then had to be taken as quickly as possible to the 'count', generally a large hall where 'counters' were waiting to begin their task of establishing the successful candidate. One could not leave the polling station throughout the day. The procedure was much the same for Municipal elections as for Parliamentary ones, except that Presiding Officers were often called upon at Parliamentary Elections to help with the 'count', when the ballot boxes were opened, their contents distributed for counting to begin. Then to await the result, listen to the speeches from the successful candidates (and the unsuccessful ones) with thanks to all who had taken part in the election.

Even more interesting, however, was serving as an 'enumerator' at the census carried out at intervals of 10 years to establish the total population of the country. A particular day (night) was used throughout the country. Every residence then had to be visited to establish who was residing there on the selected night. Return visits were sometimes necessary plus enquiries from neighbours or others to obtain the required information for the enumeration of the population. Officers in the C & E were ideal for visiting residences with their detailed knowledge of parish boundaries and the residences involved. The Board gave approval to Officers acting as enumerators. I recall that once, when acting as an enumerator, I met a band of travellers (gypsies) on the road in the parish of Chart Sutton, during the period of the census. They assured me that they had not been counted in the parish of Headcorn adjoining Chart Sutton, which they had just left, so I was able to include them all on my forms. Payment was made for the work of 'enumerating' at the rate for each complete 100 names. Fractions not included.

I was, for a number of years when residing in Poole, a member of the panel of 'Marshalls' for the annual rally of Vintage and Veteran cars organised by the Yeovil and District Motor Club, from Bristol to Bournemouth. It included motor cycles and sidecars. Always on a Sunday, to give spectators an opportunity to witness the rally en route and the final arrival on to the Promenade at Bournemouth. The Bournemouth Branch of the Civil Service Motoring Association regularly supplied Marshalls for the final stages of the rally. It was always a very jolly affair with many of the drivers in Edwardian attire, the ladies wearing large hats with scarves tied under their chins. I was always posted on the Promenade, wearing a special coat and armband to establish entitlement. The cars and even some delivery vans bearing long forgotten proprietor's names on view, entered the rally. The rally drivers came from many parts of the country, some even from abroad. Every vehicle bore a number to correspond with the printed list available for spectators to consult, describing age, owner and other details of each entrant. No. 1 was the first away from Bristol but generally not the first to arrive. Most cars bore their identification from other rallies. All were in marvellous condition, paying tribute to the care by their owners. Each worth far more than the original purchase price. I only once saw a Clyno car arrive, but it was not a fabric body model, such as I possessed as my first car. Many of the drivers had met each other previously, so there was plenty of 'chatting' going on. I was reminded that Brian had been on the London Brighton rally with his father-in-law, driving a 1902 Packard Lavassor car. Dorothy and I went to Brighton to see them arrive before they went into the hotel with June and her mother for the celebrations, with all the other drivers.

Spectators at Bournemouth were kept at a distance by barriers. Many managed to slip through to have a closer look at the

"Veterans" and to discuss with owners the "pros and cons" of owning and maintaining an ancient car. Those drivers of a car so wishing, could go to the Carlton Hotel at the conclusion of the rally, for the Mayor of Bournemouth to make the presentations to the various 'winners' in each class, 'best turned out' etc.

Among the spectators viewing the 'Veterans' on one occasion, I got into a conversation with a man who turned out to be John Hoff, a true "Man of Kent", recently arriving from Newington, the village adjoining my home in Rainham where I lived for so long. John Hoff with his wife were now residing in the newly built area of Littledown in Bournemouth, close to King's Park and Queen's Park. We became very close friends, John with his wife, Joan, both became members of the Probus Clubs. He soon became Social Secretary and very efficiently too, earning praise from all the members. He became President of Bournemouth Probus Club in 1996. He was a grand organiser. He came as my guest to Ringwood Probus. For the only time since I gave up attending Bournemouth Probus Club meetings, I attended for his first meeting as President of Bournemouth Club, as a mark of my admiration of his work as Social Secretary at Bournemouth. Through me, John and Joan Hoff met Edith Reader and became friends of hers too. It was a lucky chance that I met John Hoff when acting as a Marshall at a Veteran car rally from Bristol.

CHAPTER SIXTY
U.S.A.

In the autumn of 1991, after Dorothy's death, Paul Thistleton with his wife Alida, came over to Poole from California to visit his father, Fred. Paul had regularly visited Fred when he was an employee of Dupont, the large chemical firm manufacturing Teflon, the material used for coating saucepans etc., to prevent burning but whose main use was in the aeronautical industry for rockets and space travel. Paul had recently retired to Northern California, having been previously employed at the Dupont factory in Jacksonville, West Virginia. I never discovered the origin of the name Jacksonville or who the original Jackson was! Dupont had other factories in the USA as well as in Japan, also with interests in Holland. Paul Thistleton regularly visited Japan and sometimes Holland. These visits gave him the opportunity to break his return journeys to visit his father in Poole. Paul and Alida had met Dorothy many times in the past and always came to our flat for a meal. We were very good friends, so that Dorothy's death had cast a shadow on their lives as well. Paul and Alida had three daughters, all adults, Ruth, Anne and Adele. Ruth had married and had recently had her first baby, named Michael. Her husband was an aeronautical engineer. They lived in Kentucky. Anne was a graduate from the Massachusetts Institute of Technology, engaged in marketing. Adele was a school mistress. Alida was from California. Paul's retirement home was in Trinidad in northern California near to the larger town of Eureka on the main highway to Oregon State. During Paul and Alida's visit, the conversation turned on whether Fred would ever see his first great grandson, Michael. Fred was 95 and I was 85. Paul suggested that we take a trip to Trinidad together to see his new home and for Fred to see Michael. At first the suggested trip was more of a joke, but it developed until we were seriously considering it. I was still in the mood to get away from Bournemouth, perhaps subconsciously. Fred with his first wife and baby Paul, had emigrated to America in the late 1920's. He was fond of telling how he had seen men jumping to their death from skyscraper buildings during the great depression of 1929 and had even thought of doing the same himself! He had returned to England, again to be an accountant, first in Bournemouth and then with the Admiralty at Holton Heath near Wareham in Dorset.

Later he was transferred to Bath with the Admiralty during the late war, in the Naval Store Department, until he retired at 60, returning to Bournemouth to his bungalow at Queens Park where his wife died. She was a school mistress. His marriage to Margaret (Serenity) followed. Fred and Margaret had been to West Virginia and described Jacksonville as a 'dump'. With Paul at the factory and Alida employed as a dietician for schools plus the girls at school, Fred and Margaret had been left to their own devices most of the day, hence the term 'dump'.

The outcome of our discussions with Paul on a suggested visit to northern California to see Paul's new home in Trinidad, was that we decided to go in 1992. Fred and I would arrange our flight to San Francisco with the local travel agent, Paul to meet us in San Francisco and take us by car to Trinidad over a period of two days to allow for sight seeing en route. Paul to secure accommodation for me in the nearby hostel in Trinidad. He would also organise for me a tour of the southern States of the USA. Fred would remain with Paul and Alida during the time I was touring. Finally Paul with Fred, would meet me at the end of my tour in San Francisco for me to fly back to England with Fred. Before the start of my tour we would all go first to Shasta farther north from Trinidad towards Oregon. It was an ambitious plan for Fred and I to contemplate considering our ages, but we agreed to go.

I received from Paul, once he had returned to Trinidad, the full details of a tour by Tauck Tours, reputed to be the best tour operators in the United States. I was very pleased that he had arranged this for me, relieving me of the task.

Fred and I set out at the end of July 1992 for our visit to California and beyond. We took a hired car to Heathrow for the 12 hour flight to San Francisco. After we had taken off and had been in the air for about an hour and were conversing, Fred suddenly stopped talking, appearing to be having convulsions. I hurriedly summoned an air steward who established, very fortunately, that there was a doctor on the plane among the passengers. The doctor came and looked at Fred and called for an oxygen mask to be applied. He took Fred's pulse, finding it to be exceptionally low. He instructed me to continue take Fred's pulse for the rest of the journey to San Francisco. It hovered between 40 and 50, which from my scanty knowledge was exceptionally low. Strangely enough when we reached San Francisco, Fred recovered. It seems that the altitude at which we had flown had caused Fred a problem. He was provided with a wheel chair from the plane to pass through Customs and Imigration controls. To keep up, with Fred's rapid progress through these, I too was provided with a wheel chair. When I finally got out of this, I explained to the young lady pushing it, that I really had not required it, except to keep up with my companion. So I offered to do a little dance for her, say the 'Cha, Cha, Cha'. She seemed a little taken aback.

Fred for his part said nothing about his condition on the flight. He did not tell Paul and Alida who had met us. Neither did he mention it to me, then, or at any time since. I have never mentioned it to him. Either his mind is a complete blank over the 'convulsions' or he had decided never to refer to the matter. I think the former. With Paul and Alida we started our journey northwards.

We left San Francisco by the very impressive Golden Gate Bridge. After a short journey we stopped for the night at a 'Best Western Inn' where Paul had already booked us in. Next morning an early rise to continue northwards. Next we visited the 'Jack London National Park', commemorating Jack London, author of 'White Fang' and 'The Call of the Wild', books I had read as a boy. I recalled the older man who had described to me his time in the Klondyke, when I had shared with him a room in the crowded 'digs' in Edgbaston, Birmingham, where the landlady's husband was a Commercial Traveller in coffin furniture!

We next made a detour into the Redwood country where we could see the enormously tall trees, many of which were wide enough at ground level for a motor car to be drive through. One even had a shop, fully inside the trunk, selling souvenirs. It was quite an experience to stand with Fred inside the tree trunk. I could find no one to explain to me why these phenomenally tall trees grew in that particular part of the globe. The only answer I received was that it was due to the climate and the soil in combination. Whatever causes such beautiful trees to grow is immaterial so long as they are preserved and do not fall prey to commercial interests. The policy of the authorities is designed to prevent such happening. Young trees are encouraged to grow to replace any that die from age or other causes so that posterity will continue to enjoy the magnificent sight they present. Following the visit to the tall trees, we passed through acres and acres of vine country producing wines for which California is famous. Then to reach the small town of Eureka. I wondered why "Eureka?" Archimedes was more than 2,000 years away with the proverbial bath, but I believe his discoveries causing him to shout "Eureka", was to do with detecting the adulteration of gold. Finally we reached Trinidad and Paul's residence. Trinidad, as I recall, is an island off the coast of South America. Paul's Trinidad is reported to be so named due to it being sighted on the Feast of the Holy Trinity. These stories exist. In any case it was a very pleasant spot with seals basking in the sun, in the bay, on view from the house. It was arranged that I had 'bed and breakfast' accommodation at the hostel, only a few yards away, and to have all other meals with Paul, Alida and Fred. This lasted several days until we set out towards Oregon and Mount Shasta. During that time I went with Paul and Fred to a beach to search for garnet stones thrown up by the Pacific Ocean!! There we met a family picnicking on the beach who invited us to share with them their meal. Fred was in his element, finding someone to listen to his account of how he knew "all about America" from his stay in the 1929 depression! For my part, I discovered that the great grandmother in the party was named Cox, the same as my mother's maiden name. So I had a photograph taken of all the "Cox's" together, great grandma, grandma, mother and me in a group! I had been very sad because I was passing through the period of Dorothy's birthday, August 5th and our wedding day, August 2nd, so many years ago. I always became sad when we were not celebrating these dates together.

We arrived at Shasta safely. Near were the mountains with much snow. From this snow came the water that flowed or was transferred by dams and other means to enable the plains of California to be cultivated. The hotel was very comfortable. Fred and I were in adjoining rooms sharing a 'loo'. Paul and Alida across the lawn in another section. Early in the morning Fred went to the 'loo'. I waited because he appeared to be taking rather a long time. Fred

392

called to me for assistance. I found him with the blood from an haemorrhage showing on his pyjamas. I summoned Paul and Alida. Fred was taken to the hospital in Shasta where he stayed until Paul started on his return to Trinidad, later to be hospitalised in Eureka. I did not see him again until I returned from my Tauck Tour at San Francisco. Paul was there with Fred having decided to accompany us back to England. Fred had recovered sufficiently to make the journey home. He later entered the new Royal Hospital in Bournemouth for an operation from which he made a complete recovery at age 96!

From Shasta, I was taken by Phil and Barbara Ward, proprietors of the hotel to Redding, a nearby town for a flight to San Francisco, en route for another flight to Phoenix in Southern Arizona. On the small plane at Redding I sat at the front immediately behind the pilot's seat. A very young lady, or so she seemed to me, was sitting in the seat. I said to her "are you the driver". This appeared to amuse the other passengers. I had never before taken a flight in such a small plane. The 'driver' admitted that she was the pilot. We arrived safely at San Francisco airport, where I went in search of the next plane, to go to Phoenix. Air travel in the USA is the 'norm'. Trains now a thing of the past! To be expected in such a large country. England is just a small 'off shore' island adjacent to Europe! From Phoenix airport I took a taxi to the Arizona Biltmore Hotel where I stayed overnight before going back to Phoenix Airport to meet the Tauck Tour representative and many of the fellow tourists. After this, back to the Biltmore Hotel which was a very high class establishment. The next day we all had a tour of Phoenix plus a visit to an Indian museum.

There were 31 in the party of tourists, one couple from Cheshire in England. Of the rest, one from California, ten from New York or New York State, difficult for me to identify which except that I knew Brooklyn and Bronx are in New York, the rest I could not establish. There were two from France, six from Belgium, and three from Germany. One couple came from Egypt but gave a New York address. Six were from Florida. They were all very friendly. I fell into conversation with a man named Kelsey Stone, from Florida, formerly the Principal of a High School in Philadelphia who had travelled extensively in Europe, so we had that much in common to talk about. At the dinner in the evening he chose a steak so large he could not eat it all! Mine was smaller. There was an orchestra playing throughout with a singer said to be a relative of Nat King Cole, and he sang well. After the dinner I sat with some Americans, residents of Phoenix, a dentist with a very pretty wife. I could have danced with her to the orchestra, but dancing by diners was not possible. No room for dancing! I received an invitation to visit them in Phoenix should I return to the USA.

The next morning an early start for our tour. The hotel, 'Biltmore' was enormous. We were 'en route' for Sedona where there was an Indian Reservation. Stops were made at Montezumas Castle, formerly an Indian settlement, and at Red Rocks, very picturesque. That night the tour party stayed at the Doc Diablo Hotel where we had a formal reception to get to know each other. This was the opportunity to get to know who we were and where we came from, by each making a little speech. I made mine, offering to teach anyone interested to dance! A Mrs Esther Zimmerman, travelling with her teenage daughter, Karen, I think a Jewess, from Brooklyn, New York, made a suggestion to me (in fun) that we get married. This was a fine start to my tour! The reception party was followed by a 'barbecue' and was very jolly.

Author and tour courier, Cindy Greystoke, at identification meeting of Tauck Tour of Western United States 1992.

The following day we were off early to reach the Grand Canyon, which for me was to be the highlight of my tour. And it was. First we saw a film of an expedition down the whole length of the Canyon in the early nineteenth century. Afterwards we went to view the

394

Canyon, an awe inspiring sight. With Esther Zimmerman and her daughter Karen, I went on a helicopter flight over the Canyon where an even better appreciation of the Canyon's grandeur was possible. No other member of the tour party took an helicopter flight. I had dinner that night with Kelsey Stone and his friend Hilda Kotler, also from Florida. We stayed overnight at Thunderbird Lodge and next day were en route to Las Vegas through the desert to Bolder Dam country, still under construction. We reached Las Vegas with a drive down the 'Sunset Strip' and boulevard to the Hilton Hotel for the night. First I attended a floor show including Diana Ross, she was difficult to hear as the Hilton hotel was full of people 'playing the tables' and fruit machines. The next morning was another early start, this time by plane for San Diego, taking one hour, where we boarded another coach into the city. San Diego was most impressive with a magnificent bridge over the mouth of the harbour. American naval vessels were at anchor. The party was requested to dress smartly with collars and ties for a group photograph. We all looked different! Next was a visit to the celebrated Charlie Brown's restaurant and an elaborate meal. The following day I visited San Diego zoo but was not impressed by animals kept in cages. With some of the party I then took a cruise in the harbour where American Navy vessels were on view, some 'moth balled'. This I followed with a trip into Mexico to Tijuana with a very friendly French couple and had photographs taken in a 'donkey cart', except that the donkey was painted with stripes to look like a zebra!! The Mexican town was very dirty with streets unswept, in contrast to the cleanliness of the towns on the American side of the border. But it was an experience to have been to Mexico which I thoroughly enjoyed. We were next off, en route, to Los Angeles. I found Los Angeles an ugly sprawling town apart from the area around the 'stars' homes in Hollywood where we were not allowed to take photographs. We did, however, visit the site where film stars had recorded their 'footprints' and 'handprints' in wet concrete which when it set, remained for posterity to see, if interested! I took the opportunity to photograph those of Myrna Loy, always my favourite in past years, Sophia Loren, Marilyn Monroe, Bob Hope, Bing Crosby and Peter Sellers. These photographs are now in my album to remind me of when I visited the cinema instead of watching television! The next day the party visited Universal City for a tour of the 'theme park'. Some 'themes' seems to me very artificial, but that is what filming consists of, in my view! I was photographed with a very 'exotic' female, some said it was a 'look-a-like' of Mai West, (come up and see me sometime). The visit to Universal City was very tiring, so back to the hotel 'Century Plaza' for a hot bath and a rest. In the evening presentations were taking place for the Awards of the 'Golden Book'. I did not discover what this involved except that tickets for admission cost 175 dollars (about £90) so did not attempt to attend! There was, however, an exhibition on behalf of Iberian Airways. I saw two figures repre-senting Don Quixote and Sancho Panza, the famous characters of the Spanish author, Cervantes, in his satirical romance of chivalry and of whom it is said 'Quixote' is the only absolutely original creation over the whole of fiction!!   (For some reason I cannot understand, Don Quixote always reminds me of Fred Thistleton, or perhaps the other way round!). Don Quixote is my favourite story. I endeavoured to purchase the two figures made very expertly in papier-maché. After a deal of 'haggling' I was successful, so the two figures came back with me to England and now adorn my present residence! The figures were kindly packed for me by the Iberian Airways staff in a special carrying box. For 12 dollars each I obtained my prize! Although Don Quixote is my favourite fictional character, what I really enjoy is the poetry, (poetry is the right word), of Omar Khayyam, translated by Edward Fitzgerald, and A.A. Milne's stories of Christopher Robin, all very simple. I was introduced to the work of Omar Khayyam by a fellow apprentice, Attwood, in the early 1920's. Dorothy bought me a beautiful leather bound copy of the Rubaiyat, illustrated in colour. I have treasured it ever since. On the occasion when the bookseller from Maidstone came to my apartment in the Avenue in Poole to purchase some books I wanted to sell, he offered me £50 for my special Rubaiyat but I declined to sell. It is gold leafed and gold engraved. I have several other copies but not one so precious to me as the one Dorothy gave me. Other 'poets' I enjoy are Edward Lear, especially the 'Owl and the Pussycat' which was Edith Reader's favourite too, and of course the A.A. Milne stories of Christopher Robin which I read to both by sons when they were young and eventually presented them both with full copies of the various Christopher Robin books. I can still quote the Rubaiyat at length and sometimes do to impress my listeners. My reading tastes are very simple, except perhaps of Aldous Huxley, now I think, out of fashion.

Author with 'Mai West'. 'Look-a-like'
at Universal Studios Los Angeles, U.S.A. 1992

Living in Dorset, however, I discovered the poet, William Barnes, to whom a memorial stands in Dorchester churchyard. His poems, in pure Dorset dialect fascinate me but which I find easier to understand that I do of those of Robert Burns in the Scottish wording. My favourite is the poem "Wife a-lost", which begins:

> "Since I noo nwore do zee your feäce,
> Up Stäirs or down below"
> I'll zit me in the lwonesome pleäce
> Where flat-bough'd beech do grow:
> Below the beeches' bough, my love,
> Where you did never come,
> "An' I don't look to meet ye now
> as I do look at hwome"

All very sad, but sadness becomes normal with the loss of one's partner for 61 years.

Next on in California with Paul and Alida Thistleton and Fred, through very good agricultural country with acres of tomatoes, picked by machine, squash, pumpkins, beans and corn (in England, maize) etc. all grown by irrigation by water from hundreds of miles away, producing three crops a year in rotation. We passed many 'old fashion' missions with names revealing former Spanish origin, much as does San Diego, Los Angeles and San Francisco. All these 'missions' were selling mementoes or souvenirs, (what I generally term 'gee-gaws'). Then through some mountainous country to Shell Beach, a really beautiful spot for the night. On then towards Monterey, calling at Hearst Castle, former home of Randolph Hearst where he entertained Charlie Chaplin, Bernard Shaw, Winston Churchill and other celebrities. Finally to Monterey, via the picturesque town of Carmel where I had hoped to meet a member of the Royal Overseas League, living there pursuing his art of painting. But I was not successful. In Monterey I took a photograph of the plaque commemorating the capture of the town by USA forces from the Spanish Californians in 1840, to extend United States sovereignty. In the evening I went with other tour members to hear a 'Big Jazz Band' in the hotel and danced with three ladies, members of the tour, one French, one Belgian and the other an American. Most enjoyable!

Our next call was to Yosemite National park, another 'highlight' of the tour. We stayed at the Ahwahne Lodge a very fine hotel in Yosemite Valley. We had lunch at the Mansion House Hotel where a pianist played throughout the meal. Very good dance music so I did a little solo dance to amuse those of our party nearby! The scenery in Yosemite was simply marvellous but due to the drought, very little water from the falls. Next day I went with three others from our party on a seven and a half hour 'Grand Tour' of the Forest. Saw more giant trees. We visited the 'Eagles Nest', 'Glacia Point;, 'Half Dome', 'Three Brothers' and other rock formations, climbing at one point to over 6,000 feet above sea level. Actually, of course, not 6,000 feet above the valley below. Those not on the 'Grand Tour' missed out on what was another memorable experience.

We were off next day for a long drive to San Francisco. We saw many 'back packers' heading for Yosemite for some sort of rally. There was some evidence of forest fires around but fortunately they had not reached Yosemite National park. Our next stop was at Columbia, centre of the 1848 gold rush. The buildings were still maintained in 1848 style, with shop signs recalling status as the centre of gold mining. Some made millions, others very little. I was able to take a photograph of the Masonic Hall bearing the date 1880. We finally reached San Francisco through more rich farm land and masses of windmills generating power for the farms.

Finally, in San Francisco, where we were taken on a short tour and over the Oakwood Bridge, a marvellous engineering feat. The following day there was a Grand Tour of the city, up and down the hills that are a feature of San Francisco, through China Town, past the Cathedral where the earthquake struck in 1906 (the year of my birth), climbing to the high point giving a view of the seven hills. Finally back to Fisherman's Wharf, the most colourful area. I took a trip on the Cable car, known as the 'Trolley'. There was a 2 hour wait in the queue to get aboard. "Then Clang, Clang, went the Trolley" as the well known song records! Finally back to our hotel. The 'Trolley' is a most antiquated system devised by a Scotsman in 1898 to replace transport by horse and cart. It is still working and has become San Francisco's "trade mark" and its tourist attraction.

We had a final cocktail party on the 33rd floor of our hotel, The St. Frances, then speeches and thanks to Cindy Greystoke, our courier throughout the tour. Farewells by all our party to each other before down to the restaurant for the last dinner together. My final goodbye to Esther Zimmerman who had been a good friend throughout the tour. At last to bed for the last time in America.

The next day Paul Thistleton arrived with Fred to accompany us back to England. This time Fred showed no signs of distress at or of the altitude affecting him. We reached Heathrow on time. I was met by a senior official of the Customs staff on duty who had been noti-fied of my arrival. With Fred again in a wheelchair, I was given the same treatment, but in my case the senior official who was an old friend, pushed my wheelchair through the Customs control to the amazement of his staff on duty!! A hire car, so with Fred and Paul,, I was soon back to Poole to pick up the threads of my life in the Bournemouth, Ringwood and Ferndown area. Fred was taken into Bournemouth Hospital for his operation and fully recovered. A very tough character! We had been away in America for nearly a month.

CHAPTER SIXTY ONE
Royal Masonic
Benevolent Institution.

Life went on calmly until the onset of winter 1992, although I was troubled with the ulcers again on my ankle. Edith Reader took on the task of dressing my ankle with the permission of Poole Hospital on the days I did not attend there. I think she was keen to demonstrate her nursing skill which had been dormant since she left Canada. The ankle recovered sufficiently for me to suggest we take a trip to Portugal and Spain. We went with Saga, first to Madrid, then to Lisbon and Seville, back to Madrid, by coach, with many towns en route. Edith Reader was thrilled with the visit to the park in Seville with the many white pigeons to feed. She was a great lover of wild and tame animals and birds. Her garden at Ferndown had many bird baskets hanging for the various tits to eat the nuts she provided, although the squirrels had their share too, if the bird baskets were within reach. During this tour of Spain and Portugal, again my ankle gave me trouble and I was not able to walk as far as most of the others on the tour. But Edith did so although she was clearly having difficulties with breathing. I knew her heart condition was again a problem. The town we enjoyed visiting the most was Toledo, for its steel products work, particularly. In Lisbon we visited a night club for a meal and to see an excellent stage show with Portuguese dancing. It was my first visit to Madrid and I was agreeably surprised at its splendour. Back then to England.

Edith Reader was advised by her doctor and a Consultant to enter Bournemouth Hospital again for attention to her heart condition. I was able to visit her daily. Meanwhile I had been offered a vacancy in Zetland Court, the Royal Masonic Benevolent Institution Home in Bournemouth or alternatively in the Institution's Home in Chislehurst. The latter was very near to Colin's residence in the Royal Parade at Chislehurst. I was not happy living alone at Sunset Lodge.

I was given ample time to make a decision, but the offer of a vacancy would not be continued indefinitely. My dilemma was that I had many friends in Bournemouth and Ringwood areas whom I could visit or who could visit me should I go to Zetland Court, whereas the home at Chislehurst was almost on Colin's doorstep where he would be able to visit me and attend to any of my wants that might develop. Friends in Bournemouth would not last indefinitely whereas Colin was much younger. There is a saying that 'Blood is thicker than water'. It certainly applied in the case of "Colin versus friends". At Chislehurst, besides being so near to Colin's residence, I was but one hour away by car via the newly opened M25 motorway from Brian's residence at Worplesdon, from where he would be able to visit me instead of via the longer journey to Bournemouth. Residence at Chislehurst also was much nearer to the Medway Towns where I still had relatives, as well as nearer to Staplehurst, should I wish to visit my Masonic Lodge there. The argument against going to live at Chislehurst was that I would be distant from all my friends in Dorset especially from Edith Reader who had become such a good companion.

Edith Reader regularly went to the Cotswolds late in each summer to stay with John and Ann Heath, who came over from Toronto, Canada, each year for a holiday at Sedgeberrow near to Evesham. They had been friends of Edith in Canada long before her marriage to Harold Reader. They were acquainted with Edith's family and background. While in England for their lengthy stay each year, they visited Ferndown to stay with Edith, as well as Edith having shorter visits to Sedgeberrow to stay with them. I met the Heath's twice at Ferndown. They were a friendly couple, very fond of Edith. They knew of Edith's heart problem and shared my concern.

I decided that I would take the vacancy offered to me for residence at the Duke of Kent Court by the Royal Masonic Benevolent Institution, at Chislehurst. Edith came out of hospital and I promised that I would go down to the Bournemouth area to visit her every weekend. It was a hard decision for me to make, selling my apartment in Poole and disposing of those effects I would be unable to take to Chislehurst. After a house agent in Canford Cliffe, Poole, had failed to find a buyer, my Solicitor advised me to engage another agent in Westbourne. By a lucky chance a member of the Argyll Bowls Club who had been on holiday to Torquay with a bowls tour, had met there a lady on another bowls tour to the same hotel. She was I believe from Essex. They decided to marry and to live in Bournemouth. Before getting married, they had visited the Westbourne agent I had recently appointed. He recommended they look at my flat which was for sale. The man's name was Ben Marcus. He was a member of the Argyll Bowls Club, the Bournemouth Probus Club and the "Argyll Fellowship" that had been started in Westbourne, for men and women of the Argyll Bowls Club to keep the club together during the winter, when no outdoor bowls was possible. I had previously given advice to the Founder, who was a Past President of the Probus Club named Rodney Maunder on how to go about the formation. It was not another Probus Club, although on similar lines, with a monthly lunch, but no speakers. Membership was restricted to members of the Argyll Bowls Club, both men and women. A separate womens' bowls club had been started for ladies at the Argyll where a second green had been put down by the Bournemouth Council. Nearly all the men members of the "Argyll Fellowship Club" and some of the ladies were members also of the two Probus Clubs. But the "Argyll Fellowship" met only during the winter months when no bowling was possible on the outdoor greens.

The lady's name to be married to Ben Marcus was O'Leary, presumably of Irish extraction, whereas Ben Marcos was of the Jewish faith. Ben Marcus owned a flat in Westbourne and Mrs O'Leary a house in Essex. Both had to be sold. They visited my flat and liked it. But what decided them to purchase was that I had two garages adjoining each other. The availability of two garages was what encouraged me to purchase 20 years earlier, but even better, was that now the two garages adjoined each other. My "ploy" in obtaining a 'next door' garage from another flat owner at the cost of agreeing to pay the legal fees involved, had proved to be wise!

"Marcus and O'Leary" agreed to buy, although they were not yet married. The normal delays due to legal requirements where property was involved took place.

Edith had suffered another grievous loss in the death from cancer of her prize winning Siamese cat. She was heartbroken and nothing would console her. I called to see her every day. It was affecting her own recovery. She had the cat's body cremated and the ashes put into a casket to be buried with her when she too, "passed on". It made my prospective removal to Chislehurst difficult to contemplate.

402

Edith Reader had no relatives in England. She was entirely alone apart from her many friends. She did not want to return to Canada. I paid a visit to Chislehurst and agreed that I would take up residence there in due course when I had dealt with the disposal of my flat and contents. Then back again to Ferndown and Poole.

The sale of Sunset Lodge was finalised. Mrs O'Leary purchased some of my main bedroom furniture. My 'daily help' Daphne Knight had the beautiful three piece suite, all of which had been purchased from Maples. A local dealer specialising in 'reproduction furniture' for export to the Unites States, eagerly purchased my dining room furniture. The two boys chose any items they wanted. Colin advertised a sale for me and came down to attend to it. The flat was eventually cleared. Brian and Colin arranged for the items I wished to take to Chislehurst for my room there to be transported. These involved my bookcase, presented to me when I retired from H.M. Customs and Excise, with most of the books I valued and also the bureau bookcase with more of my books. The entire suite from my second bedroom also went to Chislehurst so that my room in the Retirement Home was furnished with my own effects instead of with the standard furniture provided by the Masonic Benevolent Institution for residents. In this way I was made to feel happy in my retirement home when I finally took up residence.

Once more I went back to Ferndown to stay with Edith who was obviously very ill. The Chislehurst Home Manager accepted that I would be away for a while. I agreed to pay the "Home's" charges for residence, which were based on the declared means of each inmate. Residence was restricted to masons or to widows or daughters of masons. In my case I had to pay the full charges. Those not able to do so were assisted by the Benevolent Institution plus 'Income Support' where entitlement was justified under Government regulations.

CHAPTER SIXTY TWO
Death of Edith Reader

Back in Ferndown, I stayed with Edith attending to her needs. After about two weeks she became much worse and I had to dial for an ambulance which took her to Bournemouth Hospital. There I visited every day, often with John and Joan Hoff. Edith was very ill, the Consultant was considering sending her to Southampton Hospital for treatment, possibly to have a 'pace-maker' fitted, but she was too ill. Edith confided in me that 'she did not think she would make it this time'. I was prepared for the worse to happen. John and Joan were with me the night Edith passed away. I was desolate, but had to deal with the consequences of her death.

I found Edith's address book with the details of her family in Canada. There was a son, Ted, living in Scarborough, Ontario. Another son, Peter, living in Saskatchewan at Moose Jaw. A daughter living at Newcastle, New Brunswick, plus granddaughters, married, with a baby great grandson! I contacted the sons and daughter by phone to advise them of their mother's death. I also advised John and Ann Heath. Also a particular friend I knew of, named Westbrook, living in Florida, U.S.A. I spent many hours on the phone to Canada. The hospital delivered Edith's body to the undertakers at Ferndown.

Rosie Wells, who was Edith's neighbour, confided in me that Edith had told her that when she died she wished her body to be sent back to Canada to be interred in the grave with her former husband, Clare. Also that she wished the casket containing the ashes of her favourite cat to be buried with her. With Rosie Wells I arranged for Edith's wishes to be carried out by the local undertaker. It was a slow process getting permission from the Canadian authorities but eventually it was dealt with as Edith had wished.

I knew that Edith's bungalow was in trust to her for her lifetime, but was to go to Harold Reader's daughters eventually. I notified them of Edith's death. The contents of the bungalow were Edith's so the disposal was a matter for Edith's solicitors, who I understood to be Dibbens in Ferndown. Edith had always kept her third bedroom under lock with no one able to enter it. With a Dibbens' representative we searched for the key without success. It was agreed that I obtained a locksmith and in the presence of an independent solicitor, to enter the bedroom. It was all very legal! The door belonged to the "Reader daughters" but the contents belonged to Edith's beneficiaries! Eventually the door was opened by a locksmith. Revealed were masses of documents and papers. Some in filing trays and some in a filing cabinet. But with much loose paper around. Very untidy. There was a cabinet with many dolls on view and much 'bric-a-brac'. It would have taken me days to sort out, but in any case it was not my responsibility. I did, however, come across a copy of a will, appointing a firm of solicitors in the Charminster area of Bournemouth to deal with Harold Reader's estate.

I visited Dibbens in Ferndown to learn that Edith had made a will, in their possession, appointing Miss Fleet, one of the firm, and a Miss Edna Harwood living in Arundel, West Sussex, as her Executors. I knew Miss Harwood, having visited her with Edith in the past to have a tour of Arundel Castle. She was a very charming lady, younger than Edith. They had been friends in Canada and I believe employed at the establishment where Edith was the Principal. I found in the bungalow, two passports in Edith's name, one for Great Britain and the other for Canada. Also I found the valuation for most of Edith's dolls by a reputable firm of valuers and auctioneers in Bournemouth. The valuation amounted to over £26,000 (twenty six thousand pounds!) I passed the valuation to Dibbens.

Edith's car, a Toyota, was in the garage and was part of Edith's estate. My involvement was nearly complete, but I had one more task to carry out.

With Rosie Wells and Edith's best friend Dorothy Whipman, who lived in Canford Cliffs, Poole, and with whom Edith had been on holiday to Madeira and the Channel Islands at different times, I had a conference with the local vicar at the church where Harold Reader had been a church warden. We decided to hold a memorial service to which Edith's many friends could attend. The church was full to overflowing. Edith's two step daughters, the daughters of Harold attended. Also, because both Brian and Colin were abroad, my two grandchildren, Adrian and Elaine attended to represent them. Afterwards I held a reception at the nearby hotel for those wishing to attend. Many of my friends who were Edith's friends too, accepted my invitation. For me, such a sad occasion. None of Edith's family came over from Canada to attend the service.

I found a home for Edith's other Siamese cat, via the Siamese Cat Society. This was at New Milton, where I went with Rosie Wells to inspect his new home. He was a valuable cat and his new owners were pleased to accept him.

One strange outcome from the Memorial Service. With Adrian and Elaine, my grand children, and with a number of others who had attended, we went to the Coach House Hotel in Ferndown where the Probus Club held its meetings, to have lunch. There my mackintosh coat was stolen and in it the keys to Edith's bungalow plus other keys. I had to return to the bungalow to borrow keys from Rosie Wells. There was a duplicate set in the bungalow which I could use once I gained admission. Weeks later my keys were returned surreptitiously, to the hotel by being left on the reception counter. I recovered them when I went down to Ferndown for a Probus Club meeting from Chislehurst. But my 'mac' never came back. It was quite a good one, so I lost out once more!

I learned from John Heath in Canada that Edith had signed there another Will. I have since learned that a decision has to be made on which Will is to be used. The domicile of Edith, either Canadian or English is a prime factor, yet to be determined. I know that I am not involved in either Will for which fact I am thankful.

I went to Arundel to go with Miss Edna Harwood to Sedgeberrow to see John and Ann Heath when they came to England on their next visit. This for the benefit of Miss Harwood, wanting to know as an English Executor what was the present situation.

John Heath was not able to give us very much information. He had attended Edith's interment, the casket containing the cat's ashes being inside the coffin. John had met members of Edith's family and from them had understood that there were four beneficiaries named in Edith's Canadian will. But probate had not been settled, the domicile of Edith being involved. The four beneficiaries were the three children of Edith plus her favourite granddaughter, "Debbie". He understood that they had expressed a wish for the English will to be used rather than the Canadian one but that this was not yet decided. Edna Harwood had no legal knowledge of what an Executor had to do. She had left all matters for Dibbens, the Solicitors in Ferndown to deal with. She was, of course, perfectly entitled to relinquish her appointment as an Executor but had not done so. Edna Harwood and I left Sedgeberrow still very much in the dark. I advised her to get into touch with Dibbens but do not know if she did so.

I heard from Rosie Wells, living next door to Edith's bungalow, that it had been sold and that the new owners were in occupation. Edith's car had been taken away, but where to, Rosie did not know. All of Edith's effects had been cleared and, as Rosie understood, sold by auction. By whom she did not know. According to Rosie, the dolls had been sent to Canada, but she could not confirm this. Those friends of Edith who had been promised a doll from the collection, by Edith, were unlikely to receive one! How Dibbens had managed to sell Edith's effects and dispose of her car without Probate being granted is, to me, a mystery. The whole matter of Edith's estate in England was clearly a matter for the named Executors, Miss Fleet (of Dibbens) and Miss Harwood, but the grant of Probate was necessary. I had no further interest in the matter, having given Miss Edna Harwood my advice. Edith had owned a diamond ring worth £1,000. The hospital authorities had passed this to Dibbens. It was presumably sent to Canada with the dolls. It was not for me to enquire about. It was Edna Harwood's responsibility unless she had relinquished her Executorship.

CHAPTER SIXTY THREE
Chislehurst.

I returned to Chislehurst to commence the final stage of my life in the care of the Royal Masonic Benevolent Institution, and the companionship of my two sons.

I took up residence in the autumn of 1993. At first I was given a very small room, quite too small for all my effects. Later I was given No. 64 a much larger room. In this I installed a second wardrobe to hold some of my many clothes; a small domestic refrigerator and a Vanity Unit, to replace the rather unsightly wash basin with many pipes on show. All at my own expense. I was determined to ensure that as this being my home, I would have it as comfortable as I could possibly make it. All domestic services are provided in the home. Cleaning, laundry, plus all meals, including an early morning cup of tea, mid-afternoon tea, mid-morning coffee and late night 'Horlicks'. Within five months I was elected Chairman of the Residents' Association, involving not very onerous duties, such as preparing and posting the programmes arranged for the Residents each week; dealing with the distribution of Christmas monetary gifts to the staff, after agreement with the Committee and the Treasurer. A sum of £1. each is collected monthly by the Hon. Treasurer from Residents, thus relieving them of making personal gifts. Also if necessary to deal with any problems thrown up in the Home or complaints from any Resident, that need to be discussed with the Home Managers. These occur very rarely and are virtually non-existent. There is a Committee of 6 Residents of whom two, the Hon. Secretary and the Hon. Treasurer occupy two of the separate eight flats which are self-contained and occupied by married couples and are self supporting in respect of meals. The rest of the Residents, some 60 or so, enjoy all the facilities the Home provides. The other four members of the Committee are all in the main building. There is a sub-committee which deals with food and agrees the menus prepared a month in advance. The committee of the Residents has delegated the Vice chairman to be a member of the food sub-committee. The system works very well. In addition to the normal residents, some of whom are in wheel chairs, there is a separate 'sick bay' where permanent or temporarily ill Residents are cared for. The staff consists of qualified nurses, semi-qualified nurses and many 'Carers'. In addition to single rooms for each Resident, there are some double rooms for married couples. All the corridors leading to the individual rooms have adequate toilet facilities plus a kitchen were the residents can, if they so wish, prepare tea or coffee, also for drying and ironing small items not sent to the Home laundry. There are three managers, The Manager, her Deputy and her Assistant Manager. All three are qualified nurses and managers appointed by RMBI.

In addition to all this, there is a very competent, "Friends of the Court Association" which is assiduous in making life for all the Residents, fit, or not so fit, or very seriously ill, happy in the Home. All "Friends" are Masons from the surrounding area, although any Mason may be a member of the "Friends" and many Lodges are paid up members of the "Friends of the Court". A "Friends of the Court" News sheet is published twice a year, giving details of activities. Nobody need really be unhappy in the Home although procedures are sometimes monotonous. At Christmas time the "Friends" really "Go to town" with gifts for each individual Resident. Two 'Fairs' are held annually, 'The Spring Fair' and 'The Autumn Fair'. There is also a 'Strawberry Tea' in June when guests may attend to enjoy the fare provided. At the Fairs there are numerous stalls where it is possible to purchase practically anything from jewellery to clothing, books, stationery, pictures, etc. to suit every taste. A type of "Jumble Sale" but better, to which guests may attend.

Entertainments are provided by visiting concert parties. Also trips out by car or minibus to places of interest. The gentlemen are invited to visit nearby Lodges as guests. At one to Hythe in Kent, with the Ladies to tea and another to Gillingham. "Never a dull moment!" I have been through the "chunnel" to France on an official outing. Also visits to the local surgery for medical attention, although the doctor or doctors allocated to the Home pay required visits. Every care is provided for.

I located the Probus Club of Eltham and was invited to a meeting followed by lunch. I could have become a member but the distance involved in attending was the deciding factor and caused me to decline the invitation. Instead I joined the local Probus Club of Chislehurst which meets in the Chislehurst Golf Club Clubhouse at Camden Place, once the residence of Napoleon III, the Empress and the Prince Imperial. Napoleon III died there in January 1873 but the Empress continued to reside at Camden Place until March 1881 when she left for extensive journeys abroad until she died in Madrid in 1920. The Prince Imperial was killed by the Zulus in June 1879 in South Africa. Camden Place became the headquarters of Chislehurst Golf Club in 1894. In the grounds at Camden Place, William Willet, a builder, erected himself a house called the 'Cedars.' He was later to be the originator of 'Summer Time' to which we are all now subjected.

To be a member of Chislehurst Probus Club one has to pay in addition to the annual subscription, £10 to the Golf Club, unless one is a member of that club. So membership of Chislehurst Probus Club was quite expensive compared with Bournemouth or Ringwood. I went with the Probus Club for a visit to Lords Cricket ground including entry to the famous 'Long Room'. This was followed by a visit to St. Paul's Cathedral where I went down into the crypt and saw once more the chapel of the "Most Excellent Order of the British Empire" of which I am a member. Also to see again where my grandson Adrian, was christened under the privileges accorded to members of the Order.

I also joined the Chislehurst and North Kent Branch of the Society of the Men of Kent and Kentish Men, which meets, generally in the Methodist Church in Prince Imperial Road in Chislehurst, one a month, besides organising visits to places of interest.

The Masonic Home has an outdoor bowls green in Holbrook Lane, very close to Shepherds Green where the Home is situated. Membership of the Duke of Kent Bowls Club is, in the main, restricted to Masons in the area. The Green is the property of the R.M.B.I. All members of the Bowls Club must also be member of the 'Friends of the Court'. Residents at the Home are entitled to free membership of the Bowls Club, but only three play bowls and so have become members of the Duke of Kent Bowls Club. I attend occasionally to play when there is a Club 'open' day, so can play with the other members. I do not put my name down to play against opponents from other clubs in matches. At my age and with some infirmity from my leg and ulcerated ankle, plus using a stick to retain my balance, I could be a liability in the team. I do, however, go to watch matches being played, especially when against another Masonic team. The Duke of Kent Club plays matches against the Masonic Bowling Association teams from West Kent, Essex, Sussex and Surrey. I have suggested that they secure a match against East Kent or West Hampshire Masonic teams, but so far this has not been arranged. It would be quite a distance for the Hampshire team to come to Chislehurst for a match.

I have joined the "White Oaks" Indoor Bowls Club which plays throughout the year at Swanley, quite close to Chislehurst. It is under the control of Sevenoaks District Council which supplies special facilities one day a week for disabled and partially disabled bowlers to play. This facility is given on Thursdays, each week to play with bowlers, all younger than I but who have some form of disability. It is an enjoyable outing for me. We play for a cup on one Thursday in each month and I have won it on two occasions. Also my son Colin has presented us with a 'Christmas Cup' which we play for annually in December. So far I have reached the final once to secure the "Runners up" trophy. It is all good exercise for me, and I meet people away from the Home for a change! I go to Swanley in my car which I am permitted to keep at the Home and have a parking area to use.

From the Home I have been able to visit Guys Hospital Dental Department where I have been fitted with new dentures to replace those supplied in 1969 and 1970 at the Victoria Hospital, East Grinstead, after my face was damaged and jaws broken in the motor accident when the policeman responsible was acquitted at Cranbrook Court by prejudiced magistrates. For my glaucoma condition I am regularly examined at Orpington Hospital at six monthly intervals. To date there has been no deterioration in my eyesight. At Orpington Hospital also, I attend for control of the recurrence of rodent ulcers (skin cancers) on my forehead. An examination carried out at Queen Mary Hospital in Sidcup for possible prostate trouble proved negative. Shortly before I left Bournemouth area, my doctor there detected slight diabetes. This is kept under control by careful dieting. No deterioration has taken place. I am examined every six months for this at my doctor's surgery. My only real problem has been the small ulcers which developed on my right ankle. For these I am treated at the surgery by the District nurse, but I have been admitted twice to Benenden Hospital in Kent under the control of a Consultant. I have been for many years a member of the Post Office and Civil Service Sanatorium Society which owns the Benenden Hospital. The hospital was under my control for the Excise when I had charge of that area of the country, part of my Station. It was quite an experience to be admitted there as a patient!. The treatment is first class. My admissions there have lasted two or three weeks and have proved effective. Unfortunately my leg has poor circulation, possibly due to the plates still affixed to the broken leg sustained in the accident. I expect I will always now be troubled by these ulcers breaking out periodically. Unfortunately I have become profoundly deaf and registered as a 'deaf person with sight'. By wearing a hearing aid, (I have one for each ear), this disability is kept under control as far as is possible. There is no cure!

CHAPTER SIXTY FOUR
Finale.

From the Home, now I am in Kent, I have been able to make many visits into the County and beyond, to call on my relatives and friends, more easily than was possible from Poole, although I have from time to time been down to the Bournemouth/Poole/Ringwood area. With My son Colin I visited the Dickensian Fair in Rochester and with him was able to stroll around the King's School area, renewing memories. We also paid a visit to Chatham Dockyard, which closed in March 1984, but reopened to the public as Chatham Historic Dockyard Trust. Much has been demolished since my time there as an apprentice. There was no sign of the Dockyard School where I strove long and hard to secure four years as a student. The school seems to have been demolished. The former Dockyard church still stands. It was there that John Boulter, son of an electrical fitter apprentice in my day, first sang as a chorister before he became a lead singer in the Television 'Black and White Minstrel Show'. The plaque recording that H.M.S. Victory, flagship of Lord Nelson, was built in No. 2 Dock at Chatham Dockyard, was missing, lost when the dockyard closed. Maybe it has gone to Portsmouth to remind visitors there that this famous ship was a product of Chatham, not Portsmouth! The visit to the dockyard brought back so many memories.

We also paid a visit to Leeds Castle to see a 'Veteran' car rally and a 'Hot Air' balloon ascent. There was the golf course where I played formerly, with Lady Bailey's permission and where Colin fished in the moat around the Castle. Possibly one of very few with permission so to do. We lunched at the Bearsted Country Club House formerly the Tudor Hotel, where Dorothy and I had danced together so many times. Our house "Orchard Gate" was looking as attractive as ever. The village had changed but the village green and pond were still there. Just many memories.

In Chatham, there were no more tramcars running. The Technical School closed, standing silent and almost derelict, opposite Institute Hill, where we struggled to carry up the cricket gear to play on the Great Lines. Opposite also on the corner, was no longer Packer's shop where we as pupils, could buy a small piece of cake at 'break' for one half penny, or a larger piece for a penny. For an "end piece" much larger, the price was three half-pence. One had to be 'well off' to afford an 'end piece'. At the rear of the shop, where my cousin, Edith Tutt's husband, was a baker's roundsman, where once had stood the yard where poor people could obtain stale loaves and yesterday's cakes for "next to nothing", so that a queue formed, no more. How times have changed! The "X" Brand clothing factory, no more! So the girl machinists no longer singing as they sewed. Near to Chatham Town Hall where Dorothy did not wait for 5 minutes, the former Marine School has disappeared. In Rochester, the Casino where I first met Dorothy, was standing empty and dejected. No longer any dancing of the 'Charleston' or doing the 'Twist' to Lew Stone's band. In Maidstone, now with two bridges over the River Medway, but with so many 'one way streets' that I became lost. The Brewery has been demolished. In Tovil, part of Maidstone, where stood the paper mill I controlled for purchase tax, was now the Lord Cornwallis Masonic Centre. With Colin, Eileen, and Nancy Henderson, the widow of John, my former colleague in the Investigation Branch, later Assistant Collector, Dover, for Customs and Excise, we attended there the Ladies Night of Staplehurst Lodge. Nancy Henderson still lives in Folkestone. She is not a dancer, but came with me, Colin and Eileen, as my partner for the Ladies Night. We have been friends for over 40 years. John and Nancy had visited Dorothy and I in our house at Bearsted. He had died in Benenden Hospital before retiring. I attended Nancy Henderson's 80th birthday party held at Beech, near Alton in Hampshire where her son, also named John, resided. He is a Computer Scientist with a degree from Oxford, a Justice of the Peace and an Examiner for the Open University. Nancy Henderson also came to Chislehurst to attend with me, the Dinner/Dance and presentation of the Duke of Kent Bowls Club prizes at the end of the bowls season. Also to the Savoy Hotel, again with Colin and Eileen, to the celebrations of those on the Roll of Honour of the Royal Masonic Benevolent Institution, of which I have become a member.

With Sybil Burkett, the widow of Tom who was my partner when we 'did' the Western Brothers (South Eastern Brothers) and was also the front end of the circus horse in Gillingham (I was the back end), I went to the C.S.M.A. Carnival show at Camber Sands, near Rye in East Sussex. There we saw the Beverley Sisters as the star attraction for the Carnival. They looked as attractive as they did when I last saw them in Liverpool at the Adelphi Theatre,. It must be over 40 years ago when I was attending a Federation Council. The delegates were staying at the Adelphi Hotel and so were the Beverley Sisters. Memories also of Dorothy with her sister and Netta Trill 'singing' 'Sisters, Sisters' in Gillingham and Maidstone. Sybil Burkett is now over 90 years old and is still cultivating her garden in Birchington-on-Sea, near Margate where she now resides.

I attended the New Year Party of the Civil Service Motoring Association in Bournemouth and stayed at the Queen's Hotel. I invited Wing Commander John Pickering, and his wife Joan together with John and Joan Hoff, Mai Butt, the widow of Major Sidney Butt, and Daphne Knight, my former helper in keeping my flat tidy, to be my guests for the Old Year Night dinner/dance and celebrations. Joan Hoff could not attend at the last minute, due to an attack of asthma. But the rest of my guests with me enjoyed the celebrations of welcoming in the New Year. John Pickering is a Past President of the Bournemouth Probus Club while John Hoff is the current President. Sidney Butt was the Probus member with whom I was compiling the history of Bournemouth Probus when he died suddenly in Southbourne, Bournemouth. It was John Pickering who at the last minute, declined the chairmanship of the Royal Overseas League after I had consented to act as his Vice Chairman.

With a number of the other Residents at the Home I went on a river cruise from Woolwich to Greenwich and return. It was interesting for me to view some of the old wharves on the Thames, now no longer in use, indeed some, such as at Canary Wharf converted to residences for 'Yuppies' or others able to afford them. What was more interesting to me was to see the Royal Naval College at Greenwich from another angle - the river. To think also that if I had been that little bit more studious and attained first place in the Dockyard School, I might have attended the College to become a

Naval Constructor! But I am sure that I would not have been so happy as I was as Excise Officer for the Weald of Kent and part of Sussex, the territory I had chosen to serve in from the first day I entered H.M. Customs and Excise!

I observed at the Royal Naval College at Greenwich that there was no statue or monument to Captain Cook whose journeys to the South Seas had established British supremacy there. There was a statue to General Wolfe, whom Captain Cook had advised from his survey of the St. Lawrence River, where best to land his troops for them to scale the Heights of Abraham so to capture Quebec and secure Canada for the British Crown. There is, however, a statue to Captain Cook at the end of 'The Mall' in London, close to Admiralty Arch.

Shortly after I took up residence in the Home, I went to the meeting of Staplehurst Lodge with a number of guests, including Colin, Ernie Nicholls and the Chairman of the 'Association of Friends of the Court', in Chislehurst, Bill Thornber. Also as my guest, Arthur Holbrook with whom I had been at school at Chatham Technical School over 70 years earlier. Many members of my original Lodge in Gillingham, The Manor of Gillingham Lodge, also attended. The occasion was the celebration of having been a mason for 60 years. The Provincial Grand Master of the Province of East Kent, came up from Folkestone to attend and present me with a 'Scroll' recording my long membership. Brian came later to attend the 'supper' that followed the meeting. Although entitled, he does not attend Masonic ceremonies by choice.

I penned an article on the name 'Barnabas' mentioning my Great Grandfather, my name, the names of several of my Great Uncles and cousins plus my father's name, that of Barnabas. And of course that I was married in St. Barnabas Church. The article has been submitted to the Masonic news for East Kent. It has not yet been published, but I am hoping that the Editor will accept it.

I have paid a visit to my cousins in Chatham, first to 'Babs' who is a teacher of dancing, mainly 'Sequence' style, the daughter of my mother's youngest sister, and with her went to her son living at Walderslade. This is the area where in my young days, the rubbish from Chatham was deposited. Now a fully built up housing estate! Also there, to visit two more girl cousins, one of whom was one of

Dorothy's baby bridesmaids at our wedding. Married to Cyril Whittaker, a descendant of the lady who came round the streets in Chatham before the first world war, 1914/19, selling shrimps and winkles from her basket for Sunday tea!. Cyril, a former shipwright in Chatham Dockyard, now retired.

The two girl cousins are the daughters of my mother's only brother. A son died without issue, so there will be no Cox's to carry on the name from my grandfather Cox's family. I have visited Dorothy's younger brother at Hove where he has retired, enjoying the re-unions with his former Air Force comrades and visiting the French Resistance personnel who sheltered him until his release by the advancing American forces from the South. He has one daughter. Dorothy's elder brother has no children. Dorothy's father's only brother had a son who died without issue. So Dorothy's name 'Brown' will die out too, but there are plenty more 'Browns' about! I have one grandson, but so far no great grandchildren. Soon, too, the name Sheppard will be no more. It is something I cannot control.

My sister, Doris, had three sons and one daughter. All named Craske. The elder was a heating engineer, the second son entered the Customs and Excise, after a little coaching from me! He became an Inspector, but left the C & E to become a financial adviser so far as I am aware. The youngest son entered first, the Inland Revenue Department; transferred to the Customs Waterguard; became an Unattached Officer from the amalgamation of the Outdoor Service with the Waterguard, and he is now a Surveyor at Maidstone with control of V.A.T.... as his burden!! My sister's daughter married an Air Force Officer who is now a British Airways pilot flying to all parts.

If I am asked, what is your greatest disappointment in life? It is the death of my baby daughter. She would, I am sure, have given both Dorothy and I, immense happiness. My second regret is that I have so few grand-children, and no great grandchildren, but this is something outside of my control.

What has given me pleasure? Apart from the happiness I derived from being an Excise Officer in the area I always coveted, my love for Dorothy controlled my life, once we were married. My greatest thrill was visiting Buckingham Palace to receive my award of the M.B.E. Why I was chosen for this, I do not know.

I enjoyed listening to the skylarks singing in the air above the fields around Wolterton Hall, in Norfolk. They reminded me of my early days hearing them sing above the Coney Banks in Luton, Chatham. There the skylark always sang above its well concealed nest in the grass below. When it swooped to land, it did so well away from the nest for fear of disclosing its position to those who would rob its precious contents. The rest of the larks journey was on foot! Maybe larks still remember that when Charles 1st imposed the first Excise duty in 1643, among the items on which the King's Excise was levied were 'larkes' eggs. When these were sold in the market, it enabled the hated King's Exciseman to collect the duty! But the bird song I enjoyed even more than the skylark, was with Dorothy when we were returning home to Bearsted after visiting my parents at Rainham. This was a nightingale that sang regularly in the thicket near to the Chiltern Hundreds public house at Peneden Heath, Maidstone, where many a smuggler "danced the hempen jig" on the gallows. It is said that in April 1824, a crowd of 40,000 watched the execution there of 4 smugglers. I wonder who counted the audience?

The nightingale was always singing late at night. We always stopped to listen. Now the thicket has gone, devoured by a huge housing estate and the nearby modern Stakis Hotel. The nightingale sings no more in the thicket! Is a housing estate more valuable than the song of a nightingale?

In May 1996 I was contacted by Vernon Cocking O.B.E., a Barrister, formerly employed in the Customs and Excise Solicitors Office. He had previously been a member of the C & E Investigation Branch. He read for the Bar. Being successful in becoming a Barrister, he was transferred by the Board to the Solicitor's Office but has now retired, living at Croydon. He was the organiser of the "Old Boys" Association for former members of the Investigation Branch. Vernon had traced my address. Vernon Cocking told me that there would be a re-union of "Old Boys" at the 'Mudlark Hotel' in Southwark in September and he invited me to attend. It seemed that the "Old Boys" had already had one meeting in the previous January of which I was unaware. I duly went to the 'Mudlark' for the September meeting. There I received a most hearty welcome and toasted as the 'doyen' of the "Old Boys" Association being 90 years of age, the oldest surviving member of the Investigation Branch. I was really embarrassed by the warmth of my reception. I made a short speech saying that in 'my day' the I.B. Staff totalled 30 Officers. The Chief Investigation Officer of the I.B. who was there as a guest, announced that the I.B., now the Investigation Division, had a staff of 1,700 due to the horrific increase in smuggling, particularly of drugs, and were being employed where necessary abroad. I knew only a few of those, present, all being much younger. Another meeting of the 'Old Boys' took place in April 1997, which I also attended and was again made very welcome.

In July 1996, I went back to Poole for the 100th birthday of Fred Thistleton. I was accommodated at Zetland Court, the R.M. B.I. Home in Westbourne, Bournemouth. Paul and Alida Thistleton had come over for the celebrations, from Trinidad, California. Fred's niece, Susan Young, the widow of a doctor, now living at Moreton-in-Marsh in the Cotswolds, was also present as well as many friends, particularly from the Civil Service Retirement Fellowship, of which Fred is still the President! The date was July 7th. Fred had received a congratulatory telegram from the Queen as well as a second one from the Queen Mother, specially sent because the Queen Mother is the Patron of the C.S. Retirement Fellowship. Three birthday cakes had been prepared bearing the figures for 100. It was a jolly party as it should have been. Fred made an adequate speech dealing with memories as a 'Victorian'. He overlooked the fact that he was less than 5 years old when Queen Victoria died! He did mention, though, the bath chairs that "clutterered up" Bournemouth in the early days of the 20th Century. He was in good form and still very sprightly. I was glad that I went, particularly so, to see Paul and Alida again. Their daughter Ruth had had a second baby, a girl. The youngest daughter, Adele is expecting one, having married. But unfortunately the middle daughter Anne and by far the most accomplished, has had a divorce. The friends that I had met at Trinidad, California had sent best wishes to Fred and to me.

In the foyer of the entrance to the Masonic Home at Chislehurst is a plaque commemorating the opening of the Home. It was by Princess Marina, Duchess of Kent, on the 26th July 1968. It brings back memories to me of another date, 29th November 1934. On that day Dorothy and I walked up the Strand in London between crowds gathered on the pavements, to the Headquarters of the Customs and Excise Federation. It was the wedding day of Prince George, Duke of Kent, to Marina, his future Duchess.

The Federation offices were at that time in Walter House, in the Strand. They overlooked the route for the Royal Processions on their way to St. Paul's Cathedral for the first Royal wedding to a foreign Princess this century. Because the Federation offices gave a first class view of the expected Royal processions, it was decided that those members of the Executive Committee who could attend should be allowed to use the view point, with their wives. Dorothy and I were making our way to Walter House. I was the youngest member of the Executive, indeed the only 'post 1926' entrant. A member, on account of my U.O. status. We saw all the Royal carriages go past Walter House. There was not a finer view in the whole of the Strand.

Included in the members of the Federation Executive, enjoying the view were 'Tommy' Morton, President, a Customs Officer in London Port, R.B. Hunter, the previous President, an Excise Officer at Hastings, T.W. Rogers, Hon. General Secretary, Excise officer in the Strand station, London West, (who later became President, when he transferred to the Excise Station in Oswestry), 'Ernie' Buck, Customs Officer, London Port, a Secretary, later to become Hon. General Secretary 'Jimmy' Cowherd, George Busey, Harry Mather, Harry Davies, and W.E. Blackborow, all of whom at different times served as Secretaries of the Federation. And myself the 'baby' on the Executive Committee, elected as Unattached Officer from Dover Collection, eventually, also to become a Secretary. 'Tommy' Morton, R.B. Hunter, and 'Ernie' Buck, each received the honour of being awarded M.B.E.'s. Like me, forgotten, some even before their demise, but each had served their fellow members of the Grade of Customs and Excise Officer to the best of their abilities.

Prince George Duke of Kent married his Princess Marina. She was able to open this Masonic Home in his memory. Prince George was killed in an aeroplane crash on the 24th August 1942 en route to Iceland. His name lives on in the R.M.B.I. Retirement Home at Chislehurst where I now have sufficient leisure time to pen my Memoirs!

420

At the Royal Naval Dockyard School at Chatham over the entrance door was carved an advice to all the students, the words:-

"Onward then, the Virtue lies"
"In the struggle, not the prize"

The author of the advice is not known to me, despite endeavouring to establish his or her identity. Maybe I have followed the advice given. The reader of my Memoirs must be the judge.

Horace Albert Barnabas Sheppard M.B.E.
Born 16th June 1906

Published April 1998